The SysAdmin Handbook

The Best of
Simple-Talk SysAdmin

First Published by Red Gate Books, 2010
This handbook was commissioned by Red Gate Software, engineers of ingeniously simple tools for optimizing your Exchange email environment. Learn more about Exchange Server Archiver and PST Importer by
visiting www.red-gate.com

Red Gate Books

Newnham House

Cambridge Business Park

Cambridge

CB2 0WZ

United Kingdom

ISBN 978-1-906434-43-4

Disclaimer

Red Gate Books, Simple-Talk.com, and the authors of the articles contained in this book are not liable for any problems resulting from the use of techniques, source code, or compiled executables referenced in this book. Users should review all procedures carefully, test first on a non-production server, and always have good backup before using on a production server.

Editors: Tony Davis, Andrew Clarke and Michael Francis

Cover Art: Paul Vlaar

Typesetting & Design: Gower Associates and Matthew Tye

Table of Contents

Virtualization 321

About the Authors

Jaap Wesselius

Jaap Wesselius is a senior Exchange consultant for DM Consultants (HTTP://WWW.DM-CONSULTANTS.NL/), a Microsoft Gold Partner with a strong focus on messaging and collaboration solutions. Prior to working for DM Consultants, Jaap worked for eight years for Microsoft Services in The Netherlands, specializing in Exchange Server. Jaap is a BSc, MCSE, MCITP, and MCT, and was awarded the Microsoft MVP Award (Exchange Server) for his contributions to the Dutch messaging and collaboration community. Besides Exchange Server, Jaap is also very active in virtualization, and is a founder of the Dutch Hyper-V community. You can reach Jaap at J.WESSELIUS@DM-CONSULTANTS.NL or JAAP@HYPER-V.NU.

Ben Lye

Ben Lye is a senior systems administrator at a multinational software company. He has over ten years' experience of supporting and administering Windows and Exchange, and has been MCSE and MCP certified since 1999. Ben is passionate about automating and streamlining routine tasks, and enjoys creating and using tools which make day-to-day administration easier.

Michael B. Smith

Michael B. Smith is a well-known author and consultant in the Exchange Server and Active Directory arenas. His most recent book is *Monitoring Exchange Server 2007 with System Center Operations Manager 2007*, published in February 2009. You can contact Michael via email at MICHAEL@THEESSENTIALEXCHANGE.COM and read his blog at HTTP://THEESSENTIALEXCHANGE.COM.

Jonathan Medd

Jonathan Medd is a Senior Technical Consultant for a large local government organisation in the UK. He has been working with Windows Infrastructure products since 1997, in the last few years particularly around Active Directory and Exchange and, most recently, virtualisation with VMware products. He has held the MCSE certification since 1998 and VMware VCP certification since 2008. In 2007, he discovered Windows PowerShell and he spends a lot of time encouraging IT pros he meets to use PowerShell by talking with them, by giving presentations to User Groups, or via posts on his blog at HTTP://JONATHANMEDD.NET. He also co-hosts a regular PowerShell podcast which contains info on how to learn PowerShell and what's going on in the PowerShell world – you can find this at HTTP://GET-SCRIPTING.BLOGSPOT.COM. You can follow him on Twitter at HTTP://TWITTER.COM/JONATHANMEDD.

Brien Posey

Brien Posey is a freelance technical writer, and a five-time Microsoft MVP. Over the last thirteen years, Brien has published literally thousands of technical articles and whitepapers, and written or contributed to dozens of books. Prior to becoming a freelance writer, Brien served as CIO for a national chain of hospitals and healthcare facilities. He has also served as a network administrator for the Department of Defense at Fort Knox, and for some of the nation's largest insurance companies.

Neil Hobson

Neil is a Principal Consultant with Silversands, a UK-based Microsoft Gold Partner and is responsible for the design, implementation, and support of Microsoft infrastructure systems, most notably Microsoft Exchange systems. He has been in the IT industry since 1987 and has worked with Exchange since V4.0 days. He has been an Exchange MVP since 2003 and spends some of his spare time helping others in various Exchange mailing lists, and the public Exchange newsgroups; he also contributes to the MSExchange Blog.

Desmond Lee

Desmond Lee specializes in end-to-end enterprise infrastructure solutions built around proven business processes and people integration across various industries. He is a popular speaker at major international events, and contributes frequently to several highly rated publications and public forums/newsgroups. Desmond is a Microsoft Most Valuable Professional (Communications Server), Microsoft Certified Trainer and founder of the Swiss IT Pro User Group, (WWW.SWISSITPRO.CH) an independent, non-profit organization for IT Pros by IT Pros championing Microsoft technologies. You can follow his IT adventures at WWW.LEEDESMOND.COM.

Nicolas Blank

Nicolas Blank is an Exchange MVP and consultant at Symbiotech (HTTP://WWW.SYMBIOTECH.CO.ZA), a consultancy that specializes in the Microsoft Infrastructure and related tools space with a strong focus on messaging, collaboration, migration, and security solutions. Nicolas currently builds solutions based on Active Directory, Exchange, Office Communication Server and a variety of third-party vendors. Nicolas consults, speaks, writes, and delivers seminars on various topics and blogs at HTTP://BLANKMANBLOG.SPACES.LIVE.COM.

William Lefkovics

William Lefkovics, B.Sc., MCSE, is the Technical Director at Mojave Media Group, LLC in Las Vegas, NV. He is the co-author of *Microsoft Exchange Server 2007: The Complete Reference* and contributes a monthly column on Outlook at Windows IT Pro Magazine.

Nathan Winters

Nathan Winters is a Unified Communications Consultant for Dimension Data; a Microsoft Gold Partner on five continents whose clients include over 70% of the Global Fortune 100. He has been working in IT for four years, and specializes in Exchange, Active Directory, and Virtualization. Recent work has included an Exchange 2007 design for several clients and an OCS 2007 voice design including Enterprise Voice. Midway through 2006, Nathan founded the Microsoft Messaging and Mobility User Group UK, which holds regular meetings in the UK to discuss topics related to Exchange. In April 2007, he was awarded an MVP (Exchange Server) for his work with MMMUG and regular contributions to the Mark Minasi Forum. He is a regular contributor to the MSExchange.org website and his other articles have been published by Penton Media (Exchange and Outlook Administrator newsletter), Microsoft (TechNet Industry Insiders) and on the MMMUG website. For more of his articles see the links below: HTTP://WWW.MMMUG.CO.UK/FILES/DEFAULT.ASPXHTTP://WWW.MSEXCHANGE.ORG/NATHAN_WINTERSHTTP://WWW.WINDOWSITPRO.COM/AUTHORS/AUTHORID/1651/1651.HTML You can contact Nathan at NATHAN@CLARINATHAN.CO.UK or through his blog at HTTP://WWW.MMMUG.CO.UK/BLOGS/NWEB.

Nirmal Sharma

Nirmal Sharma is an MCSEx3, an MCITP, and was awarded a Microsoft MVP award in Directory Services four times. He specializes in Directory Services, Microsoft Clustering, Hyper-V, SQL, and Exchange. He has been involved in Microsoft Technologies since 1994, and followed the progression of Microsoft Operating System and software. He specializes in Microsoft technologies. In his spare time, he likes to help others and share some of his knowledge by writing tips and articles. He can be reached at NIRMAL.SHARMA@MVPS.ORG.

Introduction

Over the past two years, Simple-Talk has published articles on a variety of SysAdmin topics, from Exchange to Virtualization, and including everything from Powershell to Unified Messaging.

We have brought the best of these articles together to form The SysAdmin Handbook. With over fifty articles packed into this book, it will be an essential reference for any Systems Administrator, whether you have years of experience or are just starting out.

Simple-Talk is an online technical journal and community hub for working SQL Server and .NET developers and administrators, as well as enthusiasts and those taking their first steps with these Microsoft technologies. Simple-Talk provides in-depth technical articles, opinions and commentary to more than 388,000 subscribers.

The Simple-Talk SysAdmin newsletter is a fortnightly publication. Subscribing to the newsletter means you will get the latest straightforward and practical technical articles straight to your Inbox. If you do not already receive the newsletter, subscribe for free at WWW.SIMPLE-TALK.COM/COMMUNITY/USER/ CREATEUSER.ASPX.

We would like to thank all the authors who have contributed SysAdmin articles to Simple-Talk over the past two years, as well as those who have taken their time to read the articles, and participate in the community. Because of this, we have been able to develop a successful SysAdmin community on Simple-Talk, filled with high-quality and useful technical articles.

The Simple-Talk Publishing Team

Message Hygiene in Exchange Server 2007

03 July 2008

by William Lefkovics

Around four out of every five email messages are spam. Now that the nuisance threatens to engulf what has become the normal route of business communications worldwide, all the vendors of Mail Servers are taking more active steps to confront the problem. William Lefkovics explains how Microsoft Exchange 2007 is meeting the challenge of the rising tide of spam.

A defense-in-depth approach

Unsolicited Commercial Email (UCE), or spam, is still a huge problem. Different research firms place the total percentage of spam to be anywhere from 70–90% of the total volume of email around the world. Different enterprises may see variances in either direction from this range. It is still too much.

Spam Botnets

Most spam today is distributed by networks of unsuspecting workstations infected with malware. These bots are small applications capable of, among other things, forming and sending SMTP messages en masse by remote command. Spammers typically pay for use of botnets (short for "robot networks") rather than maintaining their own. In the United States, the Federal Bureau of Investigation (FBI) has been working through "Operation Bot Roast" which identified 1 million infected hosts in the US alone, and has resulted in the arrest and conviction (or guilty pleas) of several botnet operators. (http://www. us-cert.gov/press_room/botroast_200711.html).

Microsoft, in response to this ongoing battle, improved upon their set of native tools in Exchange Server 2003 Service Pack 2. They provided a more complete system to allow administrators to eliminate known spam early in the SMTP conversation and to give them more control in assessing spam levels on more questionable messages. Exchange Server 2007 expands and improves on this defense-in-depth approach giving administrators effective sequential tools without additional software cost.

There is no silver bullet that will prevent spam from reaching Inboxes, but there are several steps Exchange administrators can take to reduce inbound spam significantly. With Exchange Server 2007, Microsoft introduced server roles. There are five roles in total – Mailbox, Client Access, Hub Transport, Unified Messaging, and Edge Transport. The Edge Transport role is intended to reside in a perimeter network and perform the majority of the inbound message hygiene functionality for the Exchange organization. The Edge Transport server is typically the gateway SMTP server for the enterprise. Assuming so, message hygiene begins here.

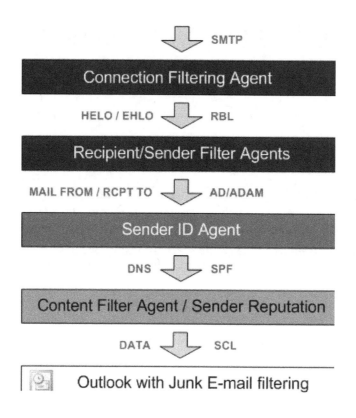

Figure 1.

Figure 1 shows the inbound flow of messages passing through the various anti-spam agent layers. Each layer implements a different test in the effort to validate messages. If 80% of messages arriving at your gateway are spam, then it certainly makes sense to drop those emails as early as possible in the SMTP conversation. The anti-spam tools available on an Exchange 2007 Edge server are shown in Figure 2.

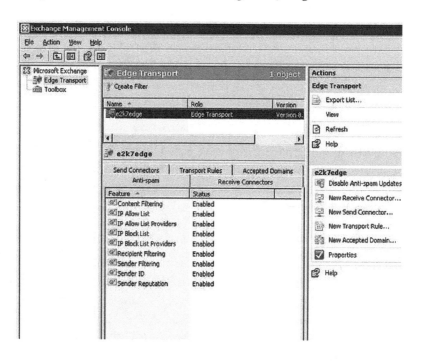

Figure 2.

Figure 2 shows the anti-spam tools available on an Exchange 2007 Edge server. Double clicking or selecting the desired anti-spam feature in the middle pane, and clicking Properties in the Action pane, will open the configuration settings for that feature. The four IP lists, allow and block, make up the Connection Filtering Agent.

Connection filtering agent

The first line of defense, and probably the most prolific one in terms of the potential volume of effective message filtering, is connection filtering.

Feel the Power!
The Exchange Management Shell (EMS) is an extension of Windows PowerShell for managing Exchange 2007. The EMC is built upon the EMS. For all the actions taken in the EMC, there is an equivalent EMS command. There is a complete set of cmdlets to manage connection filtering from the EMS. For example, `Get-IPBlockListConfig` on the Edge Server will return the IP Block list configuration.

For all the Exchange Server cmdlets run `Get-ExCommand` in the EMS. Microsoft maintains a library of these cmdlets as well. The anti-spam cmdlets can be found at HTTP://TECHNET.MICROSOFT.COM/EN-US/ LIBRARY/ BB124601(EXCHG.80).ASPX.

The Connection Filtering Agent is concerned with the source IP address of the host that is connecting on TCP Port 25. The agent references the IP address of the host making the connection request against an IP Allow List and an IP Block List. In addition it can query an IP Block List Provider or an IP Allow List Provider. If the IP address is listed on a block list, either internal or at a block list provider, and not on an allow list, then the connection is dropped. The IP Block list is maintained by the administrator. IP Block List Providers, also called Real-time Block Lists (RBLs) or DNS Block Lists (DNSBLs), maintain databases of known spam hosts.

A good strategy is to select one or two of the well known DNSBLs to complement your manual efforts to maintain corporate IP Block and IP Allow lists. Over the last five years, Spamhaus has been a solid DNSBL for me. I have also used Spamcop over that same time period. Spamcop has shown some inconsistency but has performed well over the last year or two. If you choose just one, I recommend *zen.spamhause. org*. In my company, and at clients, this step alone blocks over 55% of inbound spam messages. These are messages that my Exchange system does not have to process any farther. An independent resource for DNSBL performance can be found at HTTP://STATS.DNSBL.COM/.

Connection filtering is exceptional! That is, it allows for an Exception List. You can configure Exchange to allow messages addressed to specific SMTP addresses to pass through even if the source host IP address is on a block list. It might be a good idea to add *postmaster@yourdomain.com* to the Exception List.

Configuring Exchange 2007 to query a DNSBL is simple. From the Exchange Management Console (EMC), open the configuration settings for IP Block List Providers and select the Providers tab. The Add button opens an input box to enter the name of the DNSBL.

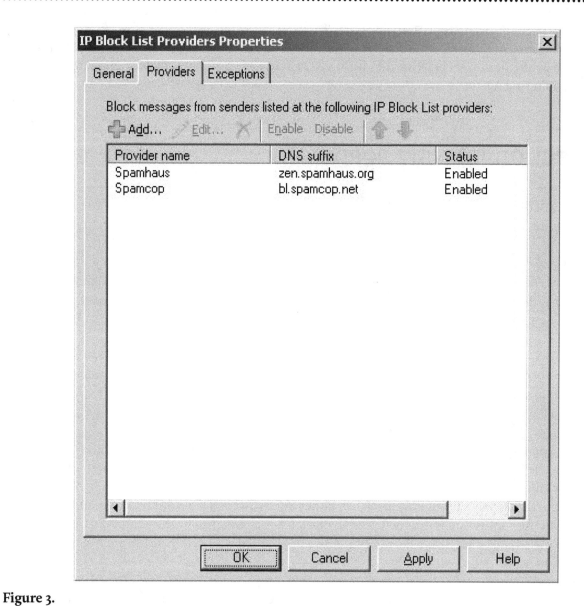

Figure 3.

Figure 3 shows the IP Block List Providers Properties window with two DNSBLs entered.

Sender filtering agent

If the message survives Connection Filtering, the administrator can have Exchange reference the sender SMTP address against a list of addresses to block. The sender address is available after the MAIL command in the SMTP conversation. Specific SMTP addresses can be blocked, or entire domains. Adding *.domain.com to the Sender Filtering list will also block all subdomains for domain.com. While the default action is to block messages, Sender Filtering can also stamp the result in the message header and allow it to pass through. Content Filtering will consider the stamp status in its rating of the message (more about that later).

The EMC has a simple interface to enter blocked senders in the Sender Filtering properties. Addresses can also be added at the EMS command line with a simple cmdlet such as:

```
>Set-SenderFilterConfig -BlockedSenders badaddress@domain.com
```

Recipient filtering agent

The next command in the SMTP transaction is the RCPT command, where the intended recipient of the message is exposed. Here we can apply a filter based on the recipient information. It is possible to block incoming messages for specific addresses, but more importantly, it is also possible to have Exchange query ADAM (or Active Directory if the Anti-spam agents are run on the Hub Transport Server) to validate the recipient address.

No Edge Server? No problem!
In the absence of an Edge Transport server, as may be the case in smaller companies, the Hub Transport role can host the Anti-Spam agents. First, on the Hub Transport Server, you must run the PowerShell script `Install-AntispamAgents.ps1`, found in the \scripts folder on the Exchange 2007 DVD or extracted download.

After the script has completed, the Exchange Transport Service must be restarted. There will now be an Anti-Spam tab for the Hub Transport Server node under the Organisation Configuration container in the Exchange Management Console. Exchange 2007 sp1 moves a couple of settings to the server container.

Selecting the check box by **Block messages sent to recipients not listed in the Global Address List** can reduce the workload of other anti-spam agents and the server in general. If Exchange Server accepts the message without validating the recipient address, and the address does not exist in the organization, then it will have to submit a Non-Delivery Report (NDR) back to the sending server.

Having the server check the directory for addresses does make it easier for spammers to perform address harvesting. The connecting server can test for a series of generic addresses in the same session. Exchange 2007 allows for a short delay when servers provide the RCPT address before replying with 550 5.1.1 to indicate user unknown. A delay of a few seconds can reduce the value of the connection to spammers while not reducing performance significantly on the Exchange side. This delay is called *SMTP Tarpitting*. It is still effective in some instances but, with the advent of spam bots, connecting hosts show little or no adverse reaction – they just seem to go on unabated. Individual enterprises should monitor Recipient Filtering to gauge its effectiveness.

Finally, the Recipient Filtering layer is also an easy place to prevent users from receiving any external email, by including their address in the Recipient Filter block list. They will still be able to send to the internet. Again, the interface in the EMC is a basic address entry form with an equivalent cmdlet such as:

```
>Set-RecipientFilterConfig -BlockedRecipients address@domain.com
```

SenderID filter agent

The anonymous nature of the SMTP protocol allows senders to use incorrect or nonexistent domains in the source address of a message. SenderID is based on the Sender Policy Framework (SPF) and uses the same DNS record format. SPF, originally called *Sender Permitted From* is outlined at *www.openspf.org* and RFC 4408. With the SenderID Filter Agent enabled, Exchange Server executes a DNS lookup for an SPF record for the sending SMTP domain. If a published SPF record is available, Exchange will be able to determine if the IP address of the SMTP source is authorized to send email for the sending SMTP domain. This anti-spoofing measure is described in RFC 4406 entitled *Sender ID: Authenticating E-Mail*. As with other message hygiene layers, the administrator can conserve resources by configuring specific exceptions. Messages from specific domains, or those addressed to certain recipients, can be configured to bypass SenderID queries.

SenderID tries to determine the correct sender address to validate against, which is not always obvious. The SenderID Filter Agent will parse the message headers applying a specific algorithm to arrive at the Purported Responsible Address (PRA). This algorithm is defined in RFC 4407 called *Purported Responsible Address in E-Mail Messages.* This also differentiates SenderID from basic SPF.

The SPF record query returns a status. SenderID only deletes or rejects a message when the status returned from the lookup is set to FAIL. This is configurable in the SenderID Properties window in the EMC. No action is taken for other status levels which include PASS, NEUTRAL, SOFT FAIL, TEMP ERROR, and PERM ERROR.

Confused with SPF record formatting?

There are a few resources online to assist in creating a properly formatted SPF record and validating an existing record. Microsoft maintains such a tool, affectionately called Sender ID Framework SPF Record Wizard found at HTTP://WWW.MICROSOFT.COM/MSCORP/SAFETY/CONTENT/. *technologies/senderid/ wizard/.*

Content filtering agent

In Exchange Server 2003, Microsoft made available a separate download called the Intelligent Message Filter (IMF) Version 1. The IMF was updated to version 2 and included in Exchange 2003 Service Pack 2. In Exchange Server 2007, the IMF is now referred to as the Content Filter Agent, which could be considered IMF v3.

Content Filtering is engaged after the previous layers have assessed the messages and after the DATA command is fulfilled in the SMTP conversation. Content Filtering is a little bit of a "black box." However, with sufficiently large samples, people have worked backwards to compile reasonable algorithms that may be in play. Microsoft has a great deal of experience with spam. Hotmail.com, msn.com, and Microsoft. com have provided almost unlimited samples from which to create an effective content filter mechanism. Microsoft calls it SmartScreen technology and it forms the basis for content filtering in Outlook as well as Exchange Server. Exchange assesses messages and tries to quantify the likeliness that the message is spam. This measurement is called the Spam Confidence Level (SCL) and is stored as an attribute of the message. Content Filtering assigns a value between 0-9 and records this in an X-header. The higher the SCL, the greater the chances the message is spam. There is also an SCL value of -1 reserved for internal and authenticated messaging.

In the Content Filtering properties window, we can add custom terms to ensure that certain messages are either blocked or allowed to pass. A pharmaceutical distributor may want to whitelist the term Viagra, for example. In addition, recipient addresses can be listed as exceptions in the filtering process, such as *postmaster@domain.com*. New to Exchange 2007 is the ability to whitelist certain senders or domains bypassing content filtering. This is not available in the EMC, but the cmdlets are intuitive. To whitelist an SMTP address, the following can be run from the EMS:

```
>Set-ContentFilterConfig -BypassedSenders address@domain.com
```

Administrators can assign one of three actions to a message, based on its SCL value: delete, reject or quarantine.

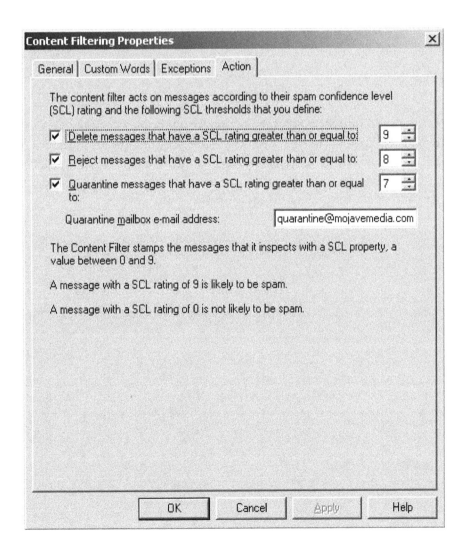

Figure 4.

Figure 4 shows the options in the EMC to assign actions, based on specific minimum SCL ratings. This also shows the current settings on my Edge Server. You will note in Figure 4 that messages with an SCL value of 7 will be quarantined to a separate mailbox. This means that SCL values of 6 or less will be have the rating appended to the header and the message passed through to the Hub Transport and on to the recipient. These settings are not required and different values may be more appropriate in different companies. Administrators should test different threshold values to see what is most effective for their enterprise.

There is also a Junk Mail Threshold for SCL messages. This is configured through the EMS only and simply determines the SCL value at which messages are moved to the Junk Mail folder of the recipient's mailbox.

The final thing I will mention is Sender Reputation. Sender Reputation is a new addition to the message hygiene efforts in Exchange Server. Exchange analyzes characteristics of SMTP sessions of unknown senders. After a sender has sent 20 messages, Exchange maintains a Sender Reputation Level (SRL) analogous to the SCL for content filtering. Sender Reputation, as implemented in Exchange 2007, is a Microsoft creation that is in its infancy and presents potentially compelling options for the future of anti-spam technologies.

Summary

Spam is a moving target. Currently there is no single tool to deploy in the enterprise that will solve this ongoing problem easily. With Exchange 2007, Microsoft provides, out of the box, a multi-faceted defense against UCE. The key to effective spam filtering, using the native Exchange Server 2007 tools, is to determine unwanted messages as early as possible in the message flow. When used together, the tools provide a competitive anti-spam solution at no additional software cost.

Using Exchange 2007 for Resource Booking

16 July 2008

by Nathan Winters

The process of booking various resources to go with a meeting room just got a whole lot easier with Exchange 2007. Nathan Winters explains Exchange's resource-scheduling functionality and offers practical advice on how you might go about configuring Exchange to allow users who are scheduling meetings to specify that such things as video conferencing, projection equipment, and refreshments are required for the meeting.

Introduction

Although previous versions of Exchange were regularly used to host mailboxes that represented resources, Exchange 2007 was the first version in which these mailboxes were actually different from normal mailboxes. This means that there is now no need to rely on add-in software such as the "Auto Accept Agent." It also means that the design process has been rather more thought through, thereby ensuring a useful solution both at the server and client end.

In Exchange 2007, it is possible to create resource mailboxes that can represent either Rooms or Equipment. These exist as disabled accounts in Active Directory and can be managed in various ways. Exchange 2007 also contains the type of *"Auto Accept Agent"* functionality that was missing from Exchange 2003. Having a mailbox type of "Resource" is useful because it makes administration separate. It allows these mailboxes to have special functionality but yet to be secure as disabled users. It is also helpful to be able to distinguish between rooms and equipment, as it is easier for users, and gives more flexibility when adding custom resource properties, as we shall see later.

With the "Availability Service" it is now possible to get real-time information about resource availability without the need to wait for public folder replication to occur (so long as Outlook 2007 is being used). To make best use of this solution, you must ensure that Outlook 2007 is being used by those who will be interacting with the resources and managing their use. This is important because much of the user interface, such as the Scheduling Assistant, is held in Outlook 2007. I would, however, be careful in rolling out Outlook 2007 to the entire user base before thorough testing is carried out. Unless you are careful, you will have dissatisfied users; this is because Outlook 2007 does not always perform as expected, especially with third-party add-ons.

Environment

My test environment consists of servers in two sites. Each site has a Mailbox server and a combined Hub-Transport and Client-Access server. Outlook 2007 and OWA 2007 are used as clients. Various users have been set up in each site, such as users, admin users (secretaries), resources (projectors), and rooms. I have configured such a test environment because it is useful to be able to show different sites with a different naming convention. Equally, I was interested to see how time zones are handled and I discovered that, in my view, this could be done better. For example, as I'll mention later, Outlook is not as flexible as I would like in helping people to arrange meetings in different time zones that require a room in each zone. You could easily test the vast majority of this functionality on a single Exchange server with a single Outlook client.

Creating or migrating resource mailboxes

The resource mailboxes can be created from the GUI or from the command line as shown below:

```
New-Mailbox -database "Siteamb1\SG1\DB1" -Name SiteA-Room1 -
OrganizationalUnit "SiteA Rooms" -DisplayName "SiteA-Room1" -
UserPrincipalName SiteA-Room1@gaots.co.uk -Room
```

If you are migrating the resource mailboxes from an Exchange 2003 system, then use one of the following commands to convert the migrated mailbox to a resource, either "room" or "equipment" as you wish.

```
Set-Mailbox -Identity Name -Type Room
Set-Mailbox -Identity Name -Type Equipment
```

Before moving on, the resource mailboxes must be set up to "auto accept" meeting requests; otherwise they will always remain as "tentative" until an operator intervenes. This is done as follows:

```
Get-Mailbox | where {$_.ResourceType -eq "Equipment"} | Set-
MailboxCalendarSettings -AutomateProcessing:AutoAccept
Get-Mailbox | where {$_.ResourceType -eq "Room"} | Set-
MailboxCalendarSettings -AutomateProcessing:AutoAccept
```

Once suitably configured as above, each resource mailbox will send an auto-accept message to meeting organizers (Figure 1). The message text can be customized to suit requirements.

Figure 1:   **Showing auto acceptance. This message can be customized.**

Feature investigation

I have now discussed how to create resource mailboxes and how to configure their basic option of responding by accepting requests. As you saw, the initial setup is really fairly simple; it is just important to remember that, when migrating from 2003, you must convert the mailbox to the new resource type. Now, let's move on and look at some of the key resource-centric features that Exchange 2007 offers.

Security and booking policies

Both security configuration and booking policies allow the administrator to grant control of resource mailboxes to certain users: those users (using Outlook Web Access) can then define how they are used. For example, it is possible to specify the maximum meeting duration, to define and allow meetings to be scheduled only during working hours and to define how to handle conflicts.

The first step is to setup the resource-admin users as "delegates" of the specific resources in each site. The command below will get mailboxes with the type Equipment or Room and with "**sitea**" in the name. It will then give Delegate access to the account "**siteaadmin**." I have repeated the steps for **siteb**:

```
Get-Mailbox -RecipientTypeDetails EquipmentMailbox, RoomMailbox | Where {$_.Name
-match "^sitea"} | Set-MailboxCalendarSettings -ResourceDelegates siteaadmin

Get-Mailbox -RecipientTypeDetails EquipmentMailbox, RoomMailbox | Where {$_.Name
-match "^siteb"} | Set-MailboxCalendarSettings -ResourceDelegates sitebadmin
```

The "delegate user" for each resource mailbox may be sent a copy of the meeting requests which go to that resource depending on policy, and they are then able to accept or reject these requests.

Next, set up the admin accounts in **sitea** and **siteb** to have full access to their respective resources. The command below is for **siteb**:

```
Get-Mailbox -RecipientTypeDetails EquipmentMailbox, RoomMailbox | Where {$_.
Name -match "^siteb"} | Add-MailboxPermission -AccessRights FullAccess -User
sitebadmin
```

With Full Admin permissions on the resource mailbox, the admin user can then open the mailbox as an additional mailbox in Outlook and have full control of all functions. Most important of these is the OWA Options/Resource Settings section of a resource mailbox. This is used to configure some of the Resource options such as: "Resource Scheduling Options," "Resource Scheduling Permissions," "Resource Privacy Options," and "Response Message." Every option that is available via the shell is also available in OWA, as shown in Figure 2.

To access the relevant mailbox in OWA you will need to access a specific URL:

HTTP://SERVERNAME/OWA/RESOURCEMAILBOX@DOMAIN.COM

... and then log in with the account which has Full Access rights. Click on the **Options** button in the top right-hand corner and then, in the left-hand pane, click on the **Resource Settings** section.

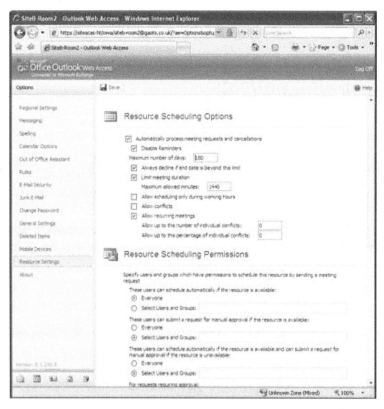

Figure 2:   The Resource Settings page in OWA options.

Once you have reached the **Resource Settings** section of the mailbox options in OWA, you can see the policies that are available. There are three policies, **BookInPolicy**, **RequestInPolicy**, and

RequestOutOfPolicy.

- **BookInPolicy** is a list of users who can schedule the resource automatically. By default it is set to Everyone.

- **RequestInPolicy** is a list of users who can request to schedule a resource and have to have it authorized by the resource administrator.

- **RequestOutOfPolicy** is a list of users who can submit a request for a resource even if it is already booked. (This might for example be used for the CEO!)

This page enables you to allow conflicts, set maximum meeting length, allow recurring meetings, customize the text of notification mails and a host of other settings.

A policy example

So, what if you want to set a policy that makes it mandatory for a delegate to authorise the request when anyone books catering?

This can be done by first setting up the delegate for the catering resource mailbox as above. Then log into OWA (also as above) and set the **These users can schedule automatically if the resource is available:** policy to **Select Users and Groups**. Set the **These users can submit a request for manual approval if the resource is available:** policy to **Everyone**. Save the settings.

At this point, when anyone tries to submit a request, the delegate user will get a mail like the one in Figure 3.

The delegate user can then accept the request (and go ahead and book the catering with the caterer).

Figure 3:   The Request info forwarded to delegates.

Meanwhile the requesting user will get a mail as in Figure 4, showing the pending request. The meeting is held as tentative, to prevent the resource being booked by someone else.

Figure 4:   The Tentative mail received by the user whilst waiting approval.

Once the delegate user approves the request, the meeting will be booked and acceptances sent out.

More info about the policies and the shell commands available can be found here:

HTTP://TECHNET.MICROSOFT.COM/EN-US/LIBRARY/AA996340.ASPX

HTTP://TECHNET.MICROSOFT.COM/EN-US/LIBRARY/BB124987(EXCHG.80).ASPX

Viewing meeting rooms

So what does this look like from the client perspective? In Outlook 2007 it is possible to see all rooms, and their availability, in one window by using the Scheduling Assistant in Outlook 2007 as shown in Figure 5.

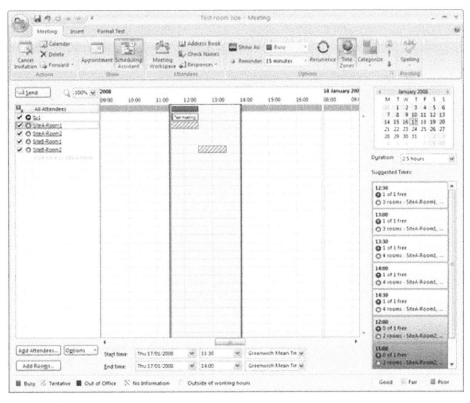

Figure 5:   The Scheduling Assistant.

All rooms can be added from the **Add Rooms** button. In the main window you will see which rooms are available. This is supplemented by the **Suggested Times** area on the right-hand side.

Although it isn't obvious, it is possible to set the meeting time zone when creating a meeting using the **Time Zones** button highlighted at the top right in Figure 5. However, it is not possible to view an additional time zone in the Scheduling Assistant as you can in the main Outlook calendar.

Scheduling resources

The **Scheduling** tab is where most bookings will take place. The basic scheduling of resources is simple. First, open a meeting request and enter a subject and, if necessary, the attendees. Next, move to the **Scheduling** tab. Use the new **Add Rooms** button to open the window as in Figure 6. This shows the **All Rooms** address list which gives a view of the capabilities of each room. As you can see, "SiteB-Room2" is listed with a capacity of two, which is a default property that can be customized on each room, using the Exchange management console, as shown in Figure 7.

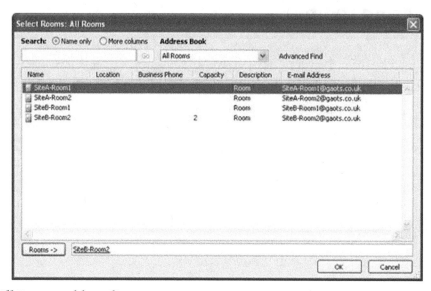

Figure 6:   The All Rooms address list.

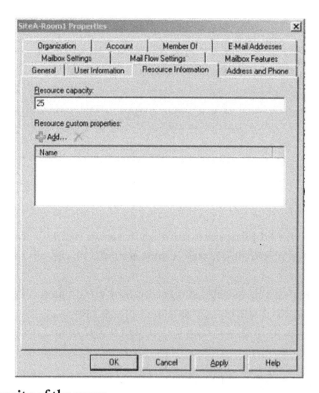

Figure 7:   Setting the capacity of the room.

If you are searching for an available room, select those with the correct properties (such as capacity), and add them. Back on the **Scheduling** tab, you can then use the **Attendees** tab to add other attendees or resources such as projectors. Figure 8 shows the booking facilities.

Figure 8: **Scheduling tab showing users, resources, and rooms.**

Custom resource properties

As I mentioned earlier, it is possible to add custom properties to resource mailboxes. If, for example, you have a catering menu and you want to use a resource mailbox to identify the menu code, then firstly create the custom resource types as follows.

First, read the current resource configuration and store it in a temporary variable called **$ResourceConfiguration** by running the following command:

```
$ResourceConfiguration = Get-ResourceConfig
```

Next, create your custom properties, in this case sandwich types – *Fish, Vegetarian, Meat*:

```
$ResourceConfiguration.ResourcePropertySchema+=("Equipment/Fish")
$ResourceConfiguration.ResourcePropertySchema+=("Equipment/Vegetarian")
$ResourceConfiguration.ResourcePropertySchema+=("Equipment/Meat")
```

Finally, update the resource configuration of your organization by using the modified resource property schema, using the following command:

```
Set-ResourceConfig -Instance $ResourceConfiguration
```

Once you have created the custom resource properties, you will then add them to the relevant resource mailbox. This can be done in the Exchange management console. The example in Figure 9 shows two catering menus.

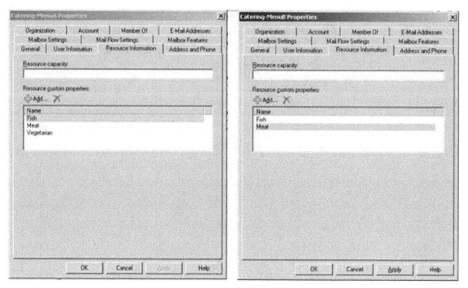

Figure 9:   Showing the method of adding custom resources.

Having done that, one way to view these extended attributes is by using the PowerShell command below:

```
Get-Mailbox -RecipientTypeDetails RoomMailbox |fl Name,ResourceCustom
```

However, with a little more investigation, I have found another more user-friendly way!

As it would appear that only the **All Rooms** address list has the right GUI part to show the **Description** field, I have edited the filter to include the EquipmentMailbox type as well.

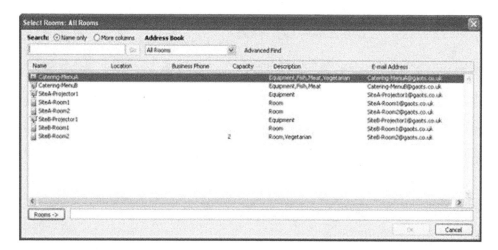

Figure 10: The combined Rooms and Equipment resources showing custom properties.

I used this command to edit the filter. The results of the filter change are shown in Figure 10.

```
Set-AddressList -Identity "All Rooms" -RecipientFilter {(Alias -ne $null -and
(RecipientDisplayType -eq 'ConferenceRoomMailbox' -or RecipientDisplayType -eq
'SyncedConferenceRoomMailbox' -or RecipientDisplayType -eq 'EquipmentMailbox'))}
```

Summary

This article describes the Exchange Resource Scheduling functionality. I realize I haven't covered every single feature, but I have aimed at doing enough to give you the skills needed to continue developing your resource booking solution using Exchange 2007.

In general, with a little investigation and some color-coding in Outlook, you can create a decent resource booking system. Of course it is not as polished as some of the third-party systems, but then a lot of them are not that great!

Some improvements are necessary in the user interface. For example, when you are adding custom resource properties you can't actually see them in Outlook unless you are modifying the **Rooms** address list. It should be possible to use the Exchange Web Services to create a custom front end for working with the "resource mailboxes" that you create. Let's hope someone does it soon.

Microsoft Exchange Server 2007: Controlling Email Messages using Exchange's Transport Rules

22 July 2008

by William Lefkovics

Some tasks that should have been easy in previous versions of Exchange just weren't. Now, with transport rules in Exchange 2007, administrators have a much improved set of tools to manage message flow.

As a long-time Exchange administrator, one of the great frustrations I have found over the years has been how difficult certain, seemingly trivial, administrative tasks are to implement in Exchange Server. It is almost embarrassing to tell management that it is not that simple to add a disclaimer to outbound SMTP messages, or insert text into the subject of certain messages, or control message flow for compliance requirements.

With Exchange Server 2007, Microsoft addresses many of these deficiencies by completely changing the underlying architecture. SMTP has been brought back into Exchange instead of extending the SMTP service in Internet Information Server (IIS). Arduous transport event sinks have been replaced by Transport Agents on the Hub Transport and Edge Transport roles. Transport rules are implemented in the Exchange 2007 architecture through Transport Agents. There is a Transport Rules Agent on all Hub Transport Servers and an Edge Transport Agent on all Edge Servers. Administrators now have a basic UI to control messages using transport rules – one of the killer features of the latest Exchange Server.

Focus of transport server roles

Edge Transport Servers perform gateway services for an Exchange organization. They are somewhat independent sentries in the perimeter of corporate networks. As such, their function in terms of transport rules focuses on message hygiene and security. Edge servers are not domain members and have no direct access to Active Directory.

Hub Transport Servers, on the other hand, are integrated in the Windows domain infrastructure and have access to Active Directory. They handle messages that remain internal to the organization, in addition to content arriving from, or departing to, an Edge Transport server. The focus of transport rules implemented on the Hub Transport role is geared toward policy enforcement and compliance.

Because of the different focus of transport rules between the Edge and Hub Transports, the actual set of rules varies between them.

Scope of transport server roles

Edge Transport servers work alone. Transport rules on the Edge are stored in a somewhat portable subset of Active Directory called Active Directory Application Mode (ADAM). A special updating mechanism called EdgeSync is used to keep ADAM fairly current for Edge with user information from AD. If there are multiple Edge servers in place, they do not share their instance of ADAM. Any updates must be performed separately to each Edge server. Different Edge Transport servers may control different connections to the Exchange organization or they may be clones of one to serve as redundant gateways for a single connection. Either way, Edge servers are not aware of each other, they are not members of the internal Exchange organization or Windows domain, and they operate independently.

By contrast, every single email message sent in an Exchange 2007 organization must pass through at least one Hub Transport Server. Even if the sender and recipient reside in the same database, the message leaves the store and passes through the transport pipeline on a Hub Transport Server before returning to the mailbox server. Transport rules are stored in Active Directory. This means (and this is important) that every Hub Transport Server accesses the same set of transport rules. Messages sent through Exchange 2007 can not bypass transport rule processing! Historically, this has been a significant obstacle for administering an Exchange messaging infrastructure that meets regulatory compliance initiatives.

Write your own Transport Agent! What do you need? All that is required to compose and implement a custom Transport Agent is a server with either the Exchange 2007 Edge Transport Role or the Hub Transport Role installed. The Microsoft .NET Framework 2.0 Software Development Kit (SDK) and a suitable IDE, such as Visual Studio 2005 or 2008 (to compile the agent to a DLL) are also needed. Microsoft provides a set of classes through the .NET Framework extensions to programmatically access, and even change, SMTP message properties at various events through the transport pipeline. A little C# or Visual Basic programming skills does help.

For more information on developing Transport Agents see the Microsoft Exchange Server 2007 SP1 SDK: WWW.MICROSOFT.COM/DOWNLOADS/DETAILS.ASPX?FAMILYID=I90F7IA4-7B5F-4A4C-99BA-9BDO32EI6EI5&DISPLAYLANG=EN or MSDN: HTTP://MSDN.MICROSOFT.COM/EN-US/LIBRARY/AA579I85%28EXCHG.80%29.ASPX

What types of messages do transport rules work against?

Almost every type of message that travels through the hub goes through transport rule processing. Standard email messages with plain text, HTML, or RTF are all accessible by the transport rule agent. Transport rules do work for digitally signed messages and encrypted or opaque messages as well, but only aspects that it can access. A rule can still read the message header even if the message body has been encrypted.

Exchange 2007 Service Pack 1 added transport rule support for IPM.Note formatted messages, as you might see from applications that generate email messages, as well as unified messaging emails, including voice mail messages, fax messages, and missed call notification messages.

Anatomy of a transport rule

Help Microsoft improve transport rules!

Ben Neuwirth at Microsoft posted a blog entry publishing a script that can be run against your transport servers to return a statistical analysis outlining which predicates and actions you use most. The script does not collect any personal data and you can review it before emailing it to Ben. The entry is found at HTTP://MSEXCHANGETEAM.COM/ARCHIVE/2008/07/07/449150.ASPX.

Transport rules are not all that different from Outlook rules in their logic. Each rule is composed of at least one condition, an Action or Actions and optionally, one or more Exceptions. If no conditions are selected, then the rule will apply to **all** messages. Where there are multiple conditions, they all must be met; however, no matter how many exceptions there are, it only takes one to prevent the rule from firing.

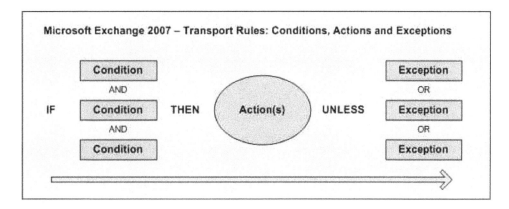

Figure 1.

Figure 1 shows this logical flow through a transport rule. Transport rules are quite flexible with a solid set of options.

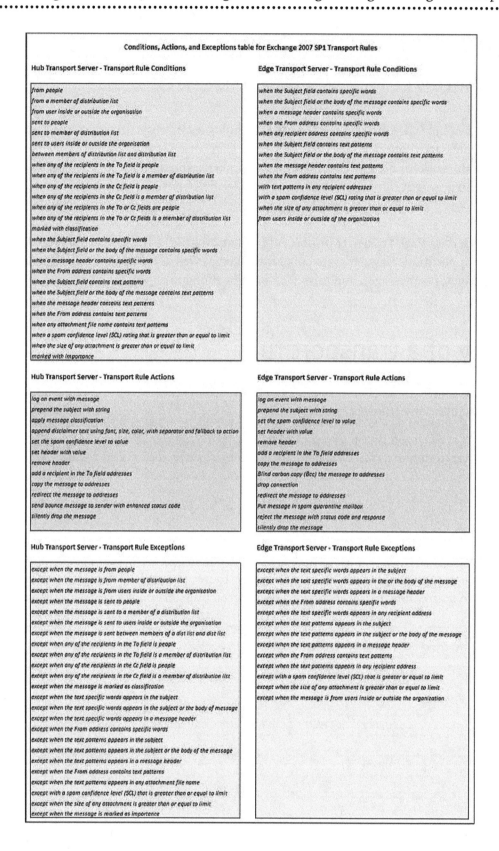

Figure 2.

Figure 2 shows the various Conditions, Actions, and Exceptions for the Edge and Hub Transport Servers. When these predicates and actions are selected, there are variables to include, such as text, addresses, and other properties. Unfortunately, you can not add your own actions or predicates to Microsoft's transport rules interface. You can develop your own custom transport agent to fulfil such a need, of course.

Regulatory compliance

Many companies these days are required to assert greater control over their messaging solutions. Regulatory agencies in various countries demand certain email communications be archived and discoverable. In addition, corporate policy may be designed to minimize liability exposure by providing employees with a working environment safe from harassment or loss of productivity through electronic communications. Transport rules in Exchange 2007 provide rudimentary solutions to assist administrators in deploying effectively compliant messaging systems. For example, archiving sensitive information may be required in some jurisdictions. Who wants to be investigated by the UK Information Commissioner's Office or the US Securities and Exchange Commission and not be able to provide the content they require?

Ethical walls

Since every message must pass through a Hub Transport Server, the hub becomes the point of message control for policy enforcement and compliance. Transport rules can fire on messages where senders or recipients belong to specific groups. This makes it easy to allow or prevent mail flow based on universal distribution group membership. A transport rule can prevent confidential email sent, either intentionally or accidentally, from the Finance department to a factory worker, simply by restricting delivery of email between those groups. This virtual blockade of email communication between groups is referred to as an Ethical Firewall or Ethical Wall. A policy may be put in place to have CFO emails, which are often of a sensitive nature, blocked from being sent to factory workers. In the rare case where the CFO needs to send something, then perhaps the HR department can send that email instead. Every company is different, and Transport rules provide some flexibility for securing the flow of email for diverse scenarios. Ethical walls using transport rules reduce the potential for confidential information to get into the wrong Inbox.

Message classifications

Note

Message Classifications are not available to Outlook clients by default. Outlook 2007 clients require Message Classifications to be exported from AD and copied to the local registry on the workstation for Outlook to access. This manual process allows administrative control on who can apply classifications to messages.

With Exchange 2007 there is a special type of server-side message categorization called Message Classification, usable with OWA 2007 and Outlook 2007 clients. These are custom labels stored in Active Directory that can be applied to email messages. Transport rules can either act upon messages with specific classifications or can assign a message classification to messages based on specific properties. Exchange 2007 actually has a few sample message classifications by default. These are not accessible through the EMC; however, they are fairly easily managed using the EMS.

To create a list of Message Classifications using the EMS type the following cmdlet:

```
[PS]C:\>Get-MessageClassification | ft
```

This will generate a simple table, as shown in Figure 3, where you can also identify a new Message Classification we added for Simple Talk articles.

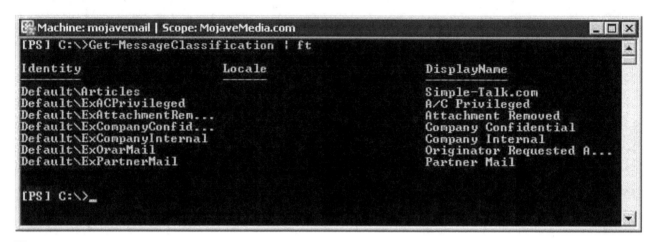

Figure 3.

Working with Message Classifications goes beyond the scope of this article. More information can be found at the source: HTTP://TECHNET.MICROSOFT.COM/EN-US/LIBRARY/AA998271(EXCHG.80).ASPX.

Creating a new transport rule

What permissions are needed to create transport rules?

Just to see the transport rules, the administrator must be delegated at least the Exchange View-Only Administrator role. To create or modify existing transport rules, the administrator must have the Exchange Organization Administrator role.

As you probably already know, the Exchange Management Console (EMC) was built upon the Exchange Management Shell (EMS). Each action performed from the EMC holds an equivalent EMS cmdlet. Transport rules can be managed from either the EMC or the EMS. We will look at both options.

Whether you are creating a new transport rule on a Hub server or an Edge server, the process is very similar. We will walk through an example using the Hub Transport Server where messages are copied to another mailbox based on keywords in the subject. On an internal Exchange 2007 server, the EMC has a few containers outlining menu options based on scope. Hub Transport rules are stored in Active Directory in the Exchange Configuration container, so they are replicated throughout the entire AD forest. Logically, transport rules are thus managed using the Hub Transport option under the Organization container in the EMC as shown in the left-hand pane in Figure 4.

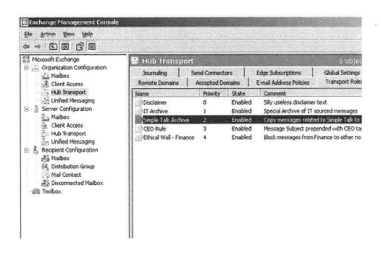

Figure 4.

Also in Figure 4, you can see that the **Transport Rules** tab in the center pane is selected.

To launch the wizard, click on the **New Transport Rule** option in the **Action** pane of the EMC.

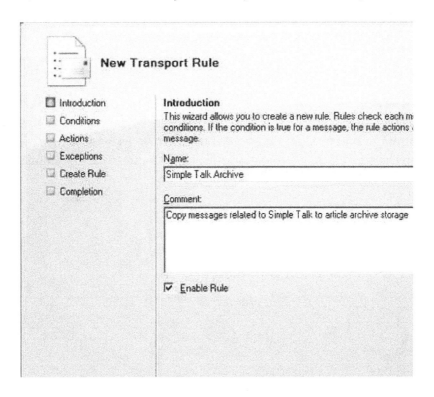

Figure 5.

Figure 5 shows the initial screen requiring a name for the rule. The description field is informational and optional, and is displayed in the EMC. The wizard walks through the conditions, actions, and exceptions for the new transport rule. For our example, the property that triggers the rule is the presence of the keywords "Red Gate" or "Simple Talk" in the message subject, as shown in Figure 6.

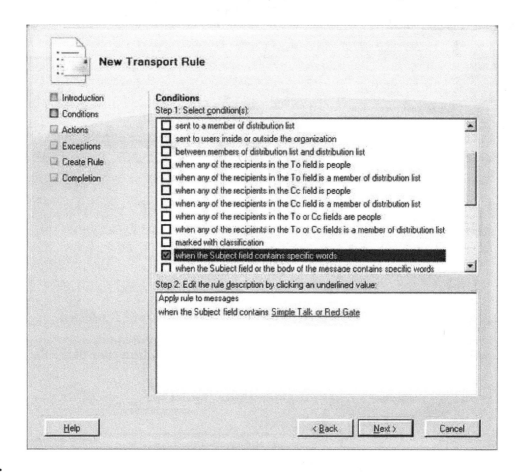

Figure 6.

This condition will result in the message being copied to an article archive mailbox (see Figure 7) unless the message has been tagged with the Message Classification "Company Confidential" (see Figure 8).

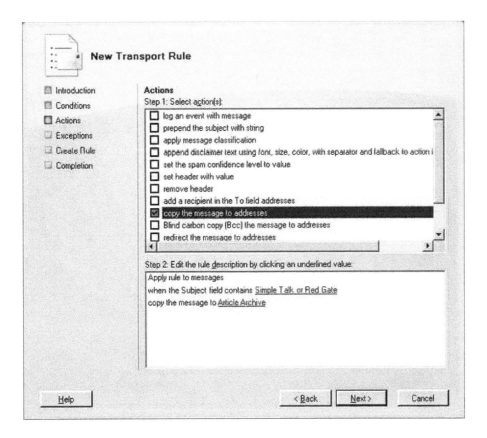

Figure 7.

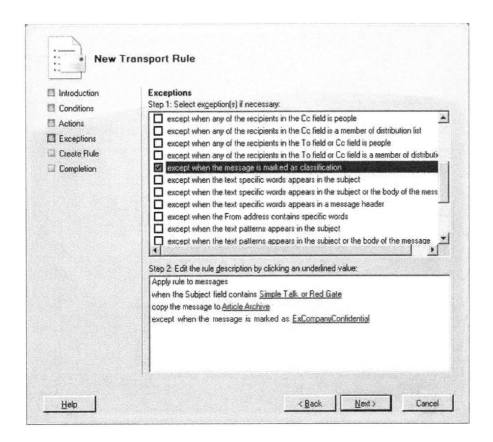

Figure 8.

The next window in the New Rule wizard is a confirmation of what has been entered (see Figure 9).

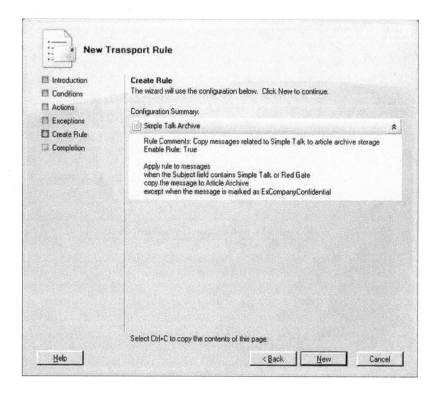

Figure 9.

Clicking New will complete the rule and present the EMS code that was used to create it (see Figure 10).

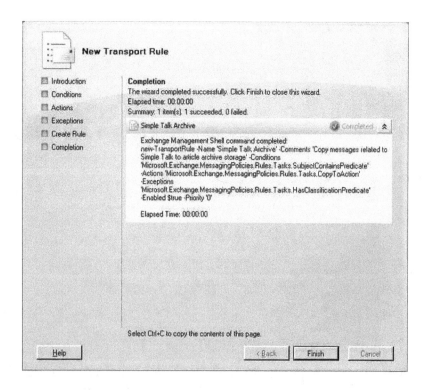

Figure 10.

CTRL+C will copy this EMS command to the clipboard. In most places in the EMC, the cmdlet is complete; however, for transport rules, the variables are not displayed in the UI. They must be assigned manually if you are entering the transport rule using the New-TransportRule cmdlet. In our example, this command is as follows:

```
[PS]C:\>
$Condition = Get-TransportRulePredicate SubjectContains
$Condition.Words = ("Simple Talk,""Red Gate")
$Action = Get-TransportRuleAction CopyTo
$Action.Addresses = @((Get-Mailbox "Article Archive"))
$Exception = Get-TransportRulePredicate HasClassification
$Exception.Classification = (Get-MessageClassification ExCompanyConfidential).
Identity

new-TransportRule -Name 'Simple Talk Archive' -Comments 'Copy messages related
to Simple Talk to article archive storage' -Conditions $Condition -Actions
$Action -Exceptions $Exception -Enabled $true -Priority '0'
```

The last parameter sets a transport rule priority. Transport rules are applied in order of priority, starting with "0." Rules are added in the order they are created. It may be necessary to move a rule up the list and this is controlled using the -priority parameter in EMS for either New-TransportRule or Set-TransportRule cmdlets. This is also easily done in the EMC by using **Change Priority** option in the **Actions** pane when the desired rule is selected.

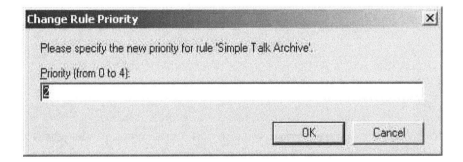

Figure 11.

Figure 11 shows the interface for entering a numerical priority from 0 (highest) to the number of rules less 1. Microsoft recommends a maximum of 1,000 rules, mostly because that is where they stopped testing. This should be more than enough for most companies.

You modify existing transport rules in much the same way – either with the EMC or EMS. The EMS uses the Set-TransportRule cmdlet for updating rules. For a list of cmdlets for managing transport rules in the EMS, see Get-Help as shown in Figure 12.

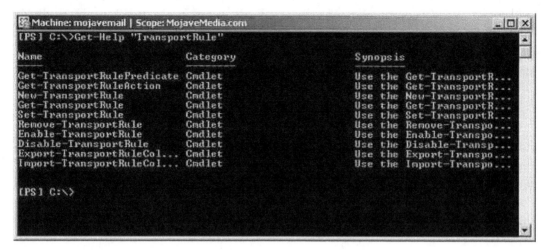

Figure 12.

Backing up transport rules

Internally, transport rules reside in AD, so they are backed up with AD. If you are going to make significant changes to transport rules, you might want to back up the set currently in place first. The EMS cmdlet `Export-TransportRuleCollection` bundles all of the transport rules into a file which can be imported later if needed. Importing overwrites the existing rules. On an Edge Server, exporting the transport rules is used as a backup mechanism, or to import them into other "cloned" Edge Transport servers.

Summary

Exchange Server 2007 takes great steps forward in controlling messages and message transport from an administrator perspective. Some tasks that were challenging or required third-party applications in previous versions of Exchange have been made more accessible through transport rules in Exchange 2007. With the Edge Server role concerned with security and the Hub Transport role focused on compliance and policy enforcement, transport rules provide a much improved set of tools for administrators to manage message flow in their Exchange organizations.

Exchange Database Technologies

22 August 2008

by Jaap Wesselius

··

One of the most misunderstood technologies in Exchange Server, regardless of its version, is the database technology. Most people, even Exchange administrators know it is something to do with ESE and tools like ESEUTIL but, once it's running, they leave it that way for the rest of their lives. It's too difficult and you'd better not touch it in case it breaks!

··

In this article, I'll explain some of the fundamentals of the Exchange Server database technology. The primary focus is on Exchange Server 2007 but, when appropriate, I'll refer to Exchange Server 2003.

What's on the disk?

When you've installed Exchange Server 2007 you will find some database files on the C:\ drive, typically in "C:\Program Files\Microsoft\Exchange Server\Mailbox\First Storage Group\" as can be seen in Figure 1.

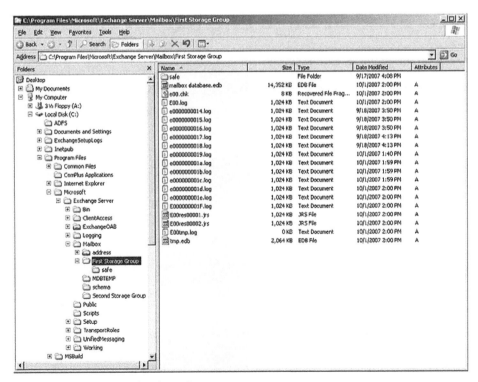

Figure 1:   Database files in a standard Exchange setup.

We can see several files in this directory:

- **mailbox database.edb** – this is the actual mailbox database where all the mailboxes are hosted. One or more mailbox databases can be hosted in one directory

- **E00.log** and subsequent log files – these are log files that are used by Exchange server for transactional processing of all information

- **e00.chk** – a checkpoint file that keeps track of the relation between the information in the log files and in the database

- **E00tmp.log** – a temporary log file

- **E00res00001.jrs** and **E00res00002.jrs** – temporary reserved log files used by Exchange server in case a Disk Full situation occurs.

These files belong together and create a so-called "Storage Group." During the installation of Exchange Server, one database is created in a Storage Group. In Exchange 2007, the Public Folder database is created in a second Storage Group. When replication technology (like LCR, CCR or SCR) in Exchange 2007 is used, then only one database per Storage Group can exist. If no replication technology is used, up to five databases can be created in each Storage Group.

So, a Storage Group is a set of one or more database files that share a common set of log files.

ESE – Extensible Storage Engine

The underlying technology used in Exchange Server is the Extensible Storage Engine, or ESE. ESE is a low-level database technology, sometimes referred to as JET database. ESE has been used for Exchange since the first version of Exchange, version 4.0 in 1997. But Active Directory, WINS, and DHCP also use a form of ESE.

The ESE database follows the ACID principle. ACID stands for:

- Atomic – A transaction is all or nothing, there is no "unknown state" for a transaction

- Consistent – the transaction preserves the consistency of the data being processed

- Isolated – a transaction is the only transaction on this data, even when multiple transactions occur at the same time

- Durable – the committed transactions are preserved in the database.

Transactions can be seen in normal life, as well. Suppose you go to the bank to transfer money from your savings account to your normal account. The money is withdrawn from your savings account and then added to your normal account and both actions are recorded and maybe printed on paper. This can be seen as one transaction. You don't want it to end in an unknown state, where the money is withdrawn from your savings account but not added to your normal account.

The same principle goes for Exchange Server. Suppose you move a message from your Inbox to a folder named "Simple Talk." From a transaction point of view it starts by adding the message to the "Simple Talk" folder, then it updates the message count from this folder, it deletes the message from the Inbox and updates the message count for the Inbox. All these actions can be seen as one transaction.

The mailbox database

The mailbox database is the primary repository of the Exchange Server information. This is where all the Exchange Server data is stored. On disk it is normally referred to as **mailbox database.edb**; in older versions of Exchange Server it is called **Priv1.edb**, but it can have any name you want.

In Exchange Server 2000 there was also a file called **Priv1.stm**, referred to as the streaming file. It was meant to store Internet messages like SMTP. These messages were saved in the streaming file and a pointer was set in the .edb file. An .edb file and a .stm file belong together and cannot exist without each other. The streaming file was removed from Exchange 2007, which was possible because of the improvements to ESE, though Exchange 5.5 also had no .stm file.

In theory, the mailbox database can be 16 TB in size, but it is normally limited to a size you can handle within the constraints of your Service Level Agreement or SLA. The recommended maximum database size of a normal Exchange Server 2007 (or earlier) is 50 GB, for an Exchange Server 2007 using Local Continuous Replication it is 100 GB, and for an Exchange Server 2007 using Continuous Cluster Replication it is 200 GB. These are sizes that can readily be used in a normal backup cycle, and can be restored in an appropriate timeframe when needed.

The data within a database is organized in a Binary Tree, or B+ Tree. A Binary Tree can be seen as an upside-down tree where the leaves are in the lower part. The actual mail data is stored in the leaves. The other pages only contain pointers. This is a very efficient way of storing data since it requires only two or three lookups to find a particular piece of data, and all pointers can be kept in memory.

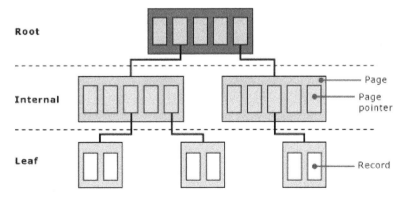

Figure 2: A Binary Tree used in Exchange Server. The actual data is stored in the leaves.

One or more Trees in a database make a table. There are several kinds of table in an Exchange server: a **Folders** table, a **Message** table, **Multiple Message Folder** tables, and an **Attachment** table.

The tables hold the information we can see in Outlook (Web Access). The tables consist of columns and records, the columns are identified as MAPI properties, the records contain the actual information.

Multiple Trees exist in one database and sometimes Trees need to be split when the Tree fills up. Exchange Server's internal processes will reorganize all information from one Tree into two Trees. This is called a "split." It is not possible to predict how many Trees will be in a particular database, but it will be hundreds or thousands of Trees. This can be seen in the header of the database which will be explained later in this article.

Database pages

A page is the smallest unit of data in an Exchange Server environment. For Exchange Server 2007, a page is 8KB in size; all earlier versions use a 4KB page size. Increasing the page size from 4KB to 8KB results in a dramatic increase in performance of the database technology. There are also several hardware storage solutions that perform much better with a page size of 8KB.

A page consists of a header, pointers to other pages, checksum information, and the actual data from Exchange Server regarding messages, attachments or folders, for example. A database file can consist of millions of pages. The total number of database pages can easily be calculated by dividing the total size of the database by the page size of 8KB. If a database, for example, is 100 GB in size, it consists of 100 GB/8KB = approximately 13.1 million pages. Each page is sequentially numbered. Whenever a new page is created it gets a new incremented number. When pages are read from the database and altered, they get a new number before being written to the log file and flushed to the database file. Needless to say, this sequential number must be a very large number. It's a 64-bit number which means 18 quintillion changes can be made to a database.

How does it fit together?

There are four parts that are import with respect to Exchange Server data:

The **internal server memory** – this is the location where all the processing of data takes place. Exchange server creates new database pages when needed and processes them. When a database page is needed from the database file it is read from the disk into memory.

The **log files** – as soon as Exchange Server has finished processing the database pages for a transaction they are immediately written to the log file in use at that moment. This is the log file called E00.log, or E01.log, E02.log and so on, depending on the Storage Group. Please remember that every Storage Group has its own set of log files starting with its own prefix like E00, E01, E02 etc. The database pages are kept in memory though, because the pages might be needed in the near future. If so, and it is still in memory, it saves the Exchange Server a disk read. A disk read is a valuable disk action that is much slower than a page read from memory. When a log file is filled it is closed and renamed to a different name. This name consists of the prefix, followed by a sequential number which is incremented every time the log file is saved. This way you can see files like E0000001.log, E0000002.log, E0000003.log, etc. Be aware that the sequence use HEX numbering – the log file that follows E0000009.log is going to be E000000A.log, not E0000010.log. The sequence number in Exchange terms is called the lGeneration number. This process is called the log file roll-over.

The **database file**, the part where the database pages are stored eventually. As stated before, a transaction is written to the log file first but it is kept in memory. When Exchange needs more memory the database pages are flushed to the database file. They are flushed from memory to the database file, they are not read from the log files and then written to the database. This is a common misunderstanding! Flushing data to the database file also occurs when pages are kept too long in memory and the gap between the log files and the database file become too large.

The difference between the transactions in the log file and the transactions in the database is monitored by the **checkpoint file**, E00.chk (for the first storage group). The checkpoint file records the location of the last transaction written to the database file. As soon as a new transaction is written to the database file, the checkpoint file location is advanced to the next location.

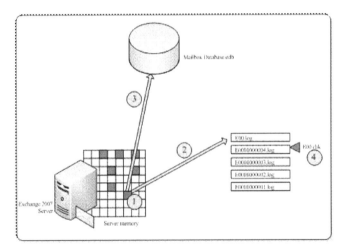

Figure 3:   Schematic overview of the working of the Exchange Server database.

The above mentioned process is the same in all versions of Exchange Server.

Note

*One serious constraint in Exchange 2003 and earlier is the 32-bit platform, which is limited to only 4 GB of memory. All processes will run in this 4 GB memory, separated into 2 GB of system and 2 GB of user space. This is relatively tight for caching purposes, especially when a large number of mailboxes are consolidated on one Exchange 2003 server. It can be tweaked using the /3GB (HTTP:// SUPPORT.MICROSOFT.COM/?KBID=823440) and the /USERVA switch (HTTP://SUPPORT.MICROSOFT. COM/?KBID=810371) in the **boot.ini** file of the Exchange Server, but it still isn't an optimal situation.*

Memory constraints will always result in a higher disk IO, and when the storage is not designed properly this will result in a bad performance. Most of the Exchange 2003 performance issues are related to bad storage design. Exchange 2007 is a 64-bit platform and memory usage on a 64-bit server is only limited by your budget. Exchange 2007 will use as much memory as possible for caching, which will result in fewer IO operations on the disk. So, the more memory in your Exchange 2007 server, the less disk IO you will see on your storage.

All transactions in an Exchange server flow through the log files. This is the only way to achieve a consistent environment. This includes everything – new messages as they arrive, the creation of new folders, moving messages between folders, deleting messages, appointments, notes, etc. All information in the mailbox goes through the log files. The creation of the mailbox (not the mailbox properties in Active Directory though!) is recorded in the log files, and even the creation of a mailbox database is recorded in the log files. This automatically means that if you lose your database and you still have all your log files available (maybe in combination with your last backup set) you can reconstruct everything up to the point you lost your database.

Note

It is very important to separate your log files and your database files. Separate them on multiple disks or multiple LUNs. If you separate them on multiple LUNs on your SAN, make sure that, under the hood multiple, separated disks are used. This will have a positive impact on your performance and it will make sure you have a recovery path when either one of the disks is lost!

One important point to remember is that the log files are always in advance of the database, so there's always data not yet written into the database. This data can cover a number of log files and this number of log files or amount of data is called the "checkpoint depth." This automatically means the database in a running state is always in a non-consistent state. To get it in a consistent state, all log files in this range are needed. This is because data is already written to the log files, but not yet to the database file.

In Exchange Server this is called a "dirty shutdown" state. When a database is dismounted it is brought into a consistent state. All data not yet written to disk is flushed to the database and all files are closed. All information is now written into the database. This is called a "clean shutdown" state of the database.

The log files needed to get the database into a consistent state or "clean shutdown" are recorded in the header of the database. The header of a database is written into the first page of the database file and contains information regarding the database. The header information can be retrieved using the ESEUTIL tool. Just enter the following command in the directory where the database file resides:

```
ESEUTIL /MH "Mailbox Database.edb"
```

Which will result in an output like this:

```
F:\SG2>eseutil /mh mbx2.edb

Extensible Storage Engine Utilities for Microsoft(R) Exchange Server
Version 08.01
Copyright (C) Microsoft Corporation. All Rights Reserved.
```

```
Initiating FILE DUMP mode...
      Database: mbx2.edb


     File Type: Database
 Format ulMagic: 0x89abcdef
 Engine ulMagic: 0x89abcdef
Format ulVersion: 0x620,12
Engine ulVersion: 0x620,12
Created ulVersion: 0x620,12
    DB Signature: Create time:07/03/2008 21:44:30 Rand:136947877 Computer:
      cbDbPage: 8192
        dbtime: 8851359 (0x870f9f)
         State: Dirty Shutdown
  Log Required: 14647-14658 (0x3937-0x3942)
  Log Committed: 0-14659 (0x0-0x3943)
 Streaming File: No
       Shadowed: Yes
     Last Objid: 6345
   Scrub Dbtime: 0 (0x0)
     Scrub Date: 00/00/1900 00:00:00
   Repair Count: 0
    Repair Date: 00/00/1900 00:00:00
Old Repair Count: 0
Last Consistent: (0x2F16,2D,181) 07/29/2008 19:34:29
    Last Attach: (0x2F17,9,86) 07/29/2008 19:34:29
    Last Detach: (0x0,0,0) 00/00/1900 00:00:00
          Dbid: 1
  Log Signature: Create time:07/03/2008 21:44:29 Rand:136951962 Computer:
    OS Version: (5.2.3790 SP 2)


Previous Full Backup:
     Log Gen: 8697-8722 (0x21f9-0x2212)
       Mark: (0x220D,1EC,162)
       Mark: 07/19/2008 22:57:43


Previous Incremental Backup:
     Log Gen: 0-0 (0x0-0x0)
       Mark: (0x0,0,0)
       Mark: 00/00/1900 00:00:00


Previous Copy Backup:
     Log Gen: 0-0 (0x0-0x0)
       Mark: (0x0,0,0)
       Mark: 00/00/1900 00:00:00


Previous Differential Backup:
```

```
    Log Gen:  0-0  (0x0-0x0)
       Mark:  (0x0,0,0)
       Mark:  00/00/1900  00:00:00

 Current Full Backup:
    Log Gen:  0-0  (0x0-0x0)
       Mark:  (0x0,0,0)
       Mark:  00/00/1900  00:00:00

 Current Shadow copy backup:
    Log Gen:  0-0  (0x0-0x0)
       Mark:  (0x0,0,0)
       Mark:  00/00/1900  00:00:00


    cpgUpgrade55Format: 0
   cpgUpgradeFreePages: 0
cpgUpgradeSpaceMapPages: 0


    ECC Fix Success Count: none
  Old ECC Fix Success Count: none
     ECC Fix Error Count: none
  Old ECC Fix Error Count: none
  Bad Checksum Error Count: none
Old bad Checksum Error Count: none


Operation completed successfully in 0.578 seconds.



    F:\SG2>
```

Plenty of interesting information regarding the database can be found in this output.

- **DB Signature** – a unique value of date, time, and an integer that identifies this particular database. This value is also recorded in the log files and the checkpoint files, and this ties them together.

- **cbDbPage** – the size of the pages used in this database. In Exchange 2007 this is 8KB, in earlier versions of Exchange Server this is 4KB.

- **Dbtime** – (part of) the number of changes made to this database.

- **State** – this files shows the state of the database, i.e. whether it is in a consistent state or not. The database in this example is in a "dirty shutdown" state (I crashed it to get the information) and it needs a certain amount of log files to get in a "clean shutdown" state.

- **Log Required** – if it is not in a consistent state, these log files are needed to bring it into a consistent state. To make this database a consistent state again, the log files E000003937.log through E000003942.log are needed. Exchange Server will perform the recovery process when mounting a database so, under normal circumstances, no Exchange Administrator action is needed.

- **Log Committed** – this entry is for a new feature in Exchange 2007 called "Lost Log Resiliency" or LLR. Under normal operation the E00.log is just an open file. When the Exchange Server crashes there is the possibility that the E00.log will be corrupted. When this happens it is no longer possible to recover the database to a consistent state because E00.log is in the "Logs Required" range. The LLR feature takes the E00.log out of the "Logs Required" range, making it possible to do a recovery even if the E00.log is lost. One important thing to note is that all information already contained in the E00.log will be lost!

- **Last ObjID** – the number of B+ Trees in this particular database. In this example there are 6,345 B+ trees in the database.

- **Log Signature** – a unique value of date, time, and an integer that uniquely identifies a series of log files. As with the database signature, this ties the database file, the log files, and the checkpoint file together.

- **Backup information** – entries used by Exchange Server to keep track of the last full or incremental (or VSS) backup that was made on this particular database.

The same kind of information is logged in the header of the log files (ESEUTIL /ML E00.LOG) and in the header of the checkpoint file (ESEUTIL /MK E00.CHK). As these file are grouped together, you can match these files using the header information.

Conclusion

A Storage Group in an Exchange Server is one or more database files, a set of log files, and a checkpoint file. These files belong together and have a tight relationship. But if you understand the basic principles of transactional logging it isn't too difficult. All information in a database is first recorded in the log files for recovery purposes, so deleting "unneeded" log files to create additional space is a bad idea since it will break the recovery process. Don't just delete these log files, but have them purged by a backup application. This way you have a recovery process using this backup and the log files that are generated after the last backup.

Bad things can happen to databases and log files in recovery scenarios. These bad things are not normally caused by Exchange Server itself, but by administrators who do not know what they are doing and do not underdstand the implications of their actions.

Install a test server, create some storage groups and mailboxes, and start playing around with the databases. See for yourself what happens during a crash and discover the databases and the header information. It will be the first step in a solid disaster recovery plan!

Message Classifications in Exchange 2007

18 September 2008

by Neil Hobson

In Exchange 2007, you can now classify your messages in any way you wish, so that, for example, you can flag messages as being sensitive information that should not be sent outside the company. You can also create transport rules for all messages of a particular category. It is an easy way of implementing email policies within a company.

Introduction

Exchange 2007 has a new feature, known as message classification, that allows users to apply a classification to a message to ensire that the actual usage of that message is understood by both the sending and receiving parties. In previous versions of Exchange, the concept of message classification has been restricted to marking messages with high, normal, or low importance. Now it's possible to not only choose between the default message classifications that ship with Exchange 2007, but also to create custom classifications, as I'll show you later.

It's important to understand that message classifications are also an Outlook 2007 feature and therefore this is the version of Outlook you need to deploy to take advantage of this feature. However, there are several configuration changes required in order to make message classifications available to Outlook 2007 clients. If you have Outlook Web Access 2007 clients, these can use message classifications without any further modifications.

As I've just mentioned, there are message classifications that are provided by default. In all, there are six default message classifications. They are: A/C Privileged, Attachment Removed, Company Confidential, Company Internal, Originator Requested Alternate Recipient Mail, and Partner Mail.

In the next section of this article I'll be showing you how to export the message classifications to an XML file that the Outlook 2007 clients within your environment can locate. This is to allow Outlook 2007 to display the classifications within email messages. Therefore, if you plan on creating new custom message classifications, you should do so before you export the classifications to an XML file. I'll be covering the creation of custom message classifications later in the article.

Creating the XML file

The first part of the process is the creation of the classification XML file that Outlook 2007 will reference. Fortunately, Microsoft has made this part of the process easy by providing a PowerShell script that can do this for you. The script is installed along with Exchange 2007 and can be found in the *\Program Files\ Microsoft\Exchange Server\Scripts* folder on the drive where you installed Exchange 2007. The script name is *Export-OutlookClassification.ps1* as you can see from Figure 1.

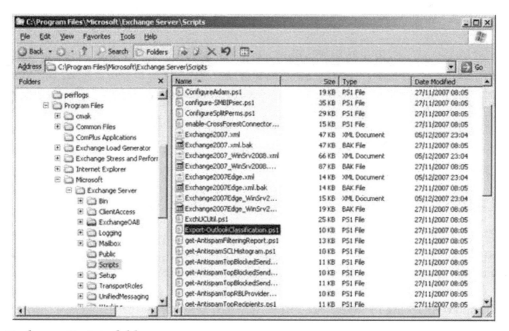

Figure 1: **Exchange Scripts folder.**

To use this script, bring up the Exchange Management Shell and run the following cmdlet:

```
./Export-OutlookClassification > c:\classifications.xml
```

As you can see from the cmdlet example, the output of the PowerShell script is redirected to a file called *C:\classifications.xml*. Of course, you are free to use a different file name if you choose. If running the cmdlet has been successful, you should be returned straight back to the command prompt; in other words, there is no "success" message per se. To prove that the cmdlet has been successful, open the classifications.xml file with Internet Explorer and check for valid contents. An example of what this file looks like when the six default message classifications have been exported is shown in Figure 2.

Figure 2:   Contents of classification.xml.

The classifications that you have exported to the XML file are those classifications that can be chosen by the users who are sending the message; they have nothing to do with the type of message classification that a user can receive. I will expand on this later in the article. Now that you have exported the classifications.xml file, there are two additional parts of the overall message classification configuration to complete. First, you need to store the classifications.xml file in a location that each Outlook 2007 client can access and, second, you need to make a registry change to each Outlook 2007 client to enable message classifications. I'll cover these two configuration elements in the next two sections of this article.

Locating the XML file

With regard to the location of the classification.xml file, you might think at first that the best location is on a network share, since you will only need to copy the file once to a specific location. However, it's actually better if you copy the file locally to each Outlook 2007 client that requires the use of message classifications. You have to consider the case of Outlook 2007 clients that run in cached mode. Outlook 2007 clients that are running in cached mode are sometimes disconnected from the corporate network, such as those users connecting via Outlook Anywhere when working from home. I'm not suggesting that the model of copying the classification XML file to every Outlook 2007 client is the best model that Microsoft could have come up with but, at the same time, this is what we, as IT professionals, currently have to work with. Therefore, you'll need to produce a good working method, such as login scripts, to distribute the XML file to all Outlook 2007 clients along with the registry change that is detailed in the next section.

Required registry modification

Once you have copied the XML file to each client machine that requires the message classification functionality, you also need to create several registry values on these same client machines. The required registry information is as follows:

```
Key:
HKEY_CURRENT_USER\Software\Microsoft\Office\12.0\Common\Policy
String Value:
AdminClassificationPath
Value:
c:\classifications.xml
This is the location of the XML file and therefore must match the file name and
location of your classification XML file.
DWORD Value:
EnableClassifications
Value:
1
This setting simply controls whether message classifications are enabled or not.
Set this to 1 to enable message classifications or 0 to disable them.
DWORD Value:
TrustClassifications
Value:
1
```

The TrustClassifications setting should be set to 1 when the user's mailbox is on an Exchange 2007 server. This setting can also be used to control the prepending of text to the message classification when sending messages to mailboxes on legacy versions of Exchange, since these versions of Exchange do not support message classifications. I will not be covering this area any further within this article.

The *Policy* key is not present by default, and so must be created. Once the new information has been entered, the registry should look like the one shown in Figure 3.

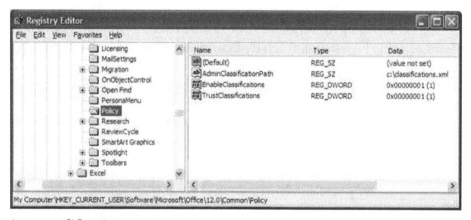

Figure 3:   Registry modifications.

Creating a classified message

Having set up classifications, creating a classified message couldn't be easier. Once you've copied the classification XML file to the Outlook 2007 client and created the required registry settings, launch Outlook 2007 and compose a new message. If you had Outlook 2007 open when making the registry changes, restart Outlook 2007 to start using message classifications.

In the new message window, you'll find the **Permission** button on the ribbon as you can see from Figure 4.

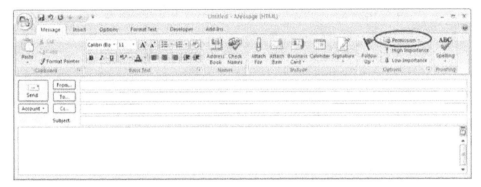

Figure 4: Outlook 2007 Permission button.

Click the small down-arrow to the right of the **Permission** button and you will be presented with the six message classification options as defined in the XML file created earlier. You can see this in Figure 5.

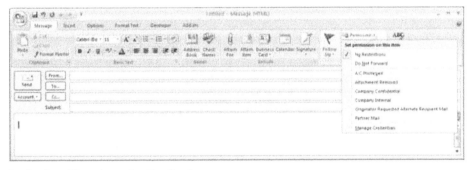

Figure 5: Default classifications in Outlook 2007.

Let's say that I choose to classify this new message as **Company Confidential**. Once I've classified my message, it appears as shown in Figure 6 below.

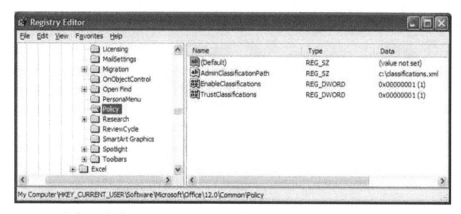

Figure 6: New message classified as Company Confidential.

What if the recipient, a user called Ann in this case, isn't enabled for message classifications and therefore doesn't have the required registry modifications in place? In this case, Ann just sees an ordinary message as shown in Figure 7.

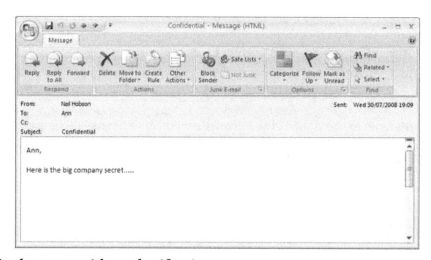

Figure 7: Received message without classification.

The message classification metadata is still associated with the message even if Ann's client is not able to show it. We can determine that this is true by adding the required registry changes and restarting Ann's Outlook 2007 client. Once this has been done, we can see the message classification is now shown as you can see in Figure 8.

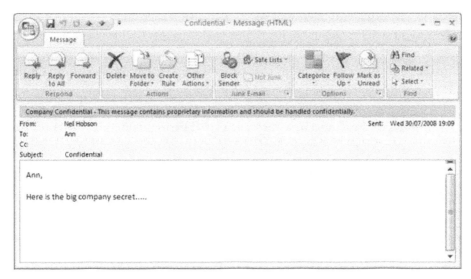

Figure 8: Received message with classification.

Creating custom classifications

The six default classifications may suffice for your needs, but there is always the chance that you will need something a little different. With that in mind, let's look at creating custom message classifications.

To create a new message classification you can use the New-MessageClassification cmdlet. In order to run this cmdlet, the account you are using must be delegated the Exchange Organization Administrator role, since you are making changes that affect the entire Exchange organization. Before we run the New-MessageClassification cmdlet, let's run the Get-MessageClassification cmdlet to confirm the presence of the default six message classifications. This is shown in Figure 9.

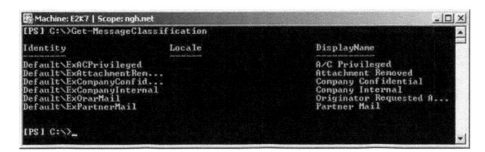

Figure 9: Default message classifications.

If you run the New-MessageClassification cmdlet without any additional parameters, you'll be prompted for three parameters to complete the creation process. They are the *Name*, *DisplayName* and *SenderDescription* parameters.

- **Name**. This is the administrative name of the classification. For example, if you want to retrieve details about the message classification with a Name attribute of Custom, you can use the Get-MessageClassification -Identity Custom cmdlet.

- **DisplayName**. This attribute is the name of the classification as seen in Outlook 2007, as shown in Figure 5.

- **SenderDescription**. This is the description that the sender of the message sees in Outlook 2007. This is the **Company Confidential** bar that you can see in Figure 8.

Figure 10 shows the process of creating a new message classification using just the three basic parameters.

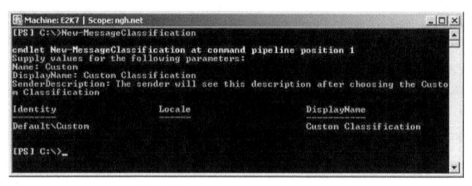

Figure 10: Creating a new message classification.

Here's something to note. Immediately after you have created this new classification, run the following cmdlet:

```
Get-MessageClassification custom | fl
```

This obtains full details about the newly created *Custom* message classification as you can see from Figure 11. What you may notice is that the *RecipientDescription* attribute is populated with the same text that we supplied for the *SenderDescription* attribute, even though we never had to specify the *RecipientDescription* information during the creation of this new message classification. This is expected behavior if you do not specify the *RecipientDescription* text during the creation of the message classification.

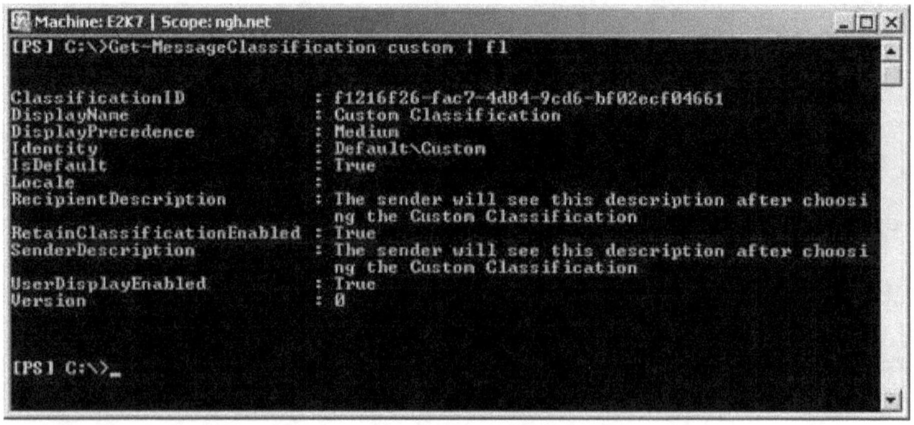

Figure 11: Custom message classification parameters and values.

As you can probably guess, the *RecipientDescription* attribute contains the text that the recipient of the message will see when opening the classified message. Once you've created the message classification, you can easily alter the parameters as with any other Exchange Management Shell cmdlet. For example, the following cmdlet alters the *RecipientDescription* attribute on the *Custom* message classification that we've recently created.

```
Set-MessageClassification Custom -RecipientDescription "The recipient will see
this description after opening a message sent with the Custom Classification"
```

Once you have configured your message classifications, you need to re-export the entire list of message classifications into a new XML file and redistribute to the Outlook 2007 clients. Therefore, you should ideally plan your custom message classifications before you export the list of classifications into an XML file for the first time. As you can see from Figure 11, once Ann opens a new message that has been classified with the *Custom* message classification, the new recipient description text is now displayed.

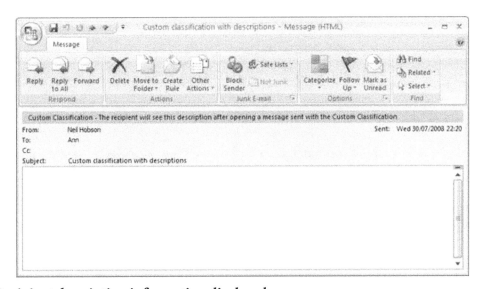

Figure 12: Recipient description information displayed.

Manipulation with transport rules

With the introduction of transport rules within Exchange 2007 (see *Microsoft Exchange Server 2007: Controlling Email Messages using Exchange's Transport Rules* by William Lefkovics, earlier in this book), you can now begin to perform really useful administrative tasks that have previously been unavailable in legacy versions of Exchange, such as adding a disclaimer to all outbound email messages or perhaps copying messages from certain individuals to an additional mailbox.

You can also use transport rules to further extend the ability of message classification. For example, suppose that we need to add specific text to the subject of a message that has been marked with our custom message classification. Let's see how we can use transport rules to do this. I'm going to use the Exchange Management Console in this example. Here's what to do.

• Run the **Exchange Management Console** and navigate to the **Organization Configuration** container.

- Under the **Organization Configuration** container you will see the **Hub Transport** container. Click this and then choose the **Transport Rules** tab as you can see in Figure 12. Note that the **Action** pane has been removed for clarity.

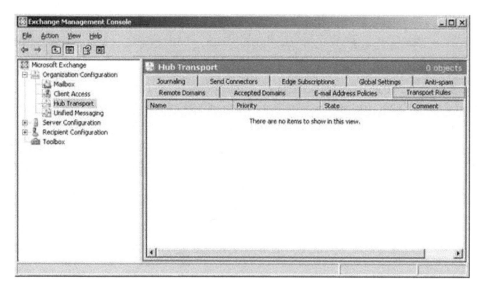

Figure 13: Transport Rules tab.

- Right-click the **Hub Transport** container and choose **New Transport Rule…** from the context menu. This invokes the new transport rule wizard.

- On the opening screen of the transport rule wizard, give your rule a suitable name and make sure that the **Enable Rule** check box remains selected. Click **Next** to advance to the next screen.

- The next screen of the wizard is the **Conditions** screen. Here, choose the **marked with classification** condition in the **Step 1** area of the screen. You should now see that, in the **Step 2** area of the screen, the **marked with classification** condition has now been added. An example is shown in Figure 13.

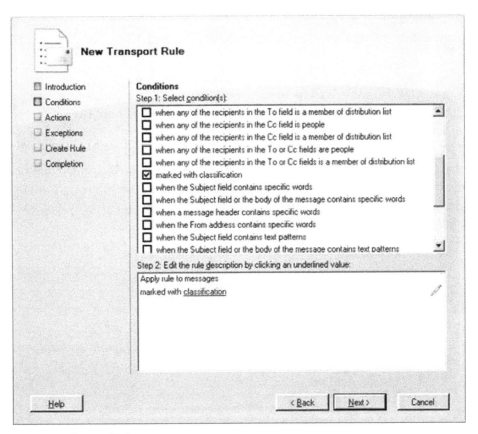

Figure 14: Transport rule conditions.

- In the **Step 2** area of this screen, click the underlined word **classification**. This brings up the **Select message classification** window shown in Figure 14. Select the relevant message classification which, in this example, is the **Custom Classification**, and click **OK**.

Figure 15: Select message classification window.

- Back at the **Conditions** window of the transport rule wizard, you should now see that the Step 2 area of the screen shows your condition as marked with **Custom**. Click **Next** to proceed through the wizard.

- You are now presented with the **Actions** screen of the wizard. In this example, we are going to add additional text to the subject line of the messages, so choose the **prepend the subject with string** option in the **Step 1** area of the screen.

- In the **Step 2** area of the **Actions** screen, click the underlined word **string** and, in the resulting **Specify subject prefix** window enter your desired text to be prepended to the subject. In this example, I'm going to add the text *Custom Classification*. If you've done everything correctly, your **Actions** screen should look like the example shown in Figure 16.

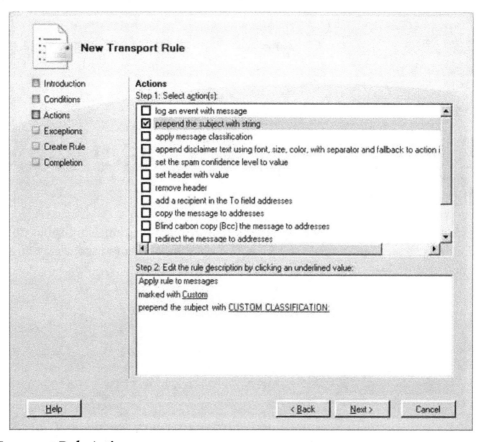

Figure 16: Transport Rule Actions.

- Clicking **Next** on the **Actions** screen takes you to the **Exceptions** screen where you can choose to apply exceptions to the rule. Within this article I'm not going to add any exceptions, so I will simply click **Next** and move on to the next screen.

- Finally we are now at the **Create Rule** screen that allows you to review your selections. If you are happy with your selections, click **New** to create the new transport rule.

- If everything has been successful, you are presented with the **Completion** screen informing you of a successful creation, as you can see in Figure 17.

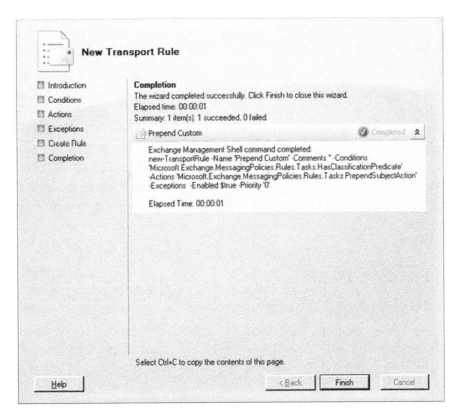

Figure 17: Transport Rule Completion screen.

The expected outcome of this transport rule is that, whenever a message is sent and is marked with the Custom message classification, the subject line of that message should be prepended with the text *Custom Classification*. As you can see from Figure 18, the transport rule works perfectly.

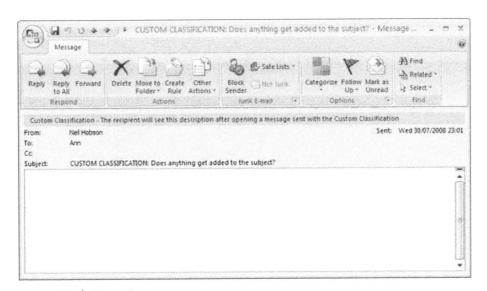

Figure 18: Transport Rule in action.

73

Summary

It's now possible for the end-users of an Exchange 2007 system to classify their messages such that recipients of those messages understand that there may be restrictions relating to the message content. For example, the message may contain sensitive information that should not be sent externally from the company. The flexibility of message classifications is further extended when you consider that transport rules can be created to perform specific actions on messages that have been classified by the users as you have seen in this article. In my experience, not every company that deploys Exchange 2007 implements message classifications but it is, nonetheless, a useful and welcome addition to the Exchange 2007 feature set, particularly for those organizations that need to comply with regulations or other email policies.

Deploying Exchange 2007 on Windows Server 2008

19 September 2008

by Nicolas Blank

Nicolas Blank recounts his experiences deploying Exchange 2007 SP1 on Windows Server 2008, when not everything worked out of the box as it should have done, and describes the fixes to the issues he faced.

My customer's scenario wasn't quite typical – he had an unstable mail server running Exchange 2003, as well as Active Directory issues, one of which included the requirement to rename the directory tree. The customer wanted a brand new environment and, in order to realize the scalability and security benefits of Microsoft's 64-bit OS, decided on Windows Server 2008. This meant I was called in to perform a "Green Fields" migration, where a new target environment is built and all users, machines, and mail are migrated to it. To complicate matters, the customer was on a tight hardware budget, meaning he could only afford a single large machine for a 200-user site.

Designing a solution

The design was relatively straightforward – since I only had a single machine available, I had to place the HUB, CAS and mailbox role onto that machine. Having all of the roles on one machine is well catered for in the available design guidance from the Exchange team at Microsoft (HTTP://TECHNET. MICROSOFT.COM/EN-US/LIBRARY/AA998891%28EXCHG.80%29.ASPX). The machine had 16 GB of memory and a quad core processor. I also had enough disks to create a decent set of mirrors for the OS, page file, logs and a RAID 5 array for the Exchange Database. SPAM handling was done at the ISP, which meant one less burden for the HUB role to handle, since the budget did not allow for additional hardware for an edge server. AV would be handled by the ISP, though this did not preclude internal attack, and I chose Forefront (HTTP://WWW.MICROSOFT.COM/FOREFRONT/DEFAULT.MSPX) to handle AV on the Exchange server to scan both existing mail in the stores and transmitted mail via the HUB role.

Building a new mail server

Server 2008 is much "lighter" on a default install than Server 2003, with fewer components deployed by default. However this default install requires me to add the roles and features required to build a multi-role Exchange Server. Instead of adding each feature through the GUI by hand, I built a batch file containing the required commands. The only reboot required would be after the installation of Active Directory Domain Services remote management tools. From the command line I ran `ServerManagerCmd -i RSAT-ADDS` to install this service, and rebooted. After which I ran the following commands in listed order in a batch file.

```
ServerManagerCmd -i PowerShell
ServerManagerCmd -i Web-Server
ServerManagerCmd -i Web-ISAPI-Ext
ServerManagerCmd -i Web-Metabase
ServerManagerCmd -i Web-Lgcy-Mgmt-Console
ServerManagerCmd -i Web-Basic-Auth
ServerManagerCmd -i Web-Digest-Auth
ServerManagerCmd -i Web-Windows-Auth
ServerManagerCmd -i Web-Dyn-Compression
ServerManagerCmd -i RPC-over-HTTP-proxy
```

Using the command line was dramatically faster than using the GUI would have been, and allowed me to script all of the required prerequisites, thereby eliminating any potential mistakes installing the prerequisites. After this l invoked the Exchange installer and, since all of the prerequisites were met, Exchange had no issues installing.

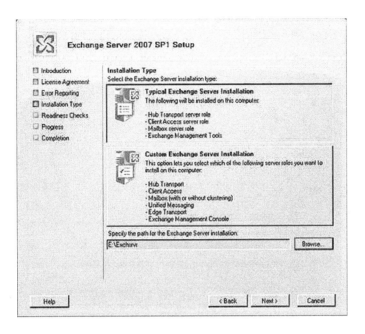

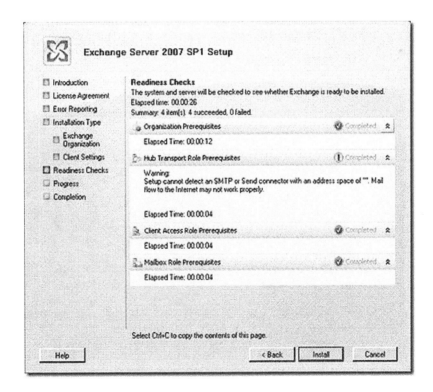

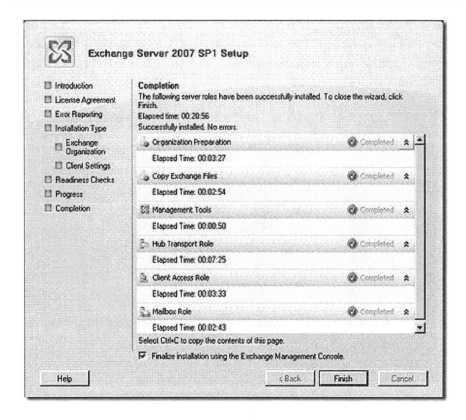

The problem, was IPv6. The last thing I added before installing Exchange was the prerequisite for the CAS role to host Outlook Anywhere and mobile clients, namely RPC over HTTP, using this command: `ServerManagerCmd -i RPC-over-HTTP-proxy`.

I noticed that RPC over HTTP didn't always work. The solution lay in the limited support for the CAS role and IPv6. Running `Netstat -a -n` from the command line gave the results below.

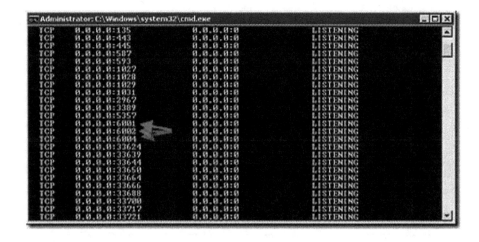

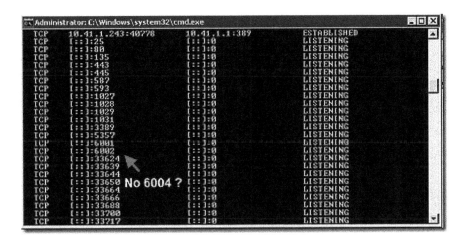

If you're familiar with IPv4, you'll know that, in the first picture, the IP stack is listening on open ports 6001, 6002 and 6004, but these ports were missing on the IPv6 stack on the same address "[::]:" . This meant that one of the core requirements for RPC over HTTP, communication with the local server, had been compromised. At first glance, the fix seems simple – surely you just disable IPv6? Correct, but that wasn't as easy as you might think.

First I had to unbind IPv6 from the Network Adapter but, just like Vista, Server 2008 requires a registry hack in order to disable the protocol altogether.

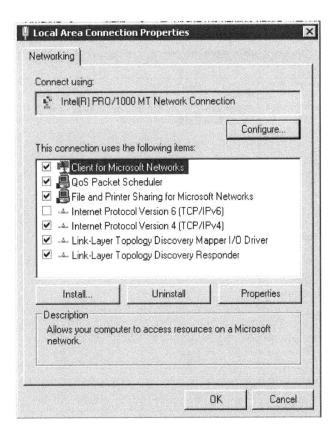

Using Regedit I navigated to: HKLM\SYSTEM\CurrentControlSet\Services\Tcpip6\ Parameters, added a DWORD32 called DisabledComponents and gave it the following value: 0xff, effectively disabling all IPv6 components. See the article at HTTP://MSEXCHANGETEAM.COM/ ARCHIVE/2008/06/20/449053.ASPX from the MS Exchange team for background.

When installing Exchange 2007 on Server 2008, using Outlook Anywhere requires using this value, but refer to the table below for other possible values.

Function	Value
Disable all IPv6 tunnel interfaces, including ISATAP, 6to4, and Teredo tunnels	0X1
Disable all 6to4-based interfaces	0X2
Disable all ISATAP-based interfaces	0X4
Disable all Teredo-based interfaces	0x8
Disable Teredo and 6to4	0xA
Disable IPv6 on non tunnel interfaces including all LAN and PPP interfaces	0X10
Disable IPv6 on all LAN, PPP, and tunnel interfaces	0X11
Prefer IPv4 to IPv6 when attempting connections	0x20
Disable IPv6 over all interfaces and prefer IPv4 to IPv6 when attempting connections	0xFF

Have a look at the IPv6 Transition Technologies Whitepaper at HTTP://TECHNET.MICROSOFT.COM/EN-US/ LIBRARY/BB726951.ASPX for more details.

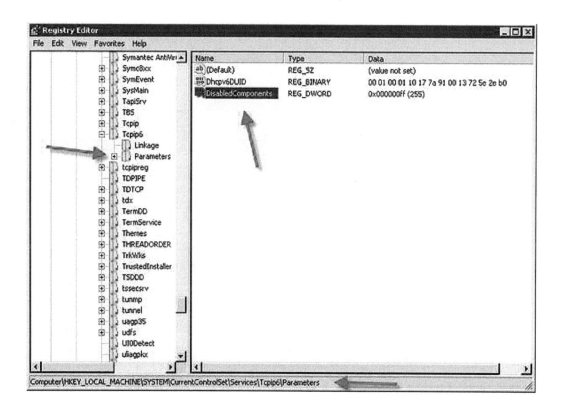

One final step was required, namely editing the hosts file to remove the IPv6 "localhost" equivalent. This meant commenting out the ::1 line by placing a # in front of it as well as manually adding the Netbios and FQDN names

```
10.41.1.243      mpmx01.ds.customerAD.com
10.41.1.243      mpmx01
127.0.0.1        localhost
# ::1            localhost
```

Note that the last line comments out the IPV6 address

> **Note**
>
> *This issue is current as of Exchange 2007 SP1 Rollup 3, though it should be resolved with Rollup 4 (if it comes out for real! See* HTTP://MSEXCHANGETEAM.COM/ARCHIVE/2008/09/11/449787.ASPX*). None of my Exchange customers run IPv6 and, even with this issue resolved, I would still disable IPv6 or any other protocol not actively used in the environment. After a reboot running* netstat -a -n *again revealed that IPv6 was, indeed, gone for good.*

Finishing the org

With that out of the way, configuring Exchange was straightforward. I added the same SMTP namespace as the original org, configured a SAN certificate for the CAS role, allowing OWA and Outlook Anywhere to communicate securely and allowed anonymous mail submission to the Receive connector, thereby enabling Internet mail. Final testing showed that I could communicate with Exchange both internally and externally. The migration proceeded smoothly after that, using Quest Migration Manager (QMM) to move both the AD user accounts, and the Exchange Mailboxes. The advantage in using this toolset over native tools, was that there was virtually no user impact, and it required no desktop visits. Depending on the timeframe required, the complexity of the migration and the amount of mail that needs to be moved, I generally prefer using third-party utilities to native utilities. I have had particular success with QMM, since it supports single or many object rollback. This allowed me to build Disaster Recovery plans that fitted the overall business requirement into the migration plan. Native tools can often be "fire and forget" and you have to hope that the end result is the one you hoped for.

It was worth noting that the original Exchange server suffered massive hardware failure the day after the migration completed and was signed off. The server drive subsystem failed catastrophically, requiring a complete replacement of all drives in the array. One of the original migration drivers was to move off the old hardware platform. Had the business decided to wait to migrate any longer, we might have experienced the hardware failure while migrating.

Conclusion

If you get the chance to upgrade, Windows Server 2008 offers a number of enhancements in the OS which benefit Exchange 2007 deployment and management greatly. Security and resilience are enhanced and Windows ships with a better IP stack allowing more RPC connections, amongst other features. This "Green Fields" migration path is particularly straightforward, but even the more complex methods are well worth following if you have the budget. A few things remain incompatible; for example, Server 2008 contains no native backup utility for Exchange 2007, and Exchange 2007 does not support the new Read Only Domain Controller feature in Server 2008. The first of these, at least, is likely to change in the near future. IPv6 is irritating, but it is quickly disabled since it offers no value over IPv4 at this point. Server 2003 is still available at the time of writing, but I wouldn't hesitate to deploy Server 2008, and gain advantages such as Hyper-V support or "free" geo-clustering with CCR and SCR clusters replicating over the WAN. It is worth remembering that Exchange is a large application, making every deployment worth planning for, irrespective of which operating system it is deployed against.

Reporting on Mobile Device Activity Using Exchange 2007 ActiveSync Logs

10 October 2008

by Ben Lye

Ben Lye takes on the often difficult task of keeping track of mobile device activity.

I was recently asked to generate reports on how many users are using mobile devices to access their Exchange mailbox, what kind of devices are being used, and how that use has changed over time. Fortunately, Exchange 2007 includes a PowerShell cmdlet which will parse the IIS log files on a client access server and produce CSV output files detailing the Exchange ActiveSync usage. So, with a small amount of effort it's possible to extract the relevant data from the Exchange logs and produce some interesting reports.

The command for exporting ActiveSync logs is intuitively called **Export–ActiveSyncLog**. It takes an IIS log file as input, and generates six CSV files as output.

Output Filename	Description
Users.csv	ActiveSync activity by user, including items sent and received, as well as device type and ID
Servers.csv	ActiveSync activity by client access server
Hourly.csv	Hour-by-hour report of ActiveSync activity
StatusCodes.csv	Summary of the HTTP response codes issued in response to ActiveSync requests
PolicyCompliance.csv	Report on device compliance with ActiveSync policy
UserAgents.csv	Summary of the different user agents used to access Exchange

For my purposes Users.csv is the most interesting part of the output as it can be used to identify who the users are, which device types are the most popular, and how much use the service is getting. It's worth noting that the data in the reports is taken from the server's perspective, so **Total Emails Sent** refers to the number of emails that the server sent to the client device.

In an Exchange environment with multiple client access servers (such as an environment with servers in multiple Active Directory sites, or one using an Internet-facing network-load-balancing array) you will need to export the logs from all client access servers which mobile devices connect to. If you have a single client access server exposed to the Internet which all mobile devices connect to, you'll only need to export the logs from that one.

To use Export-ActiveSyncLog you need:

• the Exchange Server Administrator role

• read-only access to the directory that contains the IIS log files.

This example will export the ActiveSync data from the IIS log file of September 1st 2008. It will use UTC times, and will put the output in C:\Temp\EASReports.

```
Export-ActiveSyncLog -FileName "C:\Windows\System32\LogFiles\W2SVC1\ex080901.
log" -UseGMT:$true -OutputPath "C:\Temp\EASReports"
```

That will work fine for a single log file, but what if you need to export multiple log files? Well, you can list all the log files in a directory using **Get-ChildItem,** which you can in turn pipe to the Export-ActiveSync command:

```
Get-ChildItem "C:\Windows\System32\LogFiles\W3SVC1" | Export-ActiveSyncLog -
UseGMT:$true -OutputPath "C:\Temp\EASReports"
```

This syntax will combine the data from each log file and produce a single set of CSV files covering the entire range of the input log files. Because I need to be able to report on usage over time, this approach won't give me what I need.

Another way to process multiple log files is to produce a set of CSV files for each log file. However because the CSV files would typically all use the same names, I also need to specify a prefix for the name of the output CSV files, which will ensure I get all the output. For that I use the -OutputPrefix parameter of the Export-ActiveSyncLog cmdlet.

This command will create CSV files prefixed with the name of the log file they were generated from:

```
Get-ChildItem "C:\Windows\System32\LogFiles\W3SVC1" | ForEach { Export-
ActiveSyncLog -FileName $_.FullName -OutputPath "C:\Temp\EASReports"
-OutputPrefix $_.Name.Replace(."log",""_") -UseGMT:$true}
```

Now that I have the CSV files for all my log files I can import the data into a database and run reports. For the database I have an SQL database which consists of a single table based on the Users.csv file, with the addition of an ID field as the primary key, and a date field to store the date of the log file.

Getting data from PowerShell into the database is a little bit more complicated. This PowerShell script will import all the Users.csv log files which were exported with the previous command into the SQL database.

```
# Script for importing Exchange ActiveSync Users.csv files into a SQL database

# Set up the parameters for connecting to the SQL database
$dbserver = "dbserver.company.com"
$dbname = "EASReports"
$dbuser = "dbusername"
$dbpass = "dbpassword"

# Create the ADO database object
$objConnection = New-Object -comobject ADODB.Connection

# Open the database connection
$objConnection.Open("PROVIDER=SQLOLEDB;DATA SOURCE=$dbserver;UID=$dbuser;PWD=$db
pass;DATABASE=$dbname")

# Find all the Users.csv files and import them
Get-ChildItem "C:\Temp\EASReports\*Users.csv" | ForEach {
    # Get the date from the name of the file
    $Date = ($_.Name).SubString(2,6)
    $Year = "20" + $Date.SubString(0,2)
    $Month = $Date.SubString(2,2)
    $Day = $Date.SubString(4,2)
    $Date = Get-Date -Year $Year -Month $Month -Day $Day -Hour 0 -Minute 0
-Second 0

    # Import the CSV file
    $CSVFile = Import-Csv $_

    # Get the column names from the first line of the CSV file
    $CSVFileProperties = Get-Content "$_" -totalcount 1 | % {$_.split(,"")}

    # Loop through each entry in the CSV file
    ForEach ($Entry in $CSVFile) {

        # Ignore lines with an empty Device ID
        If ($Entry."Device ID" -ne "") {
            # Construct the SQL insert statement
            $SQLString = "INSERT INTO Users ("
            Foreach ($Prop in $CSVFileProperties) {
                $SQLString = $SQLString + "[$Prop],"
            }

            $SQLString = $SQLString + "[Date]) VALUES ("
```

```
        Foreach ($Prop in $CSVFileProperties) {
            $SQLString = $SQLString + "'" + $Entry."$Prop" + "',"
        }


        $SQLString = $SQLString + "'$Date')"


        # Add the record to the database
        $null = $objConnection.Execute($SQLString)
    }



    }
}


# Close the database connection
$objConnection.Close()
```

With the data in an SQL database I can then use Excel to connect to the database and analyze the data. The resulting output looks like this:

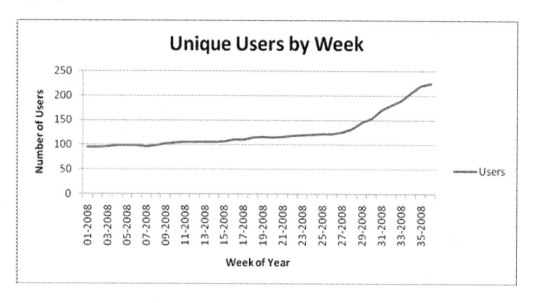

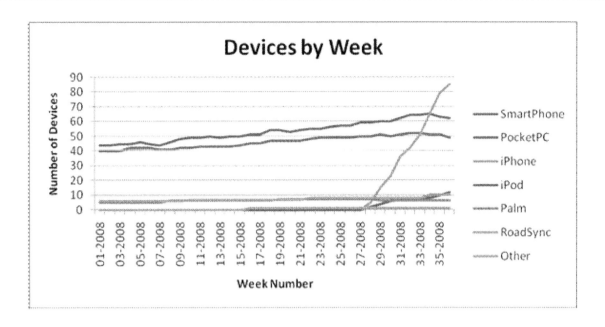

As I said at the beginning, it takes a small amount of effort to extract the data and get it into a format suitable for long-term reports but, once the pieces are in place, it's a relatively simple task.

More information on the Export-ActiveSyncLog cmdlet can be found on the Microsoft Exchange TechNet website (HTTP://TECHNET.MICROSOFT.COM/EN-US/LIBRARY/BB123821%28EXCHG.80%29.ASPX).

Online Exchange Backups

18 October 2008

by Jaap Wesselius

Here, Jaap explains online backups. These have major advantages over offline backups since the backup application does all the logic and the work for you.

In an article for Simple-Talk, entitled *Exchange Server Log File Replay*, (see WWW.SIMPLE-TALK.COM/ EXCHANGE/EXCHANGE-ARTICLES/EXCHANGE-SERVER-LOG-FILE-REPLAY/) I explained how to create an offline backup, how to check the database for consistency, how to purge the log files in a safe way and how to restore an offline backup. The major disadvantages are that the database has to be offline, it's a lot of work, and you need a very good understanding of what you're doing.

A much better solution is to use online backups. Online backups do all the work, check the database and purge the log files. And they do this all online, so there's no interruption for the end-users.

NTBackup

Windows NT, Windows 2000, and Windows 2003 have a neat little backup utility called NTBackup. NTBackup is a lightweight version of a (very old) Veritas BackupExec version. But it's cheap and it does precisely what we can expect from a backup solution.

When installing Exchange Server on a Windows 2003 Server the NTBackup application is extended with two ESE DLLs, which makes it possible to create online backups from the Exchange Server. The process is the same for all backwards versions of Windows and all backwards versions of Exchange Server. Unfortunately, Windows Server 2008 is configured with a new backup application (it's a feature that has to be installed separately) that can create snapshot backups of your Windows Server. It does not contain a plug-in for Exchange Server, so when you run Exchange Server 2007 on a Windows Server 2008 machine you have to buy a third-party application to back up your Exchange databases.

In NTBackup and all other streaming backup applications there are four types of backups:

Full backup – makes a backup of the entire mailbox database and purges the log files.

Incremental backup – only the changes made since the last full backup are backed up. Since all changes are written to the log files, only the log files since the last full backup are backed up. When finished, they are purged.

Differential backup – only the changes made since the last full backup are backed up, but the log files are not purged.

Copy backup – this is the same as a full backup, but it does not interfere with your normal backup cycle, i.e. the header information is not updated and the log files are not purged.

Creating a full backup

NTBackup creates a backup at the ESE level. This means it accesses the database through the ESE engine and not on the file level. When opening NTBackup you have to select the Microsoft Information Store. Do not select the file **mailbox database.edb** from the disk. Although this will put your mailbox database in the backup set, it will not do the necessary maintenance, and it does not prepare for restoring your file.

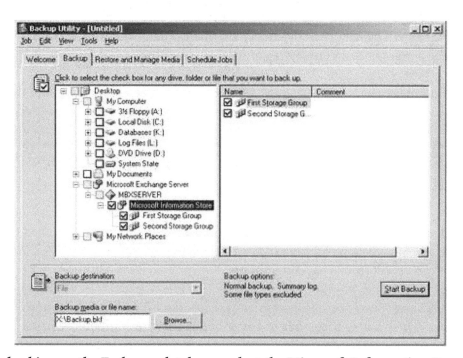

Figure 1: For backing up the Exchange databases, select the Microsoft Information Store.

When you start the backup the following things are happening:

- The current position of the checkpoint file is recorded. This location is needed for purging purposes; all log files older than the current log file can be deleted when the backup is finished. This location is recorded in the header of the database in the "Current Full Backup" section.

- NTBackup begins the backup operations and it starts reading the pages in the database. It starts with the first page and continues until it reaches the last page at the end of the database. During this operation, all pages are checked for their checksum before they are streamed to the backup media. If a page fails its checksum test, the backup operation is aborted and an error is written to the Windows Event log.

New pages that are created during the online backup will still be flushed to the database, even when they are flushed to a portion of the database that has already been backed up. This is no problem, since all transactions are still written to the log files, and thus create a recovery path. During a restore the Exchange server will correct this during a so called "hard recovery".

- When all database pages are written to the backup media, the database is safe. All information that's written to the log files needs to be written to the backup media as well. To achieve this, a "log file rollover" is forced. This means that the current log file E00.log is closed (or E01, E02, etc., depending on the storage group), a new log file is created and the lGeneration number is increased. The log files from the point recorded in Step 1 until the last log file created in Step 3 are now written to the backup media. Because of the log file "roll over" you will never see the E00.log file in the backup set.

- All log files prior to the point recorded in Step 1 are now purged from the log file disk.

- The "previous full backup" section of the database is now updated with the last information when the backup was running.

- NTBackup is now finished with the backup of the database.

When checking the database header after creating a streaming backup, you will see something like this (with irrelevant information removed):

```
K:\sg1>eseutil /mh "mailbox database.edb"

Extensible Storage Engine Utilities for Microsoft(R) Exchange Server
Version 08.01
Copyright (C) Microsoft Corporation. All Rights Reserved.

Initiating FILE DUMP mode...
     Database: mailbox database.edb

Previous Full Backup:
    Log Gen: 34-35 (0x22-0x23)
      Mark: (0x23,1D,183)
      Mark: 09/16/2008 07:50:19

Previous Incremental Backup:
    Log Gen: 0-0 (0x0-0x0)
      Mark: (0x0,0,0)
      Mark: 00/00/1900 00:00:00

Operation completed successfully in 0.101 seconds.

K:\sg1>
```

Creating an incremental backup

An incremental backup can only be created if a previous full backup is performed on the Exchange database. The process of NTBackup creating an incremental backup is as follows:

- The backup session is initialized and the ESE engine is contacted. The location of the checkpoint file is logged in the current incremental backup section.

- A log file roll-over is performed, forcing a new log file to be created.

- All log files up to the new log file are written to tape.

- All log files are purged from the disk.

- The current incremental header section of the database is updated.

- NTBackup is now finished.

If you check the header information of the database again, you will see both the header information of the full backup as well as from the incremental backup:

```
K:\sg1>eseutil /mh "mailbox database.edb"


Extensible Storage Engine Utilities for Microsoft(R) Exchange Server
Version 08.01
Copyright (C) Microsoft Corporation. All Rights Reserved.

Initiating FILE DUMP mode...
      Database: mailbox database.edb

Previous Full Backup:
      Log Gen: 34-35 (0x22-0x23)
        Mark: (0x23,1D,183)
        Mark: 09/16/2008 07:50:19

Previous Incremental Backup:
      Log Gen: 34-52 (0x22-0x34)
        Mark: (0x35,8,16)
        Mark: 09/16/2008 19:16:45


Operation completed successfully in 0.0 seconds.

K:\sg1>
```

Note

The process for a differential backup is identical to an incremental backup, except that the log files are not purged.

-1018 errors

One of the tasks performed by a streaming backup is a checksum check on all pages being streamed to tape. An incorrect page can be in the database but, as long as the page isn't touched by the Exchange server, you would never know. If the backup touches the page it sees that the checksum isn't correct. What will happen depends on the version of Exchange

In the release version of Exchange Server 2003 and earlier

The original release of Exchange Server 2003 (and earlier) does not contain any error correcting code for CRC errors. If an issue is detected the backup will fail and an error with Event ID 474 is logged in the eventlog. In the description you can read: `The read operation will fail with error -1018 (0xfffffc06)`. As per Microsoft knowledgebase article 867626 you have to perform a database repair action or restore the database from a previous backup.

In Exchange Server 2003 SP1 and later

Service pack 1 for Exchange Server 2003 contains error correcting code for checksum errors and thus can handle database pages that have an incorrect checksum. A streaming backup will check the pages and will notice any inconsistencies. Owing to the error correcting code in SP1 the backup application will continue, but will fix the page and write a notice in the eventlog with Event ID 399: `Information Store (2672) First Storage Group: The database page read from the file "G:\SG1\ priv1.edb" at offset 6324224 (0x0000000000608000) for 4096 (0x00001000) bytes failed verification. Bit 24032 was corrupted and has been corrected.`

A lot of detailed information can be found in the Microsoft Exchange Server 2003 SDK Documentation which can be found at WWW.MICROSOFT.COM/DOWNLOADS/DETAILS.ASPX?FAMILYID=5CA18D40-5A37-4A20-94AE-6A6CF6CB846D&DISPLAYLANG=EN. Also Jerry Cochran's book, *Mission-Critical Microsoft Exchange 2003: Designing and Building Reliable Exchange Servers*, is a very valuable source of information as it describes backup technologies from a programming perspective. It is sold, for example, via Amazon (see WWW.AMAZON.COM/MISSION-CRITICAL-MICROSOFT-EXCHANGE-2003-TECHNOLOGIES/DP/155558294X/ REF=PD_SIM_B_34).

Online restore

When performing an offline backup you have to take care of the database, the log files, and the checkpoint file, and take all the necessary steps in the correct order. An online backup does all the dirty work.

When performing an online restore, make sure that you mark the database for being overwritten. This is a property of the database and can be set using the Exchange Management Console.

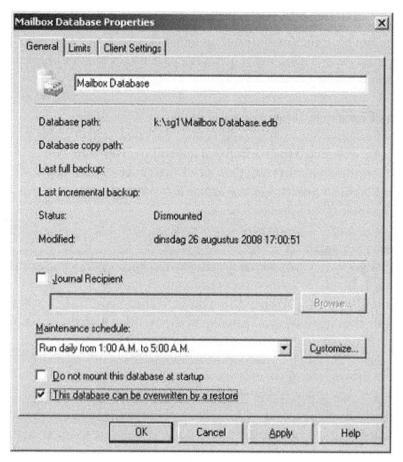

Figure 2: This database can be overwritten by a restore.

In NTBackup select the **Restore and Manage Media** tab and select the appropriate full backup set. After clicking on the **Restore** button you are presented another important Window.

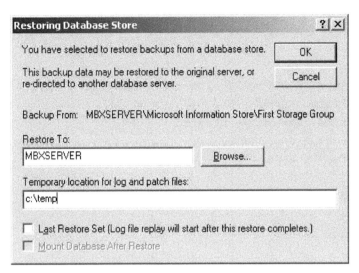

Figure 3: Is this really the last restore set? If so, checkmark the check box.

If you want to restore an incremental backup, DO NOT SELECT the **Last Restore Set**. If you do, the database is being hard recovered immediately after the restore is finished and you do not have the option any more to restore an incremental backup.

But even if this is the last restore set, I'd like to not set the check box. This allows the possibility to check the database and the log files before a hard recovery is started. The log files that were written to the backup are restored in the Temporary location path C:\temp.

When the restore is finished you will see all the log files in the directory C:\temp\first storage group (or any other storage group that you've restored) and a file called restore.env. This file contains the information needed for hard recovery and can be read using the ESEUTIL tool:

```
C:\temp\First Storage Group>eseutil /cm

Extensible Storage Engine Utilities for Microsoft(R) Exchange Server
Version 08.01
Copyright (C) Microsoft Corporation. All Rights Reserved.


     Restore log file: C:\temp\First Storage Group

        Restore Path: C:\temp\First Storage Group
          Annotation: Microsoft Information Store
              Server: MBXSERVER
     Backup Instance: First Storage Group
     Target Instance:
Restore Instance System Path:
  Restore Instance Log Path:


           Databases: 1 database(s)
       Database Name: Mailbox Database
               GUID: 10364919-F177-46D7-B5BE46D7D1B7C03F
```

```
          Source Files: k:\sg1\Mailbox Database.edb
     Destination Files: k:\sg1\Mailbox Database.edb


    Log files range: E0000000022.log - E0000000034.logog
   Last Restore Time: <none>
      Recover Status: recoverNotStarted
       Recover Error: 0x0000000000
        Recover Time: Tue Sep 16 19:34:41 2008


Operation completed successfully in 0.0 seconds.


C:\temp\First Storage Group>
```

The process to fix the database with the log files that were restored from backup is called hard recovery. You can manually start the hard recovery using the ESEUTIL /CC command. This will replay all log files in the temporary directory into the database. The database itself is already in the correct location, as you can see in the output above. When more log files exist in the normal production environment beyond the point of backup (and thus beyond the point of restore), they will be replayed into the production database as well. This will bring your database into a consistent state up to the most current point possible.

If you set the checkmark at Last Restore Set in Figure 3, this will happen automatically. The database will be hard recovered and all additional log files will be replayed as well. When finished, the database can be mounted automatically as well.

Note

This process is the same for all backup applications from major vendors that support streaming backups with Exchange Server.

VSS or snapshot backups

With Exchange Server 2007, Microsoft is shifting its backup focus from the traditional online streaming backup to VSS or snapshot backups. Why do I still spend a serious amount of time on streaming backups? Because the underlying ideas are still very important, and it gives an understanding what steps to perform in a VSS or snapshot backup.

Note

NTBackup cannot create VSS or snapshot backups from an Exchange Server database. It does, however, contain functionality to create a file level VSS backup. If you see a snapshot backup of your Exchange Server database in NTBackup it is very likely that the Exchange Server database is selected on the filesystem level and not on the Information Store level!

A snapshot is just a point in time, and at this point in time an image is created. This image can be used to roll back to in case of a disaster. The Volume Shadow Copy Service in Windows Server 2003 and later provides an infrastructure to create these point-in-time images. These images are called Shadow Copies.

There are two kinds of Shadow Copy:

- **Clone** (Full Copy or Split Mirror) – a complete mirror is maintained until an application or administrator breaks the mirror. From this moment on, the original and the clone are fully independent of each other. At this point, it is effectively frozen in time.

- **Copy on Write** (Differential Copy) – a shadow copy is created that is a differential rather than a full copy of the original data. Using the Copy on Write, a shadow copy of the original data is made before the original data is overwritten. Effectively the backup copy consists of the data in the shadow copy combined with the data on the original location. Both need to be available to reconstruct the original data.

The Volume Shadow Copy infrastructure consists of the following components:

- **Requestor** – the software that invokes the VSS and creates, breaks, or deletes the shadow copy. Typically, the requestor is the backup application.

- **Writer** – a software part that is provided by an application vendor. In our case this is provided with the Microsoft Exchange Server. A writer is responsible for providing a consistent point-in-time image by freezing or quiescing the Exchange Server at the point in time. Please note that an Exchange writer is provided for Exchange Server 2003 and higher.

- **Provider** – the interface to the point-in-time image. This can either be on a storage array (hardware provider) or in the Operating System (software provider). Windows Server 2003 provides a software provider with VSS functionality out of the box.

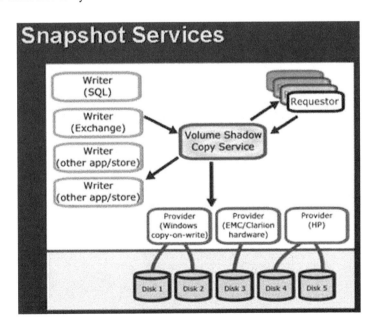

The following steps occur when a VSS backup is performed:

1. The requestor, i.e. the backup application, sends a command to the Volume Shadow Copy Service to take a shadow copy of the Storage Groups.

2. The VSS service sends a command to the Exchange writer to prepare for a snapshot backup.

3. The VSS service sends a command to the appropriate storage provider to create a shadow copy of the Exchange Storage Group. This storage provider can be a hardware storage provider or the default Windows storage provider.

4. The Exchange writer temporarily stops, or quiesces, the Storage Group, and puts them in read-only mode, and all data is flushed to the database. Also a log file roll-over is performed to make sure that all data will be in the backup set. This will hold a couple of seconds for the snapshot to be created (in the next step). All write I/Os will be queued.

5. The shadow copy is now created.

6. The VSS service releases the Exchange server to resume ordinary operations, and all queued write I/Os are completed.

7. The VSS service queries the Exchange writer to confirm that the write I/Os were successfully held during the shadow copy creation. If the writes were not successfully held, it could mean a potentially inconsistent shadow copy, and the shadow copy is deleted and the requestor notified. The requestor can retry the shadow copy process or fail the operation.

8. If successful, the requestor verifies the integrity of the backup set (the clone copy). If the clone copy integrity is good the requestor informs the Exchange Server that the backup was successful and that the log files can be purged.

***

Note

It is the responsibility of the backup application to perform a consistency check of the shadow copy. The Exchange writer does not perform this check. This is also the reason why you have to manually copy the ESE related files like ESE.DLL to the backup server.

***

Steps 1 through 6 usually take about 10 seconds, this is the time needed to create the actual snapshot. This is not the time to create a backup though. A backup application still has to create a backup to another disk or to tape, which still can take hours to complete depending on the size of the databases.

When the backup application has finished, the header information of the Exchange database is updated as well. Using ESEUTIL /MH, you can check the status of the database.

```
K:\sg1>eseutil /mh "mailbox database.edb"


Extensible Storage Engine Utilities for Microsoft(R) Exchange Server
Version 08.01
Copyright (C) Microsoft Corporation. All Rights Reserved.



Previous Full Backup:
     Log Gen: 13-14 (0xd-0xe) - OSSnapshot
       Mark: (0xF,8,16)6)6)
       Mark: 10/02/2008 14:27:30


Previous Incremental Backup:
     Log Gen: 13-16 (0xd-0x10) - OSSnapshot
       Mark: (0x11,8,16)
       Mark: 10/02/2008 14:34:25


Operation completed successfully in 0.171 seconds.


K:\sg1>
```

Note

This screen output has been edited for readability.

Microsoft does not currently offer a GUI-based VSS requestor for Exchange, and using command-line tools puts you in a difficult support situation in regards to creating restores. Microsoft is working on a solution which can be read on the Microsoft Product Group teamblog at HTTP://MSEXCHANGETEAM.COM/ARCHIVE/2008/06/18/449031.ASPX.

For testing purposes, Microsoft offers the Exchange Server 2007 Software Development Kit; the accompanying documentation can be found on the Microsoft website (HTTP://MSDN.MICROSOFT.COM/EN-US/LIBRARY/AA579095%28EXCHG.80%29.ASPX).

Microsoft also provides a VSS Software Development Kit. This SDK contains a very small test tool that is able to create VSS backups of the Exchange Storage Group. This command line tool is called BETest and can be used for test, development, troubleshooting or demonstrating VSS and Exchange 2007. More information regarding BETest can be found at HTTP://MSDN.MICROSOFT.COM/EN-US/LIBRARY/BB530721%28VS.85%29.ASPX. The Exchange product team released a blog on troubleshooting VSS issues which can be found at HTTP://MSEXCHANGETEAM.COM/ARCHIVE/2008/08/25/449684.ASPX.

Using the BETest tool you can make very basic VSS backups. The backup is written to disk (on a location you can enter on the command line) and the log files are purged. Since the responsibility of performing a consistency check is at the backup application, this check is not performed when using BETest.

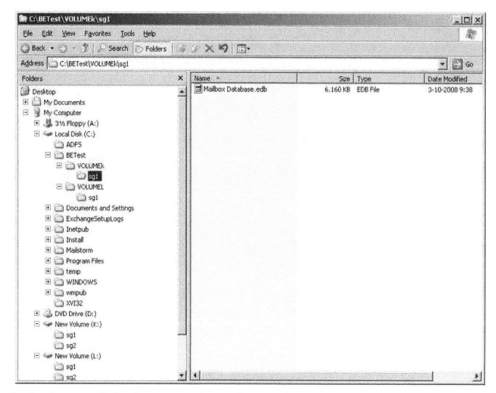

Figure 4: The backup on disk after using the BETest tool.

In the example in Figure 4, the original database location was on disk K:\ and the log files were on disk L:\.

When the database contains a faulty page you will never notice during the backup. Even the backup of the database on the disk will contain the faulty page. You have to manually perform a consistency check on the backup of the database using the ESEUTIL tool with the /K option:

```
C:\BETest\VOLUMEk\sg1>eseutil /k "mailbox database.edb"


Extensible Storage Engine Utilities for Microsoft(R) Exchange Server
Version 08.01
Copyright (C) Microsoft Corporation. All Rights Reserved.


Initiating CHECKSUM mode...
    Database: mailbox database.edb
 Temp. Database: TEMPCHKSUM2496.EDB


File: mailbox database.edb


        Checksum Status (% complete)


    0  10  20  30  40  50  60  70  80  90 100
    |----|----|----|----|----|----|----|----|----|----|
    WARNING: page 455 checksum verification failed but the corruption ( bit
```

```
35816 ) can be corrected
```

```
770 pages seen
0 bad checksums
1 correctable checksums
297 uninitialized pages
0 wrong page numbers
0x5634 highest dbtime (pgno 0x1c8)

97 reads performed
6 MB read
1 seconds taken
6 MB/second
7866 milliseconds used
81 milliseconds per read
121 milliseconds for the slowest read
30 milliseconds for the fastest read

Operation completed successfully in 0.271 seconds.


C:\BETest\VOLUMEk\sg1>
```

The Event log shows all VSS steps performed by the BETest tool but, since no checking was performed, nothing is logged in the Event log about a possible corruption!

Since this is a correctable error, you can still access the mailbox and access the message that contains this faulty page. This is automatically corrected by Exchange Server. When this happens a message is logged in the Event log with Event ID 399:

```
"MSExchangeIS (3680) First Storage Group: The database page read from the file
"k:\sg1\Mailbox Database.edb" at offset 3735552 (0x0000000000390000) (database
page 455 (0x1C7)) for 8192 (0x00002000) bytes failed verification. Bit 35816 was
corrupted and has been corrected."
```

When using an Exchange Server 2007 Continuous Cluster Replication (CCR) solution, a VSS backup solution is even more interesting. When the backup application is CCR aware it is possible to create a VSS backup against the passive copy of the CCR cluster. End-users will never even notice a backup is created because all actions are performed against the passive copy. Any performance impact will only be noticed on the passive copy, where no users reside.

VSS restore

A Volume Shadow Copy backup is created on a storage group level. Exchange Server 2003 is very rigid on restoring; it can restore to the same location, to the same server and only on a Storage Group level. Exchange Server 2007 is much more flexible, and can restore on the same location, but also to other servers or to a Recovery Storage Group, for example.

Restoring a backup is a straightforward process and basically the same as an online restore. The database is restored, the log files in the backup set are also restored and hard recovery takes place to bring the database in a consistent state. If needed, additional log files can be replayed as well to bring the database up to date to the last moment possible.

Replication and backups

One might ask if the replication technology is a good alternative for creating backups? The answer is simple and short: No!

Since there is a copy of the database in an Exchange 2007 Cluster Continuous Replication solution, there is some more time available in a disaster recovery scenario. When a database crashes, there's a copy of the database available to resume operations. But deleting messages or deleting mailboxes is a legitimate action from an Exchange point of view, and these actions will be replicated to the copy of the database as well. Also, the offsite storage that's possible with backups (to tape) is a very important factor in creating backups.

Third-party application vendors

Microsoft does offer a VSS backup solution for Exchange Server via the System Center Data Protection Manager (DPM) 2007, but Microsoft does not offer a VSS backup solution for Exchange Server out of the box like, for example, NTBackup. If you don't want to use DPM 2007 but you want to use a VSS backup solution for Exchange Server, you have rely on a third-party solution. Microsoft has several partners working with the Exchange team in Redmond to build really great products, each with its own feature set. You can find a complete list of backup partners at WWW.MICROSOFT.COM/EXCHANGE/PARTNERS/2007/BACKUP.MSPX.

Conclusion

Creating online backups has major advantages over an offline backup solution since the backup application does all the logic for you. It also checks the database for any inconsistencies and, if checksum errors are found, they are automatically corrected before the data is sent to the backup set.

Recovery from an online backup is much easier than recovery from an offline backup. The database and the log files are automatically recovered from the backup set using the so-called hard recovery. Additional log files that were created after the last backup set was created are automatically replayed, bringing the database up to date to the last moment.

A streaming backup is a default Windows 2003 solution, but Microsoft is shifting its focus from the streaming backup to the VSS (snapshot) backup due to the dramatic performance increase of VSS backups. Microsoft offers the System Center Data Protection Manager which can make backups, but it works very differently from the standard VSS Backup solution that third-party vendors offer.

In *Exchange Database Technologies* (earlier in this book), *Exchange Server Log File Replay* (WWW.SIMPLE-TALK.COM/EXCHANGE/EXCHANGE-ARTICLES/EXCHANGE-SERVER-LOG-FILE-REPLAY/), and this article, I have explained some basics about Microsoft Exchange database technologies, replaying log files, recovery techniques and backup and restore solutions.

It's your turn now to start working with this information in a lab environment, and to start thinking about a disaster recovery solution for your Exchange Server environment. Document all the steps needed when a disaster strikes, and perform regular fire drills on disaster recovery. Only this will help you recover more quickly when something bad happens in your Exchange Server environment.

Optimizing Exchange Server 2007

24 November 2008

by Brien Posey

Brien Posey ponders an "off-the-cuff" remark that Exchange 2007 runs so well with a default configuration that you don't even have to worry about optimizing Exchange any more. He decides that there is actually plenty that can be done to help Exchange to perform even better.

A couple of weeks ago, I was in Las Vegas presenting several Exchange Server sessions at one of the many IT conferences that they have out there. After one of my sessions, I was having a conversation with one of the other conference attendees. During the conversation, he made an off-the-cuff remark that Exchange 2007 runs so well with a default configuration, that you don't even have to worry about optimizing Exchange any more.

Maybe it was because I was because I was still jet lagged, or because my mind was still on the session that I had just presented, but the remark didn't really register with me at the time. Later on, though, I started thinking about his comment and, while I don't completely agree with it, I can kind of see where he was coming from.

I started working with Exchange at around the time when people were first moving from Exchange 4.0 to version 5.0. At the time, I was working for a large, enterprise class organization with roughly 25,000 mailboxes. Although those mailboxes were spread across several Exchange Servers, the servers' performance left a lot to be desired. I recall spending a lot of time trying to figure out things that I could do to make them perform better.

Although there is no denying how poorly our Exchange Servers performed, I think that the server hardware had more to do with the problem than Exchange itself. For example, one night I was having some database problems with one of my Exchange Servers. Before I attempted any sort of database repair, I decided to make a backup copy of the database. In the interest of saving time, I copied the database from its usual location to another volume on the same server.

All of the server's volumes were using "high speed" RAID arrays, but it still took about three-and-a-half hours to back up a 2 GB information store. My point is that Exchange has improved a lot since the days of Exchange 5.0, but the server hardware has improved even more dramatically. Today, multi-core CPUs, and terabyte hard drives are the norm, though they were more or less unheard of back in the day.

When the guy at the conference commented that you don't even have to worry about optimizing Exchange 2007, I suspect that perhaps he had dealt with legacy versions of Exchange on slow servers in the past. In contrast, Exchange 2007 uses a 64-bit architecture, which means that it can take full advantage of the CPU's full capabilities, and that it is no longer bound by the 4 GB memory limitation imposed by 32-bit operating systems.

Although Exchange 2007 does perform better than its predecessors, I would not go so far as to say that optimization is no longer necessary. Think about it this way: if you've got an enterprise grade Exchange Server, but you've only got 20 mailboxes in your entire organization, then that server is going to deliver blazing performance. If you start adding mailboxes, though, you are eventually going to get to the point at which the server's performance is going to start to suffer.

This illustrates two points. First, the Exchange 2007 experience is only as good as what the underlying hardware is capable of producing. Second, even if your server is running well, future growth may require you to optimize the server in an effort to maintain the same level of performance that you are enjoying now. Fortunately, there are some things that you can do to keep Exchange running smoothly. I will spend the remainder of this article discussing some of these techniques.

My approach to Exchange 2007 optimization

To the best of my knowledge, Microsoft has not published an Exchange 2007 optimization guide. They do offer some lists of post-installation tasks, but most of the tasks on the list are related more to the server's configuration than to its performance. Although there isn't an optimization guide, so to speak, the Exchange 2007 Deployment Guide lists a number of optimization techniques and, for all practical purposes, serves as the optimization guide. Since I can't cover all of the techniques listed in the guide within a limited amount of space, I want to talk about some optimization techniques that have worked for me.

As I have already explained, the underlying hardware makes a big difference as to how well Exchange is going to perform. For the purposes of this article, I am going to assume that you have already got the appropriate hardware to meet your needs. If you have insufficient hardware capabilities for the workload that the server is carrying, then these techniques may or may not help you.

The Microsoft Exchange Best Practices Analyzer

If you were to ask me what was the single most important (non-hardware-related) thing you could do to optimize Exchange Server, I would probably tell you to run the Microsoft Exchange Best Practices Analyzer (ExBPA). Although the ExBPA, shown in Figure A, was originally designed as a configuration analysis tool, and has been largely used by the IT community as a security tool, what it really does is scan your Exchange Server organization and make sure that it is configured according to Microsoft's recommended best practices. Many of Microsoft's best practices for Exchange Server are related to security, but there are plenty of performance- and reliability-related recommendations as well.

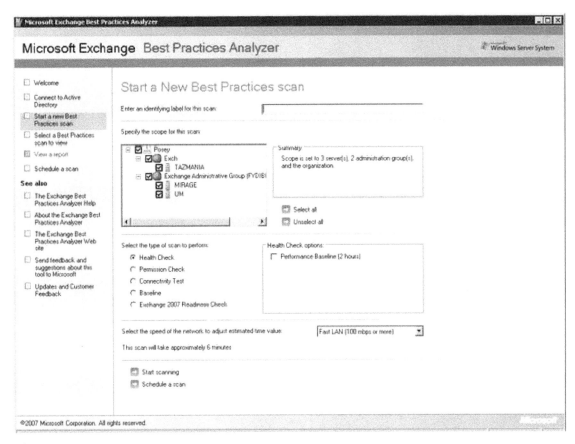

Figure A.

The Microsoft Exchange Best Practice Analyzer makes sure that your Exchange organization is configured according to Microsoft's best practices.

The ExBPA started life as a downloadable utility for Exchange 2003. Microsoft recommends this tool so strongly, though, that they actually included it in the Exchange Management Console for Exchange Server 2007, at the very top of the list of tools in the Toolbox.

One thing that you need to keep in mind is that Microsoft is a dynamic organization. They are constantly doing research on the ways that their products are being used, and sometimes their recommended best practices end up changing as a result of that research. This means that optimizing Exchange 2007 is not a "set it and forget it" operation. You need to periodically run the ExBPA to see if any of Microsoft's recommendations for your organization have changed. Keep in mind, though, that if you are using Microsoft's System Center Operations Manager or System Center Essentials, they will automatically run ExBPA on a daily basis.

Disk I/O

If you are an Exchange veteran, then you might have been a little surprised when I listed running the ExBPA as the single most important step in optimizing an Exchange Server. In every previous version of Exchange, the most important thing that you could do from a performance standpoint was to optimize disk I/O.

There are a couple of reasons why I didn't list disk optimizing disk I/O as my top priority. First, if an Exchange Server has a serious problem in which the configuration of the disk subsystem is affecting performance, then the ExBPA should detect and report the issue when you run a performance baseline scan. More importantly, though, you can always count on your users to tell you when things are running slowly.

Another reason why disk I/O isn't my top priority is because Exchange Server 2007 uses a 64-bit architecture, which frees it from the 4 GB address space limitation imposed by 32-bit operating systems. Microsoft has used this larger memory model to design Exchange 2007 in a way that drives down read I/O requirements. This improves performance for database reads, although the performance of database writes has not really improved.

Of course, that doesn't mean that the old rules for optimizing a disk subsystem no longer apply. It is still important to place the transaction logs and the databases onto separate volumes on high speed raid arrays for performance and fault tolerance reasons. Keep in mind that you can get away with using two separate volumes on one physical disk array, but doing so is not an ideal arrangement unless you divide your bank of disks into separate arrays so that each volume resides on separate physical disks.

If the same physical disks are used by multiple volumes, then fault tolerance becomes an issue unless the array is fault tolerant. That's because, if there is a failure on the array, and both volumes share the same physical disks, then both volumes will be affected by the failure.

Even if the volume is fault tolerant, spanning multiple volumes across the same physical disks is sometimes bad for performance. In this type of situation, the volumes on the array are competing for disk I/O. If you were to separate the volumes onto separate arrays or onto separate parts of an array, though, you can eliminate competition between volumes for disk I/O. Each volume has full reign of the disk resources that have been allocated to it.

Storage groups

As was the case in previous versions of Exchange, Microsoft has designed Exchange 2007 so that multiple databases can exist within a single storage group, or you can dedicate a separate storage group to each individual storage group.

Microsoft recommends that you limit each storage group to hosting a single database. This does a couple of things for you. First, it allows you to use continuous replication, which I will talk about later on.

Another thing that it does is that it helps to keep the volume containing the transaction logs for the storage group from becoming overwhelmed by an excessive number of transactions coming from multiple databases, assuming that you use a separate volume for the transaction logs from each storage group.

Using a dedicated storage group for each database means that the transaction log files for the storage group only contain transaction log entries for one database. This makes database level disaster recovery much easier, because you do not have to deal with transaction log data from other databases.

Mailbox distribution

Since Exchange Server can accommodate multiple Exchange Server databases, it means that you have the option of either placing all of your mailboxes into a single database, or of distributing the mailboxes among multiple databases. Deciding which method to use is actually one of the more tricky points of optimizing Exchange Server's performance. There are really two different schools of thought on the subject.

Some people believe that, as long as there aren't an excessive number of mailboxes, it is best to place all of the mailboxes within a single store. The primary advantages of doing so are ease of management and simplified disaster recovery.

There is also, however, an argument to be made for distributing Exchange mailboxes among multiple stores (in multiple storage groups). Probably the best argument for doing so is that if a store-level failure occurs, then not all of your mailboxes will be affected. Only a subset of the user base will be affected by the failure. Furthermore, because the store is smaller than it would be if it contained every mailbox in the entire organization, the recovery process tends to be faster.

Another distinct advantage to using multiple mailbox stores is that, assuming that each store is placed on separate disks from the other stores, and the transaction logs are also distributed onto separate disks, the I/O requirements are greatly decreased, because only a fraction of the total I/O is being directed at any one volume. Of course the flip side to this is that this type of configuration costs more to implement because of the additional hardware requirements.

As you can see, there are compelling arguments for both approaches, so which one should you use? It really just depends on how much data your server is hosting. Microsoft recommends that you cap the mailbox store size based on the types of backup that you are using. For those running streaming backups, Microsoft recommends limiting the size of a store to no more than 50 GB. For organizations using VSS backups without a continuous replication solution in place, they suggest limiting your database size to 100 GB. This recommendation increases to 200 GB if you have a continuous replication solution in place.

There are a couple of things to keep in mind about these numbers, though. First, the limits above address manageability, not performance. Second, the database's size may impact performance, but it ultimately comes down to what your hardware can handle. Assuming that you have sufficient hardware, Exchange 2007 will allow you to create databases with a maximum size of 16 TB.

If you do decide to split an information store into multiple databases, there are some hardware requirements that you will need to consider beyond just the disk configuration. For starters, each database is going to consume some amount of CPU time, although the actual amount of additional CPU overhead varies considerably.

You are also going to have to increase the amount of memory in your server as you increase the number of storage groups. Microsoft's guidelines state that a mailbox server should have at least 2 GB of memory, plus a certain amount of memory for each mailbox user. The table below illustrates the per-user memory requirements:

User type	Definition	Amount of additional memory required
Light	5 messages sent / 20 messages received per day	2 MB
Medium	10 messages sent / 40 messages received per day	3.5 MB
Heavy	Anything above average	5 MB

The 2 GB base memory, and the per-user mailbox memory requirements make a couple of assumptions. First, it is assumed that the server is functioning solely as a mailbox server. If other server roles are installed, then the base memory requirement is increased to 3 GB, and the per-user mailbox requirements remain the same.

These recommendations assume that the server has no more than four storage groups. Each storage group consumes some memory, so Microsoft requires additional memory as the number of storage groups increase.

When Microsoft released SP1 for Exchange 2007, they greatly decreased the amount of memory required for larger numbers of storage groups. For example, a server with 50 storage groups requires 26 GB of memory in the RTM release of Exchange 2007, but when SP1 is installed, the requirement drops to 15 GB. The following table illustrates how the base memory requirement changes as the number of storage groups increases.

Number of storage groups	Exchange 2007 RTM base memory requirements	Exchange 2007 Service Pack 1 base memory requirements
1–4	2 GB	2 GB
5–8	4 GB	4 GB
9–12	6 GB	5 GB
13–16	8 GB	6 GB
17–20	10 GB	7 GB
21–24	12 GB	8 GB
25–28	14 GB	9 GB
29–32	16 GB	10 GB
33–36	18 GB	11 GB
37–40	20 GB	12 GB
44–44	22 GB	13 GB
45–48	24 GB	14 GB
49–50	26 GB	15 GB

One last disk-related consideration

Exchange Server 2007 Enterprise Edition allows you to use up to 50 storage groups. I have only worked with a deployment of this size on one occasion, but made an interesting observation that I had never seen specifically pointed out in any of the documentation.

Normally, server volumes are referenced by drive letters. If you have a server with 50 stores, all on separate volumes, then you more than exhaust the available drive letters. As such, you will have to address the volumes as mount points rather than drive letters.

Backups

I don't know about you, but when I think about optimizing a server's performance, backups are not usually the first thing that comes to mind. Even so, my experience has been that you can get a big performance boost just by changing the way that nightly backups are made. Let me explain.

Most organizations still seem to be performing traditional backups, in which the Exchange Server's data is backed up to tape late at night. There are a couple of problems with this. For starters, the backup process itself places a load on the Exchange Server, which often translates into a decrease in the server's performance until the backup is complete. This probably isn't a big deal if you work in an organization that has a nine-to-five work schedule, but if your organization is a 24-hour-a-day operation, then a performance hit is less than desirable.

Another aspect of the nightly backup that many administrators don't consider is that a nightly backup almost always coincides with the nightly automated maintenance tasks. By default, each night from midnight to 4:00, Exchange performs an automated maintenance cycle.

This automated maintenance cycle performs several different maintenance tasks, including an online database defragmentation. These maintenance tasks tend to be I/O intensive, and the effect is compounded if a backup is running against a database at the same time that the maintenance tasks are running.

There are a few ways that you can minimize the impact of the maintenance cycle and the backup process. One recommendation that I would make would be to schedule the maintenance cycle so that it does not occur at an inopportune moment.

The maintenance cycle occurs at the database level. If you've got multiple databases then, by default, the maintenance cycle will run on each database at the same time. Depending on how many databases you've got, you may be able to schedule the maintenance cycle so that it is only running against one database at a time. Likewise, you may also be able to work out a schedule that prevents the maintenance cycle and the backup from running against the same database at the same time.

If you want to see the current maintenance schedule for a database, open the Exchange Management Console, and navigate through the console tree to Server Configuration | Mailbox. Next, select your Exchange mailbox server in the details pane, followed by the store that you want to examine. Right-click on the store, then select the **Properties** command from the resulting shortcut menu. You can view or modify the maintenance schedule from the resulting properties sheet's **General** tab.

Another way that you can mitigate the overhead caused by the backup process is to take advantage of Cluster Continuous Replication (CCR). Although CCR is no substitute for a true backup, CCR does use a process called log shipping to create a duplicate of a database on another mailbox server. It is possible to run your backups against this secondary cluster node rather than running it against your primary Exchange Server. That way, the primary Exchange Server is not impacted by the backup.

If you do decide to use CCR, then you will have to keep in mind that you are only allowed to have one database in each storage group. Otherwise, the option to use CCR is disabled.

The Windows operating system

Another aspect of the optimization process that is often overlooked is the Windows operating system. Exchange rides on top of Windows, so if Windows performs poorly, then so will Exchange.

One of the best things that you can do to help Windows to perform better is to place the pagefile onto a dedicated hard drive (or better yet, a dedicated array). You should also make sure that the pagefile is sized correctly. Microsoft normally recommends that the Windows pagefile should be 1.5 times the size of the machine's physical memory.

There is a different recommendation for Exchange 2007, though. Microsoft recommends that you set the pagefile to equal the size of your machine's RAM, plus 10 MB. If you use a larger pagefile, then the pagefile will eventually become fragmented, leading to poor performance.

Finally, make sure that your server is running all the latest patches and drivers. You should also take the time to disable any services that you don't need. Every running service consumes a small amount of system resources, so disabling unneeded services can help you to reclaim these resources.

Conclusion

In this article, I have explained that, while Exchange Server has improved over the years, there are still a lot of things that you can do to help Exchange to perform even better. This is especially important in larger organizations in which the server's finite resources are being shared by many different users.

Exchange Recovery Storage Groups

06 January 2009

by Jaap Wesselius

It can happen at any time: you get a request, as Admin, from your company, to provide the contents of somebody's mailbox from a backup set as part of an investigation. The Recovery Storage Group is usually the easiest way to do this. It may either mean using the Exchange Management Console or the Exchange Management Shell. Jaap explains all.

Very recently I was at a customer's site, and the Exchange administrators had received a request from the legal department to retrieve somebody's mailbox from several backup sets and create .PST files of the Inbox. The .PST files had to be handed over to the legal department. Of course the particular user was not aware of these actions.

The Exchange administrator retrieved the Exchange database files from backup (130 GB!) but had absolutely no idea how to retrieve the mailbox data out of the files. The Recovery Storage Group in Exchange Server 2003 and Exchange Server 2007 can be very useful in a situation like this.

Backup and restore

This particular customer made a full backup of their Exchange Server 2003 database every weekend, and an incremental backup was created every night. This means that during a normal night the Exchange Server database is not backed up, but the Exchange Server log files are backed up and purged from the disk. Please refer to my article, *Online Exchange Backups*, earlier in this book, for more information on these backup techniques.

If data from a mailbox out of a backup that's 14 days old needs to be retrieved, you have to get that backup set, but you cannot just simply restore the database to its original location. In order to restore the database to its original location the database needs to be dismounted and the 14-day-old backup has to be restored. This not only results in an outage but will also result in a loss of data if you're not careful, so it is not an acceptable option. Also, you have to restore the full backup made during the weekend, and possibly one or more incremental backups, depending on the date stamp you have to restore.

A Recovery Storage Group is like any other Storage Group, except for the fact that databases mounted in a Recovery Storage Group do not contain live mailboxes but only disconnected mailboxes. A Recovery Storage Group is a Storage Group that can be used for recovery purposes; you can restore a database from a backup set in a Recovery Storage Group and recover data from it.

A Recovery Storage Group and the database(s) it contains are invisible to the end-users and Outlook clients; only the administrator can access the Recovery Storage Group and the database(s) it contains.

Suppose there is a user in our Exchange Server 2003 environment named Joe Sixpack. Joe is suspected by the legal department and the legal department has requested a copy of his mailbox to check whether Joe has sent out some confidential information to the Internet. Joe's mailbox is located on an Exchange server named 2003SRVR in the default mailbox store in the first Storage Group. This Storage Group contains three databases in total. There's also a second Storage Group that hosts only one Mailbox Store.

To retrieve a copy of Joe's mailbox the IT department wants to use the Recovery Storage Group option in Exchange Server 2003.

Follow these steps to create a Recovery Storage Group in Exchange Server 2003:

- In Exchange System Manager, select and then right-click the Exchange Server 2003 object, select New and then select **Recovery Storage Group**.

- Enter the location where the transaction log files and the checkpoint file should be located. By default it is in the C:\Program Files\Exchsrvr\Recovery Storage Group directory, but it can be any location you want. Please keep in mind that there should be sufficient storage available to host the complete database and all log files. If you want to perform recovery steps using ESEUTIL, you have to take an additional storage requirement into account.

- An empty directory is created where the database and the log files will be stored.

When the Recovery Storage Group is created, the database that needs to be restored must be selected.

- In the Exchange System Manager, right-click the Recovery Storage Group and select **Add Database to Recover**.

- All mailbox databases that are known in Active Directory are displayed, so Joe's Mailbox Store should be selected, (in this example, **Mailbox Store (2003SRVR)**.

- After clicking **OK**, the Mailbox Store properties are shown. Leave these at their default values and click **OK**.

- **DO NOT MOUNT THE DATABASE.**

The database is now created in the Recovery Storage Group in Active Directory. The next step is to restore the database from the backup set.

No additional steps are needed here. When a Recovery Storage Group is created, the behaviour of an online restore is changed. The database is not restored to its original location, but it is automatically redirected to the Recovery Storage Group location that's been created earlier. Just restore the **Mailbox Store (2003SRVR)**, and it will be automatically placed in the right directory.

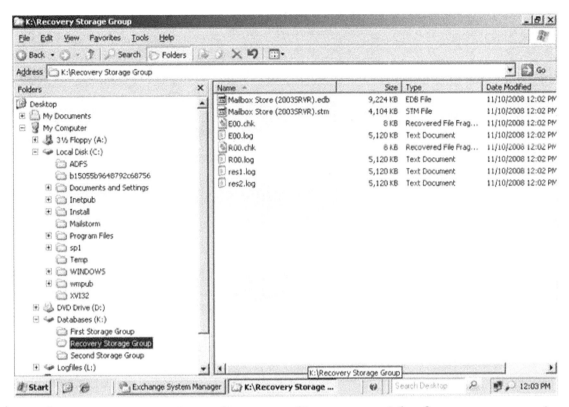

Figure 1: The Recovery Storage Group directory and its contents, right after a restore operation.

In a normal Storage Group in Exchange Server 2003 the log files have a prefix like E00, E01, E02 or E03. In a Recovery Storage Group the prefix is R00. This way it is always clear when a particular directory contains data from a Recovery Storage Group.

After the Exchange database is restored from a backup set it can be mounted. Just right-click this database in the Recovery Storage Group in the Exchange System Manager and select **Mount Store**.

Remember that the database in a Recovery Storage Group is actually an old version of the running database, so it also contains all mailboxes that are in the running database. In the Recovery Storage Group, however, these are disconnected mailboxes, i.e. the original user accounts in Active Directory are matched to the mailboxes in the running database.

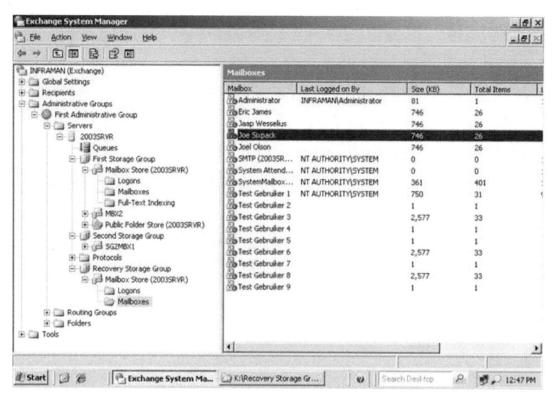

Figure 2: After mounting the database in the Recovery Storage Group, it contains disconnected mailboxes.

The last step is to create a .PST file from Joe Sixpack's mailbox. The Exchange System Manager contains some functionality to copy or merge this data into the running mailbox of the user; for creating a .PST file the free Microsoft tool, Exmerge, has to be used. This can be downloaded from the Microsoft website: HTTP://WWW.MICROSOFT.COM/DOWNLOADS/DETAILS.ASPX?FAMILYID=429163EC-DCDF-47DC-96DA-1C12D67327D5&DISPLAYLANG=EN. More information about the usage of Exmerge can be found in Microsoft knowledgebase article 327304: HTTP://SUPPORT.MICROSOFT.COM/?KBID=327304.

To retrieve the contents of Joe Sixpack's mailbox from the Recovery Storage Group follow the steps below.

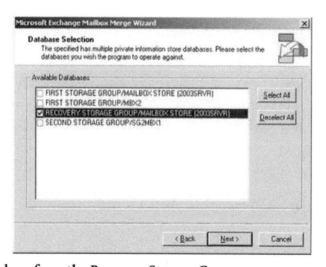

Figure 3: Select the database from the Recovery Storage Group.

- Start the Exmerge.exe utility from the local disk.

- In the Microsoft Exchange Mailbox Merge Wizard select **Extract or Import (Two Step Procedure)** and click **Next**.

- Select **Step 1: Extract data from an Exchange Server Mailbox** and click **Next**.

- In the **Source Server** window enter the servername and the domain controller name and click **Next**.

- In the **Database Selection Window** select the **Mailbox Store** in the **Recovery Storage Group**. This is the "old" store where Joe's data need to be extracted from.

- In the next window select Joe Sixpack's mailbox.

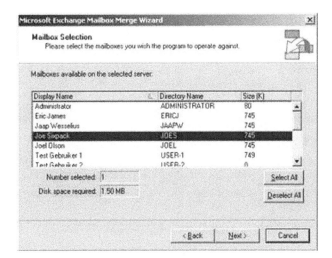

Figure 4: **Select Joe Sixpack's mailbox to retrieve the data from it.**

- In the next Window, select the locale; the default setting is English (US). The last mailbox login locale can also be selected by clicking the check box.

- Select the Folder (directory) where the .PST file will be stored. Any directory can be used.

- Save the settings (default selection) and watch the export process going on.

- When the operation is completed successfully click **Finish**.

Joe Sixpack's mailbox that was in the backup set is now saved in the .PST file on local disk. This .PST file can be handed over to the legal department for further investigation while Joe Sixpack never noticed anything about the whole operation.

Recovery Storage Group in Exchange Server 2007

The Recovery Storage Group functionality is also implemented in Exchange Server 2007, but it is not available through the default Exchange Management Console interface. To perform all operations with a Recovery Storage Group, the Exchange Management Shell needs to be used. You can use some Recovery Storage Group functionality using the toolbox in the Exchange Management Console. I will explain this later in this article.

Open the Exchange Management Shell and enter the New-StorageGroup command. Make sure that you use the -Recovery option, otherwise you'll create a regular Storage Group:

```
[PS] C:\>New-StorageGroup -Server MBXSERVER -LogFolderPath l:\rsg
-SystemFolderPath l:\rsg -Name RSG -Recovery


Name            Server         Replicated      Recovery
----            ------         ----------      --------
RSG             MBXSERVER      None            True
```

Now create the Database in using the New-MailboxDatabase cmdlet. This database has the same name as the original mailbox database that contains Joe Sixpack's mailbox:

```
[PS] C:\>New-MailboxDatabase -MailboxDatabaseToRecover "Mailbox Database"
-StorageGroup MBXSERVER\RSG -EdbFilePath "k:\rsg\mailbox database.edb"


Name            Server         StorageGroup    Recovery
----            ------         ------------    --------
Mailbox Database   MBXSERVER   RSG             True
```

The newly created database in the Recovery Storage Group should have the ability to be overwritten by a restore, so set this property:

```
[PS] C:\>Set-MailboxDatabase -Identity "MBXSERVER\RSG\Mailbox Database"
-AllowFileRestore:$TRUE
```

Before the database can be mounted, the database should be restored from the backup set. When a Recovery Storage Group is created the restore is automatically redirected to the Recovery Storage Group by the Information Store, just like in Exchange Server 2003. Restore the database using your backup application.

When the database is restored into the Recovery Storage Group directory on the disk the database can be mounted:

```
[PS] C:\>Mount-Database -Identity "MBXSERVER\RSG\Mailbox Database"
```

Now the Recovery Storage Group is created, the mailbox database is created, restored from the backup set and mounted. It is still invisible to the end-users and no one except the administrator can access the mailbox database in the Recovery Storage Group. Please remember that it is only accessible through the Management Shell, so colleagues using the regular Exchange Management Console also do not notice anything.

There is a thing you have to know, though. In the Exchange Management Console you can go to the Toolbox and enter the **Database Recovery Management**. From there, there's also the possibility to manage the Recovery Storage Group. The following tasks are available in the **Manage Recovery Storage Group** area:

- Merge or copy mailbox contents.

- Mount or dismount databases in the Recovery Storage Group.

- Remove the Recovery Storage Group.

- Set up `Database can be overwritten by restore` flag.

- Swap databases for "dial tone" scenario.

When the database is mounted, the database statistics can be requested of the database in the Recovery Storage Group with the `Get-MailboxStatistics` cmdlet. These are disconnected mailboxes and are unknown to Active Directory. As far as Active Directory is concerned, the actual mailboxes are located in the "mailbox database.edb" in the First Storage Group. Joe Sixpack's mailbox is clearly visible.

```
[PS] C:\>Get-MailboxStatistics -Database "RSG\Mailbox Database"


DisplayName         ItemCount  StorageLimitStatus   LastLogonTime
-----------         ---------  ------------------   -------------
Test User 2         145                   10-11-2008 14:18:29
Test User 4         122                   10-11-2008 14:18:29
Test User 3         129                   10-11-2008 14:18:29
Eric James          64
Test User 9         85                    10-11-2008 14:18:30
Administrator       1                     13-11-2008 15:03:25
Joel Olson          40
Test User 7         99                    10-11-2008 14:18:30
Test User 6         105                   10-11-2008 14:18:30
Test User 5         111                   10-11-2008 14:18:29
Test User 8         93                    10-11-2008 14:18:30
Test User 10        72                    10-11-2008 14:18:29
Joe Sixpack         56                    13-11-2008 17:12:21
Microsoft System Attendant 0              13-11-2008 16:34:10

SystemMailbox{10364919-F1 402
77-46D7-BEB5-3FC0B7D155A9
```

```
}
Test User 1          163                  10-11-2008 14:18:29
[PS] C:\>
```

Exchange Server 2007 SP1 has a new cmdlet to export data to a .PST file and, as such, the successor of EXMERGE that was used in Exchange Server 2003 and earlier. There are a few caveats with the `Export-Mailbox` cmdlet:

- To use this cmdlet, Outlook 2003 SP2 (or higher) has to be installed on the server where the cmdlet is run. This can be a management workstation (or a management server) with only the Exchange Management Tools installed. It should also be a 32-bit server, since the 64-bit Exchange Management Tools cannot cooperate with the 32-bit Outlook client software.

- The `Export-Mailbox` cmdlet runs only against a normal Exchange Server 2007 SP1 database and not against databases running in the Recovery Storage Group.

To overcome the second limitation, a special "recovery mailbox" can be created in an ordinary Storage Group. When this mailbox is created, the contents of Joe Sixpack's mailbox can be restored into this recovery mailbox:

```
[PS] C:\ >restore-mailbox -Identity "Recovery Mailbox" -RSGDatabase "RSG\Mailbox
Database" -RSGMailbox "joe sixpack" -TargetFolder Recover
```

When the Restore Mailbox operation is running a progress bar is shown.

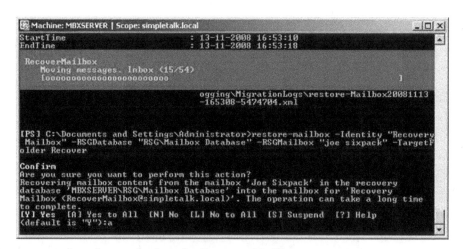

Figure 5:   The progress bar shown during the Recover Mailbox operation.

When the Restore Mailbox operation is finished, the contents of Joe Sixpack's mailbox are available in the Recovery Mailbox. When using Outlook to access this mailbox, the contents are available in the \Recover folder in the mailbox. The \Recover folder in the Recovery Mailbox can be exported using Outlook. In the File menu select the **Import and Export** option and then select **Export to a file**. Follow the wizard to complete the export to a .PST file.

When Outlook 2003 SP2 (or higher) is installed on the Management Server the Export Mailbox cmdlet can also be used:

```
Export-mailbox -identity "Recovery Mailbox" -PSTFolderPath c:\temp\joesix.pst -
IncludeFolders "\Recover"
```

This will export the contents of the \Recover folder, and therefore the recovered mailbox from Joe Sixpack to a .PST file in the C:\temp directory on the local disk.

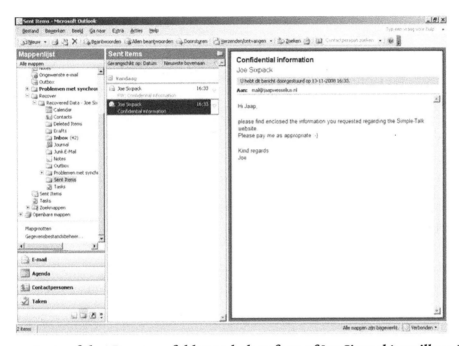

Figure 6: The contents of the \Recovery folder and, therefore, of Joe Sixpack's mailbox. Joe Sixpack did, indeed, send out sensitive information.

Recover mailbox data

Another interesting feature of the Recovery Storage Group is to recover deleted mailbox data. Suppose a user named Joel accidentally deleted important items from his mailbox and he is unable to retrieve this using the **Recover Deleted Items** option in Outlook.

To solve this problem please restore the database that holds Joel's mailbox data into the Recovery Storage Group. In Exchange Server 2003 in the Exchange System Manager go to the Recovery Storage Group and check Joel's mailbox. A disconnected mailbox should be visible. Right-click the mailbox and select **Exchange tasks**.

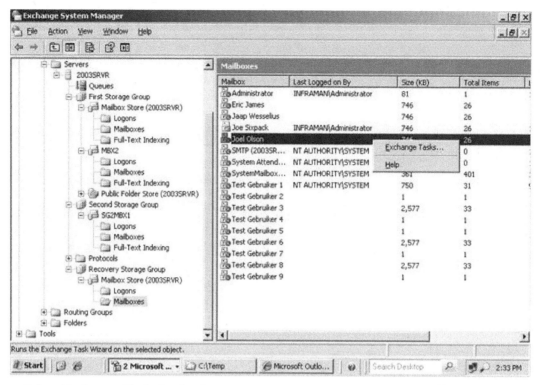

Figure 7: **Select Exchange Tasks in the Recovery Storage Group to restore mailbox data.**

After selecting **Exchange Tasks**, select **Recover Mailbox Data** (the only option available) and select the destination mailbox store. This should be the database that hold Joel's mailbox, in this case, the Mailbox Store (2003SRVR) in the first Storage Group.

Now you have two options to continue:

- **Merge Data** – when you select **Merge Data**, the data from the mailbox copy in the Recovery Storage Group will be merged into the original data. If any item exists it will be detected and will not be overwritten. Items that no longer exist (i.e. that have been deleted) will be recreated during the merge process.

- **Copy Data** – when you select **Copy Data**, the data from the mailbox copy in the Recovery Storage Group will be copied to a separate location, i.e. a special folder named **Recovered Data** followed with the data and time of the recovery process in the user's mailbox.

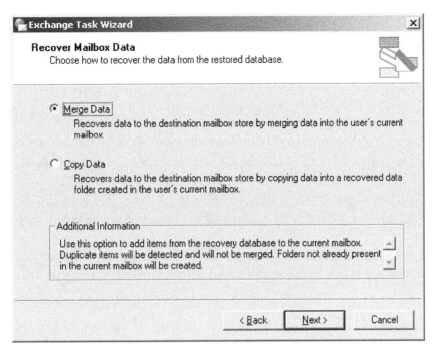

Figure 8: Merge the data into the mailbox or copy it to a "recovered data" folder in the user's mailbox.

When finished, you have recovered the mailbox data from the backup that's in the Recovery Storage Group into the user's mailbox.

With Exchange Server 2007, you have to use the Exchange Management Shell or the Database Recovery Management in the Tools option in the Exchange Management Console.

Again, restore the database that holds Joel's mailbox into the Recovery Storage Group. After restoring, you can use the `Restore-Mailbox` cmdlet in the Exchange Management Console to restore the content to Joel's mailbox.

```
[PS] C:\ >Restore-Mailbox -Identity "Joel Olson" -RSGDatabase "MBXSERVER\RSG\
Mailbox Database"

Confirm
Are you sure you want to perform this action?
Recovering mailbox content from the mailbox 'Joel Olson' in the recovery
database 'MBXSERVER\RSG\Mailbox Database' into the mailbox for 'Joel Olson
(Joelo@simpletalk.local)'. The operation can take a long time to complete.
[Y] Yes [A] Yes to All [N] No [L] No to All [S] Suspend [?] Help
(default is "Y"):a

[PS] C:\ >
```

You can also use the Exchange Management Console to recover mailbox items to Joel's mailbox.

- In the left-hand pane in the Exchange Management Console select the **Tools** option and in the middle pane select Database Recovery Management under **Disaster Recovery Tools**.

- If needed, enter the Exchange Server's name and the Domain Controller's name. Click **Next** to continue.

- After a couple of seconds some tasks are shown. Select the **Merge or Copy contents** task.

- The next window shows what database is mounted in the Recovery Storage Group; this is the Mailbox Database that was restored earlier. Click **Gather Merge Information** to continue.

- Select **Perform pre-migration tasks** to continue. If the database in the Recovery Storage Group contains a lot of mailboxes you can select **Show Advanced Options** first, to set a filter to narrow the selection.

- In the **Select Mailboxes to Copy or Merge** window, select the mailbox that needs to be restored, in this example, Joel Olson's mailbox.

- Click **Perform merge actions** to continue.

- When finished, the mailbox data have been restored to their original location.

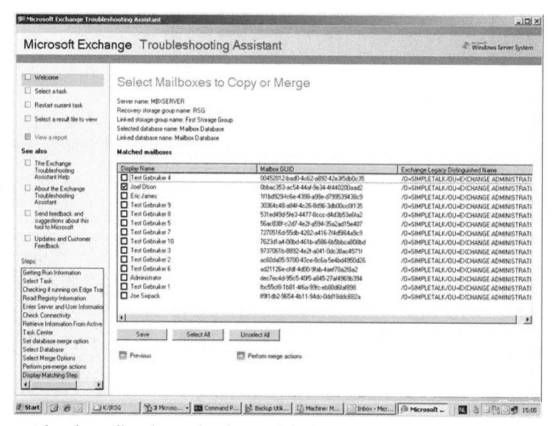

Figure 9:   Select the mailbox that needs to be restored.

Conclusion

When you need to retrieve a mailbox or mailbox content from a backup set, the Recovery Storage Group is a great tool to use. Depending on the task, you have to perform everything in the Exchange Management Console, or you may need to perform some actions in the Exchange Management Shell.

In both Exchange Server 2003 and Exchange Server 2007 it is possible to create a .PST file from a restored mailbox, but in Exchange Server 2007 it's a bit more confusing because of the usage of the Exchange Management Shell.

Before you can efficiently use the Recovery Storage Group and its purposes I would advise you to try it a couple of times, to see in what scenarios it can help you in your day-to-day Exchange Management tasks. Make sure that you document all the steps carefully. In that case you'll know exactly what steps to perform when a request is made to restore a single mailbox, either to its original location or to a .PST file.

Exchange Email Addresses and the Outlook Address Cache

12 January 2009

by Ben Lye

Because Exchange auto-complete cache uses X.500 addresses for email sent to addresses within the Exchange organization, it will bounce back messages from a re-created mailbox even after you give the user account all the old SMTP addresses. This is because the old X.500 address in the auto-complete cache is missing, and this causes Exchange to reject the messages. Ben Lye explains how to solve this common problem.

A little while ago, I had a case where, after all other troubleshooting had failed, I had to solve a mailbox corruption problem by exporting the mailbox content to a PST file, removing the existing mailbox, recreating a new mailbox, then finally importing the PST file back in. This solved the immediate problem of the corrupt mailbox, but created a new one – when Outlook users tried to email the user, either by replying to an existing message or by using Outlook's auto-completion of the user's email address, the message would bounce back to the sender. This happened even though I had re-added all the SMTP addresses that the user previously had. Email from external senders was being received properly, and replies to new messages were OK.

This problem occurs because, while the Outlook auto-complete cache stores SMTP addresses for email sent to external addresses, it uses X.500 addresses for email sent to addresses within the Exchange organisation. Even though we had given the user account all the old SMTP addresses, the old X.500 address which Outlook was sending to was missing, and this was causing Exchange to reject the messages.

The use of X.500 addresses goes back to before Exchange 2000, when previous versions of Exchange maintained their own LDAP directory. Since Exchange 2000 the mailbox's X.500 address has been stored in the **legacyExchangeDN** attribute in Active Directory. The **legacyExchangeDN** value is set when a mailbox is created, and includes the name of the Exchange administrative group where the mailbox belongs. **LegacyExchangeDN** values typically look like this:

```
/o=Organisation/ou=Administrative Group/cn= Recipients/cn=Username
```

Because the **legacyExchangeDN** value includes the administrative group name changes to admin group names will influence **legacyExchangeDN** values. For example when you upgrade from Exchange 2003 to Exchange 2007 your user-defined admin groups are replaced by a single admin group named "Exchange Administrative Group (FYDIBOHF23SPDLT)" – existing mailboxes are unaffected, but mailboxes created after the upgrade will use the new admin group name in their **legacyExchangeDN** values. (Incidentally, if you've ever wondered why the Exchange 2007 admin group has this name, or what it means, it's the phrase "EXCHANGE12ROCKS," with all the characters shifted to the right by one!)

The current X.500 address of a mailbox can be retrieved from Active Directory using a tool such as ADSI Edit, or LDP.exe, or by using the Exchange Management Shell:

```
[PS] C:\>Get-Mailbox juser | fl LegacyExchangeDN

LegacyExchangeDN : /o=Example/ou=Exchange Administrative Group
(FYDIBOHF23SPDLT)/cn=Recipients/cn=juser

[PS] C:\>
```

The X.500 address of a message sender can be retrieved using a tool such as Microsoft Exchange Server MAPI Editor (WWW.MICROSOFT.COM/DOWNLOADS/DETAILS.ASPX?FAMILYID=55FDFFD7-1878-4637-9808-1E2IABB3AE37) to open a message and get the **PR_SENDER_EMAIL ADDRESS** property:

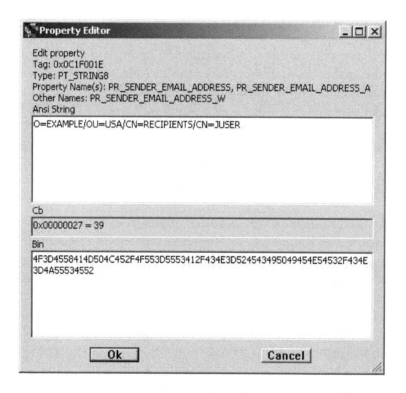

Alternatively, you can use a hex editor to open the Outlook auto-completion cache file and retrieve X.500 addresses from there. The cache is stored in a file in the user's profile, typically ...

```
%userprofile%\AppData\Roaming\Microsoft\Outlook\[Outlook profile name].NK2
```

... on Windows Vista or, on Windows 2000, XP or 2003:

```
%userprofile%\Application Data\Microsoft\Outlook\[Outlook profile name].NK2
```

There are also other tools available on the Internet which will allow viewing and editing of the content of the auto-completion cache file, but they may not expose the X.500 addresses.

Diagnostic information for administrators:

```
Generating server: demo01.example.com


IMCEAEX-_O=COMPANY_OU=USA_cn=Recipients_cn=juser@company.com
#550 5.1.1 RESOLVER.ADR.ExRecipNotFound; not found ##
```

In my case, due to our upgrade to Exchange 2007, the user's **legacyExchangeDN** value had changed from this on the old mailbox (which had been created prior to the Exchange 2007 upgrade):

```
/o=Example/ou=USA/cn=Recipients/cn=juser
```

To this on the new mailbox:

```
/o=Example/ou=Exchange Administrative Group (FYDIBOHF23SPDLT)/cn=Recipients/
cn=juser
```

Any new email sent from Outlook using the previously cached X.500 address was being rejected because the old X.500 address no longer existed in the organisation.

The solution to the problem is actually quite simple – add the old **legacyExchangeDN** X.500 address to the new mailbox as a proxy address. You can add an X.500 proxy address through the Exchange Management Console, or the Exchange Management Shell.

To add the proxy address in the console, double-click the mailbox you need to add the proxy address to, go to the Email Addresses property page, and add a new custom address.

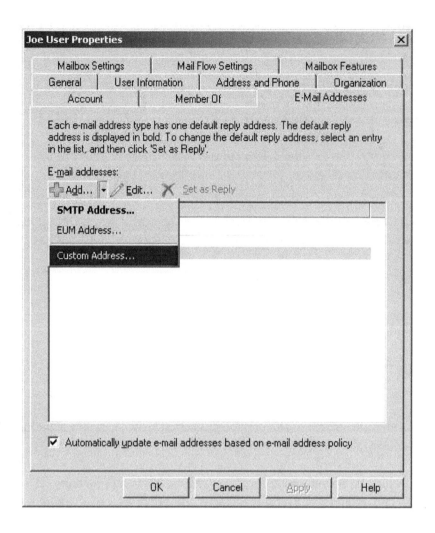

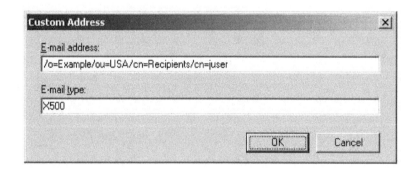

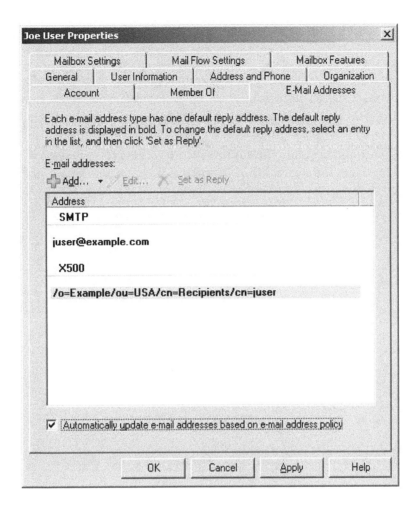

To add the proxy address in the shell we use the Get-Mailbox and Set-Mailbox cmdlets:

```
[PS] C:\>$ProxyAddresses = (Get-Mailbox juser).EmailAddresses
[PS] C:\>$ProxyAddresses += [Microsoft.Exchange.Data.CustomProxyAddress]("X500:/
o=Example/ou=USA/cn=Recipients/cn=juser")
[PS] C:\>Set-Mailbox juser -EmailAddresses $ProxyAddresses
```

Breaking these commands down:

```
[PS] C:\>$ProxyAddresses = (Get-Mailbox juser).EmailAddresses
```

...retrieves the existing proxy addresses for the mailbox and stores them in the $ProxyAddresses variable.

```
[PS] C:\>$ProxyAddresses += [Microsoft.Exchange.Data.CustomProxyAddress]("X500:/
o=Example/ou=USA/cn=Recipients/cn=juser")
```

...adds the new X.500 proxy address to the variable which contains the existing proxy addresses.

```
[PS] C:\>Set-Mailbox juser -EmailAddresses $ProxyAddresses
Updates the mailbox with the new set of proxy addresses
```

This technique can be used to solve this problem in a number of other scenarios where the **legacyExchangeDN** attribute has changed, and is not limited to mailboxes. For example, if someone leaves the Exchange organisation and you want their email to go to an external email address, you would create a contact record with the necessary SMTP proxy addresses. If you also added the **legacyExchangeDN** of the old mailbox to the contact record as an X.500 proxy address, Outlook users wouldn't get bounced messages if they used the old entry in their auto-complete caches.

Goodbye Exchange ExMerge, Hello Export-Mailbox

26 February 2009

by Ben Lye

ExMerge was a great way of exporting a mailbox to an Exchange PST file, or for removing all occurrences of an email virus, but it has now been replaced by two new Exchange Management Shell cmdlets, Export-Mailbox and Import-Mailbox which are equally as useful to have at hand.

Most Exchange administrators who've worked with Exchange prior to Exchange 2007 will be familiar with ExMerge. It was a useful tool to have available if you needed to export a mailbox to a PST file, for example, if a user left and wanted to take a copy of their mailbox with them, or you needed a PST file as an archive copy of one or more mailboxes. It was also useful if you needed to search your Exchange databases for a particular message and remove it, such as removing an email virus.

ExMerge was born in the Exchange 5.5 days as a product support tool, and was later re-released for Exchange 2003 as a web download. In Exchange 2007 ExMerge has been replaced by two new Exchange Management Shell cmdlets, `Export-Mailbox` and `Import-Mailbox`. The RTM release of `Export-Mailbox` was limited to moving messages only from one mailbox to another, but the SP1 release was enhanced to include the `export-to-PST` functionality which is familiar to ExMerge users, and that's the version I'm referring to in this article. There is no graphical interface for either `Export-Mailbox` or `Import-Mailbox`; they are only available in the shell.

It's important to note that `Export-Mailbox` is not intended for use as an Exchange migration tool. It's designed for moving mailbox content rather than an entire mailbox. If you need to migrate an entire mailbox you should use the Move-Mailbox cmdlet.

At a high level, `Export-Mailbox` can be used to

- Export mailbox content from a mailbox to another mailbox

- Export mailbox content from a mailbox to a PST file.

During mailbox exports content can be filtered by:

- Included or excluded folders

- Message sender keywords

- Message recipient keywords

- Message subject keywords

- Message and attachment content keywords

- Attachment file names

- Date range.

If you're going to use the filter options, make sure you have at least Update Rollup 4 for Exchange 2007 SP1, as this update included improvements to the filtering options.

When keyword filter options are specified, `Export-Mailbox` will first export all the messages in each from the source mailbox to the destination mailbox. The folder in the destination mailbox is then searched and messages which do not match the keyword filters are deleted. On large mailboxes this can be a time-consuming and resource-intensive operation.

Other options are available to:

- merge content from the source to the destination (the top level folder is not time stamped)

- delete content from the source mailbox after it has been exported

- include associated messages such as rules, views, and forms

- increase the number of threads

- write output to an XML log file.

The source and destination mailbox must be located on one of these versions of Exchange:

- Exchange 2007

- Exchange Server 2003 SP2 or later

- Exchange 2000 SP3 or later.

Export-Mailbox will export any items in mailbox's dumpster by converting them back to regular messages.

For multiple mailbox exports, the output of the `Get-Recipient` or `Get-Mailbox` cmdlets can be piped to `Export-Mailbox`, the **MaxThreads** parameter can be used to increase the number of mailboxes processed simultaneously.

Copying mailbox content to a subfolder in another mailbox

This might be the case if you have a user who has left, and you need to move some or all of their mailbox content into the mailbox of another user such as their co-worker, manager, or replacement, before the leaving user's mailbox is deleted.

This is the command to export the content from Joe's mailbox to a folder name "Joe" in Bob's mailbox:

```
Export-Mailbox -Identity joe@example.com -TargetMailbox bob@example.com
-TargetFolder Joe
```

The exported content will look as below.

Optionally the **AllowMerge** parameter can be used to merge the content into the target folder. When using the **AllowMerge** parameter the top-level folder isn't time-stamped, which means that the source mailbox content can be exported to the destination multiple times:

```
Export-Mailbox -Identity joe@example.com -TargetMailbox bob@example.com
-TargetFolder Joe -AllowMerge
```

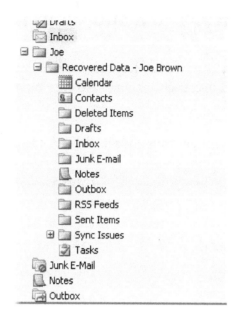

Specific folders can be included or excluded by using the **IncludeFolders** and **ExcludeFolders** parameters. For example, to include only the Inbox and Contacts folders:

```
Export-Mailbox -Identity joe@example.com -TargetMailbox bob@example.com
-TargetFolder Joe -IncludeFolders \Inbox, \Contacts
```

To export all content except for the Sent Items and Deleted Items folders:

```
Export-Mailbox -Identity joe@example.com -TargetMailbox bob@example.com
-TargetFolder Joe -ExcludeFolders "\Sent Items," "\Contacts"
```

Exporting mailbox contents to a PST file

If a user is leaving and wants to take a copy of their mailbox, you can use `Export-Mailbox` to move the data directly into a PST file.

Tip

To export mailbox content to a PST file you must run Export-Mailbox on a 32-bit Windows computer running the 32-bit version of the Exchange 2007 management tools, and Microsoft Outlook 2003 SP2 or later.

To export a user named Joe's mailbox to the PST file C:\Temp\joe.pst:

```
Export-Mailbox -Identity joe@example.com -PSTFolderPath C:\Temp\joe.pst
```

To export all the mailboxes in the sales mailbox database to individual PST files named <alias.pst>:

```
Get-Mailbox -Database "Sales Mailbox DB" | Export-Mailbox -PSTFolderPath C:\
PSTFiles
```

Searching for and removing content from a mailbox

If a virus has found its way into your Exchange organisation, or if a message has been delivered to a large number of mailboxes and you need to remove it, you can use `Export-Mailbox` to search mailboxes and remove the message.

> ### Tip
>
> *Because Export-Mailbox first copies all content to the destination mailbox before performing the search, the target mailbox can get quite large and will have a lot of I/O. It's a good idea to use a mailbox created specifically for this task, especially if you are performing the search over many mailboxes and using the MaxThreads parameter to increase the default number of threads.*

To remove any message with the words "Company confidential" in the subject line from all mailboxes on the server EXCHANGE01, processing 10 mailboxes at a time:

```
Get-Mailbox -Server EXCHANGE01 | Export-Mailbox -TargetMailbox ExportMailbox
-TargetFolder MessageCleanup -SubjectKeywords "Company confidential" -
DeleteContent -MaxThreads 10
```

To remove any messages from the sender **nasty.person@example.com** from all mailboxes on the server EXCHANGE01, processing 10 mailboxes at a time:

```
>Get-Mailbox -Server EXCHANGE01 | Export-Mailbox -TargetMailbox ExportMailbox
-TargetFolder MessageCleanup -SenderKeywords nasty.person@example.com -
DeleteContent -MaxThreads 10
```

The messages will be copied to the "MessageCleanup" folder in the target mailbox and deleted from the source mailboxes. The target folder will include a replica of the folder structure in each of the source mailboxes.

Troubleshooting Export-Mailbox

The most common problems with using Export-Mailbox are related to permissions. To use Export-Mailbox you need to be delegated the Exchange Server Administrator role, be a member of the local Administrators group for the target server, and to have full access to the source and destination mailboxes. The source and destination mailboxes must be in the same Active Directory forest.

These are some common permissions-related errors:

Error	Cause
"The specified mailbox database [Mailbox Database Name] does not exist"	The user running the Export-Mailbox command needs to be delegated the Exchange Administrator role for the Exchange server.
"Error occurred in the step: Creating target folder in the target mailbox. An unknown error has occurred. error code: -2147221233"	The user running the Export-Mailbox does not have full access to the destination mailbox.
Error occurred in the step: Moving messages. Failed to copy messages to the destination mailbox store with error: MAPI or an unspecified service provider. ID no: 00000000-0000-00000000, error code: -1056749164"	The user running the Export-Mailbox does not have full access to the source mailbox.

ExMerge may be gone, but `Export-Mailbox` is an equally useful a tool to have at hand. The flexible filtering options make it possible to do more granular exports than were possible with ExMerge, and the command shell interface makes it easy to script.

More information on `Export-Mailbox` can be found on the Microsoft TechNet website:

HTTP://TECHNET.MICROSOFT.COM/EN-US/LIBRARY/AA998579.ASPX.

More information about the dumpster can also be found on the TechNet website:

HTTP://TECHNET.MICROSOFT.COM/EN-US/LIBRARY/AA997155.ASPX.

Determining MS Exchange Disk Performance

26 March 2009

by Michael B. Smith

With an Exchange Server, how do you measure performance? How, in particular, do you go about measuring your disk subsystem's performance? Whereas the CPU Usage and Memory usage are both easy to measure, the measurement of disk performance is often described as a "black art." In fact, it isn't so difficult, as Michael Smith explains.

Performance – the big three

It is a real shame, actually. There are three major components that affect a computer's performance: the speed and power of its processor, how much memory it has, and the performance of its disk subsystem. Figuring out those first two – whether you need more memory and/or processing power – is generally pretty easy. For an example, refer to Figure 1.

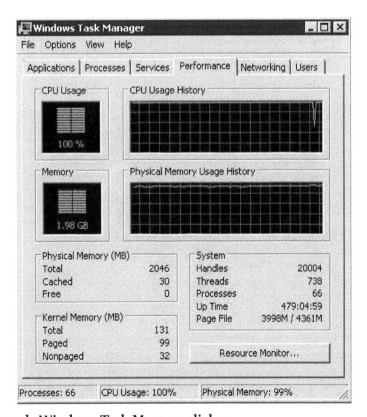

Figure 1:   The first sample Windows Task Manager dialog.

143

In Figure 1, it's pretty easy to see that the processor on this computer is overburdened. For the entirety of the CPU Usage History graphical display, the utilization of the processor was almost always 100%. Similarly, when we look at the various memory indicators, it is also pretty plain that the memory on this computer is in short supply. It takes one more indicator to be certain of that, but we can reach that conclusion based on the following indicators:

- physical memory is currently 99% utilized

- free physical memory is at zero

- the usage history shows that physical memory has constantly been highly utilized

- the page file is 92% in use (3998 MB / 4361 MB).

Now, it is often true that processor utilization and memory utilization can be tightly related. For example, if a computer has so little memory that the operating system is constantly required to move data into and out of the swap file, this tends to keep the processor utilization higher than it would be otherwise. However, since disk is so much slower than memory, it's rare that such a situation can cause a processor to be 100% utilized.

Also, you should note that physical memory being 99% utilized is not, by itself, an indication of memory depletion. Generally, Windows will try to cache system files and system data into memory, if memory is available to do so. This allows Windows to access those items much more quickly, since memory is so much faster than disk. If Figure 2, you can see another picture of that same computer, just a short while later.

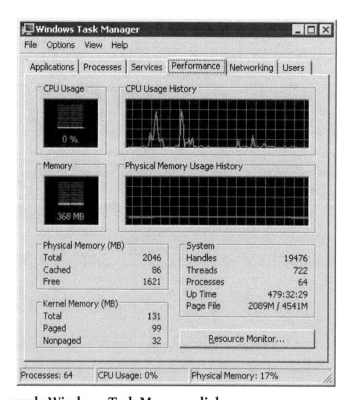

Figure 2: The second sample Windows Task Manager dialog.

In Figure 2, you see a processor that is fairly idle, with no memory pressure. The total physical memory has not changed but, in this second performance snapshot, the amount of free memory is up to 1,621 MB and the page file is only 46% in use.

Based on what we see in Task Manager, this computer should be performing very well, shouldn't it?

Of course, that is a trick question. In the first paragraph of this article, I mentioned three key contributors to performance and, so far, I've only discussed two. The third? Disk subsystem performance. Unfortunately, there is no sure-fire, single-graph view that will absolutely identify whether your disk subsystem is performing well or not. You have to do some investigation. That investigation is why some folks consider disk subsystem performance management something that is "more art than science." However, I would disagree. Diagnosing performance issues is actually very direct. Now, predicting end-user disk subsystem utilization – that is a black art!

LogicalDisk vs. PhysicalDisk

A key component of understanding how to measure the performance of an Exchange disk subsystem – or any disk subsystem – is to understand the difference between the LogicalDisk and PhysicalDisk performance objects. This is even more important than normal since these objects may, or may not, measure the same things.

The easiest way I've learned to explain them is below. Stay with me through the entire four parts of the explanation to find your "Ah-hah!" moment.

1. **LogicalDisk** – a logical disk is the unit of a disk subsystem with which Windows and users utilize a disk. When you open **Computer** (or **My Computer** for Windows 2003 and older versions of Windows) the hard disk drives shown there are logical disks.

2. **PhysicalDisk** – a physical disk is the unit of a disk subsystem which the hardware presents to Windows.

3. A logical disk may consist of multiple physical disks (think of RAID).

4. A physical disk may host multiple logical disks (think Windows partitions).

If you put all of these together, this means that, in the case where a physical disk contains only a single Windows volume, LogicalDisk and PhysicalDisk measure the same thing.

> **Note**
>
> *The highest performance disk devices currently available (Fiber Channel dual-controller disks) provide about 180 input-output operations per second (IOPS). They are quite expensive. More common enterprise class disk devices provide about 150 IOPS (for a 15K RPM SAS disk). Workstation class disk devices have much lower performance, often around only 35–50 IOPS.*

145

Somewhat confusingly, disk aggregators (this includes RAID controllers, Storage Area Networks, Network Attached Storage, iSCSI, etc.) may present many physical disks as a single logical device to Windows. However, each of these devices (known as a logical unit number or LUN) may *again* actually represent multiple logical or physical disks. Fortunately, from a Windows performance perspective, those distinctions can be ignored, at least until a specific LUN is identified as having a performance issue. In that case, in order to acquire more specific data, you will have to use performance tools from the aggregator's provider as the disk aggregators can sometimes give unpredictable results.

Is there a conclusion here? Yes, there is. The conclusion is that in the most common cases, the performance of a LogicalDisk object is what you are most interested in.

> **Note**
>
> *Lots of SAN and NAS software provides a feature called "LUN stacking" or "disk stacking" which allows multiple LUNS to exist on a single physical disk. This just complicates your life. Avoid it. Just always remember that you have to be able to identify what you are measuring and the boundaries on that measurement. If you have multiple applications accessing a single physical disk, then your performance will always be non-deterministic and difficult to predict.*

What do I measure?

Now that you know which performance object is interesting, what do you do with it?

As you probably know, any performance object is composed of a number of individual *performance counters*. A counter contains a discrete value which may be any of:

- a value that has been increasing since the last time the counter was cleared (which normally happens at system reboot)

- a value that represents the delta (change) since the last measurement

- a value that represents the percentage change since the last measurement

- a value that represents an instantaneous measurement of some item

- a value that is a percentage against some absolute (such as a time interval).

For the LogicalDisk performance object, there are 23 counters:

1. % Disk Read Time – the percent of wall-clock time spent processing read requests since the last sample.

2. % Disk Time – % Disk Read Time plus % Disk Write Time.

3. % Disk Write Time – the percent of wall-clock time spent processing write requests since the last sample.

4. % Free Space – the amount of unused space on the disk, expressed as a percentage of the total amount of space available on the disk.

5. % Idle Time – the percent of time spent idle since the last sample (that is, processing neither read nor write requests).

6. Avg. Disk Bytes/Read – the average number of bytes transferred from the disk in each read operation since the last sample.

7. Avg. Disk Bytes/Transfer – the average number of bytes transferred from or to the disk in each I/O operation since the last sample.

8. Avg. Disk Bytes/Write – the average number of bytes transferred from the disk in each write operation since the last sample.

9. Avg. Disk Queue Length – the average numbers of I/O requests (both read and write) queued for the selected disk since the last sample.

10. Avg. Disk Read Queue Length – the average number of read requests queued for the selected disk since the last sample.

11. Avg. Disk sec/Read – the average amount of time that it took for a read request to complete for the selected disk since the last sample.

12. Avg. Disk sec/Transfer – the average amount of time that it took for any I/O request to complete for the selected disk since the last sample.

13. Avg. Disk sec/Write – the average amount of time that it took for a write request to complete for the selected disk since the last sample.

14. Avg. Disk Write Queue Length – the average number of write requests queued for the selected disk since the last sample.

15. Current Disk Queue Length – the current number of I/O requests queued for the selected disk.

16. Disk Bytes/sec – the average rate, or speed, that bytes are transferred from or to the selected disk during any I/O operation.

17. Disk Read Bytes/sec – the average rate, or speed, that bytes are transferred from the selected disk during a read operation.

18. Disk Reads/sec – the average number of read requests that occur per second for the selected disk.

19. Disk Transfers/sec – the average number of I/O requests that occur per second for the selected disk.

20. Disk Write Bytes/sec – the average rate, or speed, that bytes are transferred to the selected disk during a write operation.

21. Disk Write/sec – the average number of write requests that occur per second for the selected disk.

22. Free Megabytes – the amount of unused space on the disk, expressed in megabytes.

23. Split IO/sec – if a read or write operation is too large to be satisfied in a single I/O operation, the I/O is split into multiple separate physical I/Os; this counter records how often that happens for the selected disk.

Speaking as a person who likes math, I think that all of these counters are interesting, and are worthwhile tracking over time. For example, if the **% Free Space** is decreasing on a regular basis, then you may need to plan to add more disks – or stop the expansion in some way. If your **Disk Write/sec** is trending upward, you may need to investigate why more write operations are occurring to that disk drive.

What defines good performance?

For determining whether you have adequate performance, I would suggest that there are four main counters that you need to constantly monitor. Note that in this case, I'm suggesting that the counters should be checked every one to five minutes.

Those counters are:

1. Average Disk Queue Length

2. Average Disk Read Queue Length

3. Average Disk Write Queue Length

4. Free Space (either % Free Space or Free Megabytes).

For [4], it should be obvious that if any write operations are occurring to a disk, if it fills up, performance will rapidly approach zero, the event log will starting filling with errors, and users will be calling your phone saying "Exchange is down" (or name your favorite application instead of Exchange). On the other hand, if a disk is read-only, such as a DVD-ROM database, there is no need to measure either [3] or [4]. Writes cannot occur. But that is a special case, and since we are primarily concerned with Exchange, it doesn't support any type of read-only volume.

You may find it interesting that I use the average values instead of the current values. That is because any system can be instantaneously overwhelmed. At any given moment of time, you may have 50 I/Os queued to a particular disk waiting to be satisfied; but that is unlikely to be the normal case. If that high queue value becomes the normal case, then the average values will trend quite high as well. That will serve to provide you with an absolute indication of an issue which needs to be addressed.

If the average values are not high, then you had what is called a "usage spike" in which a device was temporarily overwhelmed. And that is why we have queues anyway.

What is a high value? A high value occurs when the device cannot empty the queue. Because each I/O is variable in size, its arrival cannot be predicted, and the I/O takes a variable amount of time to complete; the point at which a device is considered saturated or overburdened with I/O requests actually occurs a little earlier than you may presume.

Now, I am not a statistician, nor do I play one on TV. However, like many of you, I took basic queuing theory in college. A device becomes saturated when its I/O queue exceeds 70% on an average basis. To put that another way: **If the average disk queue length of a device exceeds 0.70 then the performance of that disk is negatively impacting user performance.**

The overall Average Disk Queue Length is an average of the read and write average queue lengths. The read and write queues are maintained independently. A disk may (and in fact, usually will) have significantly different read and write profiles. While checking the Average Disk Queue Length is an important indicator of disk performance, if it indicates heavy usage, your first order of business is to determine whether read performance or write performance (or both) are causing the performance issue. That is the reason for my recommendation to continuously monitor all three counters.

So now you know: the best way to check your Exchange disk performance is:

• make sure there is room on the disk

• monitor the average disk queue lengths.

The next thing you may want to know is – how can I predict how my disk subsystem **should** perform? But that is a topic for another article.

Message Tracking in Exchange 2007

27 March 2009

by Ben Lye

"Where did my mail go?" In order to answer this question, to troubleshoot mail problems and to analyse mail flow, the Exchange administrator can use message-tracking logs. Ben Lye elaborates on these essential logs and explains how you can use PowerShell commands to search them for those emails that have gone adrift.

Exchange message tracking records the SMTP activity of messages being sent to and from Exchange servers running the Edge Transport or Hub Transport roles. Exchange administrators can use message tracking logs for mail flow analysis as well as troubleshooting and answering the ever-familiar, "Where did my mail go?" question.

Configuring message tracking

By default, message tracking is enabled on any exchange server which has the one or more of the Edge Transport, Hub Transport, or Mailbox roles installed. The default settings are to store up to 30 days of log files in files of up to 10 MB with a directory size limit of 250 MB.

Message tracking settings can be retrieved using the `Get-TransportServer` cmdlet for Edge and Hub transport roles and the `Get-MailboxServer` cmdlet for Mailbox server roles.

```
Machine: exchange01 | Scope: example.com                          _ □ ✕
[PS] C:\>Get-TransportServer EXCHANGE01 | fl *Message*

MessageTrackingLogEnabled                : True
MessageTrackingLogMaxAge                 : 30.00:00:00
MessageTrackingLogMaxDirectorySize       : 250MB
MessageTrackingLogMaxFileSize            : 10MB
MessageTrackingLogPath                   : C:\Program Files\Microsoft\
                                           Exchange Server\TransportRo
                                           les\Logs\MessageTracking
MessageTrackingLogSubjectLoggingEnabled  : True


[PS] C:\>_
```

To modify the message tracking settings you can use the `Set-TransportServer` and `Set-MailboxServer` cmdlets. Using these cmdlets you can:

- enable or disable message tracking (enabled by default)

- enable or disable logging of message subject lines (enabled by default)

- set the maximum age of message tracking log files (30 days by default)

- set the maximum size of the log file directory (250 MB by default)

- set the maximum size of each log file (10 MB by default)

- change the path of the log file ("C:\Program Files\Microsoft\Exchange Server\TransportRoles\Logs\ MessageTracking" by default).

If you change the path of the message tracking log directory, then new log files will be written to the new path straight away, but existing log files are not moved or copied from the old path to the new path.

Old log files are removed when either the maximum directory size has been reached, or the log file is past the maximum age. In the case of the maximum size being reached, the oldest log file is removed even though it may not have met the age limit. Because of this, if you are in a site with many users, where a lot of email is sent, you may want need to increase the maximum directory size as you might find that the log files are being deleted well before the maximum age is reached.

You can use this command to increase the maximum directory size to 2 GB and the maximum log file age to 90 days (adjust the values as appropriate for your environment):

```
[PS] C:\>Set-TransportServer EXCHANGE01 -MessageTrackingLogMaxDirectorySize 2GB
-MessageTrackingLogMaxAge 90.00:00:00
```

To configure Message Tracking you must be delegated the Exchange Organization Administrator role and be a member of the local Administrators group on the Exchange server.

Searching message tracking logs

Once message tracking is configured, using either default or custom settings, you can use the message tracking data for testing, troubleshooting, or auditing mail flow.

Logs can be searched using with the Message Tracking Tool in the Exchange Management Console or the `Get-MessageTrackingLog` cmdlet in the Exchange Management Console. Both methods use the same set of search filters, and in fact the Message Tracking Tool uses the `Get-MessageTrackingLog` cmdlet to perform the search. `Get-MessageTrackingLog` gives the option of limiting the number of results returned, and the results can be converted into different formats.

Search results can be limited using the following filters:

Name	Description
Recipients	The complete email address(es) of the message recipient(s); multiple values can be entered using a comma delimiter.
Sender	The complete email address of the message sender
Server	The server on which to search
EventID	The specific event to search for – for example, "SEND" or "DELIVER"
MessageID	Unique ID of the email message
InternalMessageID	Server-specific message ID
Subject	Subject line of the email message
Reference	Additional information for some event types
Start	Starting date/time
End	Ending date/time

To perform a search using the Message Tracking Tool, launch the Exchange Management Console, navigate to the **Toolbox** pane, and double-click **Message Tracking**. After a brief check for updates you'll be able to go to the **Welcome** screen, where you can enter search parameters to begin looking for messages in the tracking logs. While you are constructing your search, a box at the bottom of the tool shows you the Get-MessageTrackingLog command which will be used to perform the search.

To perform a search using the Get-MessageTrackingLog cmdlet, searching the server EXCHANGE01 for messages sent from john@example.com to bill@example.net, sent between 12/3/2009 and 13/3/2009:

```
[PS] C:\>Get-MessageTrackingLog -Server EXCHANGE01 -EventID SEND -Sender john@
example.com -Recipients bill@example.net -Start 12/3/2009 -End 13/3/2009
```

To perform the same search and return only the first 100 matching records:

```
[PS] C:\>Get-MessageTrackingLog -Server EXCHANGE01 -EventID SEND -Sender john@
example.com -Recipients bill@example.net -Start 12/3/2009 -End 13/3/2009
-ResultSize 100
```

If you are using Exchange 2007 SP1 you must be delegated the Exchange View-Only Administrator role to use the Get-MessageTrackingLog cmdlet. If you are using Exchange 2007 RTM you need to be delegated the Exchange Server Administrator role and be a member of the local Administrators group on the target server.

Working with the search results

Once you have a search which returns the results you need, you may want to convert those results into other formats, perhaps to use for reports or to provide information to others. PowerShell includes built-in cmdlets for re-formatting output data, and those can be used in conjunction with the Get-MessageTrackingLog cmdlet. For the **Recipients**, **RecipientStatus** and **Reference** properties it's necessary to convert the data so that it appears in the output files.

To convert the results to CSV format you can pipe the search command to the Export-CSV cmdlet. This command will create a CSV file called C:\Temp\SearchResults.csv, exporting all the available fields:

```
[PS] C:\>Get-MessageTrackingLog -Server EXCHANGE01 -EventID SEND -Sender john@
example.com -Recipients bill@example.net -Start 12/3/2009 -End 13/3/2009
| Select Timestamp, ClientIp, ClientHostname, ServerIp, ServerHostname,
SourceContext, ConnectorId, Source, EventId, InternalMessageId, MessageId,
{$_.Recipients}, {$_.RecipientStatus}, TotalBytes, RecipientCount,
RelatedRecipientAddress, {$_.Reference}, MessageSubject, Sender, ReturnPath,
MessageInfo | Export-CSV C:\Temp\SearchResults.csv
```

This command will create a CSV file including only the timestamp, event ID, sender, recipients, and subject line:

```
[PS] C:\>Get-MessageTrackingLog -Server EXCHANGE01 -EventID SEND -Sender john@
example.com -Recipients bill@example.net -Start 12/3/2009 -End 13/3/2009 |
Select Timestamp, EventID, Sender, {$_.Recipients}, MessageSubject | Export-CSV
C:\Temp\SearchResults.csv
```

Alternatively, to convert the results to HTML you can pipe the search command to the ConvertTo-HTML cmdlet. Use this command to export the results to an HTML file showing the timestamp, event ID, sender, recipients, and subject line:

```
[PS] C:\>Get-MessageTrackingLog -Server EXHUB-00-UK -EventID SEND -Sender john@
example.com -Recipients bill@example.net -Start 12/3/2009 -End 13/3/2009 |
ConvertTo-Html Timestamp, EventID, Sender, {$_.Recipients}, MessageSubject |
Set-Content C:\Temp\logs.html
```

Advanced searches

PowerShell scripts can be used to do some interesting manipulation of the message tracking log data. Here are a few examples of what can be done without much effort.

Searching across multiple servers

Get-MessageTrackingLog only searches the message tracking logs of one server. To search the logs on multiple machines we need to use a few lines of PowerShell code.

First, get the names of all the Hub Transport Servers:

```
[PS] C:\>$hubs = Get-TransportServer
```

Then pipe them into a Get-MessageTrackingLog command, in this case, looking for all email with the subject line "Important news" sent on March 13th.

```
[PS] C:\>$hubs | Get-MessageTrackingLog -MessageSubject "Important news" -Start
"13/03/2009 00:00:00" -End "13/03/2009 23:59:59"
```

This will return the message tracking information from all the Hub Transport Servers in the Exchange organisation. As with regular message tracking log searches, it's possible to output this data to a reader-friendly HTML file.

```
[PS] C:\>$hubs | Get-MessageTrackingLog -MessageSubject "Important news"
-Start "13/03/2009 00:00:00" -End "13/03/2009 23:59:59" | ConvertTo-Html
ServerHostname, Timestamp, EventID, Sender, {$_.Recipients}, MessageSubject |
Set-Content C:\Temp\logs.html
```

Reporting on email messages sent and received yesterday

Using PowerShell scripts it's possible to use the message tracking logs to create reports. This example will get the messages sent and received on the previous day for a group of mailboxes in a specific database.

```
# Get the start date for the tracking log search
$Start = (Get-Date -Hour 00 -Minute 00 -Second 00).AddDays(-1)
# Get the end date for the tracking log search
$End = (Get-Date -Hour 23 -Minute 59 -Second 59).AddDays(-1)
# Declare an array to store the results
$Results = @()
# Get the SEND events from the message tracking logs
$Sent = Get-MessageTrackingLog -Server EXCHANGE01 -EventID SEND -Start $Start
-End $End -resultsize unlimited
# Get the RECEIVE events the message tracking logs
$Received = Get-MessageTrackingLog -Server EXCHANGE01 -EventID RECEIVE -Start
$Start -End $End -resultsize unlimited
# Get the mailboxes we want to report on
$Mailboxes = Get-Mailbox -Database "EXCHANGE01\SG1\DB1"
```

```
# Set up the counters for the progress bar
$Total = $Mailboxes.Count
$Count = 1
# Sort the mailboxes and pipe them to a For-Each loop
$Mailboxes | Sort-Object -Property DisplayName | ForEach-Object {
# Update the progress bar
$PercentComplete = $Count / $Total * 100
Write-Progress -Activity "Message Tracking Log Search" -Status "Processing
mailboxes" -percentComplete $PercentComplete
# Declare a custom object to store the data
$Stats = "" | Select-Object Name,Sent,Received
# Get the email address for the mailbox
$Email = $_.WindowsEmailAddress.ToString()
# Set the Name property of our object to the mailbox's display name
$Stats.Name = $_.DisplayName
# Set the Sent property to the number of messages sent
$Stats.Sent = ($Sent | Where-Object { ($_.EventId -eq "SEND") -and ($_.Sender
-eq $email) }).Count
# Set the Received property to the number of messages received
$Stats.Received = ($Received | Where-Object { ($_.EventId -eq "RECEIVE") -and
($_.Recipients -match $email) }).Count
# Add the statistics for this mailbox to our results array
$Results += $Stats
# Increment the progress bar counter
$Count += 1
}
# Output the results
$Results
```

The script works by finding all mailboxes in the DB1 database on the Exchange server EXCHANGE01, and searching the message tracking logs to find any RECEIVE and SEND mail events. The Get-Mailbox command can be easily modified to find a different group of mailboxes or changed to return distribution groups or contacts. The script could also be modified to search across multiple servers.

More information on configuring and managing message tracking and searching message tracking log files can be found on Microsoft TechNet:

HTTP://TECHNET.MICROSOFT.COM/EN-US/LIBRARY/AA997984.ASPX

HTTP://TECHNET.MICROSOFT.COM/EN-US/LIBRARY/BB124375.ASPX

HTTP://TECHNET.MICROSOFT.COM/EN-US/LIBRARY/BB124926.ASPX

Emulating the Exchange 2003 RUS for Out-of-Band Mailbox Provisioning in Exchange 2007

08 May 2009

by Ben Lye

Exchange's Recipient Update Service was important in Exchange 2000 or 2003 in order to complete the provisioning or updating of mailboxes created from an out-of-band process or from an Active Directory User. In Exchange 2007, full provisioning is automatic, but the functionality can replaced by PowerShell scripting if it is required.

Exchange 2000 and Exchange 2003 included a component known as the Recipient Update Service or RUS. The RUS runs as a subprocess of the System Attendant, and is responsible for discovering partially provisioned mailboxes and fully provisioning them. The RUS is required because, when user accounts are configured to have a mailbox using Active Directory Users and Computers (ADUC), they only have a few key attributes assigned. When the RUS discovers these partially configured accounts, they are stamped with the remaining required attributes, and a mailbox will subsequently be created in the appropriate Exchange database when the mailbox is either logged onto or receives a message.

Many Exchange administrators who have worked with Exchange 2000 or 2003 will have experienced times when the RUS hasn't worked at all or has worked slowly and, as a result, have had problems with mailbox provisioning or updates.

In Exchange 2007, the RUS is no longer present because, when a mailbox is provisioned in either of the Exchange management tools, it is automatically fully provisioned straight away. This is great if mailboxes are only ever provisioned using the Exchange 2007 tools, but if you use an out-of-band process to provision mailboxes you will run into trouble, as those mailboxes will never be picked up and fully provisioned by Exchange 2007.

For example, in Exchange 2003 it's possible to cause a mailbox to be provisioned simply by setting the LegacyExchangeDN, Mailnickname, and homeMDB attributes on a user object. The RUS will find the user account and will finish provisioning the mailbox. If you try this with Exchange 2007 you won't get a usable mailbox.

Fortunately, there is a way to emulate the Exchange 2000/2003 RUS on Exchange 2007 using two Exchange 2007 PowerShell cmdlets, `Update-EmailAddressPolicy` which will apply an email address policy to mailboxes, and `Update-AddressList` which will update address list memberships.

The easiest way to run the "update" cmdlets is to pipe input to them from the `get` cmdlets. These

157

commands will update all email address policies and address lists:

```
Get-EmailAddressPolicy | Update-EmailAddressPolicy
Get-AddressList | Update-AddressList
```

After running these commands, the mailbox will be provisioned and will appear in the Exchange address lists, but it will appear in the Exchange Management Console as a "legacy mailbox." A legacy mailbox will still function for sending and receiving email, but it's not possible to enable or disable Exchange 2007 features such as Messaging Records Management or Unified Messaging. Legacy mailboxes can be converted to Exchange 2007 mailboxes using the Set-Mailbox cmdlet with the -ApplyMandatoryProperties parameter.

If your Exchange environment has only Exchange 2007 servers, this command will update all legacy mailboxes to Exchange 2007 mailboxes:

```
Get-Mailbox -RecipientTypeDetails LegacyMailbox | Set-Mailbox -
ApplyMandatoryProperties
```

If you have mailboxes hosted on legacy versions of Exchange and on Exchange 2007, you will need to filter the command to only touch those hosted on Exchange 2007. This command will do that by first getting only the Exchange 2007 servers, then finding all the legacy mailboxes on those servers:

```
Get-ExchangeServer |
Where{$_.AdminDisplayVersion.ToString().SubString(0, 10) -eq"Version 8."} |
ForEach{ Get-Mailbox -Server $_.Name -RecipientTypeDetails LegacyMailbox | Set-
Mailbox -ApplyMandatoryProperties}
```

The same problem exists for changes made to users outside of the Exchange Management tools. Any changes made within the Exchange 2007 tools are instantly reflected in the user's email addresses and address list membership, but changes which would impact email address policies and address list memberships that are made using out-of-band tools such as ADUC, ADSI Edit, or other tools for directly editing Active Directory, will not show up in the Exchange 2007 mailbox properties until the same "update" commands are run.

For example, if there is an email address policy which applies email addresses in the format firstname. lastname, and the last name of a user is changed using an Exchange 2007 tool, the user will instantly get a new email address with the new last name. If the same change is made using an out-of-band tool or process, then the name change will not be reflected in the user's Exchange email addresses.

This problem can also be solved by running the Update-EmailAddressPolicy and Update-AddressList cmdlets.

So, if your environment requires out-of-band mailbox provisioning or user updates, then the simplest solution is to put these three commands into a PowerShell script and schedule it to run as often as needed.

Don't forget that, if you still have mailboxes hosted on legacy Exchange servers, you need to change the last command to the filtered version shown above.

```
Get-EmailAddressPolicy | Update-EmailAddressPolicy
Get-AddressList | Update-AddressList
Get-Mailbox -RecipientTypeDetails LegacyMailbox | Set-Mailbox -
ApplyMandatoryProperties
```

To run the `Update-EmailAddressPolicy` cmdlet you need to be delegated the Exchange Server Administrator role and have local Administrator's rights for the Exchange server. To run `Update-AddressList` you need to be delegated the Exchange Organization Administrator role. To run the `Set-Mailbox` cmdlet you need to be delegated the Exchange Recipient Administrator role.

More information on the cmdlets can be found on the Microsoft TechNet website as shown below.

Update-EmailAddressPolicy – HTTP://TECHNET.MICROSOFT.COM/EN-US/LIBRARY/AA996869.ASPX.

Update-AddressList – HTTP://TECHNET.MICROSOFT.COM/EN-US/LIBRARY/AA997982.ASPX.

Set-Mailbox – HTTP://TECHNET.MICROSOFT.COM/EN-US/LIBRARY/BB123981.ASPX.

Using Exchange 2007 Transport Rules to Protect the First Entry in the Address Book

08 June 2009

by Ben Lye

Global Address Lists in MS Exchange can cause problems, because the first person in the list often gets the reply. Ben Lye shows how one can eliminate any such problems with Global Address lists by creating a mail contact, a transport rule, and a custom Delivery Status Notification.

I was recently asked to add an entry to the Outlook address book which would prevent mail being inadvertently sent to the person who normally appeared at the top of the Global Address List (GAL). This person was getting frustrated by receiving email which was clearly not intended for him.

There are several possible ways this could be achieved: a mailbox with an auto-reply or out-of-office rule, a public folder with an auto-response, a non-Exchange auto-responder, or simply a mail contact with an invalid external address, to name a few.

Ideally, I wanted the email to be stopped on Exchange without requiring an extra mailbox or public folder, and I wanted the sender should get a helpful error message. These requirements meant that a mailbox or public folder with an auto-reply rule could not be part of the ideal solution, and neither could a non-Exchange auto-responder, as that would mean that the email would have to leave the Exchange environment before being stopped. Additionally, using a contact record with an invalid address was not perfect either; because a user who emailed the contact would simply receive a rather unhelpful "address unknown" non-delivery report (NDR).

Fortunately, Exchange 2007 provides mechanisms which can be used to provide a neat solution to this problem. The solution has three parts: a mail contact which will appear at the top of the GAL, a transport rule to prevent mail being sent to the contact, and a custom delivery status notification (DSN) to provide the user with information about why their message was not delivered.

Mail Contacts are Active Directory objects which are typically used to add email addresses which are external to Exchange 2007 to the Global Address List. To create a new mail contact you must be delegated the Exchange Recipient Administrator role and the Account Operator role for the Active Directory container where you wish to create the contact.

Transport rules run on Exchange 2007 servers which have either the Hub Transport or Edge Transport role installed. They can be used to control the flow of email messages within the Exchange 2007 organization and can be used for a variety of purposes, including restricting email between certain individuals or groups, or applying a footer to all email destined for Internet recipients.

Custom DSN messages give Exchange 2007 administrators the facility to create new DSN messages for custom delivery notifications, and the ability to customize existing DSN messages. They are a useful tool if you wish to provide users with links to further information such as links to self-help knowledge base articles, or contact information for help-desk staff.

To create transport rules and custom DSN messages you must be delegated the Exchange Organization Administrator role.

The first step in implementing this solution is to create a new mail contact which has a display name that will ensure it is shown as the first entry in the GAL. An easy way to do this is to prefix the display name with a period or underscore or any other valid character which does not normally appear in Exchange display names (spaces are prohibited as leading characters in display names). We also need to specify an email address which is not in use by another email-enabled object.

The mail contact can be created in the Exchange Management Shell using the `New-MailContact` cmdlet:

```
New-MailContact -Name ."First Address Book Entry" -ExternalEmailAddress
"firstaddressbookentry@example.com" -Alias "firstaddressbookentry"
```

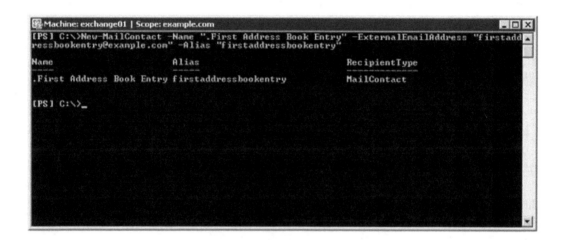

The new mail contact will appear in the Outlook address book:

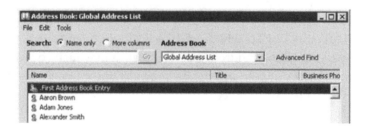

The second step is to create a new custom delivery status notification (DSN) message which will be sent to anybody who emails the new mail contact. Custom DSN messages can contain plain text or HTML, and, in this case, will provide useful information to the user, pointing out that their message probably did not reach the intended recipient.

We'll create a DSN message for DSN code 5.7.10, which is the first available enhanced status code (the valid range is 5.7.10 through 5.7.999 inclusive).

The Exchange Management Shell cmdlet for creating DSN messages is New-SystemMessage:

```
New-SystemMessage -DsnCode 5.7.10 -Text 'You have accidentally sent an email to
the first entry in the Outlook Global Address List.<br>You may wish to resend
your message to the correct recipient.' -Internal $True -Language en
```

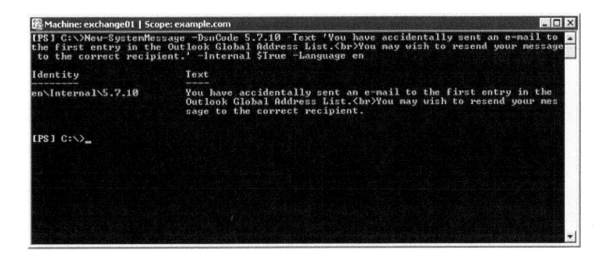

The final step is to create a new transport rule which will send the new DSN message to anybody who emails the new mail contact.

Transport rules consist of three components: conditions, actions, and exclusions. To create a new transport rule we must, as a minimum, specify the action to be taken but, in this case, we'll specify a condition and an action. The transport rule can be created in the Management Shell using these commands, incorporating the New-TransportRule cmdlet:

```
$Condition = Get-TransportRulePredicate SentTo
$Condition.Addresses = @(Get-MailContact ."First Address Book Entry")
$Action = Get-TransportRuleAction RejectMessage
$Action.RejectReason = "E-mail to the first entry in the GAL is not allowed."
$Action.EnhancedStatusCode = "5.7.10"
New-TransportRule -Name "Block e-mail to the first entry in the GAL" -Conditions
@($Condition) -Actions @($Action) -Priority 0
```

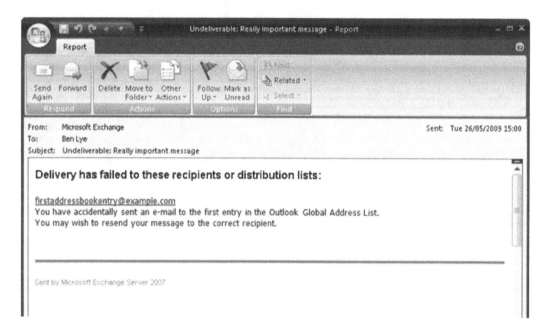

With the new mail contact in the Global Address List, the new DSN created, and the transport rule set up, if you sent a test email message to the new contact you will receive this NDR message back:

Using this solution, my objectives have been met: I didn't have to create a mailbox or public folder, the email message doesn't leave the Exchange environment, and the sender receives a useful error message.

For more information about creating mail contacts:
HTTP://TECHNET.MICROSOFT.COM/EN-US/LIBRARY/AA997220.ASPX.

For more information about custom DSN messages:
HTTP://TECHNET.MICROSOFT.COM/EN-US/LIBRARY/AA998878.ASPX.

For more information about transport rules:
HTTP://TECHNET.MICROSOFT.COM/EN-US/LIBRARY/AA995961.ASPX.

An Introduction to Messaging Records Management

07 July 2009

by Ben Lye

There are a number of features in Exchange that can be used in creative ways to solve problems in Exchange as they crop up. Ben Lye recently found a great use for Messaging Records Management when he hit the problem of a meeting-room mailbox that stopped replying to booking requests. Here, he shows how to apply policies that apply to all folders of a particular type, and how to schedule a regular task to do it.

Messaging Records Management (MRM) is a feature of Exchange 2007 which lets administrators define policies to control the storing of email data. Essentially, MRM allows you to create folder-level rules which determine how long messages stored in that folder should be retained. MRM policies can be applied to default mailbox folders or custom mailbox folders, but applying policies to custom folders requires the use of Enterprise CALs.

MRM can be used to ensure compliance with company policy or legal requirements, or other regulations. MRM can also be used as an administrative tool.

I recently had to fix an issue with a meeting room mailbox which had stopped replying to booking requests. It turned out that the mailbox was over the database's default Prohibit Send quota, so it was unable to send any messages. The problem was that all the old meeting requests, which had been deleted after they had been processed by the Calendar Attendant, were still in the Deleted Items folder, and that was causing the mailbox to exceed its quota.

The quick fix was to empty the Deleted Items folder, but this didn't really fix the root cause of the problem – the mailbox would continue to grow over time. Another option was to apply a higher quota, but this would just make the problem come back again later when the new quota was reached. Ideally, I wanted to find a way to make sure that deleted messages in resource mailboxes were permanently removed.

This is where MRM comes in – as well as applying policies for storing email messages, MRM can be used to apply policies to *delete* email messages. To solve the problem with my resource mailbox, I created an MRM policy which would automatically remove messages from the Deleted Items folders of all resource mailboxes.

There are five steps to setting up an MRM policy:

- choose the folder you want the policy to apply to

- create the managed content settings for the folder

- create a managed folder mailbox policy

- apply the managed folder mailbox policy to the mailboxes

- schedule the managed folder assistant to run.

To set up the MRM settings and policies you must be delegated the Exchange Organization Administrator's role.

I already know that I want to apply the policy to the Deleted Items folder. However, I want to create a new managed folder so that if there are future needs for different managed content settings on the Deleted Items folder in other mailboxes, they can be accommodated. Because the Deleted Items folder is a default folder I can use managed default folders.

To create a new managed default folder we use the New-ManagedFolder cmdlet

```
New-ManagedFolder -Name "Deleted Items (30-day limit)" `
 -DefaultFolderType "DeletedItems"
```

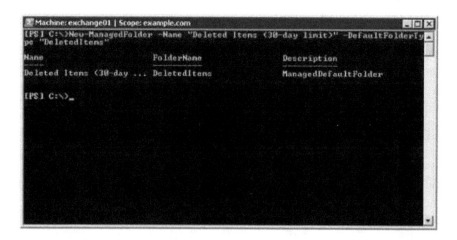

With the new managed folder created, the next thing to do is create the managed content settings. The managed content settings define the actual retention criteria.

Creation of the managed content settings can be done through either the Exchange Management Console or the Exchange Management Shell.

I want settings which will remove items from the Deleted Items folder 30 days after they were received by the resource mailbox. The deleted messages should be available for recovery according to the database's standard deleted item recovery policy.

To create the managed content settings we will use the New-ManagedContentSettings cmdlet:

```
New-ManagedContentSettings -Name "Remove Deleted Items After 30 Days" `
-FolderName "Deleted Items (30-day limit)" `
-MessageClass * `
-RetentionEnabled $true `
-RetentionAction DeleteAndAllowRecovery `
-AgeLimitForRetention 30 `
-TriggerForRetention WhenDelivered
```

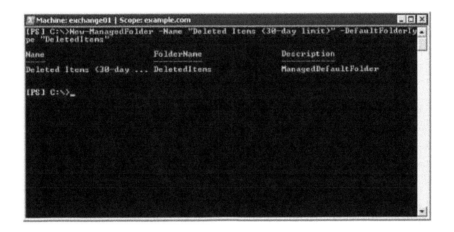

Because a mailbox can only have one managed folder mailbox policy applied, managed folder mailbox policies are used to group managed folder content settings so that multiple settings can be applied to a mailbox. The next step is to create the managed folder mailbox policy.

To create a new policy containing the new deleted item managed content settings we use the New-ManagedFolderMailboxPolicy cmdlet:

```
New-ManagedFolderMailboxPolicy -Name "Resource Mailbox Policy" `
-ManagedFolderLinks "Deleted Items (30-day limit)"
```

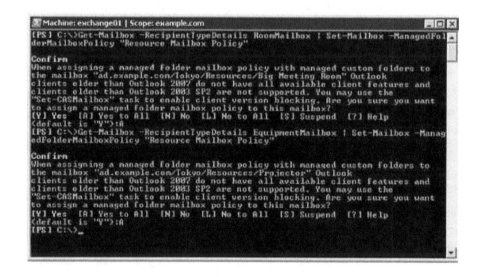

The next step is to apply the new managed folder mailbox policy to the resource mailboxes using the Set-Mailbox cmdlet (once for room resources and once for equipment resources). You will be warned that Outlook clients prior to Outlook 2007 do not support all MRM features, and clients older than Outlook 2003 SP2 are not supported:

```
Get-Mailbox -RecipientTypeDetails RoomMailbox |
Set-Mailbox -ManagedFolderMailboxPolicy "Resource Mailbox Policy"
Get-Mailbox -RecipientTypeDetails EquipmentMailbox |
Set-Mailbox -ManagedFolderMailboxPolicy "Resource Mailbox Policy"
```

The final step is to schedule the managed folder assistant (the process which actually enforces the policy) to run. This is done with the Set-MailboxServer cmdlet.

Each Exchange server only has one schedule for the managed folder assistant, and you should schedule it to run as often as needed to meet you requirements. To run the managed folder assistant on all Exchange 2007 mailbox servers daily between 1 a.m. and 3 a.m. the command would be:

168

```
Get-ExchangeServer |
Where { $_.AdminDisplayVersion.ToString().SubString(0, 10) -eq "Version 8." `
-and $_.ServerRole -eq "Mailbox" } |
ForEach { Set-MailboxServer -Identity $_.Identity `
-ManagedFolderAssistantSchedule "Sun.1:00 AM-Sun.3:00 AM," `
"Mon.1:00 AM-Mon.3:00 AM," "Tue.1:00 AM-Tue.3:00 AM," `
"Wed.1:00 AM-Wed.3:00 AM," "Thu.1:00 AM-Thu.3:00 AM," `
"Fri.1:00 AM-Fri.3:00 AM," "Sat.1:00 AM-Sat.3:00 AM" }
```

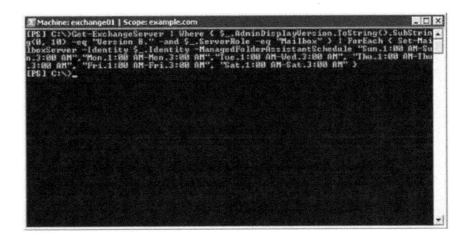

The managed folder assistant can also be started on demand using the Start-ManagedFolderAssistant cmdlet. Running the managed folder assistant can be a resource-intensive process, and it should be scheduled to run during off-peak hours.

The application of this MRM policy will ensure that my resource mailboxes will remain small, as the content of their Deleted Items folders will be automatically removed.

More information on Messaging Records Management and messaging policies can be found in Microsoft TechNet: HTTP://TECHNET.MICROSOFT.COM/EN-US/LIBRARY/AA998599.ASPX.

Restricting Outlook Client Versions in Exchange 2007

29 July 2009

by Ben Lye

There are good reasons for preventing old versions of Outlook from connecting to Exchange Server. You'll probably, at least, want to do it for security. Before you do so, you'll also need know what versions are out there being used so you can make sure that blocking of legitimate users is prevented. Ben Lye explains how it is done.

Outlook has been around for a long time, and there are many versions with different features and varying levels of security fixes. It's not always desirable to let any version of Outlook connect to Exchange Server as you may require your clients to utilize a specific feature set, such as Messaging Records Management, or to have certain security fixes. You may also have corporate policy which dictates that a particular version or versions of Outlook are used.

Fortunately, Exchange has the ability to restrict which versions of Outlook can connect, by blocking MAPI client versions, a feature which was introduced in Exchange 2000 Service Pack 1. In Exchange 2007, MAPI client blocking can be implemented on a per-server basis using a registry change, or on a per-mailbox basis using the Exchange Command Shell.

Additionally, Microsoft recommends implementing Outlook client blocking as a best practice, and if you run the Exchange Best Practices Analyzer against a server which does not have client blocking enabled, it will suggest that you configure it.

Determining which client versions are in use

Before implementing client version blocking it's a good idea to know which versions are in use. With this information you can tell which clients need to be upgraded to a newer version before blocking is implemented, or simply which clients will no longer be able to connect after it is implemented. In Exchange 2007 client version information is retrieved using the `Get-LogonStatistics` cmdlet.

`Get-LogonStatistics` accepts a mailbox, a mailbox database, or a server name as input, and returns statistics including user name, logon time, last access time, client name, and client version.

For example, to list the client versions used to access a single mailbox, the command is:

```
Get-LogonStatistics JSmith | ft UserName,ClientVersion,LogonTime
```

To list the client versions for all clients connecting to a specific server:

```
Get-LogonStatistics -Server SERVER01 | ft UserName,ClientVersion,LogonTime
```

To list the client versions for all clients on all mailbox servers, and export the results to a CSV file:

```
Get-MailboxServer | Get-LogonStatistics | `
Select UserName,ClientName,ClientVersion,LogonTime | `
Export-Csv -Path ExchangeClientVersions.csv
```

Once you have identified the clients in use in your organisation and taken any remedial action necessary, you can move on to blocking any further access by unwanted clients.

Determining which client versions to block

The client version is determined by the version of Emsmdb32.dll on the client. This is not necessarily the same as the Outlook version, or the version of any other DLL or executable files. This table shows the version of Emsmdb32.dll for major releases or updates of Outlook since the release of Office XP.

Release	Emsmdb32.dll version
Office XP RTM	10.0.2627.1
Office XP SP1	10.0.3416.0
Office XP SP2	10.0.4115.0
Office XP SP3	10.0.6515.0
Office 2003 RTM	11.0.5604.0
Office 2003 SP1	11.0.6352.0
Office 2003 SP2	11.0.6555.0
Office 2003 SP3	11.0.8161.0
Office 2007 RTM	12.0.4518.1014
Office 2007 SP1	12.0.6211.1000
Office 2007 SP2	12.0.6423.1000

Table 1: Emsmdb32.dll version by Office release.

Here are some important points to note.

- The MAPI client version numbers listed in Table 1, and those in the results of the `Get-LogonStatistics` cmdlet, are in the format x.0.y.z. When specifying MAPI versions to be blocked, you must use the format x.y.z. For example, the version number for Outlook 2003 RTM becomes 11.5604.0.

- When setting per-server restrictions it is very important to avoid restricting clients with version numbers 6.y.z, as Exchange Server makes use of MAPI for server-side component connections, and uses MAPI versions within the 6.y.z range (with the version number potentially varying by Exchange component and patch level). This does not apply to per-mailbox restrictions.

- Microsoft recommends that, at a minimum, you block all MAPI clients with version numbers equal to or earlier than 5.3164.0.0.

Single versions are blocked by specifying the version in the format *<version>*, an open-ended range is blocked by using the format -*<version1>* or *<version2>*-, and a specific inclusive range is blocked by using the format *<version3>*-*<version4>*. Multiple sets of client versions can be disabled using a comma or semicolon separated list.

Range type	Example	Effect
<version>	11.5604.0	Block the specified MAPI version.
-<version>	-11.0.0	Block the specified version number, and all previous versions.
<version>-	11.0.0-	Block the specified version number, and all newer versions.
<version>-<version>	11.0.0-11.9.9	Block the specified version numbers, and all clients between the specified versions.

Table 2:   **Example client version blocking syntax.**

Some example blocking settings to use:

Blocking setting	Effect
11.5604.0	Block Outlook 2003 RTM.
-5.9.9;7.0.0-11.9.9	Block all clients older than Outlook 2007.
12.0.0-	Block all versions of Outlook starting with Outlook 2007 and including all future versions.
-5.3164.0	Block Microsoft recommended Outlook versions.
-5.99;7.0.0-	Block all MAPI clients, except for Exchange Server components.

Table 3:   **Example client version blocking settings.**

173

Implementing the blocking settings

As mentioned earlier, restrictions can be implemented per-server or per-mailbox. Per-server restrictions are implemented via a registry change, and per-mailbox restrictions are implemented via the Exchange Management Shell – it is not possible to use the Exchange Management Console.

If both server and mailbox restrictions are used, the most restrictive combination of both settings applies; additionally, a server restriction cannot be overridden by a mailbox setting.

For example:

Server restriction	Mailbox restriction	Net effect
-5.3164.0	-11.9.9	Mailbox can only be accessed using Outlook 2007
-5.9.9;7.0.0-	11.0.0-11.9.9	Mailbox cannot be accessed by any MAPI client (which is not executing on the Exchange server)

Table 4: Cumulative effect of restrictions.

To implement a per-server restriction

Note

Incorrectly editing the registry can cause serious problems that may require you to reinstall your operating system. Problems resulting from editing the registry incorrectly may not be able to be resolved. Before editing the registry, back up any valuable data.

You need to be a local administrator on the Exchange server in order to edit the registry.

- Start the registry editor on your Exchange 2007 Mailbox server.

- Locate the HKEY_LOCAL_MACHINE\SYSTEM\CurrentControlSet\Services\MSExchangeIS\ ParametersSystem registry key.

- Right-click **ParametersSystem**, select **New**, and then select **String value**.

- Name the new string value *Disable MAPI Clients*.

- Right-click **Disable MAPI Clients**, and then click **Modify**.

- Enter the restriction setting, for example -5.9.9;7.0.0-11.9.9.

- Close the registry editor.

The change will be effective within 15 minutes or, to make it effective immediately, you can restart the Microsoft Exchange Information Store service. Once the change takes effect, any existing client connections which do not meet the version requirements will be terminated.

To implement a per-mailbox restriction

The `Set-CASMailbox` cmdlet is used to implement per-mailbox restrictions. To use the `Set-CASMailbox` cmdlet you must be delegated the Exchange Recipient Administrator role.

To prevent a mailbox from using Outlook clients prior to Outlook 2007 the command is:

```
Set-CASMailbox JSmith -MAPIBlockOutlookVersions "-11.9.9"
```

To remove a restriction for a mailbox:

```
Set-CASMailbox JSmith -MAPIBlockOutlookVersions $null
```

To prevent all mailboxes in a particular database from using clients other than Outlook 2007 RTM:

```
Get-Mailbox -Database "SERVER01\SG1\Database 1" | `
Set-CASMailbox -MAPIBlockOutlookVersions "-12.4518.1013;12.4518.1015-"
```

When an Outlook 2003 or Outlook 2007 user tries to connect with a restricted client version they will receive the message: **Your Exchange Server administrator has blocked the version of Outlook that you are using. Contact your administrator for assistance**.

Users of older clients will receive the message: **Cannot start Microsoft Outlook. The attempt to log on to the Microsoft Exchange Server computer has failed**.

More information on these cmdlets can be found in TechNet:

Get-LogonStatistics – HTTP://TECHNET.MICROSOFT.COM/EN-US/LIBRARY/BB124415.ASPX.

Set-CASMailbox – HTTP://TECHNET.MICROSOFT.COM/EN-US/LIBRARY/BB124415.ASPX.

Exchange Backups on Windows Server 2008

24 August 2009

by Jaap Wesselius

NTBackup lives no more, replaced by VSS backups. Unfortunately, Windows Server Backup didn't work with Exchange Server 2007 until now. Exchange Server 2007 Service Pack 2 contains a backup plug-in that makes it possible. Although pretty limited compared to full backup applications like Microsoft Data Protection Manager or Symantec Backup Exec, it does what you want it to do: it creates backups. Jaap explains.

In one of my earlier articles, *Online Exchange Backups,* (HTTP://WWW.SIMPLE-TALK.COM/EXCHANGE/ EXCHANGE-ARTICLES/ONLINE-EXCHANGE-BACKUPS/) I discussed the online backup options in Exchange Server 2007, streaming backups using the Backup API (Application Programming Interface) and snapshot backups using VSS. This article was written for Exchange Server 2007 running on Windows Server 2003.

Windows Server 2008 is a different story, since it has a new feature called Windows Server Backup, and NTBackup is discontinued. Windows Server Backup creates Volume Shadow Service (VSS) backups, but it is not Exchange aware. So, for backing up your Exchange Server 2007 mailbox databases running on Windows Server 2008, you are dependent on third-party products. No out-of-the-box solution like NTBackup in Windows Server 2003 is available in Windows Server 2008.

Now that Exchange Server 2007 Service Pack 2 (WWW.MICROSOFT.COM/DOWNLOADS/DETAILS.ASPX?DISPLA YLANG=EN&FAMILYID=4C4BD2A3-5E50-42B0-8BBB-2CC9AFE3216A) is available, this has changed. Amongst other new features and functionality, Microsoft has added a new backup plug-in that makes it possible to create snapshot backups using VSS from Windows Server Backup. I'll show you how.

Windows Server Backup

Windows Server Backup is a feature in Windows Server 2008. You can install Windows Server Backup using the Server Manager, select **Features** and click **Add Features**. Scroll down, select **Windows Server Backup Features** and click **Install**. If needed, you can expand **Windows Server Backup Features** and select the **Command-line Tools** as well. When the setup has finished, the Windows Server Backup utility shows up in the Administrative Tools menu.

When you open Windows Server Backup nothing special appears. There's no indication that you can back up Exchange Server 2007.

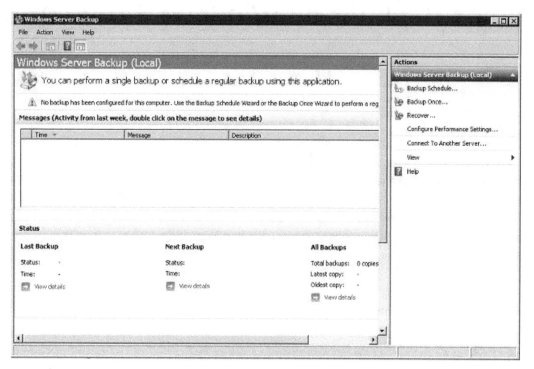

Figure 1: **Windows Server Backup. There's no indication about the Exchange awareness.**

Windows Server Backup can back up only on Volume level. When you have a default installation you can back up the entire system disk, including the C:\Program Files\Microsoft\Exchange directory. Since Windows Server Backup is aware of Exchange Server 2007 Service Pack 2, the Exchange databases will be backed up, the database will be checked for consistency and the log files will be purged.

There might be scenarios where the database and the log files are placed on a separate disk. In this example, I've located the database in G:\MDB1 and the accompanying log files in G:\LOGS1. The Public Folder database is located in G:\MDB2 and the accompanying log files in G:\LOGS2. This way you can backup only the database and the log files.

In the Windows Server Backup, in the **Actions** pane click **Backup Once...** . When the Backup Once Wizard opens, click **Next** to continue. You can select a **Full Server** backup or a **Custom** backup. Select the Custom backup if you only want to back up the Exchange database and the log files, and click **Next** to continue.

In the **Select Items** window you can select the G:\ disk where the database and the log files are located. Remove the check at **Enable System Recovery** to unselect the System disk and click **Next** to continue.

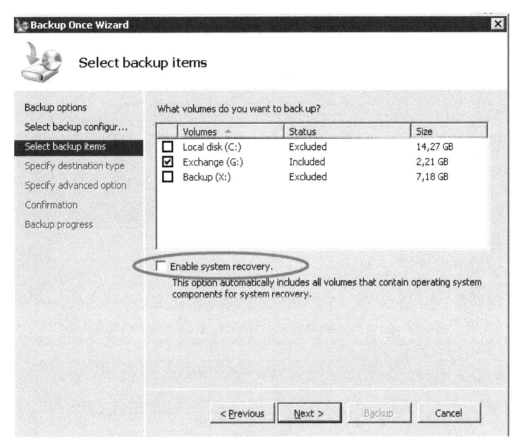

Figure 2: Remove the checkmark at "Enable System Recovery" to deselect the C:\ Drive.

The backup itself can be placed on any disk, except the disk that's being backed up and the System Disk. If you want to back up to disk you have to create an additional disk on the server. It's also possible to back up to a Remote Share. In this example, I'll write the backup to another disk. Click **Next** to continue.

Select the Backup destination (X: in this example) and click **Next** to continue.

It is possible to create a VSS Copy Backup or a VSS Full Backup. A VSS Copy Backup is a full backup of the database, but the header information will not be updated with backup information and the log files will not be deleted. You can select this option when you want to create a backup using Windows Server Backup, but you don't want to interfere with other backup solutions running on this particular server. If you select VSS Full Backup, a full backup will be created, the database header information will be updated with the backup information, and the log files will be purged (if the consistency check succeeds). In both options the database will be checked for consistency.

Select **VSS Full Backup** to create a full backup of the Exchange database and click **Next** to continue.

Check the confirmation page and click **Backup** to start the actual backup process.

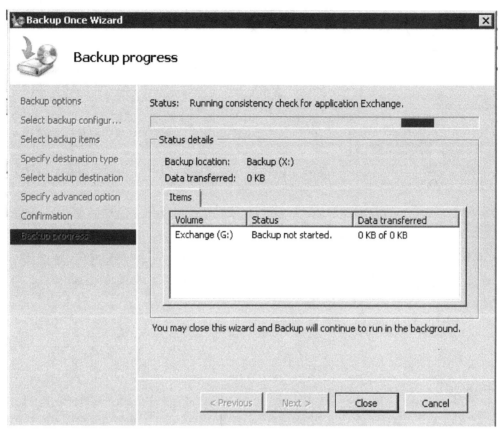

Figure 3: **The status bar is the only indication you're running an Exchange Server backup.**

The only way to see if the actual Exchange backup is performed is by looking at the console. You can see, at the Status bar: **Running consistency check for application Exchange**. You can close the Backup Once Wizard and the backup will continue to run.

If you check the Application log in the Event Viewer, you'll see entries about the backup from the Shadow Copy service and the Exchange VSS writer about the backup. Please check my other article (WWW. SIMPLE-TALK.COM/EXCHANGE/EXCHANGE-ARTICLES/ONLINE-EXCHANGE-BACKUPS/) for detailed information regarding the VSS backup process.

When you check the header information of the Exchange database, you'll find information about the backup as well:

```
G:\MDB1>eseutil /mh "mailbox database.edb"

Extensible Storage Engine Utilities for Microsoft(R) Exchange Server
Version 08.02
Copyright (C) Microsoft Corporation. All Rights Reserved.

Initiating FILE DUMP mode...
     Database: mailbox database.edb

   File Type: Database
```

```
   DB Signature: Create time:07/02/2009 12:38:52 Rand:172660 Computer:
      cbDbPage: 8192
        dbtime: 1172010 (0x11e22a)
         State: Clean Shutdown
  Log Required: 0-0 (0x0-0x0)
 Log Committed: 0-0 (0x0-0x0)
 Log Signature: Create time:07/06/2009 08:19:40 Rand:239950899 Computer:
    OS Version: (6.0.6001 SP 1)


 Previous Full Backup:
     Log Gen: 208-227 (0xd0-0xe3) - OSSnapshot
       Mark: (0xE4,8,16)
       Mark: 07/20/2009 21:00:08


 Previous Incremental Backup:
     Log Gen: 0-0 (0x0-0x0)
       Mark: (0x0,0,0)
       Mark: 00/00/1900 00:00:00


 Operation completed successfully in 0.110 seconds.


 G:\MDB1>
```

[**Note. This output has been edited for readability.**]

Windows Server Backup can only back up active Exchange Servers. This means that it is not aware of a Continuous Cluster Replication (CCR) environment and, therefore, you cannot back up the passive node of CCR Cluster. Microsoft Data Protection Manager (DPM) 2007, or other third-party products like Backup Exec, can back up the passive node and therefore reduce the load of the active node of the cluster.

Backup schedules

It becomes more interesting to use Windows Server Backup when you can schedule backups and create a backup once a day, for example, without any hassle.

Open the Windows Server Backup application, and in the Actions pane select **Backup schedule...** . Like the Backup Once Wizard you can select a Full Server backup or a Custom Backup. If you select Custom Backup it is possible to select the disk containing the Exchange Server database and log files. When creating a backup schedule the system volume will be included by default. It is not possible to deselect it.

The next step is to specify the backup time. You can create a backup once a day or multiple times a day.

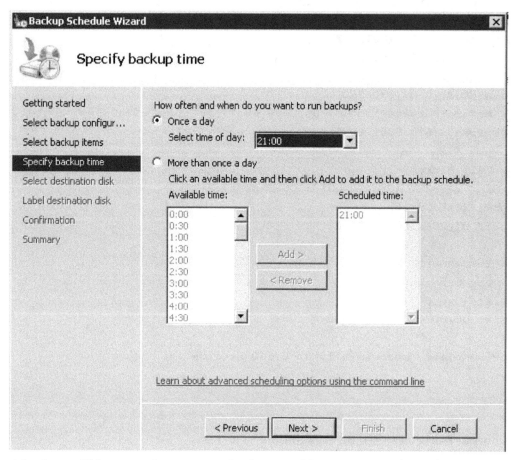

Figure 4: **A backup will be created at 9 p.m. It is also possible to create multiple backups.**

When selecting the destination disk, it will be formatted by Windows Server Backup and all information on the disk will be lost. The drive doesn't get a drive letter during format, but you can still see it through Disk Management in the Server Manager.

Note

Although you can select "Always create an incremental backup" in the Windows Server Backup application it is not possible to do this for Exchange. You can only create full backups, in the Backup Once and in the Backup Schedule option.

Restore the Exchange backup

When you want to restore the previous backup, open the Windows Server Backup and click on **Recover...** in the Actions Pane. You can select what data you want to recover. In this example, select **This Server 2007MBX01**. Click **Next** to continue.

If you have setup a backup schedule you can select a date and time of the backup you want to restore.

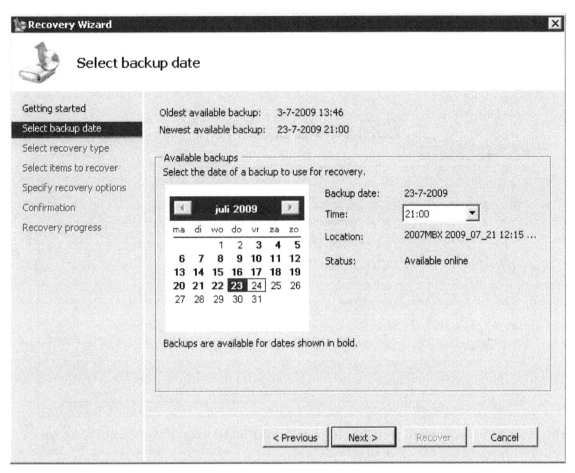

Figure 5:   Select the backup you want to restore.

Click **Next** to continue.

In the **Select recovery type** window you can select the kind of information that needs to be restored. Since this is an Exchange database restore, select **Applications** and click **Next** to continue.

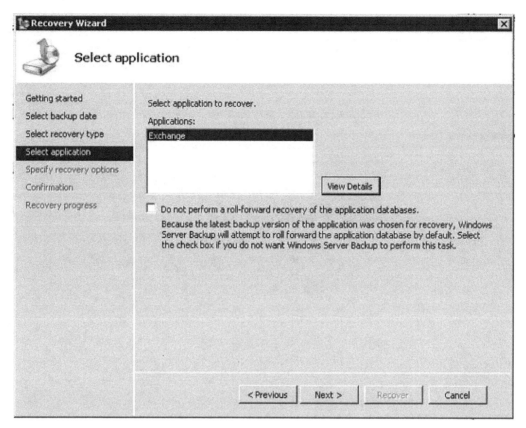

Figure 6: **Select the application you want to restore information for. If you do not want to roll forward log files, tick the check box.**

Select **Recover to original location** to restore the database to its original location. Do not forget to tick the **This database can be overwritten by a restore** check box in the database properties in Exchange Management Console. If you fail to do so, the restore of the database will fail.

In the Confirmation window check your selections and click **Recover** to start the restore process.

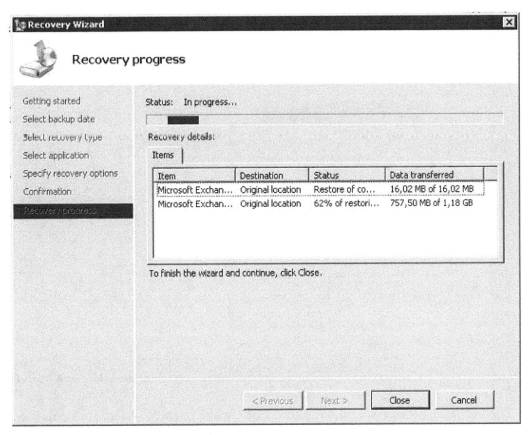

Figure 7: You can check the progress of the restore process.

Information stored in log files newer than the database (and thus not restored with the database) will be automatically rolled forward. When possible the recovery process will automatically replay, or roll forward all available log files from the restore point up to the latest possible point in time.

There's an easy way to check this. Create a full backup of your mailbox database. When the backup is successfully finished send a couple of messages to yourself. Make them easy to identify. Dismount the database and restore the database from the backup. The messages you just sent are not in this backup, but in the log files written after the creation of the backup. These log files will be automatically replayed. When you log on to the mailbox after the restore of the database you'll find the messages again, even if they weren't in the actual backup.

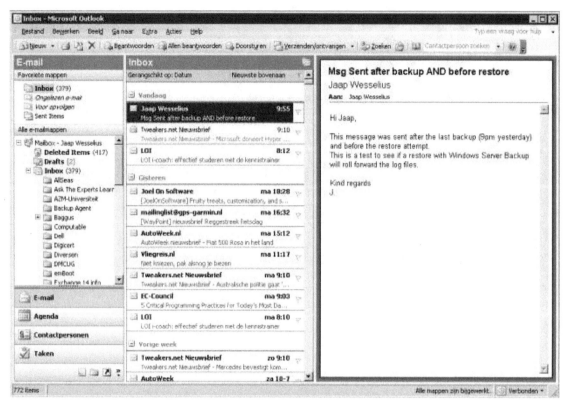

Figure 8:   The last three messages were not part of the backup but were rolled forward from
the log files.

Conclusion

Exchange Server 2007 Service Pack 2 will contain a backup plug-in that makes it possible to use Windows Server Backup in Windows Server 2008 to create Exchange Server backups. Although pretty limited compared to full backup applications like Microsoft Data Protection Manager or Symantec Backup Exec, it does what you want it to do: create backups. You can create backups manually or create a schedule for the backup application to run. It is a backup to disk solution; backup to tape is not available.

It can restore backups and it can roll forward log files after a restore, so the basic functionality is available. Nothing more, nothing less.

> **Note**
>
> *Fellow MVP Michael B. Smith created a couple of scripts that are capable of creating backups of Exchange Server 2007 running on Windows Server 2008, without the need of Windows Server Backup. You can find his solution at* HTTP://THEESSENTIALEXCHANGE.COM/BLOGS/MICHAEL/. ARCHIVE/2009/04/11/BACKING-UP-EXCHANGE-2007-ON-WINDOWS-2008.ASPX.

Monitoring and Scheduling Exchange 2007 Database Online Maintenance

25 August 2009

by Ben Lye

To keep the Exchange database healthy, it is important to make sure that online maintenance and online defragmentation are running properly, or are at least conforming to Microsoft's recommendations. Ben shows how easy it is to automate the maintenance and monitor the defragmentation task.

Exchange database maintenance is an important part of keeping Exchange healthy. Exchange Server automates online maintenance tasks and runs them based on the schedule specified by the Exchange administrator.

The online maintenance tasks are:

- purge mailbox database and public folder database indexes

- maintain tombstones

- clean up the deleted items dumpster

- remove public folders that have exceeded the expiry time

- remove deleted public folders that have exceeded the tombstone lifetime

- clean up conflicting public folder messages

- update server versions

- check Schedule+ Free Busy and Offline Address Book folders

- clean up deleted mailboxes

- clean up reliable event tables.

For detailed information on these tasks, refer to Microsoft TechNet *Maintaining Mailbox Databases and Public Folder Databases* at HTTP://TECHNET.MICROSOFT.COM/EN-US/LIBRARY/BB123760.ASPX.

If one of these maintenance tasks is performed on a database then online defragmentation will be performed on that database.

If the online maintenance tasks are unable to complete in a single schedule window, the tasks will be suspended and then resumed in the next window. In this way, maintenance is guaranteed to eventually complete. However, it is important to make sure that the scheduled maintenance windows are properly configured so that the maintenance tasks are able to complete regularly.

When scheduling online maintenance there are several guidelines to consider:

- online maintenance should be scheduled for times when there is little activity on the database

- online maintenance must not run at the same time as a backup (online defragmentation cannot start while a backup is in progress)

- online defragmentation should be able to complete at least once every two weeks

- online maintenance schedules for databases in the same storage group should not overlap (Microsoft recommends a 15-minute gap between maintenance schedules).

The default online maintenance schedule is nightly from 1 a.m. to 5 a.m. To aid in customizing the online maintenance schedule, the Windows event log can be used to see how often online defragmentation is completing and Performance Monitor counters can be used to check the efficiency of online defragmentation. This data can be used to adjust the online maintenance schedule to give more or less time.

Event log entries for online defragmentation

There are five events relating to online defragmentation starting and stopping. The events are logged in the Application log with a source of "ESE" and a category of "Online Defragmentation."

Event ID	Description
700	Online defragmentation is beginning a full pass
701	Online defragmentation has completed a full pass
702	Online defragmentation is resuming defragmentation
703	Online defragmentation has completed a resumed pass
704	Online defragmentation has been interrupted

Events 701 and 703 indicate a complete pass. In the case of Event 703, completion of a resumed pass, the event text will include information about how long defragmentation took to complete, and how many times it was invoked.

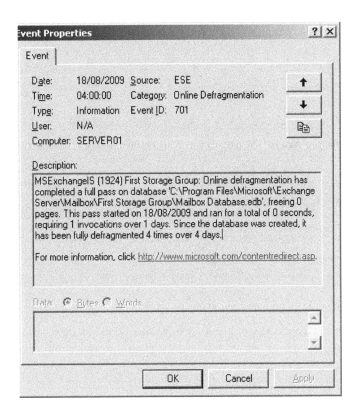

To make it easier to check how often online maintenance completes the Exchange Management Console and a PowerShell script which you can find at WWW.SIMPLE-TALK.COM/IWRITEFOR/ARTICLEFILES/787-CHECK-ONLINEDEFRAG.PS1.TXT can be used to parse the Application log.

This script will search the event log for online defragmentation messages for each database on the server on which it's run (or the clustered mailbox server if running on a cluster node) and return the amount of time taken to complete online defragmentation of each database.

```
# Script to check the status of Exchange database online defragmentation tasks
# Written by Ben Lye
#
# The script will parse the event log of the local machine looking for online
# defrag related messages. Messages are parsed to determine when online defrag
# last finished for each database and how long it took to complete.
#
# The script needs to be run on an Exchange 2007 mailbox server or mailbox
# cluster node If the script is run on a cluster node it should be the active
# node, or event log replication needs to be enabled (this is the default).


# The $records variable defines the number of events to retrieve from the log
# It can be increased or decreased according to the needs of a particular
server.
# The script will run faster if fewer records are retrieved, but data may not be
```

```
# found for all databases.
$records = 10000


# Get the hostname
$hostname = Get-Content env:computername


# Check if the local machine is an Exchange mailbox server
$mbserver = Get-MailboxServer -Identity $hostname -ErrorAction SilentlyContinue


# Check if the local machine is a member of a mailbox cluster
$cms = Get-ClusteredMailboxServerStatus -ErrorAction SilentlyContinue


# Exit the script if the local machine is not a mailbox server or a CMS node
if (-not $mbserver -and -not $cms) {
    Write-Host "The machine $hostname is not a server an Exchange mailbox
server." `
        -ForegroundColor Red
    Write-Host "This script must be run on a mailbox server or mailbox cluster
node." `
        -ForegroundColor Red
    break
}


# Determine the server name to enumerate the databases
if ($cms) {
    # This server is a cluster node, the database server name is the name of the
CMS
    $dbserver = $cms.ClusteredMailboxServerName
} else {
    # This server is a mailbox server - the database server name is the local
hostname
    $dbserver = $hostname
}


# Get the mailbox databases from the server
$mbdatabases = Get-MailboxDatabase -Server $dbserver `
    | Sort-Object -Property Name


# Get the public folder databases from the server
$pfdatabases = Get-PublicFolderDatabase -Server $dbserver `
    | Sort-Object -Property Name


# Create an array for the databases
$databases = @()


# Check if mailbox databases were found on the server
If ($mbdatabases) {
```

```
   # Loop through the databases
   ForEach ($mdb in $mbdatabases) {
      # Create an object to store information about the database
      $db = "" | Select-Object Name,Identity,EdbFilePath,DefragStart,DefragEnd,

         DefragDuration,DefragInvocations,DefragDays


      # Populate the object
      $db.Name = $mdb.Name.ToString()
      $db.Identity = $mdb.Identity.ToString()
      $db.EdbFilePath = $mdb.EdbFilePath.ToString()


      # Add this database to the array
      $databases = $databases + $db
   }
}


# Check if public folder databases were found on the server
If ($pfdatabases) {
   # Loop through the databases
   ForEach ($pfdb in $pfdatabases) {
      # Create an object to store information about the database
      $db = "" | Select-Object Name,Identity,EdbFilePath,DefragStart,DefragEnd,

         DefragDuration,DefragInvocations,DefragDays


      # Populate the object
      $db.Name = $pfdb.Name.ToString()
      $db.Identity = $pfdb.Identity.ToString()
      $db.EdbFilePath = $pfdb.EdbFilePath.ToString()


      # Add this database to the array
      $databases = $databases + $db
   }
}


# Retrieve the events from the local Application log, filter them for ESE
messages
$logs = Get-EventLog -LogName Application -Newest $records | `
   Where {$_.Source -eq "ESE" -and $_.Category -eq "Online Defragmentation"}


# Create an array for the output
$output = @()


# Loop through each of the databases and search the event logs for relevant
messages
ForEach ($db in $databases) {
```

191

```
    # Create the search string to look for in the Message property of each log
entry
    $s = "*" + $db.EdbFilePath + "*"


    # Search for an event 701 or 703, meaning that online defragmentation
finished
    $end = $logs | where {
        $_.Message -like "$s" -and ($_.InstanceID -eq 701 -or $_.InstanceID -eq
703)
    } | select-object -First 1


    # Search for the first event 700 which preceeds the finished event
    $start = $logs | where {
        $_.Message -like "$s" -and $_.InstanceID -eq 700 -and $_.Index -le $end.
Index
    } | select-object -First 1


    # Make sure we found both a start and an end message
    if ($start -and $end) {

        # Get the start and end times
        $db.DefragStart = Get-Date($start.TimeGenerated)
        $db.DefragEnd = Get-Date($end.TimeGenerated)

        # Parse the end event message for the number of seconds defragmentation
ran for
        $end.Message -match "total of .* seconds" >$null
        $db.DefragDuration = $Matches[0].Split(" ")[2]

        # Parse the end event message for the number of invocations and days
        $end.Message -match "requiring .* invocations over .* days" >$null
        $db.DefragInvocations = $Matches[0].Split(" ")[1]
        $db.DefragDays = $Matches[0].Split(" ")[4]

    } else {

        # Output a message if start and end events weren't found
        Write-Host "Unable to find start and end events for database," $db.
Identity `
            -ForegroundColor Yellow
        Write-Host "You probably need to increase the value of `$records." `
            -ForegroundColor Yellow
        Write-Host

    }
    # Add the data for this database to the output
```

192

```
    $output = $output + $db
}


# Print the output
$output
```

Microsoft recommends that, in large organisations with large databases (150–200 GB) and many storage groups (up to 20) on a single server, online defragmentation should complete at least once every two weeks for each database. In smaller organizations with smaller databases, it should complete more often.

In either case, if online defragmentation is completing within two days, then it is probably safe to shorten the online maintenance window for the database. If defragmentation is not completing within 14 days, the online maintenance window should be lengthened.

Performance monitor counters for online defragmentation

Exchange 2007 includes the following performance counters for monitoring online defragmentation:

- MSExchange Database ==> Instances\Online Defrag Average Log Bytes.

- MSExchange Database ==> Instances \Online Defrag Log Records/sec.

- MSExchange Database ==> Instances \Online Defrag Pages Dirtied/sec.

- MSExchange Database ==> Instances \Online Defrag Pages Preread/sec.

- MSExchange Database ==> Instances \Online Defrag Pages Read/sec.

- MSExchange Database ==> Instances \Online Defrag Pages Re-Dirtied/sec.

- MSExchange Database ==> Instances \Online Defrag Pages Referenced/sec.

Exchange 2007 Service Pack 1 adds these two additional counters:

- MSExchange Database ==> Instances \Online Defrag Pages Freed/Sec.

- MSExchange Database ==> Instances \Online Defrag Data Moves/Sec.

The two interesting counters are "Online Defrag Pages Read/sec" and "Online Defrag Pages Freed/Sec." These two counters can be monitored during an online maintenance window and the average values compared to determine if the window should be increased or decreased.

If the ratio of Pages Read:Pages Freed is greater than 100:1 then the online maintenance window can be decreased; if the ratio is less than 50:1 then the maintenance window should be increased; and if the ratio is between 100:1 and 50:1 there is no need to change the window.

To use these counters, extended ESE performance counters must be enabled, which is done by adding a new registry value.

> *Note*
>
> *Incorrectly editing the registry can cause serious problems that may require you to reinstall your operating system. Problems resulting from editing the registry incorrectly may not be able to be resolved. Before editing the registry, back up any valuable data.*

- Start the registry editor on your Exchange 2007 Mailbox server.

- Locate the HKEY_LOCAL_MACHINE\SYSTEM\CurrentControlSet\Services\ESE\Performance registry key.

- Right-click **Performance**, select New, and then select **DWORD value**.

- Name the new DWORD value *Show Advanced Counters*.

- Double-click **Show Advanced Counters**.

- In the **Value data** field, enter 1.

- Close the registry editor.

Once the extended ESE performance counters are enabled, Performance Monitor can be used to log the counter data to a file.

- Start Performance Monitor on the Exchange 2007 mailbox server (or the active cluster node in a CCR cluster) by clicking **Start ▸ Programs ▸ Administrative Tools ▸ Performanc**e.

- Expand **Performance Logs and Alerts** and select **Counter Logs**.

- Right-click **Counter Logs** and select **New log settings**.

- Enter a name for the new counter, such as *EDB Defrag*, and click **OK**.

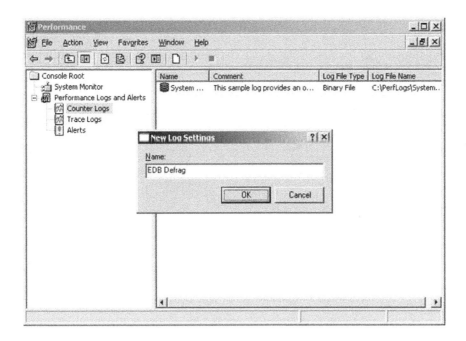

- Click the **Add Counters** button, and then select **MS Exchange Database ==> Instances** from the **Performance object** drop-down.

- Select the **Online Defrag Pages Freed/sec** and the **Online Defrag Pages Read/sec** counters from the list, select the **Information Store** storage groups, and click the **Add** button.

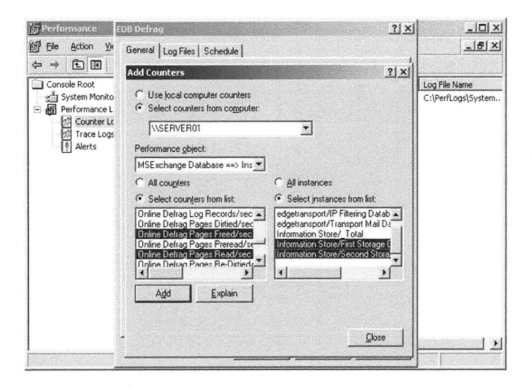

- Click **Close**.

- On the **Log Files** tab change the Log file type to Text File (Comma delimited) and uncheck **End file names with**.

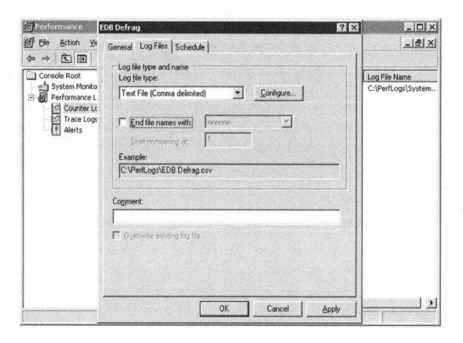

- On the **Schedule** tab, set the start time to a few minutes before the start of the next run of online maintenance, and the end time to a few minutes after the end.

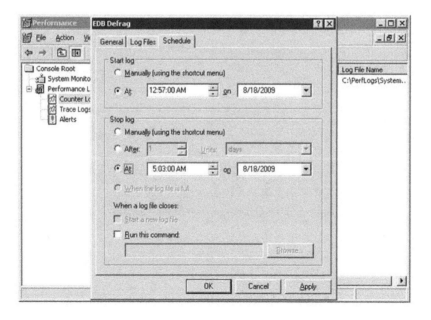

- Click **OK** and then close Performance Monitor.

The next time online maintenance runs, the performance counter data will be gathered. This data can then be analyzed by looking at the average ratio of pages read to pages freed.

The resulting CSV file will look similar to this:

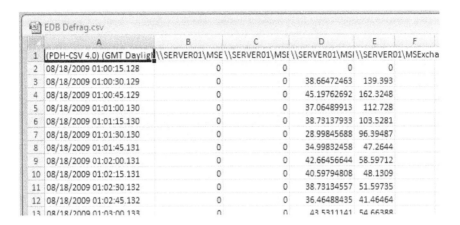

To determine the Pages Read:Pages Freed ratio, the data is averaged over the duration of the maintenance window, and the average pages read/sec is divided by the average pages freed/sec. This gives the number of pages freed/sec for every one page read/sec.

For example, if the average pages read/sec is 545, and the average pages freed/sec is 6, the ratio is 90:1 and the online defragmentation window is appropriately set.

Setting the online maintenance window

The online maintenance window is configured per database and can be set using either the Exchange Management Console or the Exchange Management Shell.

To configure the maintenance window using the console:

- launch the Exchange Management Console

- expand **Server Configuration** and select the **Mailbox** node

- select the server where the database is located, then select the database

- right-click the database and select **Properties**

- select a predefined schedule from the **Maintenance Schedule** list or, to create a custom schedule, select **Use Custom Schedule**, and then click **Customize**.

- Click OK to close the **Properties** window.

Alternatively, use the `Set-MailboxDatabase` PowerShell cmdlet to set the maintenance window.

This command will configure the maintenance window of the database **Mailbox Database** on server **SERVER01** to run every day from 3 a.m. to 4 a.m. local time using the shell:

```
Set-MailboxDatabase -Identity "SERVER01\Mailbox Database" `
-MaintenanceSchedule Sun.03:00-Sun.04:00, Mon.03:00-Mon.04:00, `
Tue.03:00-Tue.04:00, Wed.03:00-Wed.04:00, Thu.03:00-Thu.04:00, `
Fri.03:00-Fri.04:00, Sat.03:00-Sat.04:00
```

With a relatively small amount of monitoring and analysis it is reasonably easy to ensure that online maintenance is running effectively and efficiently, helping to ensure that your Exchange databases stay in good shape.

The techniques I've shown here should help you to check that online maintenance and online defragmentation are running optimally, or are at least conforming to Microsoft's recommendations.

Exchange 2010 High Availability

18 September 2009

by Neil Hobson

In April 2009, Microsoft released a public beta of Exchange 2010, the latest and greatest version of a part of its unified communications family of products. In August 2009, a feature complete Release Candidate version was released for public download. In this article, Neil Hobson takes a look at some of the high availability features of Exchange 2010.

For many years, Exchange only offered a high availability solution based on the shared storage model, whereby use of Microsoft clustering technologies protected against server-based failure, but did nothing to protect against storage failures. Although there were improvements to this form of high availability in Exchange 2007, where it was known as a Single Copy Cluster (SCC), the real changes to high availability in Exchange 2007 came with the introduction of a technology known as continuous replication. With this technology, transaction logs are shipped from one copy of a database to another, which allows an organization to deploy an Exchange high availability solution that also deals with storage failure. This storage failure protection was available on a single server with the use of Local Continuous Replication (LCR) and was also available across servers with the use of Cluster Continuous Replication (CCR). Therefore, with LCR, CCR and SCC, Exchange 2007 administrators had three different high availability methods open to them. It was also possible to cater for site failure with an extension to the continuous replication technology that was known as Standby Continuous Replication.

I won't go into detail on these Exchange 2007 solutions here, as I've covered them in a article called *Exchange 2007 High Availability*, available on the Simple-Talk website at HTTP://WWW.SIMPLE-TALK.COM/ EXCHANGE/EXCHANGE-ARTICLES/HIGH-AVAILABILITY-IN-EXCHANGE-2007/. However, the bottom line is that many organizations have deployed technologies such as CCR in order to provide high availability, and technologies such as SCR to provide site resilience.

From my experiences, more organizations have deployed CCR in preference to SCC, and it comes as no surprise to learn that SCC has been dropped entirely from Exchange 2010. As you will shortly see, the continuous replication technology lives on in Exchange 2010, but there are many changes in the overall high availability model.

With Exchange 2007 Service Pack 1, a full high availability solution was generally deployed using a total of four servers. Two servers were installed as a single CCR environment, giving high availability for the users' mailboxes. The other two servers were deployed as combined Hub Transport and Client Access Servers, and were configured as a load-balanced pair. The reason for this was simply that, if the mailbox server role was clustered, it was not possible to implement the additional Exchange 2007 server roles, such as the Hub Transport and Client Access Server role, on the server running the mailbox role. For the larger enterprises, this wasn't an unreasonable approach but, for the smaller organizations, a total of four servers sometimes seemed to be overkill for an internal messaging system. To address this specific issue, Microsoft has designed Exchange 2010 such that all server roles can be fully redundant with as few as two servers, providing you have deployed an external load balancer for incoming Client Access Server connections. In other words, it's now possible to combine the mailbox server role with other roles such as the Hub Transport and Client Access Server roles. Of course, larger organizations will still be likely to implement dedicated servers running the various server roles, but this is something that will definitely help the smaller organizations to reduce costs. Remember, though, the external load balancer requirement for incoming Client Access Server connections.

With this in mind, let's get going and look at some of the high availability features of Exchange 2010. Don't forget that this is a high-level look at the new features; in later articles on Simple-Talk, we'll be diving much more deeply into these features and how they work. Right now, the idea with this article is to get you to understand the concepts behind these new features, and to allow you to do some initial planning on how you might use them in your organization.

Database availability groups

Perhaps one of the most important new terms to understand in Exchange 2010 is the *Database Availability Group (DAG)*. The DAG is essentially a collection of as few as 1 (although 2 is the minimum to provide a high availability solution) and up to 16 mailbox servers that allow you to achieve high availability in Exchange 2010.

DAGs use the continuous replication technology that was first introduced in Exchange 2007 and are effectively a combination of Cluster Continuous Replication (CCR) and Standby Continuous Replication (SCR). DAGs make use of some of the components of Windows Failover Clustering to achieve high availability but, to reduce overall complexity, these cluster elements are installed automatically when a mailbox server is added to a DAG and managed completely by Exchange. For planning reasons, it's important to understand that the DAG forms the boundary for replication in Exchange 2010. This is a key difference over SCR in Exchange 2007, where it was possible to replicate outside of a CCR environment to a standalone server in a remote data center. However, you should also be aware that DAGs can be split across Active Directory sites if required, meaning that DAGs can therefore offer high availability within a single data center as well as between different data centers.

An important component to a DAG is the file share witness, a term that you will be familiar with if you have implemented a CCR environment in Exchange 2007. As its name suggests, the file share witness is a file share on a server outside of the DAG. This third server acts as the witness to ensure that quorum is maintained within the cluster. There are some changes to the file share witness operation as we shall discuss later in this section. When creating a DAG, the file share witness share and directory can be specified at the time; if they are not, default witness directory and share names are used. One great improvement over Exchange 2007 is that you do not necessarily need to create the directory and the share in advance, as the system will automatically do this for you if necessary.

As with Exchange 2007, the recommendation from Microsoft is to use a Hub Transport Server to host the file share witness so that this component will be under the control of the Exchange administrators. However, you are free to host the file share witness on an alternative server as long as that server is in the same Active Directory forest as the DAG, is not on any server actually in the DAG, and also as long as that server is running either the Windows 2003 or Windows 2008 operating system.

A DAG can be created via the New-DatabaseAvailabilityGroup cmdlet or via the New Database Availability Group wizard in the Exchange Management Console. The DAG must be created before any mailbox servers are added to it, meaning that, effectively, an empty container is created which is represented as an object in Active Directory. For example, Figure 1 shows a newly created DAG, called DAG1, in Active Directory as viewed using ADSI Edit.

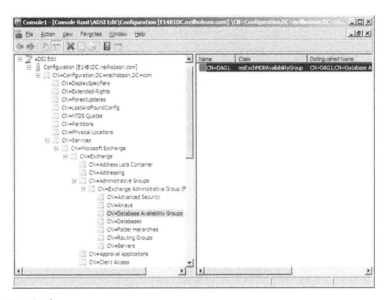

Figure 1:   ADSI Edit DAG view.

You can see that a DAG has an object class of **msExchMDBAvailabilityGroup** and that the actual Database Availability Group container location is found under the Exchange 2010 administrative group container. Bringing up the properties of the DAG object in ADSI Edit reveals the important configuration items such as the file share witness share and directory names as you can see in Figure 2.

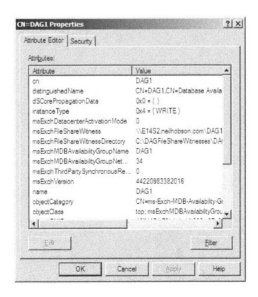

Figure 2:   DAG properties.

Once a DAG has been created, mailbox servers can be added to it as required. This is another simple process that can be achieved by right-clicking the DAG object in the Exchange Management Console and choosing the **Manage Database Availability Group Membership** option from the context menu. The corresponding Exchange Management Shell cmdlet is the Add-DatabaseAvailabilityGroupServer cmdlet. For example, to add the mailbox server called E14B1S1 to a DAG called DAG1, you'd run the following cmdlet:

```
Add-DatabaseAvailabilityGroupServer -Identity DAG1 `
   -MailboxServer E14B1S1
```

Since DAGs make use of several Windows Failover Clustering components, it comes as no surprise to see that the Enterprise Edition of Windows Server 2008 is required on mailbox servers that are added to a DAG, so do ensure that you take this into account when planning your Exchange 2010 implementation.

When creating a DAG, there are options around network encryption and compression that can be set. This is possible because Exchange 2010 uses TCP sockets for log shipping, whereas Exchange 2007 used the Server Message Block (SMB) protocol. For example, it's possible to specify that the connections that occur using these TCP sockets are encrypted. Equally, it's also possible to decide that these same connections also use network compression.

Mailbox servers and databases

Inside each DAG, there will normally exist one or more mailbox servers, although it is possible to create an empty DAG as discussed earlier within this article. On each mailbox server in the DAG, there will typically exist multiple mailbox databases. However, one of the key differences between Exchange 2010 mailbox servers and their Exchange 2007 counterparts is that Exchange 2010 mailbox servers can host active and passive copies of different mailbox databases; remember that, in Exchange 2007, an entire server in a CCR environment, for example, was considered to be either active or passive. However, in Exchange 2010, the unit of failover is now the database and not the server, which is a fantastic improvement in terms of failover granularity. Consider the diagram in Figure 3.

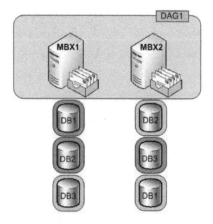

Figure 3:   Database copies.

202

In Figure 3, you can see that a DAG named DAG1 consists of two mailbox servers called MBX1 and MBX2. There are a total of three active mailbox databases, shown in green, across both servers, and each active mailbox database has a passive copy, shown in orange, stored on the alternate server. For example, the active copy of DB1 is hosted on the server called MBX1, whilst the passive copy of DB1 is hosted on the server called MBX2. The passive copies of mailbox databases are kept up to date via log shipping methods in the same way that was used in Exchange 2007, such as between the two cluster nodes within a single Exchange 2007 CCR environment. As you might expect, the active copy of the mailbox database is the one which is used by Exchange. Within a DAG, multiple passive copies of a mailbox database can exist, but there can only be a single active copy. Furthermore, any single mailbox database server in a DAG can only host one copy of any particular mailbox database. Therefore, the maximum possible number of passive copies of a mailbox database is going to be one less than the number of mailbox servers in a DAG, since there will always be one active copy of the mailbox database. For example, if a DAG consisted of the maximum of 16 mailbox servers, then there could be a maximum of 15 passive copies of any single mailbox database. However, every server in a DAG does **not** have to host a copy of every mailbox database that exists in the DAG. You can mix and match between servers however you wish.

As mentioned earlier in this section, the unit of failover in Exchange 2010 is now the database. However, if an entire mailbox server fails, all active databases on that server will need to failover to alternative servers within the DAG.

One other vital piece of mailbox database information that you should consider in your planning for Exchange 2010 is the fact that database names are now unique across the forest in which Exchange 2010 is installed. This could be a problem in organizations that have deployed Exchange 2007 with the default database name of *mailbox database*. Therefore, if you are going to be transitioning from Exchange 2007 to Exchange 2010 in the future, take time now to investigate your current database naming standards.

The Active Manager

At this point, you might be wondering how Exchange 2010 determines which of the mailbox databases is considered to be the active copy. To manage this, each mailbox server in a DAG runs a component called the Active Manager. Specifically, one mailbox server in the DAG will be the Primary Active Manager (PAM) whilst the remaining mailbox servers in the DAG will run a Secondary Active Manager (SAM). We will discuss the relationship between clients, Client Access Servers and the active copy of the mailbox database in the next section, as there are some significant changes in this area too. To view the Active Manager information, you can use the `Get-DatabaseAvailabilityGroup` cmdlet and pipe the results into the format-list cmdlet. In other words, you will need to run the following cmdlet:

```
Get-DatabaseAvailabilityGroup | fl
```

Some of the information returned with the `Get-DatabaseAvailabilityGroup` cmdlet references real-time status information about the DAG and one of the parameters returned is the **ControllingActiveManager** parameter. This parameter will show you which server is currently the PAM. It's the job of the PAM to decide which of the passive copies of the mailbox database should become the active copy in the event of an issue with the current active copy. In an environment consisting of many passive copies of mailbox databases, there will naturally be many choices of suitable mailbox databases available to the PAM. As might be expected, the PAM is able to determine the best copy of the mailbox database available for use and it does this via many different checks in order to minimize data loss. Each SAM also has an important part to play, as they inform other services within the Exchange 2010 infrastructure, such as Hub Transport Servers, which mailbox databases are currently active.

Client access server changes

In Exchange 2007, Outlook clients connect directly to the mailbox servers, whilst other forms of client access, such as OWA, Outlook Anywhere, POP3, IMAP4 and so on, connect via a Client Access Server. The Client Access Server is then responsible for making the connection to the mailbox server role as required. In Exchange 2010, one other fundamental change over previous versions of Exchange is that Outlook clients no longer connect directly to the mailbox servers.

On each Client Access Server, there exists a new service known as the RPC Client Access Service that effectively replaces the RPC endpoint found on mailbox servers and also the DSProxy component found in legacy versions of Exchange. The DSProxy component essentially provides the Outlook clients within the organization with an address book service either via a proxy (pre-Outlook 2000) or referral (Outlook 2000 and later) mechanism. A likely high availability design scenario will therefore see a load-balanced array of Client Access Servers deployed, using technologies such as Windows Network Load Balancing or third-party load balancers, which will connect to two or more mailbox servers in a DAG as shown in Figure 4.

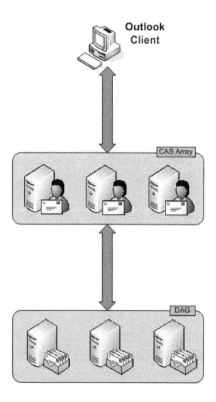

Figure 4: CAS array.

When an Outlook client connects to an Exchange 2010 Client Access Server, the Client Access Server determines where the active copy of the user's mailbox database is located, and makes the connection with the relevant server. If that particular mailbox database becomes unavailable, such as when the administrator wishes to take the database offline or it fails, one of the passive copies will become the new active copy as previously described within this article. It's the Client Access Server that loses the connection to the old active copy of the mailbox database; the actual connection from the client to the Client Access Server is persistent which is obviously good from a user-experience point of view. Then, the Client Access Server will fail over to the new active mailbox database in the DAG as directed by the PAM.

Summary

In this article, we've taken a high-level look at some of the new Exchange 2010 high availability features and how they come together to provide an overall high availability solution. If you're planning on looking at Exchange 2010, it makes sense to start understanding these new features and how they can benefit your organization. Also, there are other interesting features available in Exchange 2010 that further serve to increase the overall high availability and reliability of the messaging environment, such as shadow redundancy in the Hub Transport Server role. In future articles on Simple-Talk, we'll be covering these areas in much more detail.

Implementing Cluster Continuous Replication: Part 1

23 September 2009

by Brien Posey

Imagine that you're researching Cluster Continuous Replication, looking for a simple, direct guide to the basics of getting it set up and running. What do you do if everything you find is either too specialised, or goes into far more detail than you need? If you're Brien Posey, and you can't find that practical, to-the-point article, you roll up your sleeves and write it yourself. To kick off, he tackles the rather tedious task of setting up a majority node set cluster.

A few weeks ago, someone asked me to help them with an Exchange Server deployment. In order to make the deployment a bit more robust, they wanted to cluster their mailbox servers using Cluster Continuous Replication, or CCR. Although I had set up CCR a few times in the past, it had been a while since I had done one, so I decided to look online to re-familiarize myself with the process.

As I looked around on the Internet, I began to realize that there weren't any articles that met my needs. Some of the articles that I found only covered part of the process. Others covered the entire process but contained a lot more material than I wanted. Nobody had published a simple article, written in plain English, which described the procedure of setting up CCR from start to finish. That being the case, I decided to write one myself.

Planning the cluster

As you may already know, CCR is not a feature that you can enable on a whim. That's because CCR makes use of a majority node set cluster. You have to create the cluster at the operating system level. Only then can you install Exchange and create a clustered mailbox server. Since that is the case, I want to start out by showing you how to plan for and set up the cluster. In Part 2 of this article, later in the book, I will show you how to install Exchange onto the cluster that you have created, and how to perform a manual failover on the cluster.

The server hardware and software

The first step in the planning process is to make sure that you have the required hardware. Generally speaking, the requirements for setting up CCR are roughly the same as for creating any other mailbox server. The biggest difference is that you will need two of everything. CCR does not make use of shared storage like a single copy cluster does, so you will need two servers, and each of the servers will have to have sufficient disk resources to accommodate the mailbox database and the transaction logs. As is the case with a non-clustered mailbox server, you should place the database and the transaction logs on separate disks in accordance with Microsoft's best practices for Exchange.

Your two servers don't have to be completely identical to each other, but they should at least have similar capabilities. Remember that, at any time, either one of the servers could be acting as the active cluster node, so it is important to make sure that both servers have hardware that is sufficient to host the mailbox server role in an efficient manner.

Although not an absolute requirement, I recommend installing two NICs in each of the servers. It is also worth noting that Microsoft won't support CCR unless you use two NICs in each node. One of the NICs will be used for communications with the rest of the network, and the other will be used for communications between cluster nodes. The installation steps outlined in this article assume that each server has two NICs.

Finally, you must ensure that you have the necessary software licenses. You will need two copies of Windows Server Enterprise Edition and two copies of Exchange 2007 Enterprise Edition (clustering is not supported in the Standard editions), plus any necessary client access licenses. For the purposes of this article, I will be using Windows Server 2008 and Exchange Server 2007 with SP1.

Other cluster resources

The next step in planning the cluster is to set aside the necessary names and IP addresses. Believe it or not, you are going to have to use five different names and seven different IP addresses.

The first step in setting up the cluster is going to be to install Windows on to both of the cluster nodes. At this point in the process your servers are not cluster nodes, but rather just a couple of Windows servers. Like any other Windows Servers, you are going to have to assign a name to both of the servers. You are also going to have to assign each of the servers an IP address. That accounts for two of the four names and two of the six IP addresses.

As you will recall, we have two NICs in each of the servers. You must assign an IP address to both of the secondary NICs. The IP addresses that you used for the primary NICs should fall into the same subnet as any other machines on the network segment. The addresses assigned to the secondary NICs should belong to a unique subnet, although it is permissible to connect a crossover cable directly between the two cluster nodes

So far we have used two of our four names, and four of our six IP addresses. The next name and IP address are assigned to the cluster. This name and IP address are used to communicate with the cluster as a whole, rather than with an individual cluster node.

Finally, you will need to set aside a name and an IP address to be assigned at the Exchange Server level to the clustered mailbox server. The IP address for the cluster and the IP address for the clustered mailbox server should fall into the same subnet as the other computers on the network segment. You will only be using the alternate subnet for cluster level communications between the two nodes over the secondary network adapters.

The table below should help to give you a clearer picture of how the various names and IP addresses will be used. You don't have to use the same names and addresses as I am. They are just samples.

	Name	Primary NIC	Secondary NIC
Cluster Node 1	Node1	192.168.0.1	10.1.10.11
Cluster Node 2	Node2	192.168.0.2	10.1.10.12
MNS Cluster	WinCluster	192.168.0.3	
Clustered Mailbox Server	Exch1	192.168.0.4	

Another thing that you are going to need before you begin creating the cluster is a cluster service account. You should create a dedicated account in your Active Directory domain, and set its password so that it never expires.

One last thing that I want to mention before I show you how to create the cluster is that the Clustered Mailbox Server role cannot be combined with any other Exchange Server roles. Since every Exchange 2007 organization requires at least one Hub Transport Server and client access server, you will need at least one additional Exchange 2007 server in your organization.

Creating the cluster

Now that I have explained what resources you will need, I want to go ahead and show you how to create the cluster. This section assumes that you have already installed Windows Server 2008 onto both cluster nodes, assigned the appropriate names and IP addresses to the two nodes, and joined the nodes to your domain.

Configuring the first cluster node

Your cluster is going to consist of two separate nodes, and the setup procedure is going to be different for the two nodes. That being the case, I am going to refer to the first cluster Node as Node 1, and the second cluster node as Node 2. When the configuration process is complete, Node 1 will initially act as the active cluster node.

With that said, let's go ahead and get started by configuring Node 1. Begin the process by logging into the server with administrative credentials, and opening a Command Prompt window. Now, enter the following command:

```
Cluster /Cluster:<your cluster name> /Create /Wizard
```

For example, if you chose to call your cluster WinCluster, then you would enter:

```
Cluster: /Cluster:WinCluster /Create /Wizard
```

This command tells Windows that you want to create a new cluster named WinCluster, and that you want to use the wizard to configure the cluster.

Windows will now launch the New Server Cluster Wizard. Click **Next** to bypass the wizard's Welcome screen. Now, select your domain from the Domain drop-down list. Verify that the cluster name that is being displayed matches the one that you typed when you entered the Cluster command, and then click **Next**.

Windows will now perform a quick check to make sure that the server is ready to be clustered. This process typically generates some warnings, but those warnings aren't usually a big deal so long as no errors are displayed. The warnings are often related to 1394 firewire ports being used as network interfaces, and other minor issues.

Click **Next** to clear any warning messages, and you will be prompted to enter the IP address that you have reserved for the MNS cluster. Enter this IP address into the space provided, and then click **Next**.

You will now be prompted to enter your service account credentials. Enter the required username and password, and click **Next**.

At this point, the wizard will display a summary screen. With virtually every other wizard that Microsoft makes, you can just take a second to verify the accuracy of the information, and then click **Next**. In this case, though, you need to click the **Quorum** button instead. After doing so, you must set the quorum type to **Majority Node Set**. After doing so, click **OK**, followed by **Next**. When the wizard completes, click **Next**, followed by **Finish**. You have now created the first cluster node!

Adding the second node to the cluster

Now that we have created our cluster, we need to add Node 2 to it. To do so, log in to Node 2 as an administrator, and open a Command Prompt window. When the window opens, enter the following command:

```
Cluster /Cluster:<your cluster name> /Add /Wizard
```

For example, if you called your cluster WinCluster, you would enter this command:

```
Cluster /Cluster:WinCluster /Add /Wizard
```

Notice that this time we are using the /Add switch instead of the /Create switch because our cluster already exists.

Windows should now launch the Add Nodes Wizard. Click **Next** to clear the wizard's Welcome screen. You must now select your domain from the Domain drop-down list. While you are at it, take a moment to make sure that the cluster name that is being displayed matches what you typed.

Click **Next**, and you will be prompted to enter the name of the server that you want to add to the cluster. Enter the server name and click the **Add** button.

Click **Next**, and the wizard will perform a quick check to make sure that the server is ready to be added to the cluster. Once again, it is normal to get some warning messages. As long as you don't receive any error messages, you can just click **Next**.

At this point, you will be prompted to enter the credentials for the cluster's service account. After doing so, click **Next**.

You should now see the familiar configuration summary screen. This time, you don't have to worry about clicking a **Quorum** button. Just click **Next**, and Windows will add the node to the cluster. When the process completes, click **Next**, followed by **Finish**.

Some additional configuration tasks

Now that we have created our Majority Node Set Cluster, we need to tell Windows which NICs are going to be used for which purpose. To do so, select the Cluster Administrator console from Node 1's Administrative Tools menu. When the Cluster Administrator starts, take a moment to make sure that both of your cluster nodes are listed in the Cluster Administrator's console tree.

Now, navigate through the console tree to <your cluster name> | Cluster Configuration | Networks | Local Area Connection. This container should display IP addresses for both cluster nodes. Take a moment to verify that the addresses that are listed are the ones that fall into the same subnet as the other servers on the network segment. Now, right-click on the **Local Area Connection** container, and choose the **Properties** command from the resulting shortcut menu. When the properties sheet opens, make sure that the **Enable this Network for Cluster Use** check box is selected. You must also select the **Client Access Only (Public Network)** option. When you have finished, click **OK**.

Now, we have to check the other network connection. To do so, navigate through the console tree to <your cluster name> | Cluster Configuration | Networks | Local Area Connection 2. Make sure that when you select the Local Area Connection 2 container, the details pane displays both cluster nodes, and the IP addresses that are listed are associated with the private subnet.

At this point, you must right-click on the **Local Area Connection 2** container, and select the **Properties** command from the resulting shortcut menu. When Windows opens the properties sheet for the connection, make sure that the **Enable This Network for Cluster Use** check box is selected. You must also select the **Internal Cluster Communications Only (Private Network)** option. When you are done, click **OK** and close the Cluster Administrator.

Creating a majority node set file share witness

The problem with a Majority Node Set cluster is that the active node must be able to communicate with the majority of the nodes in the cluster, but there is no way to have a clear majority in a two node cluster. Windows can't allow a single node to count as the majority, because otherwise a failure of the communications link between the two cluster nodes could result in a split brains failure. This is a condition in which both nodes are functional, and each node believes that the other node has failed, and therefore tries to become the active node.

In order to prevent this from happening, we must create a Majority Node Set File Share Witness. The basic idea behind this is that we will create a special file share on our Hub Transport Server. In the event of a failure, the share that we create will be counted as a node (even though it isn't really a node) in determining which cluster node has the majority of the node set.

To create the Majority Node Set File Share Witness, go to your Hub Transport Server, open a Command Prompt window, and enter the following commands:

```
C:
CD\
MNS_FSW_CCR
Net Share MNS_FSW_CCR=C:\MNS_FSW_CCR /Grant:<your service account name>,Full
CACLS C:\MNS_FSW_CCR /G Builtin\Administrators:F <your service account>:F
```

When Windows asks you if you are sure, press **Y**.

What we have done is created a folder on our Hub Transport Server named C:\MNS_FSW_CCR. We then created a share named MNS_FSW_CCR, and gave our service account full access to the share. Finally, we gave the built-in Administrator account and the service account full access to the folder at the NTFS level.

Now, go to Node 1 and open a Command Prompt window. You must now enter the following commands:

```
Cluster <your cluster name> Res "Majority Node Set" /Priv MNSFileShare=\\<your
hub transport server's name>\MNS_FSW_CCR
Cluster <your cluster name> group "Cluster Group" /move
Cluster <your cluster name> group "Cluster Group" /move
Cluster <your cluster name> Res "Majority Node Set" /Priv
```

The first command in this sequence tells Windows to use the share that we have created as the Majority Node Set File Share Witness. When you enter this command, you will receive an error message telling you that the properties were stored, but that your changes won't take effect until the next time the cluster is brought online.

The easiest way to get around this problem is to move the cluster group from Node 1 to Node 2 and then back to Node 1. That's what the second and third commands in the sequence above accomplish for us.

The last command in the sequence above simply causes Windows to display the private properties for the Majority Node Set. The first line of text within the list of properties should make reference to the share that we have created for our Majority Node Set File Share Witness. This confirms that the cluster is using our Majority Node Set File Share Witness.

Conclusion

As you can see, creating a Majority Node Set Cluster can be a bit tedious. In Part 2 of this article, we will wrap things up by installing Exchange Server onto our cluster and then working through the failover procedure.

The Active Directory Recycle Bin in Windows Server 2008 R2

23 September 2009

by Jonathan Medd

It has always been a curse as well as a blessing that Active Directory has allowed the rapid removal of whole branches. Until now, administrators have looked in vain for an "undo" function after having accidentally deleted an entire division of their company. At last, with Windows Server 2008 R2, comes a way to roll back changes, as long as you are handy with Powershell.
Jonathan Medd explains.

Since Active Directory was included as part of Window Server 2000, administrators have often asked for a simple way to roll back mistakes, ranging from the incorrect deletion of the wrong user account to the accidental removal of thousands of objects by deleting an OU. Before the release of Windows Server 2008 R2 there were a number of ways using built-in or third-party methods to restore Active Directory objects, but typically they were not as quick or complete as, say, retrieving a deleted email or file.

Microsoft has included with their release of Windows Server 2008 R2 the facility, under the correct conditions, to enable a Recycle Bin for Active Directory and allow simple restoration of objects which have been erroneously removed. In this article we will briefly cover some of the options prior to 2008 R2, and then examine how to enable the new Recycle Bin and restore objects from it.

Pre-Windows Server 2008 R2

The 2008 R2 Recycle Bin for Active Directory is a great motivating point for upgrading your forest and domain(s) to the latest version, but this is not always a quick process in many enterprises, so it is worth knowing what options are available prior to this version. Like many things it's a lot better to examine and plan for possible resolutions before a significant mistake happens that you need to deal with. Retrieving Active Directory objects typically falls into two available categories, authoritative restore from a backup or tombstone reanimation.

Authoritative restore

The Microsoft KB article 840001 (HTTP://SUPPORT.MICROSOFT.COM/KB/840001) details how to perform the restoration of a user account using a system state backup of a domain controller. Typically, you would use a global catalog so that you can also restore all group membership information.

Tombstone reanimation

The above article also details how to recover an account when you don't have a system state backup, by using tombstone reanimation which was introduced with Windows Server 2003 – you can retrieve objects from the Deleted Objects container where they are kept after deletion until their tombstone period expires. Obviously regular system state backups of Active Directory are critical for your full disaster recovery procedures, but taking advantage of tombstone reanimation means you can get objects back quicker than having to go through the full authoritative restore process.

You could use the procedure in the article, which utilises the ldp.exe tool, but there are other methods around which you may find simpler.

- The article itself links to a Sysinternals tool, **ADRestore** (HTTP://TECHNET.MICROSOFT.COM/EN-US/SYSINTERNALS/BB963906.ASPX), which is a command line tool for reanimating objects.

- The free **ADRestore.Net**, a GUI tool made by Microsoft PFE Guy Teverovsky. HTTP://BLOGS.MICRO-SOFT.CO.IL/BLOGS/GUYT/ARCHIVE/2007/12/15/ADRESTORE-NET-REWRITE.ASPX.

- Quest produces a freeware product **Object Restore for Active Directory**, an easy to use GUI tool. HTTP://WWW.QUEST.COM/OBJECT-RESTORE-FOR-ACTIVE-DIRECTORY/ (Note: there is a commercial version with more features, **Recovery Manager for Active Directory**.)

- Quest also produces a cmdlet library for managing Active Directory with Windows PowerShell (HTTP://WWW.QUEST.COM/POWERSHELL/ACTIVEROLES-SERVER.ASPX). As of version 1.2, a number of the cmdlets had a tombstone parameter added to them so that a search of objects would also include items which have been tombstoned. These results could then be piped through to the new cmdlet `Restore-QADDeletedObject` to undelete the object represented by the tombstone. For instance the command `Get-QADUser -Tombstone -LastChangedOn ((Get-Date).adddays(-1)) | Restore-QADDeletedObject` would restore all user accounts deleted yesterday.

The drawback with tombstone reanimation is that, because most of the object's attributes are removed at the time of the object's deletion, a restored object using this method requires many properties of the account, such as address fields and group membership, to be manually repopulated. Whilst this is obviously preferable to re-creating an account from scratch, it does not make for a quick overall process. However, you will at least get back the objectGUID and objectSid attributes, which means there would be no need to reconfigure a user's workstation profile.

The original release of Windows Server 2008 introduced snapshot backups for Active Directory. You can take point-in-time snapshots of your Active Directory with the **NTDSUTIL** command line utility which utilizes Volume Shadow Copy to provide a snapshot. It is then possible to mount this snapshot using different ports on the same domain controller as the live Active Directory database and use standard tools to compare the two. This could really make the tombstone reanimation a lot simpler because, after restoring the object, you could view two versions of Active Directory Users and Computers side by side, and view the properties of the restored object from a previous time, so making it simpler to repopulate properties.

The Directory Service Comparison Tool (HTTP://LINDSTROM.NULLSESSION.COM/?PAGE_ID=11) takes advantage of these snapshots and makes the repopulation process more streamlined.

For those with Microsoft Exchange messaging environments, once you have the Active Directory account back, you can use the **Reconnect Mailbox** feature within Exchange to tie the restored account back up with the mailbox. This is, of course, providing you have a similar tombstone retention period for mailboxes as you do for AD accounts.

Active Directory Recycle Bin

The real reason you decided to read this article, though, was not so that we could spend time going over all the possible options for how you can piece together restored AD objects, but rather to find out how the Recycle Bin is going to make your life as an Active Directory administrator easier without necessarily the need for these different tools. The key differences from previous versions of Windows Server are that, by default, you get all of the attributes back, and the tools to use are PowerShell cmdlets, which are quickly becoming a more essential part of every Windows administrator's standard toolkit.

Firstly, though, the Active Directory Recycle Bin is not enabled by default and has certain domain- and forest-wide requirements before it can be enabled. All domain controllers within the Active Directory forest must be running Windows Server 2008 R2, and the functional level of the Active Directory forest must be Windows Server 2008 R2.

Naturally organizations are typically cautious when upgrading Active Directory, and these types of infrastructure projects don't tend to happen quickly, but the Recycle Bin could be one of the features which gives you more weight behind a decision. You should also be aware, though, that enabling the Recycle Bin is a onetime only move; there's no easy way to disable it again, so careful consideration of this decision must be taken.

It's worth noting that, if you are making a fresh forest install of Windows Server 2008 R2, the Active Directory schema will already include all of the necessary attributes for the Recycle Bin to function. If, however, you are upgrading your domain controllers from previous versions of Windows Server, then you will need to run the well-known procedure of `adprep /forestprep` and `adprep /domainprep` (for each domain) and possibly `adprep /domainprep /gpprep` (for Group Policy preparation) before you can introduce Windows Server 2008 R2 domain controllers into the environment.

So, let's go ahead and run through all the steps we need to get the Recycle Bin enabled. Firstly, ensure that all your domain controllers are running Windows Server 2008 R2, and then you need to use PowerShell. The great news with Windows Server 2008 R2 is that version 2 of PowerShell is installed by default, and is placed directly on your taskbar.

After you have installed Active Directory Domain Services, the Active Directory specific cmdlets are available to use via a module. Modules are essentially the evolution of snap-ins from version 1 of PowerShell. To access these cmdlets, you can either open the Active Directory specific version of the PowerShell console from the Administrative Programs menu, or the method I would prefer, use the `Import-Module` cmdlet.

Tip

You could add the expression PS> `Import-Module activedirectory` *to your PowerShell profile so that the cmdlets are available every time you open PowerShell.*

Once complete, all of the Active Directory cmdlets will be at your fingertips. As previously discussed we now need to get the functional level of the forest up to the level of Windows Server 2008 R2. The most common way to do this previously was through Active Directory Domains and Trusts.

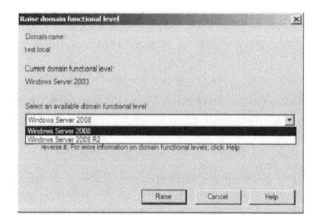

Now, though, we can do this through PowerShell. The `Get-ADForest` cmdlet will return information about your forest and the `Set-ADForestMode` cmdlet will enable you to raise the current functional level – since it is such a significant change to your environment, you will be prompted to confirm that you wish to go ahead.

```
PS> Get-ADForest | Set-ADForestMode –ForestMode Windows2008R2Forest
```

Now that our forest is at the correct functional level, we can enable the Recycle Bin. To do so, we use the `Enable-ADOptionalFeature` cmdlet. This must be either run on the DC with the Domain Naming Master FSMO role or directed at that server with the `-server` parameter. Again, you will be prompted to confirm your command, since the action is irreversible.

```
PS> Enable-ADOptionalFeature 'Recycle Bin Feature' -Scope
ForestOrConfigurationSet -target 'test.local'
```

Now that we have the Recycle Bin enabled, it's time to go check out how we recover some deleted objects. In this environment we have a very simple AD structure with a couple of test accounts to illustrate the example.

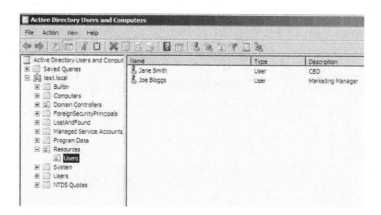

Let's take the situation where an administrator accidently deletes the **Users** OU. One of the most common reasons this can happen is because it is actually possible to delete OUs from the Group Policy Management tool, not just Active Directory Users and Computers – so an administrator might think they are removing a GPO and, in a bad moment, delete the wrong item and remove a whole OU. The administrator is prompted for what they are about to do, but I have seen it happen more than once!

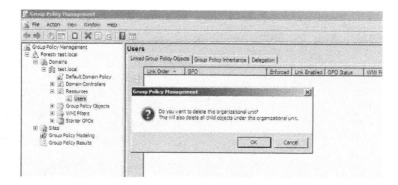

The initial release of Windows 2008 Server actually included a new check box **Protect object from accidental deletion**. In the example of the OU below, any attempt to delete the OU will be met with an **Access is denied** response and the administrator will actually have to remove the tick from that check box before the OU can be deleted.

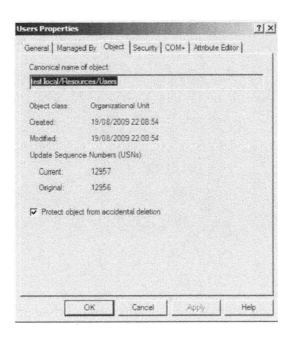

However, what you would naturally expect to happen as a consequence of the **Protect object from accidental deletion** would be that any user or computer account created in that protected OU would also be supported by the same mechanism. Unfortunately, by default, they are not so, as good practice, you would either need to build that into your account creation process or programmatically check and set that check box on all accounts in the OU on a regular basis.

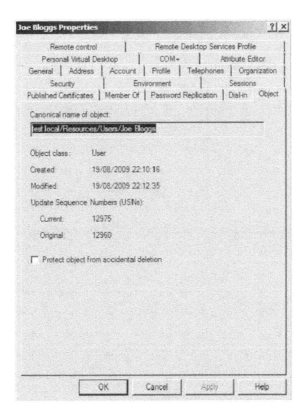

Consequently, in the above example if we accept the warning to delete the OU, we are greeted with an **Access is denied** message since the OU has protection set.

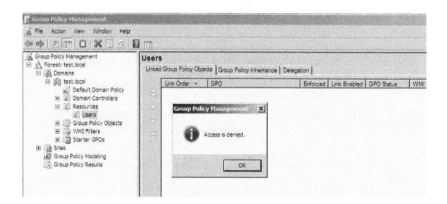

So we were saved from deleting the OU, but all of the unprotected child objects were deleted.

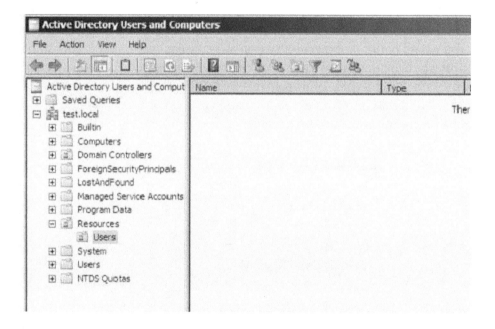

(For the purposes of this article, I now remove the **Users** OU, by first clearing the check box for protecting the object from accidental deletion.)

We can browse the current contents of the Active Directory Recycle Bin using the Get-ADObject cmdlet, directing it at the Deleted Objects container and using the -includeDeletedObjects parameter.

```
PS> Get-ADObject -SearchBase "CN=Deleted Objects,DC=test,DC=local" -
ldapFilter "(objectClass=*)" -includeDeletedObjects | Format-List
Name,ObjectClass,ObjectGuid
```

We can see from the resultant output that we have both the **Users** OU in there and the two user accounts. So let's try restoring one of the user accounts back. To do so we need the Restore-ADObject cmdlet and supply the ObjectGuid property of the user account.

```
PS> Restore-ADobject -identity 2df74fba-7e86-4f75-b16d-5725ef45a45f
```

Oh dear, it failed to restore, but PowerShell tells us that it failed because the object's parent no longer exists either, i.e. we need to first restore the **Users** OU. (An alternative would be to use the -targetpath parameter and re-direct the restore to a different OU.)

To restore the **Users** OU we can use the same cmdlet (Restore-ADObject) as to restore users; just supply the ObjectGuid of the OU.

```
PS> Restore-ADObject -identity 20142376-8a48-4b56-9972-0e64eb9e9a0f
```

The **Users** OU returns.

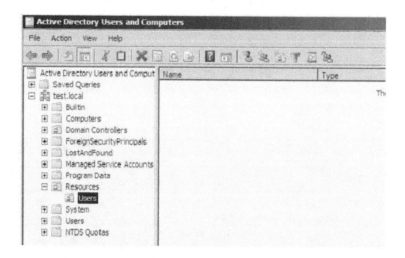

Now, we just need to get those user accounts back. Rather than have to type out the ObjectGuid for each account we wish to restore, we can instead create a search which will match all of the accounts we wish to restore, then use the PowerShell pipeline to send those results to the `Restore-ADObject` cmdlet.

```
PS> Get-ADObject -ldapFilter "(lastKnownParent=OU=Users,OU=Resources,DC=test,DC=
local)" -includeDeletedObjects | Restore-ADObject
```

The user accounts are back in the **Users** OU.

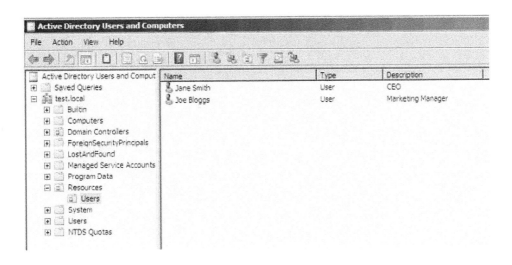

If we check the properties of the account we can confirm that, different from tombstone reanimation, we get all of the properties back.

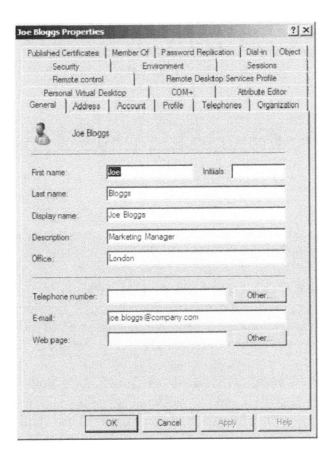

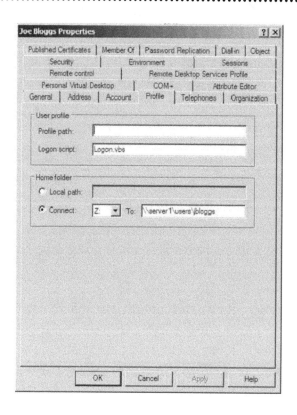

Active Directory Recycle Bin PowerPack for PowerGUI

Although the Recycle Bin is a great new feature within Windows Server 2008 R2, Microsoft is already getting feedback that there is no GUI for managing it. Whilst a lot of administrators are comfortable with PowerShell, some may still prefer to use a GUI-based management tool for these tasks. Fortunately, a great tool to plug this gap has already been provided by the community; PowerShell MVP Kirk Munro has created the Active Directory Recycle Bin PowerPack for PowerGUI (HTTP://WWW.POWERGUI.ORG/ENTRY.JSPA?CATEGORYID=21&EXTERNALID=2461). This free tool has bundled up scripts using the previously demonstrated Active Directory PowerShell cmdlets and provides a graphical front end for administration.

Simply download the PowerGUI tool plus the Active Directory Recycle Bin PowerPack and import it into PowerGUI. Open up the PowerPack and you will have a graphical view of the current contents of the Recycle Bin, with the ability to drill down through Organisational Units. Options, for restoring single items or recursively, are provided in the **Actions** column as well as alternate restoration paths and emptying items from the Recycle Bin.

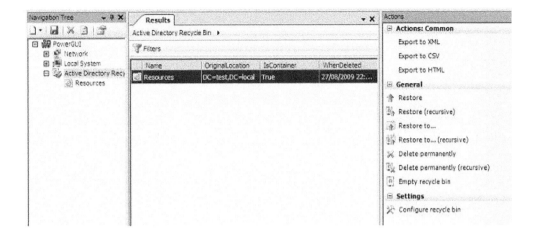

It is also possible to use the **Configure recycle bin** action to set the values for **DeletedObjectLifetime**, the amount of days objects reside in the Recycle Bin, and **TombstoneLifetime**, the amount of days objects can be restored using tombstone reanimation after they have left the Recycle Bin. In Windows Server 2008 R2 both of these values default to 180 days; in some earlier versions of Windows Server this value was 60 days; and if you upgrade those domain controllers it will remain the same, so you may wish to change the values – you can use the **Modify** action to do this.

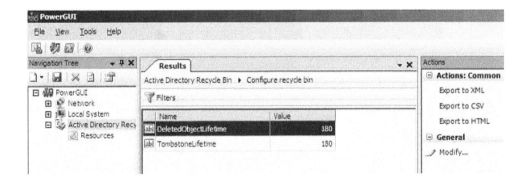

For this example I have deleted from Active Directory the **Resources** and **Users** containers and the two user accounts which you can see nicely in the screenshot below using PowerGUI.

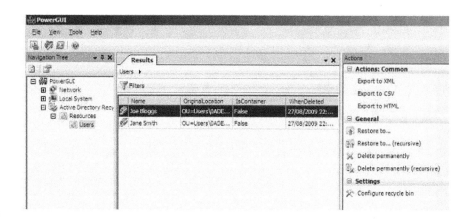

This time, we will restore the account **Joe Bloggs**, but to an alternative location using the **Restore to...** action. This is done in PowerShell using the `-targetpath` parameter of the `Restore-ADObject` cmdlet. Simply input the path to the Organisational Unit you wish to restore the object to. In this example, we use the default **Users** container as the target location.

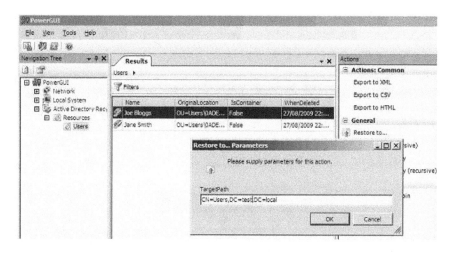

The user has been restored to the alternate location; this is particularly useful if we did not wish to bring back the entire OU(s) as we did previously.

If, however, you do wish to bring back the contents of an entire OU and everything below it, there is an action, **Restore (recursive)**.

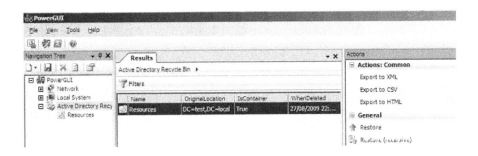

Using the **Restore (recursive)** action in this scenario brings back both the **Resources** and **Users** OUs as well as the single account remaining in it, **Jane Smith**.

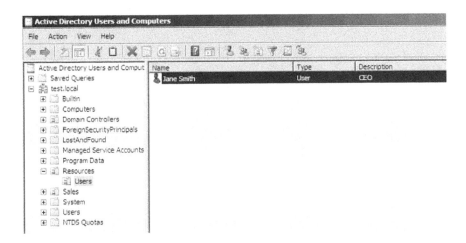

Hopefully, in a future release of Windows Server, this functionality will be provided out of the box. The most natural home would be a viewable container within Active Directory Users and Computers but, until then, the Recycle Bin PowerPack for PowerGUI will prove very useful.

Summary

One of the most requested features for a long time with Active Directory has been a Recycle Bin. Microsoft has finally delivered this with the release of Windows Server 2008 R2. It may not be a feature that enterprises get to use for a little while, given the system requirements of all 2008 R2 Domain Controllers and your Active Directory Forest at 2008 R2 functional level, but it could be one of those compelling reasons that enables you to pursue an upgrade.

Administration is via the new Active Directory PowerShell cmdlets which Microsoft is using to provide a consistent command-line interface across all of their products. Although currently there is no native GUI for these administration tasks, the Active Directory Recycle Bin PowerPack for PowerGUI enables administrators to leverage the underlying PowerShell functionality and provide a graphical interface for carrying out these tasks.

Using Group Policy to Restrict the Use of PST Files

08 October 2009

by Ben Lye

Outlook PST files are a problem for Exchange users, and offer no benefits over Exchange mailboxes. You have to use them on a local drive, they are difficult to back up, and tricky for the administrator to manage. It is possible to use Exchange Group Policy settings to limit the use of PST files, and thereby alleviate some of the difficulties they cause.

Outlook Personal Folder Files (PST files) are a data store that can be used by all versions of Outlook to store email data. PST files have long been seen as a way to archive mail out of an Exchange mailbox, often to get the mailbox under a quota limit. However, the use of PST files causes Exchange administrators some serious pain when it comes to managing email.

Here, briefly, are some of the problems with PST files.

- Microsoft does not support using PST files over a LAN or WAN network (HTTP://SUPPORT.MICROSOFT.COM/KB/297019). Using PST files located on network shares can slow down Outlook and can cause corruption of the PST file.

- Anti-virus countermeasures cannot be implemented on PST files as easily as Exchange Server mailbox databases.

- It is difficult to accurately report on PST file use, making reporting on organisational mail storage and planning for future growth difficult.

- Managing content of PST files is difficult. Exchange Server provides tools to manage the content of mailboxes (such as Messaging Records Management) and to export or remove data from mailboxes (such as the Export-Mailbox cmdlet) but there are no such tools to manage the content of PST files.

- Local PST files are difficult to back up, making them vulnerable to data loss.

Fortunately for the Exchange administrator, it is possible to restrict the ability to use PST files. There are two settings available, and both can be applied using Group Policy registry changes: **PSTDisableGrow** and **DisablePST**. PSTDisableGrow prevents new data being added to existing PST files, and DisablePST prevents users from creating or opening PST files altogether.

231

Description	Registry Path	Registry Value
Disable PST files	HKEY_CURRENT_USER\Software\Policies\Microsoft\Office\12.0\Outlook	DisablePST
Prevent PST file growth	HKEY_CURRENT_USER\Software\Policies\Microsoft\Office\12.0\Outlook\PST	PstDisableGrow

Table – PST Restriction Registry Values

Note that the registry paths are specific to Outlook versions. "12.0" refers to Outlook 2007, the registry path for Outlook 2003 would be .".\Office\11.0\Outlook" and so on.

In an environment where PST files already exist, these settings can be applied separately or together to phase out their use. The first step could be to implement restrictions on the growth of PST files using PSTDisableGrow which would allow users to access existing data but not allow it to be added to. Subsequently, all PST file use could be disabled by implementing DisablePST.

In a new Exchange environment, or one where PST files are not used (and the Exchange administrator wants to keep it that way), the DisablePST setting can be applied on its own to stop users being able to add PST files to Outlook. In any Exchange environment it is probably worth considering implementing a server-side archiving solution before disabling PST files. Server-side archiving has many benefits compared to PST files and, as many users are determined to keep large quantities of historic email, it is better to have a managed solution than unmanaged, ad hoc PST file use – a scenario often know as "PST hell."

If you are ready to disable PST file use, the settings can be applied to Outlook 2007 with Group Policy using the Office 2007 Group Policy Administrative Templates.

Applying PST Group Policy for Outlook 2007

Download the Office 2007 ADM Templates and extract the files:
HTTP://WWW.MICROSOFT.COM/DOWNLOADS/DETAILS.ASPX?FAMILYID=92D85I9A-EI43-4AEE-8F7A-E4BBAEBAI3E7&DISPLAYLANG=EN

- Launch the Group Policy Management Console, click **Start ▸ Administrative Tools ▸ Group Policy Management**.

- Expand the Forest, Domains, and domain containers then select Group Policy Objects.

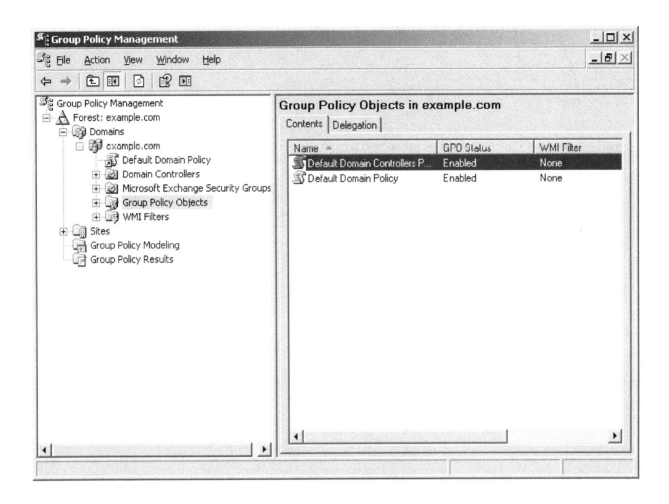

- Right-click **Group Policy Objects** and select **New**. Give the new GPO a name, for example, **PST Policy**, and click OK. (Skip this step if you want to add these settings to an existing GPO.)

- Right-click **PST Policy** (or the existing policy you wish to edit) and choose **Edit**.

- Expand **User Configuration**, right-click **Administrative Templates** and choose **Add/Remove Templates**.

- Click the **Add** button and browse to the location of the files extracted in step 2. Open the **ADM** folder and the appropriate language subfolder (en-us for English), select the file named outlk12.adm and click **Open**.

- Click **Close** to close the **Add/Remove Templates** dialog box.

- Expand **User Configuration\Administrative Templates\Microsoft Office Outlook 2007\Miscellaneous\PST Settings**.

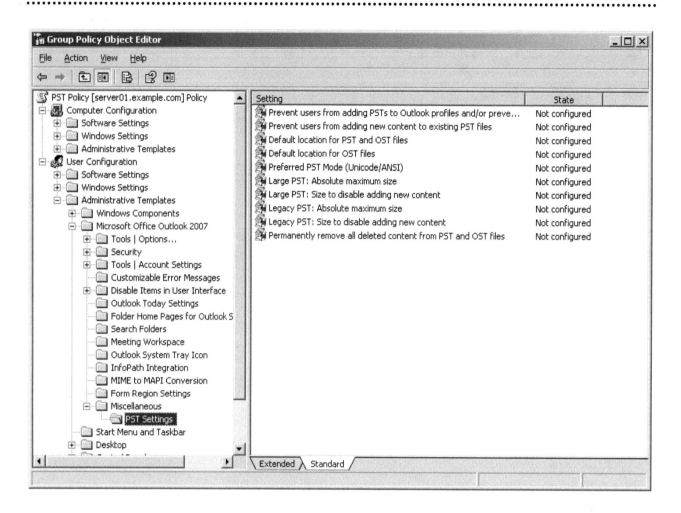

- To implement the DisablePST restriction enable the **Prevent users from adding PSTs to Outlook profiles...** setting and set the option to **Only Sharing-Exclusive PSTs can be added**. This will allow PST files for applications such as SharePoint lists, but will prevent user-created PST files from being added.

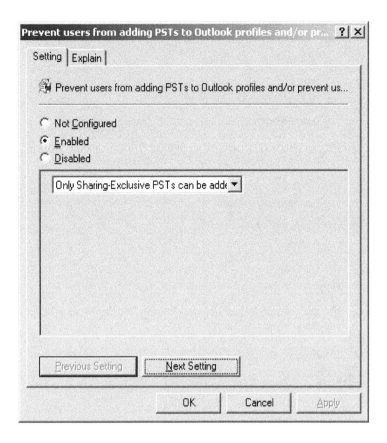

- To implement the PSTDisableGrow restriction, enable the **Prevent users from adding new content to existing PST files** setting.

If the PSTDisableGrow setting is implemented, users will still be able to create and open PST files, but they will not be able to add any data to any PST files. If they try, they will receive this error message:

If the DisablePST setting is implemented, the user will see changes in the Outlook user interface. While any PST files which were already loaded will remain part of the profile, the options to create new PST files or to open any other existing PST files will no longer be in the menu. Archive options will also be removed.

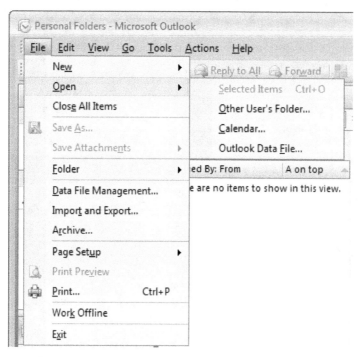

DisablePST not implemented.

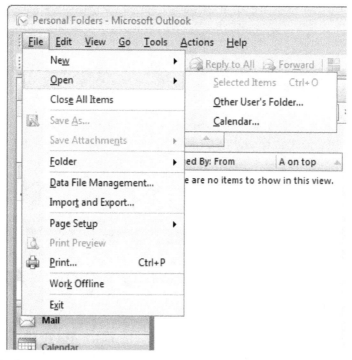

Disable PST implemented.

PST files can be a headache for Exchange administrators, but they don't have to be. With easily-applied Group Policy settings, the use of PST files can be limited, and the problems they cause can be eradicated.

Introduction to Exchange Server 2010

22 October 2009

by Jaap Wesselius

What's new in Exchange Server 2010, and what features from Exchange Server 2007 have been deprecated? What has been done to further integrate Exchange with Active Directory? In an extract from his new book, Jaap gives a rooftop view of Exchange's new features and their significance, and spells out the main reasons why it is worth upgrading.

First things first – let's cover some basic background: Exchange Server 2010 is an email and calendaring application that runs on Windows Server 2008 and, like its predecessor Exchange Server 2007, can also integrate with your phone system. It is the seventh major version of the product and, while not revolutionary, it does include some important changes and lots of small improvements over Exchange Server 2007.

The scalability of Exchange Server 2010 has improved, especially when compared to the complex storage requirements of Exchange Server 2007. The user experience has also improved in Outlook Web App, and a lot of complex issues have seen solved, or the complexity has been removed, to make the administrator's life much easier.

In this article I will give a brief overview of what's changed in Exchange Server 2010, what the new features are, what features have been removed, and how it makes your life as an Exchange administrator easier.

Under the hood: what's changed?

- By far the most important change with respect to Exchange Server 2007 is the new Database Availability Group. This will allow you to create multiple copies of an Exchange Server database within your organization, and you are no longer bound to a specific site (like in Exchange Server 2007), but can now stretch across multiple sites. Microsoft has also successfully transformed Cluster Continuous Replication and Stand-by Continuous Replication into a new "Continuous Availability" technology.

- While on the topic of simplifying, a lot of SysAdmins were having difficulties with the Windows Server fail-over clustering, so Microsoft has simply "removed" this from the product. The components are still there, but they are now managed using the Exchange Management Console or Exchange Management Shell.

- With the new Personal Archive ability, a user can now have a secondary mailbox, acting as a personal archive – this really is a .PST killer! You now have the ability to import all the users' .PST files and store them in the Personal Archive, and using retention policies you can move data from the primary mailbox to the archive automatically, to keep the primary mailbox at an acceptable size, without any hassle.

- To deal with ever-growing storage requirements, Microsoft also made considerable changes to the underlying database system. All you will need to store your database and log files with Exchange Server 2010 is a 2 TB SATA (or other Direct Attached Storage) disk. As long as you have multiple copies of the database, you're safe! And the maximum supported database size? That has improved from 200 GB (in an Exchange Server 2007 CCR environment) to 2 TB (in a multiple database copy Exchange Server 2010 environment). If you haven't yet considered what your business case will look like when upgrading to Exchange Server 2010, bear in mind that this will truly save a tremendous amount of storage cost – and that's not marketing talk!

- Installing Exchange 2010 is not at all difficult, and configuring a Database Availability Group with multiple copies of the Mailbox Databases is just a click of the mouse (you only have to be a little careful when creating multi-site DAGs). Even installing Exchange Server 2010 into an existing Exchange Server 2003 or Exchange Server 2007 environment is not that hard! The only thing you have to be aware of is the additional namespace that shows up. Besides the standard namespace, like webmail.contoso.com and Autodiscover.contoso.com, a third namespace shows up in a coexistence environment: legacy.contoso.com. This is used when you have mailboxes still on the old (i.e. Exchange Server 2003 or Exchange Server 2007) platform in a mixed environment.

- Lastly, for a die-hard GUI administrator, it might be painful to start managing an Exchange environment with the Exchange Management Shell. Basic management can be done with the graphical Exchange Management Console, but you really do have to use the Shell for the nitty-gritty configuration. The Shell is remarkably powerful, and it takes quite some getting used to, but with it you can do fine-grained management, and even create reports using features like output-to-HTML or save-to-.CSV file. Very neat!

Getting started

Exchange Server 2010 will be available in two versions:

- **Standard Edition**, which is limited to hosting 5 databases.

- **Enterprise Edition**, which can host up to 100 databases.

However, the available binaries are identical for both versions; it's the license key that establishes the difference in functionality. Exchange Server 2010 is also only available in a 64-bit version; there is absolutely no 32-bit version available, not even for testing purposes. Bear in mind that, as 64-bit-only software, there's no Itanium version of Exchange Server 2010.

Exchange Server 2010 also comes with two Client Access License (CAL) versions:

- **Standard CAL** – this license provides access to email, calendaring, Outlook Web App and ActiveSync for Mobile Devices.

- **Enterprise CAL** – this is an additive license, and provides Unified Messaging and compliance functionality, as well as Forefront Security for Exchange Server and Exchange Hosted Filtering for anti-spam and anti-virus functionality.

This is not a complete list. For more information about licensing, check the Microsoft website at www. MICROSOFT.COM/EXCHANGE.

What's been removed from Exchange Server 2010?

As always, as new features come, old features go. There are inevitably a few that have found themselves on the deprecated list this time around, and so will not be continued in Exchange Server 2010 and beyond. Since this is a much shorter list than the new features, we'll start here.

There are some major changes in Exchange Server clustering: in Exchange Server 2007 you had **LCR** (Local Continuous Replication), **CCR** (Cluster Continuous Replication) and **SCR** (Standby Continuous Replication) – three different versions of replication, all with their own management interfaces. All three are *no longer available* in Exchange Server 2010.

Windows Server Fail-over Clustering has been removed in Exchange Server 2010. Although seriously improved in Windows Server 2008, a lot of Exchange Administrators still found the fail-over clustering complex and difficult to manage. As a result, it was still prone to error and a potential source of all kinds of problems.

Storage Groups are no longer available in Exchange Server 2010. The concepts of a database, log files and a checkpoint file are still there, but now it is just called a Database. It's like CCR in Exchange Server 2007, where you could only have one database per storage group.

Due to major re-engineering in the Exchange Server 2010 databases, the **Single Instance Storage** (SIS) is no longer available. This means that when you send a 1 MB message to 100 recipients, the database will potentially grow by 100 MB. This will surely have an impact on the storage requirements in terms of space, but the performance improvements on the Database are really great. I'll get back to that later.

What's new in Exchange Server 2010?

Exchange Server 2010 contains a host of improvements and a lot of new features, as well as minor changes and improvements. Over the coming sections, I'll provide an overview of the most significant updates and additions.

Outlook Web App

The most visible improvement for end-users is Outlook Web App (previously known as Outlook Web Access). One of the design goals for the Outlook Web App was a seamless cross-browser experience, so users running a browser like Safari, even on an Apple MacBook, should have exactly the same user experience as users running Internet Explorer.

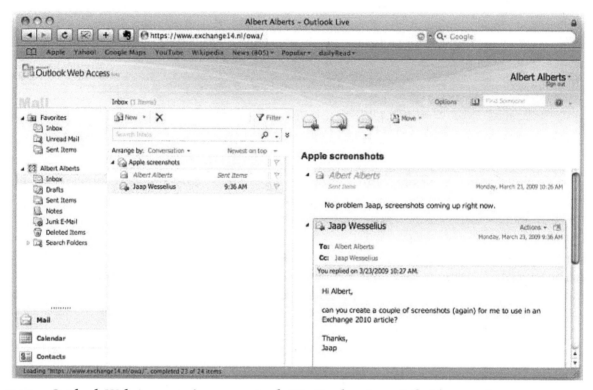

Figure 1:   Outlook Web App running on an Apple MacBook using a Safari browser!

Outlook Web App offers a very rich client experience and narrows the gap between a fully-fledged Outlook client and Outlook Web Access. To reinforce that experience, a lot of new features have been introduced. To name a few: Favorites, Search Folders, attaching messages to messages, integration with Office Communicator, a new Conversation View (which works very well!), integration with SMS (text) messages and the possibility to create Outlook Web Access policies, which give the Exchange organization administrator the ability to fine-tune the user experience. The Web App is a feature which you will find mentioned throughout the book.

High availability

The Exchange Server 2007 Cluster Continuous Replication (CCR) and Standby Continuous Replication (SCR) features are now combined into one new feature called **database availability**.

Database copies exist, just as in an Exchange Server 2007 CCR environment, and are created in a Database Availability Group, but it is now possible to create multiple copies. The replication is not on a server level as in Exchange Server 2007 but on a database level, which gives the Exchange administrator much more fine control and granularity when it comes to creating a high available Exchange organization. The servers in such a Database Availability Group can be at the same location, or other locations to create an offsite solution. There's also no longer any need to install the Microsoft Cluster Service (MSCS) before setting up the Database Availability Group, as all cluster operations are now managed by Exchange.

Exchange core store functionality

Compared to Exchange Server 2003, Exchange Server 2007 dramatically decreased the I/O on the disk subsystem (sometimes by 70%). This was achieved by increasing the Exchange database page size from 4 KB to 8 KB and by using the 64-bit operating system. The memory scalability of the 64-bit platform makes it possible to use servers with huge amounts of memory, giving them the opportunity to cache information in memory instead of reading and writing everything to the disk.

One of the design goals of Exchange Server 2010 was to use a single 1 TB SATA disk for the mailbox database *and* its log files. Another goal was to allow multi-GB mailboxes without any negative performance impact on the server. To make this possible, the database schema in Exchange Server 2010 has now been flattened, making the database structure used by the Exchange Server much less complex than it was in Exchange Server 2007 and earlier. As a result, the I/O requirements of an Exchange Server 2010 server can be up to 50% less than for the same configuration in Exchange Server 2007.

As a result of the flattened database schema, Microsoft has removed Single Instance Storage (SIS) from Exchange Server 2010, but the improvements in performance are much more significant, and more than adequate compensation for the (comparatively minor) loss of SIS.

Microsoft Online Services

Microsoft is gradually moving "into the cloud." Besides an Exchange Server 2010 implementation on premise, it is now also possible to host mailboxes in a datacenter; you can host your mailboxes with your own ISP, or with Microsoft Online Services.

Exchange Server 2010 can be 100% on premise, 100% hosted, or it can be a mixed environment, with some percentage of your mailboxes hosted and the rest on premise. This is, of course, fully transparent to end-users, but it has its effects on the administration. Instead of managing just one, on-site environment, you'll have to manage the hosted organization as well. This can all be handled through Exchange Server 2010's Exchange Management Console, where you can connect to multiple forests containing an Exchange organization.

New administration functionality

As a consequence of the major changes made to the High Availability features of Exchange Server 2010, the Exchange Management Console has also changed rather significantly.

Due to the new replication functionality, the Mailbox object is no longer tied to the Exchange Server object, but is now part of the Exchange Server 2010 organization. Also, since the concept of Storage Groups is no longer relevant, their administration has been removed from both the Exchange Management Console and the Exchange Management Shell. PowerShell cmdlets like New-StorageGroup, Get-StorageGroup, and so on, have also all been removed, although the options of these cmdlets have been moved into other cmdlets, like database-related cmdlets.

Speaking of which, Exchange Server 2010 also runs on top of **PowerShell Version 2**. This version not only has a command line interface (CLI), but also an Interactive Development Environment (IDE). This enables you to easily create scripts and use variables, and you now have an output window where you can quickly view the results of your PowerShell command or script.

In addition to PowerShell V2, Exchange Server 2010 also uses **Windows Remote Management** (WinRM) Version 2. This gives you the option to remotely manage an Exchange Server 2010 server without the need to install the Exchange Management Tools on your workstation, and even via the Internet!

One last small but interesting new feature is **Send Mail**, allowing you to send mail directly from the Exchange Management Console – ideal for testing purposes.

Exchange control panel

It is now possible to perform some basic Exchange management tasks using the options page in Outlook Web Access; not only on the user's own properties, but also at an organizational level. With this method, it is possible to create users, mailboxes, distribution groups, mail-enabled contact, management email addresses, etc.

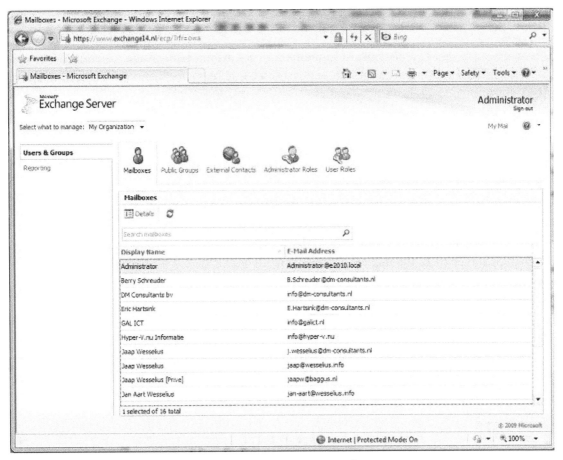

Figure 2: The Exchange control panel for basic management functions.

Active Directory Rights Management

Active Directory Rights Management Service lets you control what users can do with email and other documents that are sent to them. It is possible, for example, for classified messages to disable the "Forward" option to prevent messages being leaked outside the organization. With Exchange Server 2010, new features have been added to the Rights Management Services, such as:

- **integration with transport rules** – a template for using RMS to protect messages over the Internet

- **RMS protection for voice mail messages** coming from the Unified Messaging Server Role.

Active Directory is discussed throughout this book, as the Exchange Server 2010 has a much closer relationship with AD than previous versions of Exchange Server.

Transport and routing

With Exchange Server 2010 it is possible to implement **cross premises message routing**. When using a mixed hosting environment, Exchange Server 2010 can route messages from the datacenter to the on-premise environment with full transparency.

Exchange Server 2010 also offers (at last) **enhanced disclaimers**, making it possible to add HTML content to disclaimers to add images, hyperlinks, etc. It is even possible to use Active Directory attributes (from the user's private property set) to create a personal disclaimer.

To create a highly available and reliable routing model, the Hub Transport Servers in Exchange Server 2010 now contain **Shadow Redundancy**. A message is normally stored in a database on the Hub Transport Server and, in Exchange Server 2007, the message is deleted as soon as it is sent to the next hop. In Exchange Server 2010, the message is only deleted *after* the next hop reports a successful delivery of the message. If this is not reported, the Hub Transport Server will try to resend the message.

For more High Availability messaging support, the messages stay in the transport dumpster on a Hub Transport Server, and are only deleted if they are successfully replicated to all database copies. The database on the Hub Transport Server has also been improved on an ESE level, resulting in a higher message throughput on the transport level.

Permissions

Previous versions of Exchange Servers relied on delegation of control via multiple Administrative Groups (specifically, Exchange Server 2000 and Exchange Server 2003) or via Group Membership. Exchange Server 2010 now contains a **Role Based Access Model (RBAC)** to implement a powerful and flexible management model.

Messaging policy and compliance

As part of a general compliance regulation, Microsoft introduced the concept of Managed Folders in Exchange Server 2007, offering the possibility to create some sort of compliancy feature. This has been enhanced with new interfaces in Exchange Server 2010, such as the option of tagging messages, cross mailbox searches and new transport rules and actions.

Mailbox archive

Exchange Server 2010 now contains a personal archive; this is a secondary mailbox connected to a user's primary mailbox, and located in the same Mailbox Database as the user's primary mailbox. Since Exchange Server 2010 now supports a JBOD (Just a Bunch of Disks) configuration, this isn't too big a deal, and the Mailbox Archive really is a great replacement for (locally stored) .PST files.

Unified Messaging

The Exchange Server 2010 Unified Messaging Server Role integrates a telephone system, like a PABX, with the Exchange Server messaging environment. This makes it possible to offer Outlook Voice Access, enabling you to interact with the system using your voice, listen to voice-mail messages, or have messages read to you. Exchange Server 2010 offers some new functionality like **Voicemail preview**, **Message Waiting Indicator, integration with text (SMS) messages**, additional **language support**, etc. Unified Messaging is, unfortunately, a little outside the scope of this book, so you won't find me going into too much detail later on.

Exchange Server 2010 and Active Directory

As far as Active Directory is concerned, its minimum level needs to be on a Windows Server 2003 level, both for the domain functional level as well as the forest functional level. This might be confusing, since Exchange Server 2010 only runs on Windows Server 2008 or Windows Server 2008 R2, but that's just the actual server which Exchange Server 2010 is running on!

The Schema Master in the forest needs to be Windows Server 2003 SP2 server (Standard or Enterprise Edition) or higher. Likewise, in each Active Directory Site where Exchange Server 2010 will be installed, there must be *at least* one Standard or Enterprise Windows Server 2003 SP2 (or higher) server configured as a Global Catalog server.

From a performance standpoint, as with Exchange Server 2007, the ratio of 4:1 for Exchange Server processors to Global Catalog server processors still applies to Exchange Server 2010. Using a 64-bit version of Windows Server for Active Directory will naturally also increase the system performance.

Note

It is possible to install Exchange Server 2010 on an Active Directory Domain Controller. However, for performance and security reasons it is recommended not to do this and, instead, to install Exchange Server 2010 on a member server in a domain.

Active Directory partitions

A Windows Server Active Directory consists of one forest, one or more domains, and one or more sites. Exchange Server 2010 is bound to a forest, and therefore one Exchange Server 2010 Organization is connected to one Active Directory forest. The actual information in an Active Directory forest is stored in three locations, also called partitions:

- **Schema partition** – this contains a "blue print" of all objects and properties in Active Directory. In a programming scenario this would be called a class. When an object, like a user, is created, it is instantiated from the user blueprint in Active Directory.

- **Configuration partition** – this contains information that's used throughout the forest. Regardless of the number of domains that are configured in Active Directory, all domain controllers use the same Configuration Partition in that particular Active Directory forest. As such, it is replicated throughout the Active Directory forest, and all changes to the Configuration Partition have to be replicated to all Domain Controllers. All Exchange Server 2010 information is stored in the Configuration Partition.

- **Domain Partition** – this contains information regarding the domains installed in Active Directory. Every domain has its own Domain Partition, so if there are 60 domains installed, there will be 60 different Domain Partitions. User information, including Mailbox information, is stored in the Domain Partition.

Delegation of control

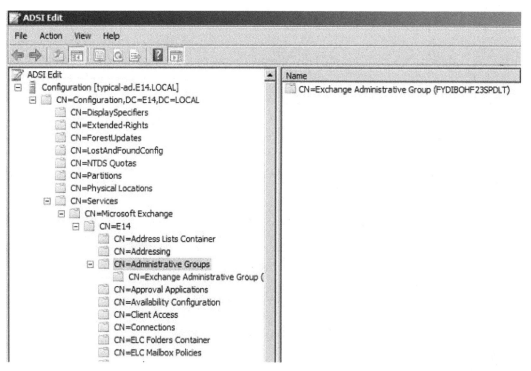

Figure 3: The Configuration partition in Active Directory holds all information regarding Exchange Server 2010 in an Administrative Group.

In Exchange Server 2003, the concept of "Administrative Groups" was used to delegate control between different groups of administrators. A default First Administrative Group was created during installation, and subsequent Administrative Groups could be created to install more Exchange 2003 servers and delegate control of these servers to other groups. The Administrative Groups were stored in the Configuration Partition so all domains and thus all domain controllers and Exchange servers could see them.

246

Exchange Server 2007 used Active Directory Security Groups for delegation of control, and only one Administrative Group is created during installation of Exchange Server 2007, called "Exchange Administrative Group (FYDIBOHF23SPDLT)." All servers in the organization are installed in this Administrative Group. Permissions are assigned to Security Groups and Exchange administrators are member of these Security Groups.

Tip

Just shift all letters in the word **FYDIBOHF23SPDLT** *to the left and you get* **EXCHANGE12ROCKS.**

Exchange Server 2010 uses the same Administrative Group, but delegation of control is not done using Active Directory Security Groups, as Microsoft has introduced the concept of "Role Based Access Control" or RBAC.

Active Directory Sites

Exchange Server 2010 uses Active Directory Sites for routing messages. But what is an Active Directory site?

When a network is separated into multiple physical locations, connected with "slow" links and separated into multiple IP subnets then, in terms of Active Directory, we're talking about sites. Say, for example, there's a main office located in Amsterdam, with an IP subnet of 10.10.0.0/16. There's a Branch Office located in London, and this location has an IP subnet of 10.11.0.0/16. Both locations have their own Active Directory Domain Controller, handling authentication for clients in their own subnet. Active Directory site links are created to control replication traffic between sites. Clients in each site use DNS to find services like Domain Controllers in their own site, thus preventing using services over the WAN link.

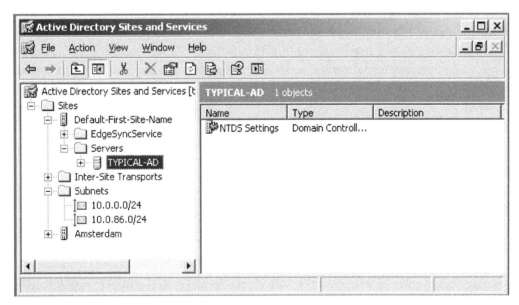

Figure 4: Two subnets in Active Directory, one for the main office and one for the Amsterdam datacenter.

247

Exchange Server 2010 uses Active Directory sites for routing messages between sites. Using our current example, if there is an Exchange Server 2010 Hub Transport Server in Amsterdam, and an Exchange Server 2010 Hub Transport Server in London, then the IP Site Links in Active Directory are used to route messages from Amsterdam to London. This concept was first introduced in Exchange Server 2007, and nothing has changed in Exchange Server 2010.

Exchange Server 2003 used the concept of Routing Groups, where Active Directory already used Active Directory Sites; Active Directory Sites and Exchange Server Routing Groups are not compatible with each other. To have Exchange Server 2003 and Exchange Server 2010 work together in one Exchange organization, some special connectors have to be created – the so-called Interop Routing Group Connector.

Exchange Server coexistence

It is very likely that large organizations will gradually move from an earlier version of Exchange Server to Exchange Server 2010, and Exchange Server 2010 can coexist, in the same forest, with (both) Exchange Server 2007 and Exchange Server 2003. It is also possible to move from a mixed Exchange Server 2003 and Exchange Server 2007 environment to Exchange Server 2010.

Please note that it is not possible to have a coexistence scenario where Exchange Server 2000 and Exchange Server 2010 are installed in the same Exchange Organization. This is enforced in the setup of Exchange Server 2010. If the setup detects an Exchange Server 2000 installation, the setup application is halted and an error is raised.

Integrating Exchange Server 2010 into an existing Exchange Server 2003 or Exchange Server 2007 environment is called a "transition" scenario. A "migration" scenario is where a new Active Directory forest is created where Exchange Server 2010 is installed. This new Active Directory forest is running in parallel to the old Active Directory with a previous version of Exchange Server. Special care has to be taken in this scenario, especially when both organizations coexist for any significant amount of time. Directories have to be synchronized during the coexistence phase, and the free/busy information will need to be constantly synchronized as well, since you'll still want to offer this service to users during the coexistence period.

This is a typical scenario when third-party tools like Quest are involved, although it is not clear at the time of writing how Quest is going to deal with Exchange Server 2010 migration scenarios.

Exchange Server 2010 server roles

Up until Exchange Server 2003, all roles were installed on one server and administrators were unable to select which features were available. It was possible to designate an Exchange 2000 or Exchange 2003 server as a so-called "front-end server," but this server was just like an ordinary Exchange server acting as a protocol proxy. It still had a Mailbox Database and a Public Folder database installed by default.

Exchange Server 2007 introduced the concept of "server roles" and this concept is maintained in Exchange Server 2010. The following server roles, each with a specific function, are available in Exchange Server 2010:

- Mailbox Server (MB) role

- Client Access Server (CAS) role

- Hub Transport Server (HT) role

- Unified Messaging Server (UM) role

- Edge Transport Server (Edge) role.

These server roles can be installed on dedicated hardware, where each machine has its own role, but they can also be combined. A typical server installation, for example in the setup program, combines the Mailbox, Client Access and Hub Transport Server role. The Management Tools are always installed during installation, irrespective of which server role is installed.

By contrast, the Edge Transport Server role cannot be combined with any other role. In fact, the Edge Transport Server role cannot even be part of the (internal) domain, since it is designed to be installed in the network's Demilitarized Zone (DMZ).

There are multiple reasons for separating Exchange Server into multiple server roles:

- **enhanced scalability** – since one server can be dedicated for one server role, the scalability profits are huge; this specific server can be configured and optimized for one particular role, resulting in a high performance server

- **improved security** – one dedicated server can be hardened for security using the Security Configuration Wizard (SCW); since only one server role is used on a particular server, all other functions and ports are disabled, resulting in a more secure system

- **simplified deployment and administration** – a dedicated server is easier to configure, easier to secure and easier to administer.

I will explain each server role in detail, in the following sections.

Mailbox Server role

The Mailbox Server role is the heart of your Exchange Server 2010 environment. This is where the Mailbox Database and Public Folder Database are installed. The sole purpose of the Mailbox Server role is to host Mailboxes and Public Folders; nothing more. In previous versions of Exchange Server, including Exchange Server 2007, Outlook clients using MAPI still connected directly to the Mailbox Server Role, but with Exchange Server 2010 this is no longer the case. MAPI clients now connect to a service called

"MAPI on the Middle Tier" (MoMT), running on the Client Access Server. The name MoMT is still a code name and will have been changed before Exchange Server 2010 is released.

The Mailbox Server role does not route any messages, it only stores messages in mailboxes. For routing messages, the Hub Transport Server role is needed. This latter role is responsible for routing all messages, even between mailboxes that are on the same server, and even between mailboxes that are in the same mailbox database.

For accessing mailboxes, a Client Access Server is also always needed; it is just not possible to access any mailbox without a Client Access Server.

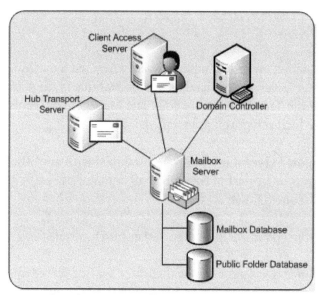

Figure 5:   The Mailbox Server role is hosting mailboxes and public folders.

Note that Internet Information Server is needed on a Mailbox Server role in order to implement the Role Based Access Control model (RBAC) even if no client is accessing the Mailbox Server directly.

As I mentioned, Storage Groups no longer exist in Exchange Server 2010, but mailboxes are still stored in databases, just like in Exchange Server 2007. Although rumors have been circulating for more than ten years that the database engine used in Exchange Server will be replaced by a SQL Server engine, it has not happened yet. In the same way, in earlier versions of Exchange Server, the Extensible Storage Engine (ESE) is still being used, although major changes have been made to the database and the database schema.

By default, the first database on a server will be installed in the directory: C:\Program Files\ Microsoft\ Exchange Server\V14\Mailbox\Mailbox Database <<identifier>>.

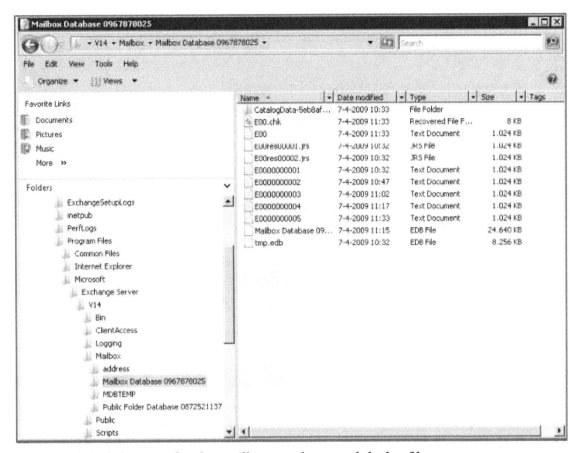

Figure 6: **The default location for the Mailbox Databases and the log files.**

The <<identifier>> is a unique number to make sure that the Mailbox Database name is unique within the Exchange organization.

It is a best practice, from both a performance and a recovery perspective, to place the database and the accompanying log files on a dedicated disk. This disk can be on a Fiber Channel SAN, an iSCSI SAN, or on a Direct Attached Storage (DAS) solution. Whilst it was a design goal to limit the amount of disk I/O to a level where both the database and the log files could be installed on a 1 TB SATA disk, this is only an option if Database Copies are configured and you have at least two copies of the Mailbox Database, in order to avoid a single point of failure.

Client Access Server role

The Client Access Server role offers access to the mailboxes for all available protocols. In Exchange Server 2003, Microsoft introduced the concept of "front-end" and "back-end" servers, and the Client Access Server role is comparable to an Exchange Server 2003 front-end server.

All clients connect to the Client Access Server and, after authentication, the requests are proxied to the appropriate Mailbox Server. Communication between the client and the Client Access Server is via the normal protocols (HTTP, IMAP4, POP3, and MAPI), and communication between the Client Access Server and the Mailbox Server is via Remote Procedure Calls (RPC).

The following functionality is provided by the Exchange Server 2010 Client Access Server:

- HTTP for Outlook Web App

- Outlook Anywhere (formerly known as RPC/HTTP) for Outlook 2003, Outlook 2007 and Outlook 2010

- ActiveSync for (Windows Mobile) PDAs

- Internet protocols POP3 and IMAP4

- MAPI on the Middle Tier (MoMT)

- Availability Service, Autodiscover and Exchange Web Services. These services are offered to Outlook 2007 clients and provide free/busy information, automatic configuration of the Outlook 2007 and Outlook 2010 clients, the Offline Address Book downloads and Out-of-Office functionality.

Note

SMTP Services are not offered by the Client Access Server. All SMTP Services are handled by the Hub Transport Server.

At least one Client Access Server is needed for each Mailbox Server in an Active Directory site, as well as a fast connection between the Client Access Server and the Mailbox Server. The Client Access Server also needs a fast connection to a Global Catalog Server.

The Client Access Server should be deployed on the internal network and not in the network's Demilitarized Zone (DMZ). In order to access a Client Access Server from the Internet, a Microsoft Internet Security and Acceleration (ISA) Server should be installed in the DMZ. All necessary Exchange services should be "published" to the Internet, on this ISA Server.

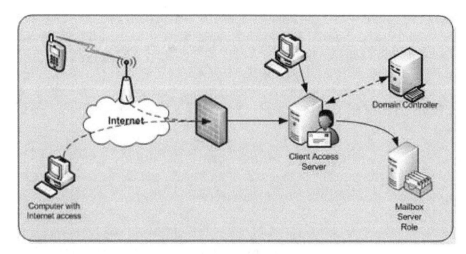

Figure 7:   The Client Access Server is responsible for providing access to (Internet) clients. The ISA Server is not in this picture.

Hub Transport Server role

The Hub Transport Server role is responsible for routing messaging, not only between the Internet and the Exchange organization, but also between Exchange servers within your organization.

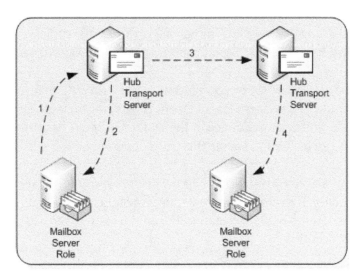

Figure 8:   The Hub Transport Server is responsible for routing all messages.

All messages are always routed via the Hub Transport Server role, even if the source and the destination mailbox are on the same server, and even if the source and the destination mailbox are in the same Mailbox Database. Figure 8 shows how this works.

1. A message is sent to the Hub Transport Server.

2. A recipient on the same server as the sender means the message is sent back.

3. When the recipient is on another mailbox server, the message is routed to the appropriate Hub Transport Server.

4. The second Hub Transport Server delivers the message to the Mailbox Server of the recipient.

The reason for routing all messages through the Hub Transport Server is simply compliancy. Using the Hub Transport Server, it is possible to track all messaging flowing through the Exchange organization and to take appropriate action if needed (legal requirements, HIPAA, Sarbanes-Oxley, etc.). On the Hub Transport Server the following agents can be configured for compliancy purposes:

* Transport Rule agents – using transport rules, all kinds of actions can be applied to messages according to the rule's filter or conditions. Rules can be applied to internal messages, external messages or both.

* Journaling agents – using the journaling agent, it is possible to save a copy of every message sent or received by a particular recipient.

Since a Mailbox Server does not deliver any messages, every Mailbox Server in an Active Directory site requires a Hub Transport Server in that site. The Hub Transport Server also needs a fast connection to a Global Catalog server for querying Active Directory. This Global Catalog server should be in the same Active Directory site as the Hub Transport Server.

When a message has an external destination, i.e. a recipient on the Internet, the message is sent from the Hub Transport Server to the "outside world." This may be via an Exchange Server 2010 Edge Transport Server in the DMZ, but the Hub Transport Server can also deliver messages directly to the Internet.

Optionally, the Hub Transport Server can be configured to deal with anti-spam and anti-virus functions. The anti-spam services are not enabled on a Hub Transport Server by default, since this service is intended to be run on an Edge Transport Service in the DMZ. Microsoft has supplied a script on every Hub Transport Server that can be used to enable their anti-spam services if necessary.

Anti-virus services can be achieved by installing the Microsoft Forefront for Exchange software. The anti-virus software on the Hub Transport Server will scan inbound and outbound SMTP traffic, whereas anti-virus software on the Mailbox Server will scan the contents of a Mailbox Database, providing a double layer of security.

Edge Server role

The Edge Server role was introduced with Exchange Server 2007, and provides an extra layer of message hygiene. The Edge Transport Server role is typically installed as an SMTP gateway in the network's DMZ. Messages from the Internet are delivered to the Edge Transport Server role and, after anti-spam and anti-virus services, the messages are forwarded to a Hub Transport Server on the internal network.

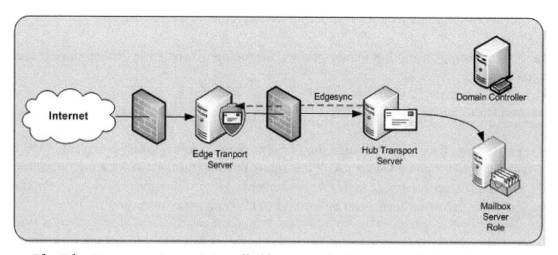

Figure 9:   The Edge Transport Server is installed between the Internet and the Hub Transport Server.

The Edge Transport Server can also provide the following services:

- Edge transport rules – like the transport rules on the Hub Transport Server, these rules can also control the flow of messages that are sent to, or received from the Internet when they meet a certain condition.

- Address rewriting – with address rewriting, the SMTP address of messages sent to, or received from, the Internet can be changed. This can be useful for hiding internal domains, for example, after a merger of two companies, but before one Active Directory and Exchange organization is created.

The Edge Transport Server is installed in the DMZ and cannot be a member of the company's internal Active Directory and Exchange Server 2010 organization. The Edge Transport Server uses the Active Directory Lightweight Directory Services (AD LDS) to store all information. In previous versions of Windows this service was called Active Directory Application Mode (ADAM). Basic information regarding the Exchange infrastructure is stored in the AD LDS, like the recipients and the Hub Transport Server which the Edge Transport Server is sending its messages to.

To keep the AD LDS database up to date, a synchronization feature called EdgeSync is used, which pushes information from the Hub Transport Server to the Edge Transport Server at regular intervals.

Unified Messaging Server role

The Exchange Server 2010 Unified Messaging Server role (see Figure 10) combines the mailbox database and both voice messages and email messages into one store. Using the Unified Messaging Server role it is possible to access all messages in the mailbox using either a telephone or a computer.

The phone system can be an IP based system or a "classical" analog PBX system although, in the latter case, a special Unified Messaging IP Gateway is needed to connect the two.

The Unified Messaging Server role provides users with the following features:

- Call Answering – this feature acts as an answering machine. When somebody cannot answer the phone, a personal message can be played after which a caller can leave a message. The message will be recorded and sent to the recipient's mailbox as an .mp3 file.

- Subscriber Access – sometimes referred to as "Outlook Voice Access." Using Subscriber Access, users can access their mailbox using a normal phone line and listen to their voicemail messages. It is also possible to access regular mailbox items like messages and calendar items, and even reschedule appointments in the calendar.

- Auto Attendant – using the Auto Attendant, it is possible to create a custom menu in the Unified Messaging system using voice prompts. A caller can use either the telephone keypad or his or her voice to navigate through the menu.

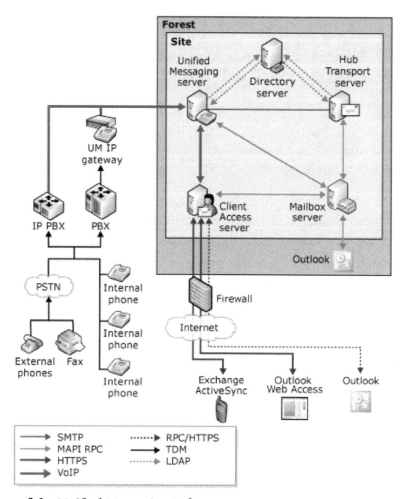

Figure 10: Overview of the Unified Messaging Infrastructure.

The Unified Messaging service installed on the Unified Messaging Server role works closely with the Microsoft Exchange Speech Engine Service.

This Speech Engine Service provides the following services:

- Dual Tone Multi Frequency (DTMF) also referred to as the touchtone (the beeps you hear when dialing a phone number or accessing a menu).

- Automatic Speech Recognition.

- Text-to-Speech service that's responsible for reading mailbox items and reading the voice menus.

The Unified Messaging Server role should be installed in an Active Directory site together with a Hub Transport Server, since this latter server is responsible for routing messaging to the Mailbox Servers. It should also have a fast connection to a Global Catalog server. If possible, the Mailbox Server role should be installed as close as possible to the Unified Messaging Server role, preferably in the same site and with a decent network connection.

Summary

Exchange Server 2010 is the new Messaging and Collaboration platform from Microsoft, and it has a lot of new, compelling features. The new High Availability, management and compliancy features make Exchange Server 2010 a very interesting product for the Exchange administrator. In fact, the new features in Exchange Server 2010 will generally result in *less* complexity, which is always a good thing!

The whole eBook can be downloaded from WWW.RED-GATE.COM/SPECIALS/EXCHANGE/ESA_EXCHANGE2010. HTM?UTM_SOURCE=SIMPLETALKARTICLE&UTM_MEDIUM=WEBLINK&UTM_CONTENT=2010EBOOKOCT09.

Implementing Windows Server 2008 File System Quotas

19 November 2009

by Ben Lye

··

File system quotas are used to restrict the amount of space users can consume, or to report on the space consumed by them. They are useful for reporting on those users or folders that are consuming large amounts of disk space on a file server. Ben Lye shows that file system quotas are quick and easy to set up, with three different methods available for configuring them.

··

Disk quotas have been available in Windows since Windows 2000 was released, and could be used by administrators to limit the amount of space users could use on an NTFS volume. Disk quotas are based on file ownership rather than folder structure and, because of this, they are not particularly useful in all situations. For example, if your server had a single storage volume and you need to apply quotas to different folders on the volume then disk quotas will not help.

File system quotas, which were first introduced in Windows Server 2003 R2, and are a part of the File Server role in Windows Server 2008 (and Windows Server 2008 R2), offer many benefits over disk quotas. With file system quotas we can set quotas for specific folders on the volume, we can use templates to ensure consistent application of quotas, and we can set quotas which are automatically applied to all sub-folders of a folder.

Additionally, file system quotas are useful, not just for limiting the amount of space users can consume, but also for reporting on space used – quotas can be set with so-called "soft" limits which are used for monitoring, rather than enforcing limits. This functionality can be extremely useful for quickly determining which users or folders are consuming large amounts of disk space on a file server.

Quota thresholds can be configured so that users or administrators receive notifications when quotas have been reached or are about to be reached. Multiple thresholds can be configured for individual quotas, and actions can include sending email messages, logging to the Windows event log, running commands or scripts, or generating storage reports.

In Windows Server 2008 file system quotas are managed with the File Server Resource Manager (FSRM) console (which is installed as a role service in the File Services role), the command line utility `dirquota`, or with Windows PowerShell using a COM API.

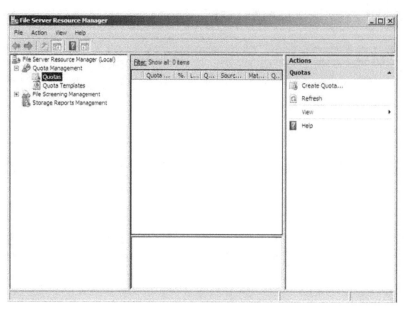

Figure: Windows Server 2008 File Server Resource Manager.

There are two kinds of quota available: hard quotas, which set a limit and enforce it, and soft quotas, which set a limit but only report on it. Soft quotas are useful for monitoring disk space use. Quotas are commonly applied using quota templates, which are a mechanism for easily applying the same quota settings to one or more folders. Quota templates are the recommended way to configure quotas and the FSRM (File Server Resource Manager) includes some example templates which cover a range of scenarios, including using both hard and soft quota types.

Before we start to configure quotas which will generate email messages, the quota File Server Resource Manager needs to be configured with an SMTP server and, optionally, the default administrator recipients, and the default "From" address.

Like all aspects of quota management, the FSRM settings can be applied using three different tools, and you can choose the method appropriate to your needs.

To configure FSRM using the FSRM console:

- Launch the File Server Resource Manager.

- Select the root node, labelled **File Server Resource Manager**.

- In the Action Pane click **Configure Options...**

- Enter an SMTP server and, if desired, configure the other settings.

- Click the **OK** button.

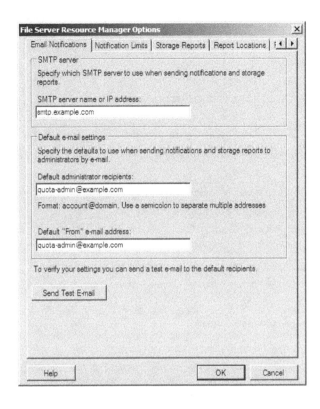

To configure FSRM using the command line:

• Open an elevated Command Prompt window.

• Enter the command: "dirquota admin options /From:quota-admin@example.com / AdminEmails:quota-admin@example.com /SMTP:smtp.example.com."

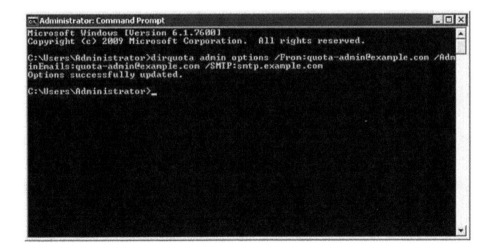

To configure FSRM using Windows PowerShell:

• Open Windows PowerShell.

• Enter these commands (or save them as a script and run it):

```
# Create a new COM object to access the FSRM settings
$fsrm = New-Object -com Fsrm.FsrmSetting

# Set the default administrators e-mail address
$fsrm.AdminEmail = "quota-admin@example.com"

# Set the from address
$fsrm.MailFrom = "quota-admin@example.com"

# Set the SMTP server
$fsrm.SmtpServer = "smtp.example.com"
```

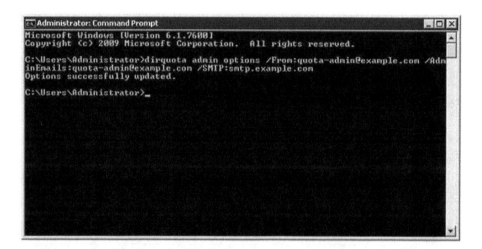

Quota Example – Home directories with a 5 GB limit

A common use of file system quotas is to put limits on the size of user's personal storage space (folders which are often referred to as home directories) on a file server. The requirements of this scenario are to limit the space each user can use to 5 GB, alert administrators when 90% of the quota has been reached, and automatically apply quotas to new home directories. The solution requires the implementation of new quota template and an auto apply quota.

Step 1: Create the new quota template

The first step is to create a new template, which we will use later to apply the quota to the file system. Using a template means we can easily make changes to all folders where we have applied the template quota settings. The template can be created using the FSRM, the **dirquota** command-line tool, or PowerShell, meaning you can choose the tool with which you feel comfortable and which fits most of your scenarios.

To create the new quota template using the FSRM:

- Launch the File Server Resource Manager.

- Expand **Quota Management ▸ Quota Templates**.

- In the **Action Pane** click **Create Quota Template**.

- Enter the template name and set the space limit.

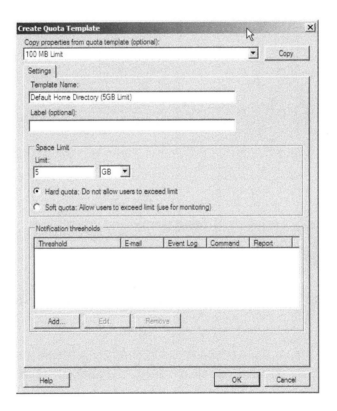

Note

*To set a soft quota (for monitoring only) check the **Soft Quota** radio button.*

- Click the **Add** button to add a notification threshold.

- Set the notification percentage to 90, check **Send e-mail to the following administrators**, and enter an appropriate destination email address. You can also customise the message text.

- Click the **OK** button twice.

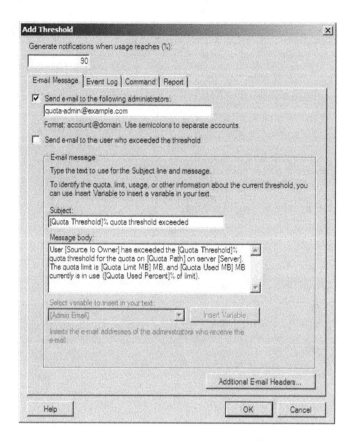

To create the new quota template using the **dirquota** command line utility:

- Open an elevated command prompt (or Windows PowerShell) window.

- Create a text file called notification.txt containing the text of the notification message.

- Enter this command:

```
dirquota Template Add /Template:"Default Home Directory (5GB Limit)" /Limit:5GB
/Type:Hard /Add-Threshold:90 /Add-Notification:90,M,notification.txt
```

```
Administrator: Command Prompt                                    _ □ X

Microsoft Windows [Version 6.1.7600]
Copyright (c) 2009 Microsoft Corporation.  All rights reserved.

C:\Users\Administrator>dirquota Template Add /Template:"Default Home Directory (
5GB Limit)" /Limit:5GB /Type:Hard /Add-Threshold:90 /Add-Notification:90,M,notif
ication.txt

Template successfully added.

C:\Users\Administrator>_
```

Note

*To set a soft quota (for monitoring only) change "/**Type:Hard**" to "/**Type:Soft**"*

To create the new quota using Windows PowerShell:

• Open Windows PowerShell.

• Enter these commands (or save them as a script and run it):

```
# Create a new COM object to access quota templates
$fqtm = New-Object -com Fsrm.FsrmQuotaTemplateManager

# Create a new template object
$template = $fqtm.CreateTemplate()

# Set the template's name
$template.Name = "Default Home Directory (5GB Limit)"

# Set the quota limit
$template.QuotaLimit = 5GB

# Set the quota type to hard limit (the flag for a hard limit is 0x100)
$template.QuotaFlags = $template.QuotaFlags -bor 0x100

# Add a quota threshold
$template.AddThreshold(90)
```

265

```
# Add a threshold e-mail action
$action = $template.CreateThresholdAction(90, 2)

# Set the e-mail message recipient
$action.MailTo = "[Admin Email]"

# Set the e-mail message subject
$action.MailSubject = "[Quota Threshold]% quota threshold exceeded"

# Set the e-mail message text
$action.MessageText = "User [Source Io Owner] has exceeded the [Quota
Threshold]% " + `
"quota threshold for the quota on [Quota Path] on server [Server]. The quota
limit " + `
"is [Quota Limit MB] MB, and " + ` "[Quota Used MB] MB currently is in use
([Quota " + `
"Used Percent]% of limit)."
```

Note

To set a soft quota (for monitoring only) change "$template.QuotaFlags = $template.QuotaFlags -bor 0x100" to "$template.QuotaFlags = $template.QuotaFlags -bxor 0x100" to disable the hard limit flag.

```
Windows PowerShell
Copyright (C) 2009 Microsoft Corporation. All rights reserved.

PS C:\> $fqtm = New-Object -com Fsrm.FsrmQuotaTemplateManager
PS C:\> $template = $fqtm.CreateTemplate()
PS C:\> $template.Name = "Default Home Directory (5GB Limit)"
PS C:\> $template.QuotaLimit = 5GB
PS C:\> $template.QuotaFlags = $template.QuotaFlags -bor 0x100
PS C:\> $template.AddThreshold(90)
PS C:\> $action = $template.CreateThresholdAction(90, 2)
PS C:\> $action.MailTo = "[Admin Email]"
PS C:\> $action.MailSubject = "[Quota Threshold]% quota threshold exceeded"
PS C:\> $action.MessageText = "User [Source Io Owner] has exceeded the [Quota Thresho
ld]% quota threshold " +
>> "for the quota on [Quota Path] on server [Server]. The quota limit is [Quota Limit
 MB] MB, and " + `
>> "[Quota Used MB] MB currently is in use ([Quota Used Percent]% of limit)."
>>
PS C:\> $template.Commit()
PS C:\>
```

Step 2: Create the quota

The next step is to use the new quota template to apply the quota to the file system.

In this example, we'll say that the home directories are all subfolders of C:\Home. Because we want any new home folders to automatically have the quota applied, we need to create an Auto apply Quota. Auto apply quotas are applied to all existing subfolders and any future folders.

To create the quota using the FSRM:

- Launch the File Server Resource Manager.

- Expand **Quota Management ▸ Quotas**.

- In the Action Pane click **Create Quota**.

- Enter the quota path and choose the appropriate template.

- Click the **Create** button.

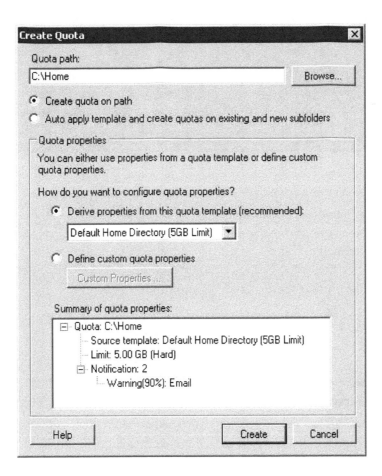

To create the quota using the **dirquota** command line tool:

- Open an elevated command prompt window.

- Create a text file called notification.txt containing the text of the notification message.

- Enter this command:

```
dirquota autoquota add /Path:C:\Home /SourceTemplate:"Default Home Directory (5GB
Limit).
```

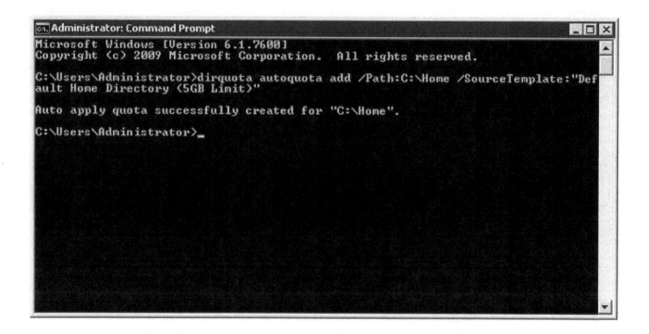

To create the quota using Windows PowerShell:

- Open Windows PowerShell

- Enter these commands (or save them as a script and run it):

```
# Create a new COM object to access quotas
$fqtm = New-Object -com Fsrm.FsrmQuotaManager

# Create the new quota
$quota = $fqtm.CreateAutoApplyQuota("Default Home Directory (5GB Limit)," "C:\
Home")

# Save the new quota
$quota.Commit()
```

```
Administrator: Windows PowerShell                                    _ □ X
Windows PowerShell
Copyright (C) 2009 Microsoft Corporation. All rights reserved.

PS C:\> $fqtm = New-Object -com Fsrm.FsrmQuotaManager
PS C:\> $quota = $fqtm.CreateAutoApplyQuota("Default Home Directory (5GB Limit)", "C:
\Home")
PS C:\> $quota.Commit()
PS C:\> _
```

Quota exceptions / folder-specific quotas

Naturally there will be occasions when a folder needs to be excluded from a template or auto apply quota. In these situations you can easily add a specific quota for that folder, to either increase the limit, or to disable the quota entirely.

To create the quota exception using the FSRM:

- Launch the File Server Resource Manager.

- Expand **Quota Management ▸ Quotas**.

- Select the folder you wish to make the exception for.

- In the Action Pane click **Edit Quota Properties...**

- Enter new limit for the quota.

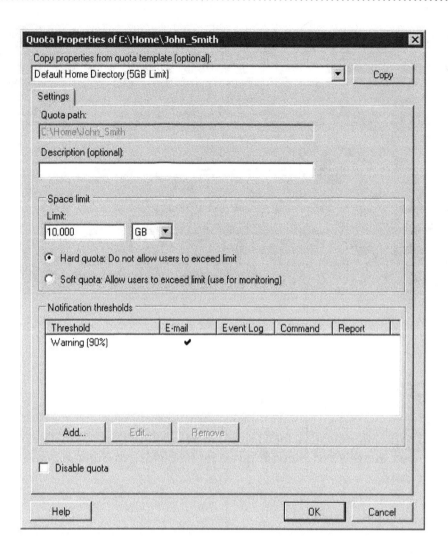

- Click **OK**.

Note

*Check the **Disable quota** box to disable the quota.*

To create the quota exception using the **dirquota** command line tool:

- Open an elevated command prompt window.

Enter the command:

```
"dirquota quota add /Path:C:\Home\John_Smith /SourceTemplate:"Default Home
Directory (5GB Limit)" /Limit:10GB /Overwrite"
```

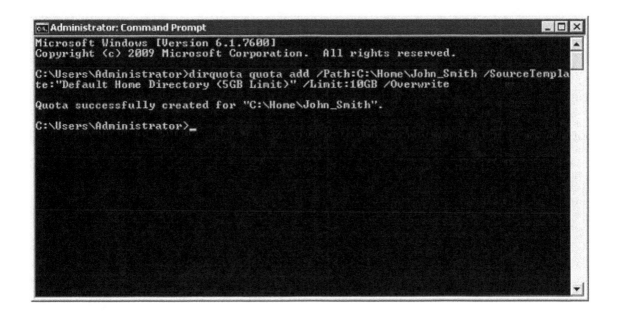

Note

*To disable the quota append the command with /**status:disabled**.*

To create the quota exception using Windows PowerShell:

* Open Windows PowerShell.

* Enter these commands (or save them as a script and run it):

```
# Create a new COM object to access quotas
$fqtm = New-Object -com Fsrm.FsrmQuotaManager

# Get the existing quota
$quota = $fqtm.GetQuota("C:\Home\John_Smith")

# Set the new quota limit
$quota.QuotaLimit = 10GB

# Save the quota
$quota.Commit()
```

Note

*To disable the quota, insert the line $**quota.QuotaFlags** = $**quota.QuotaFlags** -**bor 0x200** before saving the quota.*

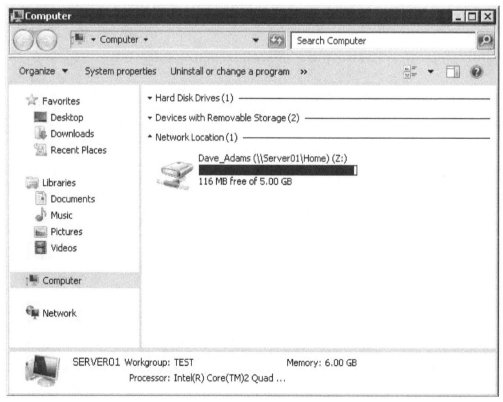

How quotas affect clients

When a client maps a network drive to a folder which has a hard quota applied, the size of the volume and the amount of available disk space shown is equal to the quota settings.

Figure: Mapped drive showing hard quota limit as volume size.

When a hard quota is met or exceeded clients will receive a message telling them that the volume is out of disk space.

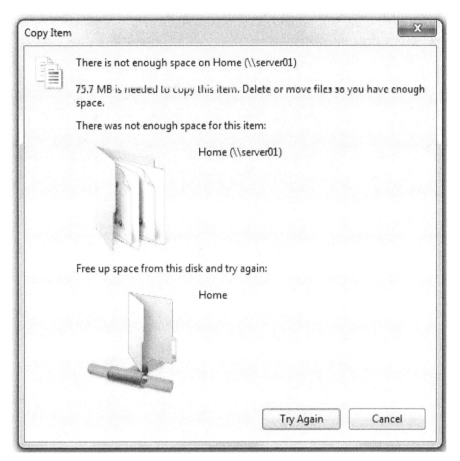

Figure: **Insufficient disk space message.**

Viewing quotas

Administrators can view hard and soft quotas using FSRM, and viewing quotas this way can be a quick method for finding large folders or large consumers of space.

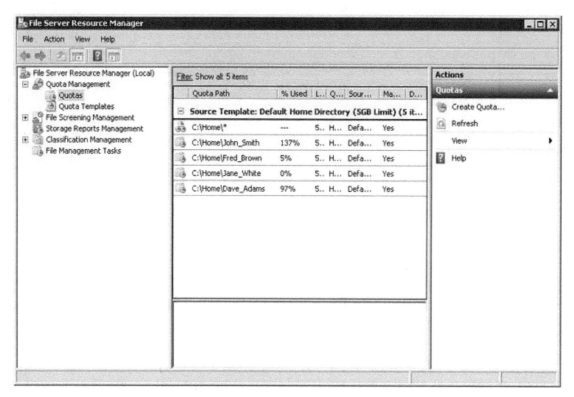

Figure: **Quotas in File Server Resource Manager.**

Summary

File system quotas are quick and easy to set up, with three different and flexible methods available for configuring them. Properly applied, they can be a good tool to help ensure efficient use of storage resources, a convenient countermeasure against storage waste, and a useful tool for reporting on storage utilisation. There is an I/O performance penalty for using quotas, but the benefits will probably outweigh the small performance cost.

More information about File Server Resource Manager is available in Microsoft TechNet:
HTTP://TECHNET.MICROSOFT.COM/EN-US/LIBRARY/CC771092%28WS.10%29.ASPX.
More information about the **dirquota** command line tool is also available in TechNet:
HTTP://TECHNET.MICROSOFT.COM/EN-US/LIBRARY/CC754836%28WS.10%29.ASPX.
More information about the COM API for working with FSRM is available in MSDN:
HTTP://MSDN.MICROSOFT.COM/EN-US/LIBRARY/BB972746%28VS.85%29.ASPX.

Implementing Cluster Continuous Replication: Part 2

19 November 2009

by Brien Posey

Cluster continuous replication (CCR) helps to provide a more resilient email system with faster recovery. It was introduced in Microsoft Exchange Server 2007 and uses log shipping and failover. Configuring Cluster Continuous Replication on a Windows Server 2008 requires different techniques to Windows Server 2003. Brien Posey explains all.

In Part 1 of this article, I showed you how to configure Windows to form a Majority Node Set Cluster. Although the procedure that I gave you works well, it is intended for use with Windows Server 2003. You can also host a clustered mailbox server on Windows Server 2008, but the procedure for creating the cluster is quite a bit different from what you saw in the first article. In this article, I want to show you how to create the required cluster on Windows Server 2008.

In the previous article, I spent a long time talking about the hardware requirements for building a cluster, and about the cluster planning process. This same information roughly applies to planning for a Windows Server 2008 cluster. You are still going to need two similar servers with two NICs installed. The requirements for the number of names and IP addresses that I covered in Part 1 also remain the same. Once again, I will be referring to the cluster node that is initially active as Node 1, and the node that initially acts as the passive node as Node 2.

Deploying the Failover Cluster feature

Before you can configure Windows 2008 Servers to act as clusters, you must install the Failover Cluster feature. To do so, begin by opening the Server Manager, and selecting the **Features** container. Click the **Add Features** link, and Windows will display a list of the various features that you can install. Select the **Failover Clustering** check box, as shown in Figure A, and click **Next**.

At this point, you will see a warning message telling you that a server restart will be required. You don't have to do anything to acknowledge the message, though. Just click the **Install** button to install the feature. When the installation process completes, click **Close** and reboot your server if necessary. Now, perform this procedure on your second cluster node.

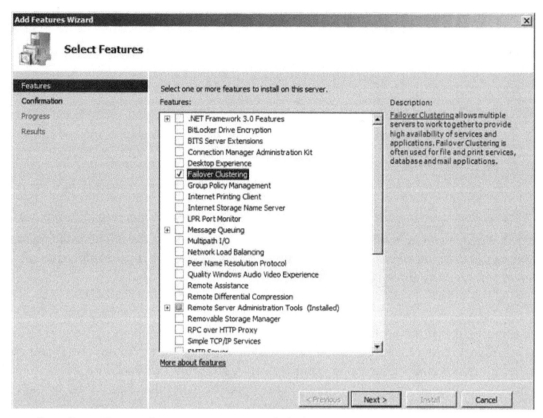

Figure A: Select the Failover Clustering option, and click Next.

The Failover Cluster management console

When we set up clustering in Windows Server 2003, we used a wizard for the configuration process, but we had to call the wizard from the command line via the Cluster command. Although the Cluster command still exists in Windows Server 2008, the individual commands that I showed you in Part 1 for invoking the cluster wizard no longer work. The good news is that you don't have to launch the wizard from the command line. In Windows Server 2008, Microsoft gives you an administrative tool that you can use to perform various clustering functions. You can access this tool by selecting the Failover Cluster Management command from the server's Administrative Tools menu.

Creating the cluster

You are now ready to create your cluster. As before, we are going to be creating an active and a passive node, which I will be referring to as Node 1 and Node 2. We can get started by opening the Failover Cluster Management Console on Node 1. When the console opens, click the **Create Cluster** link, found in the console's Management section. When you do, Windows will launch the Create Cluster Wizard.

Click **Next** to clear the wizard's Welcome dialog, and the wizard will prompt you to enter the names of the cluster nodes. Enter the name of Node 1, and click the **Add** button. Once Windows validates the server's name and adds it to the list, repeat the process by entering the name of Node 2 and clicking the **Add** button. When both cluster nodes have been added to the list, click **Next**.

You should now see a dialog warning you that Microsoft does not support the use of clusters unless the cluster configuration can be validated. You are now presented with the option of running a validation wizard. Choose the option labeled **Yes, When I Click Next, Run Configuration Validation Tests, and Then Return to the Process of Creating the Cluster**.

Click **Next**, and the wizard will take you to an introductory dialog, as shown in Figure B, that describes the validation process. Go ahead and click **Next** to move on. You are now asked if you want to run all of the validation tests, or if you want to select specific tests to run. Choose the option to run all of the tests and click **Next**. You should now see a screen that confirms the tests that you are about to perform. Click **Next** to begin the validation tests. When the validation tests complete, you may receive some warnings (particularly in regard to storage), but you should not receive any errors. Click **Finish**.

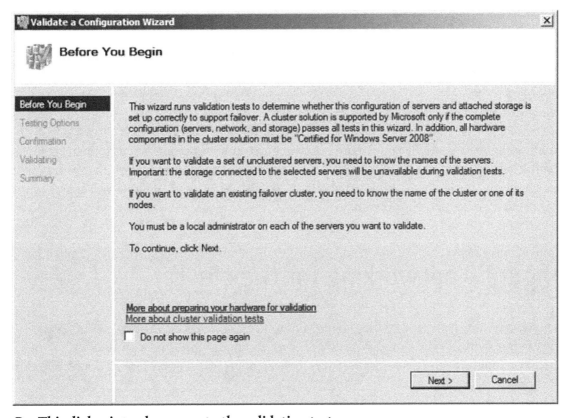

Figure B: This dialog introduces you to the validation tests.

Now that the validation is complete, Windows returns us to the Create Cluster wizard. At this point, you must enter the name and IP address that you wish to assign to the cluster, as shown in Figure C. Be sure to make note of which names and addresses you use, because you will need to reference them again later on.

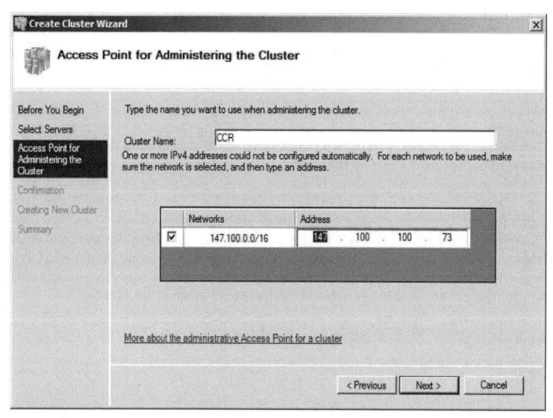

Figure C: Enter the name and IP address that you want to assign to the cluster.

After entering the cluster's name and IP address, click **Next**, and you should see a summary screen outlining the details of the cluster that you are creating. Take a moment to read the summary and make sure that everything is correct. Assuming that all is well, click **Next**, and Windows will create your cluster. When the process completes, click **Finish**.

Configuring networking for the cluster

Now that you have finished creating the cluster, you must make sure that the network adapters are configured properly for the cluster. Windows Server 2008 normally does a pretty good job of automatically configuring the network interfaces for you, but it is still important to double-check the configuration.

Navigate through the Failover Cluster Management Console to **Failover Cluster Management | <your cluster name> | Networks**. You should now see listings for both of your network segments, as shown in Figure D. They should be listed as Cluster Network 1 and Cluster Network 2 respectively.

Right-click on Cluster Network 1, and choose the **Properties** command from the shortcut menu. When you do, you will see a properties sheet for the connection. Make sure that this connection isn't the private segment that you are reserving for communication between cluster nodes.

Now, verify that the **Allow Cluster to Use this Connection** option is selected. You should also make sure that the **Allow Clients to Connect Through This Network** check box is selected. Click **OK** to close the Properties sheet.

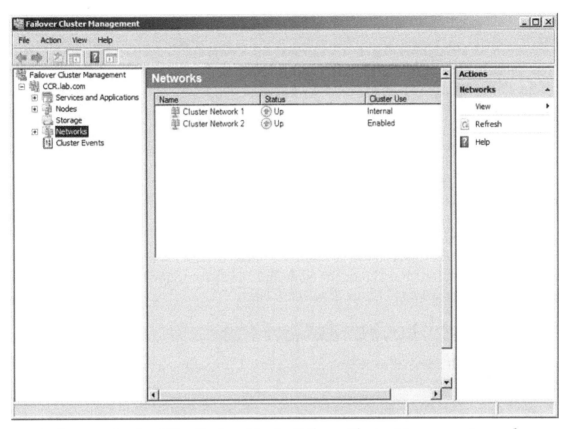

Figure D: Both networks should be displayed in the Failover Cluster Management console.

Now, right-click on Cluster Network 2, and select the **Properties** command from the resulting shortcut menu. This network connection should be the private segment that services the cluster nodes. Once again, you want to make sure that the **Allow Cluster to Use This Network Connection** option is selected. However, the **Allow Clients to Connect Through This Network** option should not be selected. Click **OK** to close the Properties sheet and return to the Failover Cluster Management Console.

Configure the node and file share majority quorum

In the previous article, I explained that a majority node set cluster has to have more than two nodes, because otherwise there is no node majority in a failover situation. Since CCR only works on two node clusters, though, we need to create a file share witness on our Hub Transport Server. This allows the file share that we create to take the place of the third cluster node.

The first thing that we need to do is to create a share on a Hub Transport Server that can be used as the file share witness. To do so, go to your Hub Transport Server, and open a Command Prompt window. You must now enter the following commands:

```
C:
CD \
MD FSM_DIR_CCR
Net Share FSM_DIR_CCR=C:\FSM_DIR_CCR /Grant:<cluster name>$, FULL
CACLS C:\FSM_DIR_CCR /G BUILTIN\Administrators:F <cluster name>$:F
```

In the code above, we are granting the cluster access to the FSM_DIR_CCR folder on our Hub Transport Server. You will notice that, every time I reference the cluster name, I am putting a dollar sign after the cluster name. The dollar sign tells Windows that we are granting access to a computer account rather than to a user account.

Now that we have prepared our Hub Transport Server, we need to configure the cluster quorum settings. To do so, go back to one of your cluster nodes and open the Failover Cluster Management Console. Once the console opens, right-click on the listing for your cluster, and select the **More Actions | Configure Cluster Quorum Settings** commands from the resulting shortcut menus.

At this point, Windows will launch the Configure Cluster Quorum wizard. Click **Next** to clear the wizard's Welcome screen, and you will be taken to a screen that asks you to select the quorum configuration that you want to use. Choose the **Node and File Share Majority (for clusters with special configurations)** option, as shown in Figure E, and click **Next**.

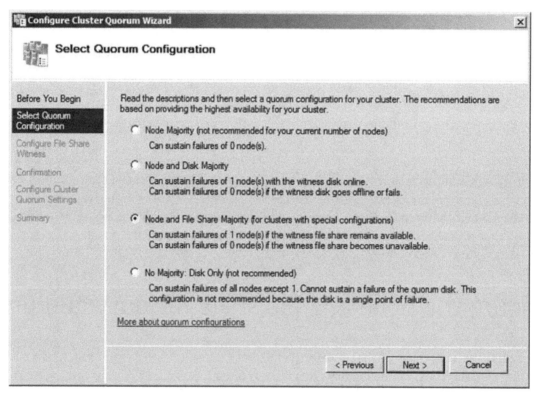

Figure E: Choose the **Node and File Share Majority (for clusters with special configurations) option.**

Choose the node and file share majority option

The next screen that you will encounter asks you for the path to the file share that you want the cluster to use. Enter the path to the share that you created earlier in UNC format (\\<your Hub Transport Server's name)\FSM_DIR_CCR). You can see an example of this in Figure F. Click **Next**, and the wizard will take you to a confirmation screen. Take a moment to make sure that the information that is presented on this screen appears correct, and then click **Next**. Windows will now configure the quorum settings. When the process completes, click **Finish**. Enter the path to the file share that you created.

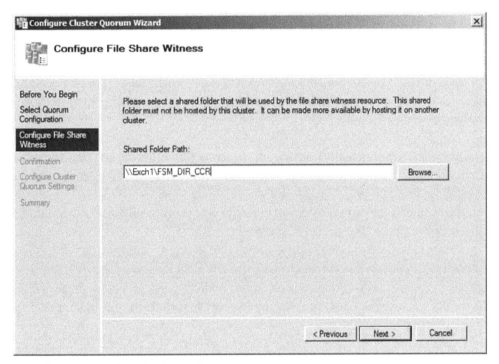

Figure F: Enter the path to the file share that you created.

Installing Exchange Server

Now that we have created our cluster, it is time to install Exchange Server 2007. There are a few things that you need to take into account before beginning the installation process.

For starters, I am assuming that both of your cluster nodes have the Exchange Server prerequisites installed. You should also keep in mind that the Clustered Mailbox Server role cannot coexist on a server with any other Exchange Server roles. This means that, as a minimum, you will already need to have an Exchange 2007 Hub Transport Server and client access server in place before deploying your clustered mailbox server.

One last thing that you need to keep in mind is that, if you are going to be installing Exchange onto a Windows Server 2008 based cluster, then you must install Exchange 2007 SP1 or higher. You can't install the RTM release and then upgrade to SP1 later on. You must start with SP1 or higher. If you are going to be installing Exchange onto Windows Server 2003, then you can install Exchange 2007 with or without the service pack, although it is always preferable to use the latest service pack.

Configuring the active node

The process for setting up the active node isn't all that different from configuring a typical mailbox server. Since we must begin by setting up the active node, you should perform these steps on Node 1.

Begin the installation process by double-clicking on Setup.exe. When the Exchange Server 2007 splash screen appears, click on **Step 4: Install Microsoft Exchange Server 2007 SP1**. This will cause Setup to launch the installation wizard.

The first screen that you will see is really nothing more than a welcome screen. You can just click **Next** to skip it. You will now be prompted to accept the server's license agreement. After doing so, click **Next**.

The next screen that you will encounter asks you whether you want to enable error reporting. This is really up to you. After you make your decision, click **Next**.

The following screen will ask you if you want to perform a typical Exchange Server installation or a custom installation. You can only configure a clustered mailbox server by performing a custom installation. Therefore, choose the **Custom Exchange Server Installation** option, and click **Next**.

You will now be prompted to select the Exchange Server roles that you want to install. Select the **Active Clustered Mailbox Role** check box, as shown in Figure G. When you do, all of the other options will be grayed out, because the clustered mailbox server role cannot coexist with any other Exchange Server role.

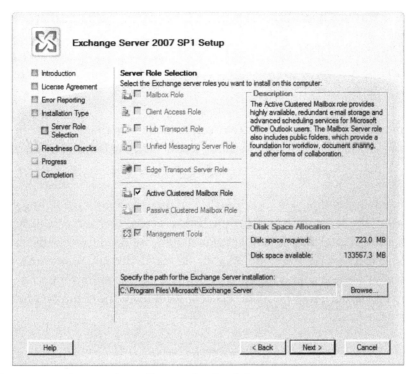

Figure G: Select the Active Clustered Mailbox Role check box.

Click **Next**, and Setup will ask you what type of clustered mailbox server you want to create. Choose the **Cluster Continuous Replication** option. Before continuing, you must enter the name that you want to assign to your clustered mailbox server, as shown in Figure H. This is the name that will be unique to Exchange Server.

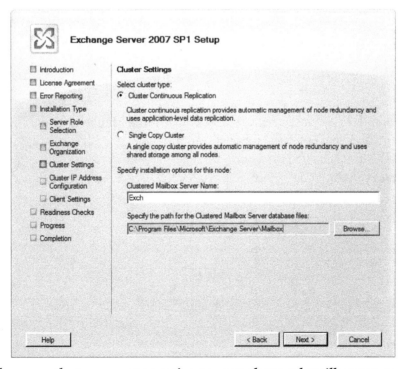

Figure H: Enter the name that you want to assign to your clustered mailbox server.

283

Choose the **Cluster Continuous Replication** option and then enter the name that you want to use for your clustered mailbox server.

Click **Next**, and you will be prompted to enter the server's IP address. You should enter the IP address that will be unique to Exchange Server.

Click **Next**, and Setup will perform a prerequisite check to make sure that all of the necessary components are in place. Assuming that the check succeeds, click the **Install** button to begin the installation process.

When the installation process completes, click **Finish**. You may see a message telling you that a restart is required before placing the server into production. If you receive such a message, just click **OK** to acknowledge it. Rather than restarting the server immediately, we need to stop the clustered mailbox server service, and move it to our passive node. As you will recall, though, we haven't actually installed Exchange onto the passive node yet. This makes things a little bit messy, but it isn't going to cause us any problems. My personal preference is to perform this operation from the command line, but you can use the Failover Clustering Console.

To stop the Clustered Mailbox Service, open the Exchange Management Shell, and enter the following command:

```
Stop-ClusteredMailboxServer <your clustered mailbox server name> -StopReason
Setup -Confirm:$False
```

Stopping the Clustered Mailbox Service allows our passive node to take ownership of the service. You can now safely restart Node 1. When the node restarts, though, Node 2 still has ownership of the clustered mailbox server. To fix this, open a command prompt window (not EMS) and enter the following command:

```
Cluster Group <your clustered mailbox server name> /Move:<the name of node 1>
```

Once the move has completed, we just need to start the Clustered Mailbox Service. To do so, open the Exchange Management Shell and enter the following command:

```
Start-ClusteredMailboxServer <your clustered mailbox server name>
```

Installing the passive node

Now that our active node is operational, we can install our passive node. Begin the installation process by double-clicking on Setup.exe. When the Exchange Server 2007 splash screen appears, click on **Step 4: Install Microsoft Exchange Server 2007 SP1**. This will cause Setup to launch the installation wizard.

The first screen that you will see is really a welcome screen. You can just click **Next** to skip it. You will now be prompted to accept the server's license agreement. After doing so, click **Next**.

The next screen asks you whether or not you want to enable error reporting. This is up to you. After you make your decision, click **Next**.

The following screen will ask you if you want to perform a typical Exchange Server installation or a custom installation. You can only configure a clustered mailbox server by performing a custom installation. Therefore, choose the **Custom Exchange Server Installation** option, and click **Next**.

You will now be prompted to select the Exchange Server roles that you want to install. Select the **Passive Clustered Mailbox Role**. Once again, the other roles will be grayed out to prevent you from selecting them, but the management tools will be installed automatically. You also have the option on this screen of specifying a database path. If you do enter a non-default path, it must match the path used by the active node.

Click **Next**, and Setup will perform a readiness check to make sure that the server has been properly prepared. When the readiness check completes, click the **Install** button. When the installation completes, click **Finish**.

Once again, you will receive a message telling you that your server needs to be restarted. This time, though, you can restart the server without having to do anything special, because this is a passive node.

Conclusion

In this article I have explained how to deploy Cluster Continuous Replication in a Windows Server 2008 environment. In Part 3, which you will find at WWW.SIMPLE-TALK.COM/SYSADMIN/EXCHANGE/ IMPLEMENTING-CLUSTER-CONTINUOUS-REPLICATION.-PART-3/ I will conclude the series by showing you various techniques for managing your cluster.

Active Directory Management with PowerShell in Windows Server 2008 R2

19 November 2009

by Jonathan Medd

One of the first things you notice with Windows Server 2008 R2 is that PowerShell 2.0 has become central to the admin function There is a powerful Active Directory module for PowerShell that contains a provider and cmdlets that are designed to allow you to manage Active Directory from the command line. Now, you can also use versions for previous versions of Windows Server.

Windows Server 2008 R2 and Windows 7 both ship with PowerShell 2.0 installed by default, a fact which begins to demonstrate how important a consistent command-line interface is becoming to Microsoft products. Which is why you as a sysadmin should be aware that, in order to excel as a Windows administrator in the 21st Century you will need to get to grips with PowerShell. Starting with products like Exchange Server 2007 and System Center Virtual Machine Manager (SCVMM), moving into the core OS with Windows 2008 R2 and Windows 7, other product groups are now providing PowerShell support with their latest releases.

Active Directory Domain Services in Windows Server 2008 R2 ships with PowerShell support via cmdlets and a provider; in addition the new Active Directory Administrative Center is built on top of Windows PowerShell technology. In this article, we will look at how you can use these new tools to more effectively manage your environment.

Active Directory scripting

When responsible for an Active Directory environment, the larger it becomes, the more likely it is you are going to want to use some kind of automation tool to manage it effectively, rather than being constantly clicking through a GUI interface to complete the same repetitive tasks. Even in environments of 100 users if you were tasked to provision 10 new users last thing on a Friday night, ready for a Monday morning, would you really want to click through the New User Wizard 10 times, and could you guarantee you wouldn't make any typing mistakes? Prior to the release of 2008 R2, some of the typical options for automating Active Directory with scripting were:

- VBScript. There are hundreds of examples on the Internet, one of the best resources being the Microsoft Script Center (HTTP://TECHNET.MICROSOFT.COM/EN-US/SCRIPTCENTER/DEFAULT.ASPX).

- PowerShell using ADSI, similar to how the VBScript examples are put together.

- PowerShell using .NET Directory Services Classes.

- PowerShell using Quest's Active Directory cmdlets (see WWW.QUEST.COM/POWERSHELL/ACTIVEROLES-SERVER.ASPX).

Each approach had its good and bad points, but going forward using the PowerShell cmdlets which ship as part of Active Directory in Windows Server 2008 R2 will be the route to take, given that this will be Microsoft's focus for administrators, rather than the examples above.

Active Directory Web Services

Introduced natively as part of Active Directory in Windows Server 2008 R2 is a new service, Active Directory Web Services. This technology permits remote management of any local directory service instance using web service protocols, which by default uses TCP port 9389. This service is included as part of an Active Directory Domain Services (or Active Directory Lightweight Directory Services) installation and is configured to run as an automatic service alongside the main ADDS service.

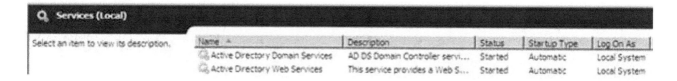

The Active Directory PowerShell cmdlets and provider which ship with Windows Server 2008 R2 are included as part of a module (modules are essentially the evolution of snap-ins from version 1 of PowerShell) and use this Web Service to manage Active Directory.

The good news for organisations who will not be immediately upgrading their Active Directory environments to Windows Server 2008 R2 and are currently running either Windows Server 2003 SP2 (or R2 SP2) or Windows Server 2008, with or without SP2, is that this Web Service has been made available as a Release To Web update (see WWW.MICROSOFT.COM/DOWNLOADS/DETAILS.ASPX?DISPLAYLANG=EN&FAMILYID=008940C6-0296-4597-BE3E-1D24C1CF0DDA). This means that you can have the same automation experience today with your current environment without going through the upgrade process for Active Directory which typically, for most organisations, involves significant planning and quite possibly cost.

There are some system requirements for this downlevel release which you should be aware of before you go diving straight in:

- .NET Framework 3.5 with SP1 must be installed on the Windows Server 2003 or 2008 Domain Controller.

- PowerShell 2.0 for Windows Server 2003 or 2008 must be installed, it's available from Knowledge Base (KB) article 968929 (HTTP://SUPPORT.MICROSOFT.COM/KB/968929).

- For Windows Server 2003 and 2008 based Domain Controllers, you must download and install the hotfix that is described in KB article 969166 (HTTP://SUPPORT.MICROSOFT.COM/KB/969166).

- For Windows Server 2003& based Domain Controllers, you must download and install the hotfix that is described in KB article 969429 (HTTP://SUPPORT.MICROSOFT.COM/KB/969429).

- For Windows Server 2008 based Domain Controllers without SP2, you must download and install the hotfix that is described in KB article 967574 (HTTP://SUPPORT.MICROSOFT.COM/KB/967574/).

Note that it is not possible to install the Active Directory module on these downlevel servers and you will, instead, require a Windows Server 2008 R2 or Windows 7 instance to remotely manage these systems with the Active Directory module. Whilst it is not a requirement that you install the Web Service on every single downlevel Domain Controller, you may run into issues if you do not give enough coverage across your Domain Controllers. The majority of the Active Directory cmdlets, though, do include a **Server** parameter which allows you to specify a particular Domain Controller to connect to.

Getting started

Once you have the Active Directory Web Service installed, either as part of a native Windows Server 2008 R2 installation, or using one of the downlevel versions as described above, you can start to manage Active Directory with the PowerShell module. To use this module, you can either Remote Desktop to connect to a Domain Controller in your environment or, more typically (and also better practice), use tools on your management workstation.

To do this from a Windows 7 based workstation you obviously already have PowerShell 2.0 installed by default. You should also install the Microsoft Remote Server Administration Tools (RSAT) for Windows 7 (WWW.MICROSOFT.COM/DOWNLOADS/DETAILS.ASPX?FAMILYID=7D2F6AD7-656B-4313-A005-4E344E43997D&DISPLAYLANG=EN). Amongst the many tools available in this package for remotely managing Windows Server is the Active Directory PowerShell module. After installation of RSAT the feature can be turned on by navigating to **Control Panel**, **Programs and Features**, **Turn Windows Features On** or **Off**.

The next step is to open a PowerShell session and use the `Import-Module` cmdlet to enable the use of the ActiveDirectory module. If this is something you would regularly use on your management workstation then it would be well worth your while to add this line to your PowerShell profile so that this module is available to you in every session without having to type the command `Import-Module ActiveDirectory`.

```
Windows PowerShell
Windows PowerShell
Copyright (C) 2009 Microsoft Corporation. All rights reserved.

PS C:\Users\Jonathan> Import-Module ActiveDirectory
```

Active Directory provider

Windows PowerShell 1.0 shipped with a number of providers which gave you access to navigate and update data stores, such as the file system or the registry in the Windows OS. Some other products also lend themselves to the concept of a provider and, in Windows Server 2008 R2, the Active Directory module ships with a provider. This provider allows you to traverse and update Active Directory just as if you were using the old style command prompt to navigate the Windows file system.

After importing the ActiveDirectory module, running the cmdlet `Get-PSProvider` will display the list of providers available to you on the system.

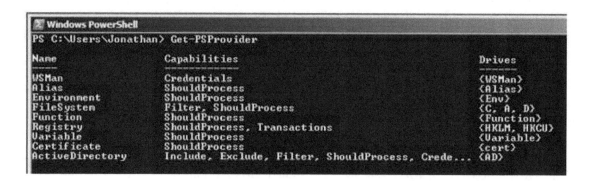

To begin you can use the familiar **cd** (which is an alias in PowerShell for **Set-Location**) to change your location to that of the Active Directory hierarchical navigation system.

You can use other familiar commands to navigate your way around and make changes. We can use the well-known **dir** to show us what is available. Then **cd 'DC=test,DC=local'** to start exploring the domain and then **dir** again will give a well-known view to that seen when first opening the Active Directory Users and Computers GUI tool.

If we then drill down further into the **Users** OU below the **Sales** OU we can observe some user accounts again by using **dir**.

This time we would like to update the Description field for the Joe Bloggs user account to read "Marketing Manager." To do that, we can use the `Set-ItemProperty` cmdlet with the path to the object we wish to change and the values we wish to set:

```
Set-ItemProperty -Path "CN=Joe Bloggs" -Name Description -value "Marketing
Manager"
```

We can then read this property back with the `Get-ItemProperty` cmdlet:

```
Get-ItemProperty -Path "CN=Joe Bloggs" -Name Description
```

Or in a GUI view:

Active Directory cmdlets

There are 76 cmdlets which make up the Active Directory module in Windows Server 2008 R2. You can view details of them via the Get-Command cmdlet and specifying the module of interest:

```
Get-Command -Module ActiveDirectory
```

The best way to learn about what each one does is to check them out in your test environment, and also use the built-in PowerShell help documentation via the Get-Help cmdlet.

For example, Get-Help Get-ADUser -Full will give you detailed information about the cmdlet and how you should go about using it.

> **Tip**
>
> *I often find using the* **-Examples** *parameter of the* **Get-Help** *cmdlet to be a great kick start to learning how a cmdlet works; rather than wade through the text help you can instantly see how you might use it via some examples.*

So let's check out some of these cmdlets.

Creating user accounts

Earlier in the article, we talked about how, when creating even a small number of users, repeatedly working through an individual wizard for each one could be a dull task and prone to consistency mistakes. Let's say the HR department supplies you with a CSV file containing information about ten new users and needs you to create these accounts ASAP before Monday.

	A	B	C	D	E	F	G
1	Name	SamAccountName	Description	Department	EmployeeID	Path	Enabled
2	John Smith	john.smith	Sales Manager	Sales	45896	ou=users,ou=sales,dc=test,dc=local	$true
3	Jane Bloggs	jane.bloggs	Sales Director	Sales	45897	ou=users,ou=sales,dc=test,dc=local	$true
4	Freddie Montana	freddie.montana	Sales Assistant	Sales	45898	ou=users,ou=sales,dc=test,dc=local	$true
5	Jo Clark	jo.clark	Administrator	Sales	45899	ou=users,ou=sales,dc=test,dc=local	$true
6	Mark Brown	mark.brown	Account Manager	Sales	45900	ou=users,ou=sales,dc=test,dc=local	$true
7	Anne Wilson	anne.wilson	Marketing Manager	Marketing	45901	ou=users,ou=marketing,dc=test,dc=local	$true
8	George Maker	george.maker	Marketing Director	Marketing	45902	ou=users,ou=marketing,dc=test,dc=local	$true
9	Lisa Taylor	lisa.taylor	Marketing Assistant	Marketing	45903	ou=users,ou=marketing,dc=test,dc=local	$true
10	Joanne Martin	joanne.martin	Administrator	Marketing	45904	ou=users,ou=marketing,dc=test,dc=local	$true
11	Clive Mason	clive.mason	Administrator	Marketing	45905	ou=users,ou=marketing,dc=test,dc=local	$true

For simplicity's sake, we'll keep it to a few basic properties like **Name** and **Description**, though of course you could, and normally would, have significantly more. Let's also say, to make your life easier, you've added a few extra columns of your own like the **SamAccountName** and the **Path** (OU) where you would like the account to be created.

We can take of advantage of a standard PowerShell cmdlet `Import-CSV` which will read in a standard CSV file and create a set of objects based on the data inside the file. We can then send the results of this cmdlet down the pipeline to the `New-ADUser` cmdlet from the ActiveDirectory module and create the ten accounts in a matter of seconds.

```
Import-CSV C:\scripts\users.csv | New-ADUser
```

It really is as simple as that and now you can also leave early on that Friday night like everyone else! Some of the results of those commands are shown below, nicely created in the OU specified in the CSV file.

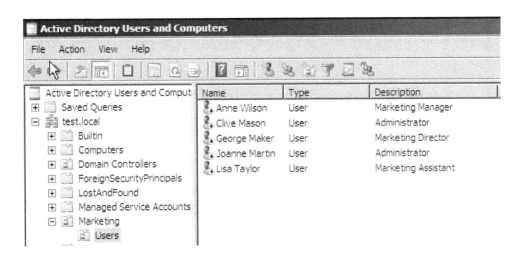

You might be wondering how we made the leap from the information specified in the CSV to the `New-ADUser` cmdlet without having to specify any parameters with this cmdlet. In fact you could create a new user account with something like this:

```
New-ADUser -Name "John Smith" -SamAccountName "john.smith" -Description "Sales
Manager" -Department "Sales" -EmployeeID "45896" -Path "ou=users,ou=sales,
dc=test,dc=local" -Enabled $true
```

We have actually taken advantage of something known as "Pipeline Parameter Binding." Since we gave the columns in the CSV file the same names as the parameters of the New-ADUser cmdlet and these parameters "Accept Pipeline Input ByPropertyName" PowerShell is clever enough to match them up and use them. It's almost as if someone has thought to try and make your administrator life just that little bit easier.

Administering groups

Another frequent maintenance task for the Active Directory administrator is the upkeep of groups and, in particular, membership of them. Let's take the scenario of the newly created Marketing user accounts and a request to add all of them to the "Marketing Application" group which is used to provide access to one of their main tools.

Again you could do that through Active Directory Users and Computers, edit the membership of the "Marketing Application" group and manually enter all of their names to add them to the group. Or you could be smart, use the Get-ADUser cmdlet with a filter to select those users, pipe the results to the standard PowerShell cmdlet ForEach-Object and then use the Add-ADGroupMember cmdlet to populate the group. OK, it might not make that big a difference for only five users, but imagine if that was five thousand.

```
Get-ADUser -filter * -SearchBase "ou=users,ou=marketing,dc=test,dc=local" |
ForEach-Object {Add-ADGroupMember -Identity 'Marketing Application' -Members $_}
```

Note

The $_ at the end of that command refers to the "current object in the pipeline", i.e. imagine it cycling through each of those users in the filter and substituting that user account for $_ each time.

The results of those cmdlets displayed below in the GUI view of the group.

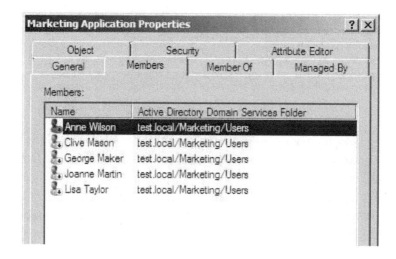

Fine-grained password policies

You may be aware that in Windows Server 2008 a new feature was introduced, whereby you were able to add multiple password policies into a single domain. In previous versions of Windows Server, there was a restriction of a single password policy in a domain and, consequently, many organisations ended up deploying multiple domains just for that reason.

So a great new feature, but unfortunately the management tool for configuring these new password policies was – wait for it – ADSI Edit! Whilst there were a number of freeware tools available around the time 2008 shipped which made this easier for the administrator, there are now out-of-the-box PowerShell cmdlets with Windows Server 2008 R2 to help you manage these policies.

The first cmdlet deals with the Default Domain Password Policy Get-ADDefaultDomainPasswordPolicy, and will retrieve information about the policy which will apply to all users unless there are any fine-grained policies.

```
Administrator: Windows PowerShell
PS C:\Windows\system32> Get-ADDefaultDomainPasswordPolicy

ComplexityEnabled           : True
DistinguishedName           : DC=test,DC=local
LockoutDuration             : 00:40:00
LockoutObservationWindow    : 00:20:00
LockoutThreshold            : 0
MaxPasswordAge              : 10.00:00:00
MinPasswordAge              : 1.00:00:00
MinPasswordLength           : 8
objectClass                 : {domainDNS}
objectGuid                  : 5e9a036b-e89a-4b35-97e9-1bd049454405
PasswordHistoryCount        : 24
ReversibleEncryptionEnabled : False
```

There's an equivalent Set-ADDefaultDomainPasswordPolicy which will allow you to make changes to any of the above settings.

You could, though, have done all of this through Group Policy Editor. The real gains come from being able to create and manage a Fine-Grained Password Policy. To create a new fine-grained password policy called "Standard Users PSO" and policy settings defined as per the parameter values, use the code below.

```
New-ADFineGrainedPasswordPolicy -Name "Standard Users PSO" -Precedence
500 -ComplexityEnabled $true -Description "Standard Users Password
Policy" -DisplayName "Standard Users PSO" -LockoutDuration "0.00:12:00"
-LockoutObservationWindow "0.00:15:00" -LockoutThreshold 10
```

In the above example the Lockout parameters should be specified in the format Day.Hour:Minutes:Seconds, i.e. LockoutDuration has been set to 12 minutes.

Fine-grained password policies are applied to Users or Groups so, to apply the **Standard Users PSO** policy to the **Marketing Users** group, the `Add-ADFineGrainedPasswordPolicySubject` cmdlet is available to you. To make this change, use:

```
Add-ADFineGrainedPasswordPolicySubject 'Standard Users PSO' -Subjects 'Marketing
Users'
```

Of course you may now have more than one fine-grained password policy.

To view details of them all, use:

```
Get-ADFineGrainedPasswordPolicy -Filter {name -like "*"}
```

and you will see results similar to those shown below so that you can compare them.

Consequently, some users may have more than one policy applied to them, so how do you tell which policy affect them?

- If a user is directly linked to a particular policy, then that policy wins. Generally, it is bad practice to link a policy directly to a user; groups should be used for more effective management.

- If a user is a member of different groups which each have different policies applied to them, then the policy with the lowest **Precedence** value will win.

- If there are no fine-grained policies created, then the **Default Domain Policy** will apply.

The best way to determine what policy will be applied to a user is to use the `Get-ADUserResultantPasswordPolicy` cmdlet.

For example, George Maker is in the **Marketing Users** and **High Security Users** groups, both of which have different fine-grained password policies applied to them. By running the command:

```
Get-ADUserResultantPasswordPolicy -Identity 'George.Maker'
```

we will be given the resulting answer of which password policy will be applied to him. In this case, it's the **High Security Users PSO** which is applied, because it had the lowest precedence value.

FSMO roles

In an Active Directory environment, all Domain Controllers are equal, although some are more equal than others. There are five roles known as Flexible Single Master Operation roles which typically will live on different domain controllers.

- Domain Naming Master.

- Schema Master.

- Infrastructure Master.

- PDCEmulator.

- RID Master.

You can use the Get-ADForest and Get-ADDomain cmdlets to determine which Domain Controllers are holding these roles. (In my test environment there is only one DC, but you get the idea.)

Whilst you could use the Netdom.exe command line tool to obtain the same information, you would need to use an alternative command line tool Ntdsutil.exe, with a different style and syntax, to transfer a FSMO role between Domain Controllers.

Consequently, by using the `Move-ADDirectoryServerOperationMasterRole` cmdlet to transfer FSMO roles between Domain Controllers, the administrator using the PowerShell module benefits from a consistent command line experience.

```
Move-ADDirectoryServerOperationMasterRole -Identity "2008R2DC2"
 -OperationMasterRole PDCEmulator,RIDMaster
```

Further information

If you want to know more, the best place to look is the Active Directory PowerShell Blog at HTTP://BLOGS.MSDN.COM/ADPOWERSHELL/DEFAULT.ASPX maintained by the team who put the module together. Also, I have made an Active Directory PowerShell Quick Reference Guide which you might find useful for getting started or as a handy reference to keep by your desk. You can find it at WWW.JONATHANMEDD.NET/2009/10/ACTIVE-DIRECTORY-POWERSHELL-QUICK-REFERENCE-GUIDE.HTML.

Summary

Windows Server 2008 R2 ships with both PowerShell 2.0 and an Active Directory module containing a provider and cmdlets to enable you to manage Active Directory from the command line. This module has also now been made available for downlevel versions of Windows Server, making it more readily accessible to those who might not be in a position to upgrade their Active Directory environments just yet.

It is very well worth spending some time with this module, even if you're just getting to grips with the basics; it will help make you a better and more effective administrator of Active Directory.

Upgrade Exchange 2003 to Exchange 2010: Part 1

11 December 2009

by Jaap Wesselius

In this article, the first of two in which Jaap describes how to move from Exchange Server 2003 straight to Exchange Server 2010, he shows what is required before moving mailboxes from Exchange Server 2003 to Exchange Server 2010. He shows how to upgrade Active Directory, install both Exchange Server 2010 and certificates, and set up the Public Folder replication. Details of the second article can be found at the end of this article.

Microsoft released Exchange Server 2010 in October 2009, and this new version of Exchange Server contains a lot of compelling new features such as the new High Availability, the facility to store your Exchange databases on JBOD (Just a Bunch of Disks), the archiving option and the new Outlook Web App. Oh, and do not forget the new Windows Mobile 6.5 and its new mail client.

If you have an Exchange Server 2003 environment, you may want to skip Exchange Server 2007 and move directly to Exchange Server 2010. The easiest way to achieve this is to integrate Exchange Server 2010 into the existing Exchange Server 2003 environment, a so called intra-organizational migration. This is also known as transitioning from Exchange Server 2003 to Exchange Server 2010. But what does it take, and what issues might arise? This is Part 1 of a series of two about moving from Exchange Server 2003 to Exchange Server 2010, and in this document I'll show you what's needed before you start moving mailboxes from Exchange Server 2003 to Exchange Server 2010.

Exchange Server 2003

Suppose we have a fictitious company called Inframan, which is a consulting company specializing in bridges, tunnels, buildings, etc. Inframan has approximately 500 employees; 50 employees are working in the office, and 450 employees are working "in the field." Employees within the office have their own desktop which connects to an Exchange 2003 Mailbox Server using Outlook 2003 and Outlook 2007. Employees outside the office connect to the office using their company laptops with Outlook 2007 and Outlook Anywhere, and with Windows Mobile devices. When needed, they can use their PC at home to use Outlook Web Access to access their mailbox. Typical usage profile is "light," and approximately 25 messages are received and 10 messages are sent per day, per user. Behind the firewall is an ISA Server 2006 acting as a reverse proxy to publish all Exchange Services to the Internet. Inframan's environment will look something like the following figure.

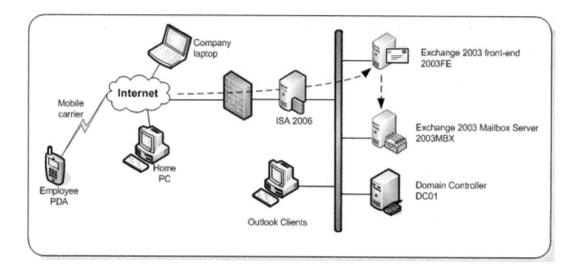

Inframan is using only one namespace for accessing all services from the Internet: webmail.inframan.nl. This is used for Outlook Web Access, Outlook Anywhere and Windows Mobile devices.

Recently, Inframan has been thinking about upgrading to Exchange Server 2007, but decided to move directly to Exchange Server 2010.

Coexistence with Exchange Server 2010

Exchange Server 2010 can easily coexist in an Exchange Server 2003 organization, as long as the Exchange Server 2010 prerequisites below are met.

- The Active Directory forest needs to be in Windows Server 2003 forest functionality mode.

- All domains that contain Exchange recipients need to be in Windows Server 2003 domain native mode.

- The Global Catalog Servers and the Active Directory Schema Master need to be at a minimum level of Windows Server 2003 SP1 (which equals to Windows Server 2003 R2).

- The Exchange 2003 organization needs to be running in "native mode."

Be careful when upgrading your Active Directory Domain Controllers, since not all versions are supported to run with Exchange Server 2003. For a complete overview check the Microsoft Technet Site at HTTP://TECHNET.MICROSOFT.COM/EN-US/LIBRARY/EE338574.ASPX.

Inframan will build two new Exchange Server 2010 servers, one combined Hub Transport Server / Client Access Server, and one dedicated Mailbox Server. These servers will be installed in the same Windows Server 2003 Active Directory domain as the Exchange Server 2003 organization. This will greatly improve the ease of moving mailbox from Exchange Server 2003 to Exchange Server 2010.

Moving from Exchange Server 2003 to Exchange Server 2010 in the same Active Directory forest is called transitioning. Building a new Active Directory forest with a new Exchange Server 2010 organization and moving mailboxes from the old Active Directory to the new Active Directory is called migrating.

The interim messaging environment, where both Exchange Server 2003 and Exchange Server 2010 coexist in the same Active Directory domain will look like this:

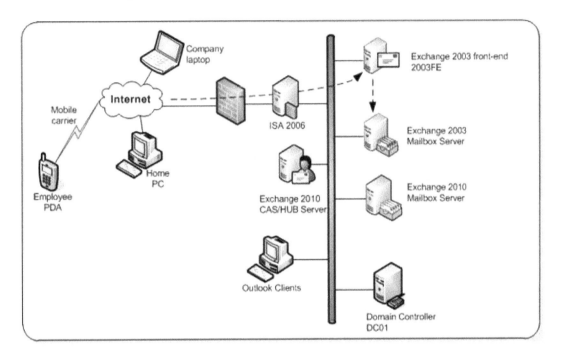

In Exchange Server 2007, Internet clients could connect to the Exchange Server 2007 Client Access Server while the mailbox was still on Exchange Server 2003. The Client Access Server retrieves the data out of the mailbox and sends it back to the Internet client. In Exchange Server 2010, this has changed. When a client connects to Exchange Server 2010, it actually connects to the Exchange Server 2010 Client Access Server and, if the mailbox is still on the Exchange Server 2003 Mailbox Server, then the client is redirected to the Exchange Server 2003 front-end server. This front-end server then handles the connection request. This automatically means the namespaces of the Exchange environment will change. For Inframan this means that the following namespaces are used:

HTTPS://WEBMAIL.INFRAMAN.NL – this is used by all Internet clients that connect to the Exchange environment. This name is not different than in the Exchange Server 2003 namespace, but it will now point to the Exchange Server 2010 Client Access Server.

HTTPS://AUTODISCOVER.INFRAMAN.NL – this is used by Outlook 2007 and (Outlook 2010) clients for autodiscover purposes.

HTTPS://LEGACY.INFRAMAN.NL – this will be the new namespace for the Exchange Server 2003 front-end server. This automatically means that the namespace for the Exchange Server 2003 front-end server is going to change!

The servers that will hold the Exchange Server 2010 server roles have the following prerequisites:

- The servers need to be running on Windows Server 2008 or Windows Server 2008 R2.

- .NET framework 3.5 with SP1 needs to be installed.

- PowerShell 2.0 needs to be installed.

- Office 2007 Filter packs needs to be installed for the Hub Transport Server role and the Mailbox Server role.

Make sure, after installing Windows on the servers, that they are up to date with the latest hotfixes and service packs.

The first step for Exchange Server 2010 Server is to upgrade the Active Directory schema to contain the Exchange Server 2010 extensions. This is achieved by using the Exchange Server 2010 setup application followed by a number of parameters:

Setup.com /PrepareLegacyExchangePermissions – Exchange Server 2003 uses the Recipient Update Service to stamp the user with the appropriate Exchange attributes during provisioning. This is replaced in Exchange Server 2010 by Email Address Policies. The /PrepareLegacyExchangePermissions parameter changes security settings so that both the Recipient Update Service and Email Address Policies can coexist in the same Active Directory.

Setup.com /PrepareSchema – this command upgrades the Active Directory schema to include the Exchange Server 2010 extensions. This can be checked by using ADSI Edit and checking the value of the UpperRange parameter of the CN=ms-Exch-Schema-Version-Pt object in the Schema. This should have one of the following values:

Value	Corresponding Exchange version
6870	Exchange Server 2003 RTM
6936	Exchange Server 2003 service pack 2
10628	Exchange Server 2007 RTM
11116	Exchange Server 2007 service pack 1
14622	Exchange Server 2007 service pack 2
14622	Exchange Server 2010 RTM

Note that the value is the same in Exchange Server 2007 Service Pack 2 and in Exchange Server 2010 RTM – this is because Exchange Server 2007 Service Pack 2 will install the Exchange Server 2010 schema extensions.

Setup.com /PrepareAD – this command upgrades the Exchange organization, which is stored in the configuration partition in Active Directory to support Exchange Server 2010. In Exchange Server 2003, information is stored in the "First Administrative Group" or perhaps more if you created additional Administrative Groups. The Exchange Server 2010 setup application will create a new Administrative Group called "Exchange Administrative Group (FYDIBOHF23SPDLT)" where all Exchange Server 2010 configuration information is stored. This will be visible in the Exchange Server 2003 System Manager, as in the figure below.

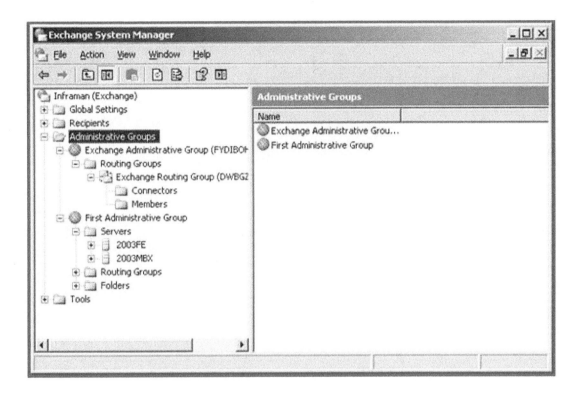

Setup.com /PrepareDomain – this is the last step in preparing the Active Directory, and will create all necessary groups in the domain being prepared.

When Active Directory is fully prepared, we can continue with installing the first Exchange Server 2010 server in the environment. For our example, this has to be the combined Hub Transport and Client Access Server. Start the graphical setup program (setup.exe) and download the Language File bundle if needed. If you select **Install only languages from the DVD**, only the language setting of your DVD (for example English or French) will be available. This is used not only for the language of the Exchange Server, but also the available language settings for the clients being used.

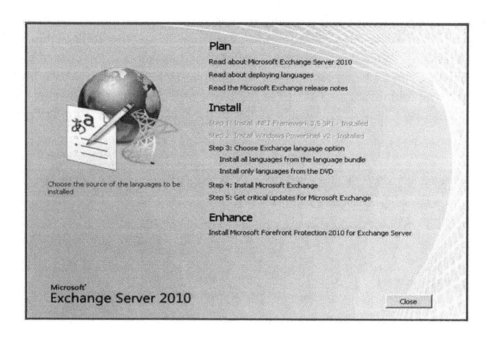

During the installation of the combined Hub Transport and Client Access Server, a so-called "custom setup" will be used. This means we can select which server roles will be installed. In the Inframan example the following needs to be selected during setup (see following diagram).

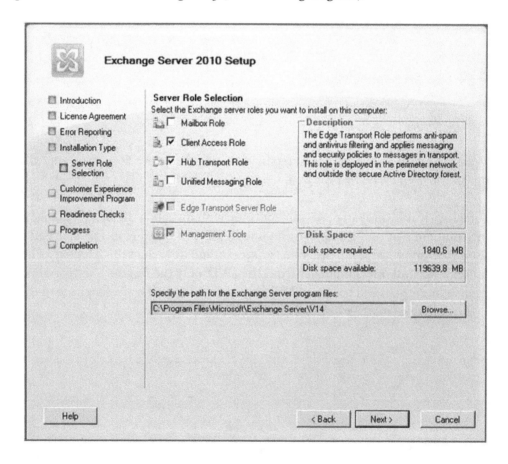

When continuing the setup application, a window will be shown asking if this Client Access Server is Internet facing and, if so, what the external domain will be. This is an important step, because it configures the Client Access Server automatically with the appropriate settings. Check the **The Client Access server role will be Internet-facing** option and enter the external domain name. This is *webmail.inframan.nl* in our example.

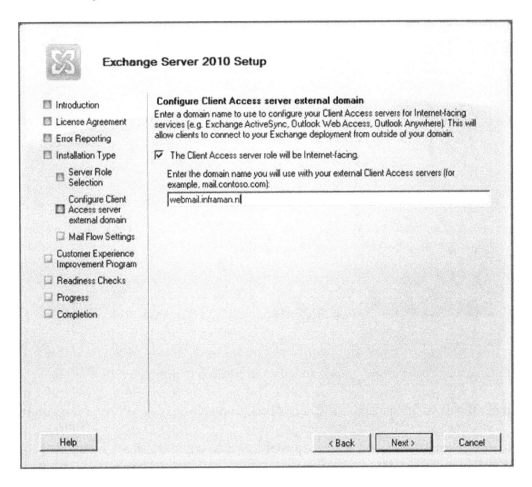

Exchange Server 2003 uses Routing Groups to determine the proper way to route messages, while Exchange Server 2010 uses Active Directory sites for routing. These are not compatible with each other, so a legacy Routing Group Connector will be created within Exchange Server 2010. This legacy connector connects Exchange Server 2010 with Exchange Server 2003 so messages can be sent between the two Exchange versions. During setup of the first Hub Transport Server, an Exchange Server 2003 Hub Server needs to be selected. This is the server the legacy Routing Group Connector will connect to.

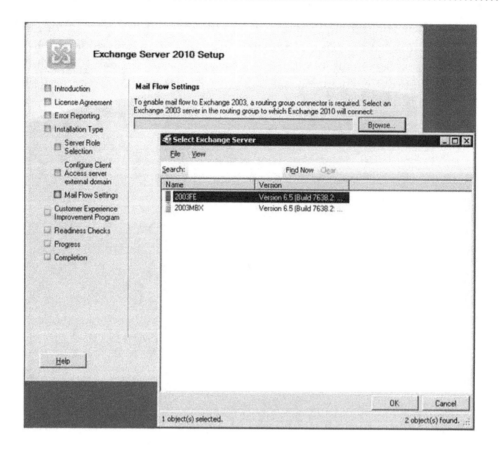

Note that this choice can be changed and/or added to after setup is complete.

Now finish the setup wizard and install the Client Access and Hub Transport Server roles on this server.

It is also possible to use the command-line setup application to set up the above mentioned configuration. Open a command prompt, navigate to the installation media and enter the following command:

```
Setup.com /mode:install /roles:ht,ca,mt /ExternalCASServerDomain:
webmail.inframan.nl /LegacyRoutingServer:2003FE.inframan.local
```

Mailbox storage design

Before installing the Exchange Server 2010 Mailbox Server role, a proper storage design has to be made. Microsoft has recently released the new storage calculator, which is now called the "Exchange 2010 Mailbox Server Role Requirements Calculator" and can be downloaded from HTTP://MSEXCHANGETEAM. COM/ARCHIVE/2009/11/09/453117.ASPX.

The Requirements Calculator needs to be used for a proper storage design. The following variables are used in the Requirements Calculator for our example.

Variable	Value
Number of mailbox servers	1
Number of mailboxes	500
Usage profile	Light
Average message size	75 KB
Personal Archive	0 MB
Mailbox Size	1024 MB
Deleted items retention	14 days

The Requirements Calculator will show the following results:

Variable	Value
Number of Databases/server	4
Number of mailboxes/database	125
Log files generated/day/mailbox	20
Mailbox server internal memory	8 GB
Database size plus overhead	177 GB
Total Log file size plus overhead/database	11 GB
Total database size	707 GB
Total log file size	42 GB
Total LUN size databases	972 GB
Total database required IOPS	72
Total LUN size log files	53 GB
Total log required IOPS	14

An interesting part of Exchange Server 2010 is the database technology. Microsoft has made significant changes to the database structure to lower the disk performance requirements. It should be sufficient to run the Mailbox databases and its accompanying log files from SATA disks.

In the Requirements Calculator there's the possibility to enter the disk configuration. For the new Inframan Mailbox server, 7,200 RPM SATA disks with a capacity of 500 GB will be used for storing the databases, and 7,200 RPM SATA disks with a capacity of 250 GB will be used for storing the log files. This disk configuration is not exactly a high-end configuration, but it is by far the most cost-effective solution.

The Requirements Calculator contains a tab called **Storage Design**. When using the above mentioned values, the Calculator recommends a RAID 1/0 configuration with 6 SATA disks for storing the mailbox databases and a RAID 1/0 configuration with 2 SATA disks for storing the log files.

Installing the Mailbox Server role

When the storage solution has been properly designed and implemented, the Exchange Server 2010 Mailbox Server role can be installed. As with the Client Access and Hub Transport Server roles, make sure you download the Language Pack during setup. Select a Custom setup and select only the **Mailbox Server role** when you get to the **Server Role selection** window. Finish the setup wizard and install the Mailbox Server role. After installation of the second server, the organization is ready to be configured, and we can prepare to start moving mailboxes from Exchange Server 2003 to Exchange Server 2010.

Configuring the Exchange Server 2010 servers

When both Exchange servers are installed it is time to configure the Exchange environment properly before Exchange Server 2010 can be used and mailboxes can be moved. The following need to be configured:

- Relocate the Mailbox Databases on the new storage solution.

- Unified Communications certificate on the Client Access Server.

- New server certificate on the Exchange 2003 front-end server.

- OWA 2010 needs to be configured for use with Exchange Server 2003.

- Public Folder replication.

- A send and receive connector also has to be configured, but I will describe this in the next article, showing how mail flow is changed from Exchange Server 2003 to Exchange Server 2010.

Relocate the mailbox databases

On the new Mailbox Server there are two drives, from a hardware perspective configured as outlined before. These drives are F:\ for the mailbox databases and the public folder database and Drive G:\ for the log files.

To change the location of the mailbox database open the Exchange Management Console and navigate to **Database Management**, which can be found in the **Organization Configuration**. Right-click the database and select **Move Database Path**. Change the database file path to a directory on Drive F:\ and change the log folder path to a directory on Drive G:\. Repeat this step for the public folder database.

If needed, create new databases and locate the new database file on Drive F:\ and the accompanying log files on Drive G:\.

Unified Communications certificate

On the Exchange Server 2010 Client Access Server, a new third-party Unified Communications certificate needs to be installed. According to Microsoft Knowledge Base article 929395 (HTTP://SUPPORT.MICROSOFT. COM/KB/929395) the following Certificate Authorities are supported for use with Unified Communications certificates:

Entrust – WWW.ENTRUST.NET/MICROSOFT/

Digicert – WWW.DIGICERT.COM/UNIFIED-COMMUNICATIONS-SSL-TLS.HTM

Comodo – WWW.COMODO.COM/MSEXCHANGE.

However, most SSL Certificate Authorities can generate UC/SAN certificates that will work just fine. New in Exchange Server 2010 is the possibility to request certificates using the Exchange Management Console. Open the Exchange Management Console and select the **Server Configuration** in the navigation pane. Select the **Exchange Server 2010 Client Access Server** and create a new certificate request. For our environment we have to use the following domain names in our certificate:

* WEBMAIL.INFRAMAN.NL

* AUTODISCOVER.INFRAMAN.NL

* LEGACY.INFRAMAN.NL.

During the coexistence phase, Internet clients will connect to the Exchange Server 2010 Client Access Server while their mailbox is still on Exchange Server 2003. The client request will then be redirected to the old Exchange Server 2003 front-end server. This server will therefore get a new FQDN (Fully Qualified Domain Name) and thus need a new certificate. This new FQDN will be LEGACY.INFRAMAN.NL.

OWA configuration

During installation of the Exchange Server 2010 Client Access Server all settings have been configured for use on the Internet. The only thing that needs to be configured is the coexistence information for Outlook Web App. The Client Access Server needs to be configured in case a mailbox is still on Exchange Server 2003 and the client needs to be redirected to the Exchange Server 2003 front-end server.

On an Exchange Server 2010 server enter the following Management Shell command:

```
Set-OWAVirtualDirectory <CASHUB01>\OWA "
-ExternalURL https://webmail.inframan.nl/OWA "
-Exchange2003URL https://legacy.inframan.nl/exchange
```

This will make sure that, when a user connects to Exchange Server 2010 Client Access Server for Outlook Web Access, and the mailbox is still on Exchange 2003, the client will be redirected to the old Exchange Server 2003 front-end server.

Public folder replication

During installation of the mailbox server, a new Exchange Server 2010 mailbox database will be automatically created. After installation, you have to make sure that this database is moved from the default location to an alternate location for recovery and performance reasons.

A new public folder database will also be automatically created on the new mailbox server. The hierarchy, which is the structure of all public folders will be automatically replicated between all public folder databases in the entire organization. The content replication of the public folders will have to be configured manually though.

To replicate the Offline Address Book and Free/Busy folders from Exchange Server 2003 to Exchange Server 2010 open the Exchange System Manager on the Exchange Server 2003 server and navigate to the **System Folders** in the **Folders** folder in the **First Administrative Group**. Navigate to the first **Offline Address Book** folder, right-click it and select **All Tasks...**, then Manage Settings.

If you want to toggle between the system folders and the normal public folders, navigate to the public folders, right-click the public folders and select **View System Folders** or **View Public Folders**.

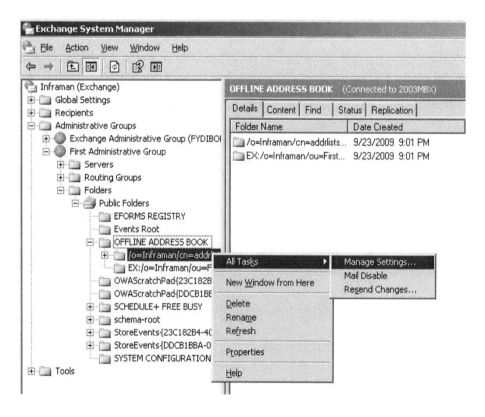

The Manage Public Folder Settings wizard will appear. Click **Next** on the welcome page and select **Modify lists of replica servers**. Follow the wizard, and add the Exchange Server 2010 Mailbox Server role as a new replica. When finished, the folder and all its subfolders will be replicated to the Exchange Server 2010 public folder database. Repeat this step for the second Offline Address Book folder and the Schedule+ Free Busy folder.

Notes

*When the **Manage Settings** option is not available you can select **Properties** and select the replication tab to add the Exchange Server 2010 Public Folder Database.*

Replication of public folders can take quite some time.

The (default) public folders that are located on the Exchange Server 2010 Mailbox Server should be replicated to the Exchange Server 2003 Mailbox Server. To accomplish this, log on to the Exchange Server 2010 Mailbox Server, open the Exchange Management console, and navigate to the Tools node. Under the **Tools** node open the Public Folder Management console.

Right-click the **Offline Address Book** in the results pane, select Properties and click the **Replication** tab.

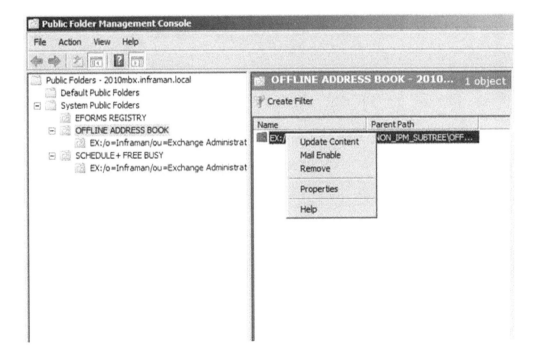

Add the Exchange Server 2003 Mailbox Server to the replica list. The contents will now be replicated to the Exchange Server 2003 Mailbox Server. Be aware that public folder replication is a low priority mechanism, so it takes some time before both public folder databases are in sync.

Repeat these steps for the Schedule+ Free Busy folder.

Summary

In this first article of two, I explained what steps are needed before you can start moving mailboxes from Exchange Server 2003 to Exchange Server 2010. In this article, the Active Directory was upgraded, two servers with Exchange Server 2010 were installed, certificates were installed and the Public Folder replication was set up.

In the next article (which you can find at WWW.SIMPLE-TALK.COM/SYSADMIN/EXCHANGE/UPGRADE-EXCHANGE-2003-TO-EXCHANGE-2010-%E2%80%93-PART-II), I cover the actual movement of the mailboxes and the steps that are needed to decommission the Exchange 2003 servers, like moving the Offline Address Book generation server and conversion of Recipient Policies and Address Books.

Customizing the Outlook Address Book

17 December 2009

by Ben Lye

It is possible to change the fields in the Outlook address book to make them a better fit for your organisation. Exchange provides templates for Users, Contacts, Groups, Public Folders, and Mailbox Agents that are downloaded to Outlook. Any changes will be visible in the address book. As usual with Exchange, careful planning before you make changes pays dividends, as Ben Lye explains.

I was recently asked if it was possible to change the information fields which are displayed in the Outlook Address Book for users – the person making the request wanted to add an additional telephone number field on the General and Phone/Notes property pages to display an internal extension.

This kind of customisation is probably something that many Exchange organisations can benefit from, and the changes to the Outlook Address Book can be implemented easily within Exchange using the Exchange Details Template Editor.

The Details Template Editor is an MMC snap-in which provides a GUI for editing the object properties which are displayed when an object is opened from the address book. Details of templates can be modified for Users, Contacts, Groups, Public Folders, and Mailbox Agents. The Advanced Find search dialogue box can also be edited. Each of the six template types can be modified in 50 different languages. The Details Template Editor is installed along with the Exchange Management Tools.

To start the Details Template Editor in Exchange 2007 RTM:

- On the taskbar, click **Start**, and then click **Run**.

- Type *mmc* in the **Open** field.

- On the **Console** menu bar, click **File**, and then click **Add/Remove Snap-in**.

- In **Add/Remove Snap-in**, on the **Standalone** tab, click **Add**.

- In **Add Standalone Snap-in**, select **Details Templates Editor** from the list of available stand-alone snap-ins, and then click **Add**.

- Click **Close** to close the **Available Snap-ins** dialog box, and then click **OK** on the Add/Remove Snap-in dialog box.

To start the Details Template Editor in Exchange 2007 SP1 or SP2 or Exchange 2010 either use the method above, or:

- Launch the **Exchange Management Console**.

- Select **Toolbox** in the console tree.

- Double-click **Details Templates Editor** in the results pane.

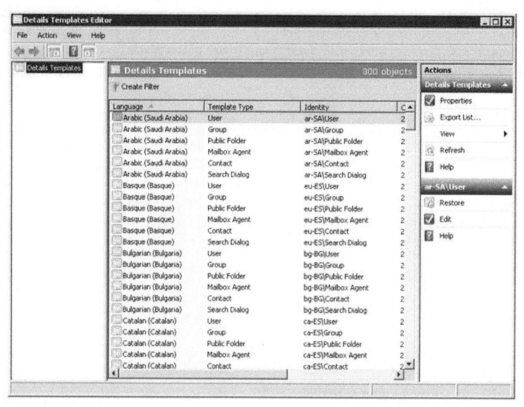

Figure: **Exchange Details Templates Editor.**

....

Note

In order to use the Details Templates Editor, you need to be delegated the Exchange Organization Administrator role.

....

In my case, I needed to edit the **English User** template. To open the template for editing, double-click it and the template editor window is shown.

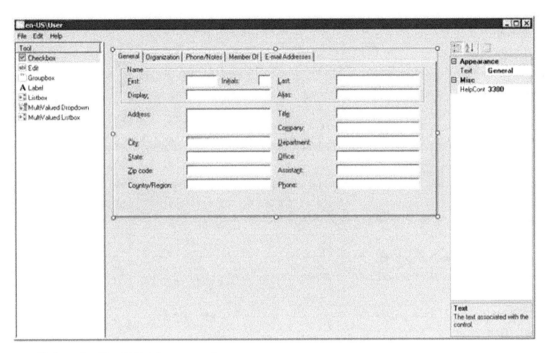

Figure: **Editing the English User template.**

The template editor is divided into three panes: the toolbox pane on the left, the designer pane in the center, and the properties pane on the right. New fields can be added to the template by selecting the appropriate element type in the toolbox pane, placing the element in the designer pane, and linking it to an object attribute in the properties pane. The properties pane can also be used for fine-grained control over the size and position of elements, as well as tab order and text size.

Note

*The template editor does not include any Undo functionality – you cannot undo any changes made in the editor, but the template can be reverted back to default settings. Templates are restored by right-clicking the template to be restored and selecting **Restore**.*

The object attributes which can be displayed on a template are limited to those provided by Microsoft. While it is technically possible to extend the set of attributes by modifying the Active Directory schema, doing so is not supported by Microsoft. If additional attributes which are not in the standard set are required, the supported method of displaying the data is to use one of the fifteen Exchange extension attributes.

In my case, I wanted to use the Active Directory attribute **IpPhone**, which had already been populated with the IP telephone numbers for our staff. As this attribute is not one included in the standard set, I had to copy the data to another attribute which could be used. To do this, I copied the data from the IpPhone attribute on each user record in AD to the Exchange extension attribute extensionAttribute1. The easiest way to do this in the Exchange Management Shell is with a short script.

This script will copy the value of the IpPhone attribute to the Exchange extensionAttribute1 attribute for all enabled user objects:

```
# Script to copy the IpPhone attribute the extensionAttribute1 attribute
# Written by Ben Lye - 07 December 2009

# Find the users in AD using an ADSI search method
$searcher = new-object DirectoryServices.DirectorySearcher([ADSI]"")

# Filter for enabled user accounts with a value in the IpPhone attribute
$searcher.filter = "(&(IpPhone=*)(objectCategory=person)(!(useraccountcontr
ol:1.2.840.113556.1.4.803:=2)))"

# Return the sorted results
$objects = $searcher.findall() | Sort-Object -Property cn

# Loop through all the objects that the search returned
ForEach ($object in $objects) {

    # Store some attribute values into variables
    $ipphone = $object.properties.ipphone
    $extensionattribute1 = $object.properties.extensionattribute1
    $dn = $object.properties.distinguishedname
    $adspath = $object.properties.adspath

    # If IpPhone is not equal to extensionAttribute1 then process this object
    If ($ipphone -ne $extensionattribute1) {
        # Get the ADSI object
        $adsiobject = [ADSI]"$adspath"

        # Set the attribute
        $adsiobject.extensionattribute1 = $ipphone

        # Commit the changes
        $adsiobject.SetInfo()

        # Output what just changed
        Write-Host $dn ":" $extensionAttribute1 "-->" $IpPhone
    }
}
```

Once the data is in an attribute which can be exposed via the details templates, then modifying the templates is relatively easy. An existing element can be relabelled and linked to the new data, or a new element can be added. When modifying or adding elements, you must match the element type to the AD field type – single-valued elements (check box or edit box) must be used for single-valued AD attributes (such as primary telephone number fields), and multi-valued attributes (list box, multivalued dropdown and multivalued list box) should be used for multi-valued AD attributes (such as "other" telephone number fields). Mismatching single and multi-valued elements and AD attributes will result in data not displaying.

I decided to replace **Assistant** on the **General** tab of the user details with the new IP phone number. To complete my changes, I opened the English user details template, changed the label text from **Assistant** to **IP phone**, and changed the **AttributeName** property of the element from **ms-Exch-Assistant-Name** to **ms-Exch-Extension-Attribute-1**.

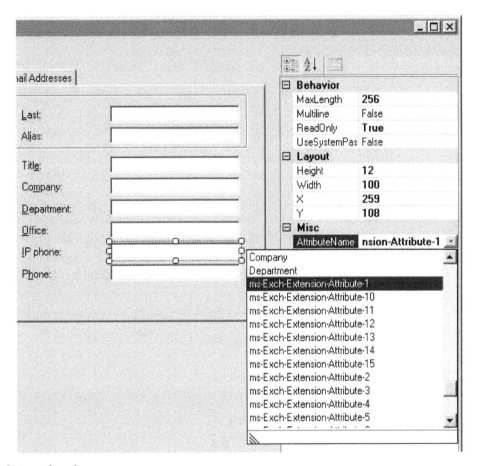

Figure: Editing the elements.

After saving the change to the template, the changes are immediately available to Outlook clients which are not in cached mode. Cached-mode clients will need to wait for the Offline Address Book to be updated and a full download of the Offline Address Book to occur (which, by default, in Outlook 2007 is only attempted once in a 13-hour period). The server update of the offline address book can be forced to run by running Get-OfflineAddressBook | Update-OfflineAddressBook and Get-ClientAccessServer | Update-FileDistributionService -Type OAB in the Exchange Management Shell.

Once the server-side update has run, and the client has downloaded the new templates, the changes will be visible in the Address Book.

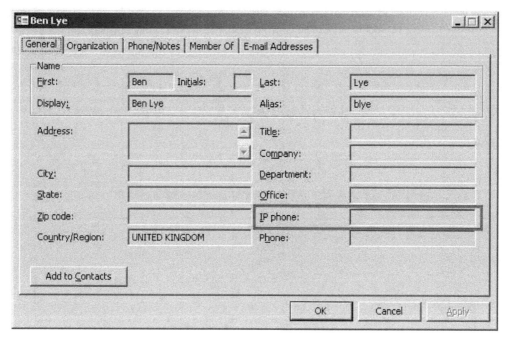

Figure: **The new details template in Outlook.**

Editing the details templates is relatively easy but, like all things Exchange, careful planning will make implementing the changes much easier. When planning for template changes it's important to know what type of data you intend to add to the templates, and to understand that, while not all data in AD can be exposed directly to the Outlook Address Book, there are workarounds available.

More information on customising the Outlook Address Book by editing the details templates is available in Microsoft TechNet at HTTP://TECHNET.MICROSOFT.COM/EN-US/LIBRARY/BB124525.ASPX.

Virtual Exchange Servers

20 November 2008

by Jaap Wesselius

Microsoft now supports running Exchange Server 2007 in server virtualization environments, not just on Hyper-V, but on any virtualizing solution that is validated in the Server Virtualization Validation Program.
Before virtualizing Exchange Server, you will need to be clear about the business advantages, and consider the size of the installation, otherwise the results can be a disappointment.

Virtualization is a hot topic these days. Microsoft released Windows Server 2008 Hyper-V just before the summer, and Hyper-V is Microsoft's answer to the supremacy of VMware ESX Server. Customers have been running applications like Microsoft Exchange Server on VMware for years now, despite the formal support statement from Microsoft that this wasn't supported. Okay, there was a "commercially reasonable effort" support, but that was basically it.

This has changed since Hyper-V was released. All server virtualization products that are validated in the SVVP (Server Virtualization Validation Program, see HTTP://WINDOWSSERVERCATALOG.COM/SVVP. ASPX?SVVPPAGE=SVVP.HTM) are now fully supported by Microsoft. Needless to say, all major virtualization vendors have signed up to this program, so all recommendations regarding virtualization are not only valid for Hyper-V but for all vendors in the SVVP program.

Microsoft has a list of all Microsoft applications that are supported in a Virtual Machine, this list is published via KB Article 957006 (HTTP://SUPPORT.MICROSOFT.COM/KB/957006/). There are some remarks in this document, and one of them is for running Exchange Server in a virtualized environment. And that's exactly what I want to talk about.

Note

The official Support Policies and Recommendations for running a virtualized Exchange server can be found at HTTP://TECHNET.MICROSOFT.COM/EN-US/LIBRARY/CC794548.ASPX.

Windows Server 2008 Hyper-V

Hyper-V is a hypervisor product. A hypervisor is a very small software layer that's situated between the operating system and the hardware. In terms of "small," Hyper-V is less than 1 MB in size.

Install Windows Server 2008 (X64 only!) on "Designed for Windows" hardware. Make sure that this hardware supports hardware virtualization, and that you have a correct BIOS version (including the Execute Bit Disabled option). All Class-A servers should be capable for Hyper-V, but be careful with the low-end servers. I have seen budget servers with Pentium IV processors that are not capable of running Hyper-V! But I have also seen laptops with, for example, an Intel Core2Duo processor that are capable of running Hyper-V (don't expect a real-world performance though). The server should have enough internal memory and disk space to facilitate the use of Virtual Machines.

After installing Windows Server 2008, you have to install Hyper-V. Hyper-V is a server role and can be installed using the Server Manager. The Hypervisor slides between the Operating System and the hardware and, after a reboot, the system is ready. Note that the original Operating System has now become a Virtual Machine as well! This Virtual Machine is called the root or parent partition. This is a special partition since it controls all other Virtual Machines on this host. These VMs are called child partitions. Special care should be taken with the parent partition, and no applications should be installed on it. The best solution for the parent partition is to use Windows Server 2008 Server Core which only has a command-line interface. There are a few graphical tools like timedate.cpl for setting the timezone and time/date information, and there's also Notepad for creating batch files. But the general interface is the command line. Windows Server 2008 Server Core has low overhead, it has a small memory footprint and it has a small attack surface. It is more difficult to manage, though, especially for the average Windows administrator.

There are some additions to the host Operating System when Hyper-V is installed. A VSP (Virtual Service Provider) is installed. This is a piece of software that gives a Virtual Machine access to hardware resources. The VSP is connected to the VMBus, an in-memory bus used for communications between parent and child partitions. Every child partition has its own VMBus for safety reasons.

VMWorker processes are also installed on the parent partition. These are used for non-native Hyper-V Virtual Machines; they cannot use the VMBus or VSP interfaces. Hardware resources are emulated on the host in the VMWorker processes for these types of Virtual Machines.

Native Hyper-V Virtual Machines offer the best performance. Whenever possible, try to use native Virtual Machines. Supported server operating systems running as a native Virtual Machines are:

*   Windows Server 2008

*   Windows Server 2003 SP2 and higher

*   Windows Server 2000 SP4

*   SUSE Linux 10d.

To integrate the native Virtual Machine with Hyper-V, special drivers need to be installed in the Virtual Machine. These drivers let the Virtual Machine use the new VMBus structure as can be seen in Figure 1. These drivers are called Synthetic Drivers and are part of the Integration Components of Hyper-V.

Other operating systems also run very well in Hyper-V, but they use hardware emulation instead of the new VMBus structure.

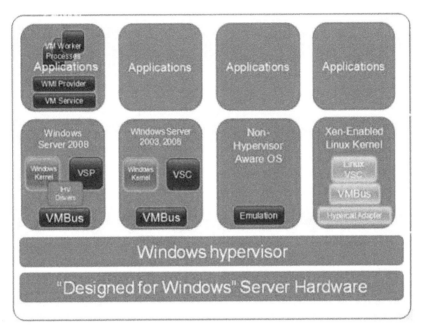

Figure 1:   Windows Hypervisor structure with multiple VMs. Note the Emulation part in the 3rd VM.

So, the original Windows Server 2008 image becomes a Virtual Machine as well, but this one should not be used for production purposes. For running Exchange Server in a virtual environment, we need to install a new native Virtual Machine that's capable of using the new VMBus structure. Never install Exchange Server in the parent partition.

Virtual Exchange servers

That being said, we want to create a fully supported virtualized Exchange Server environment. As stated before, the official support policies can be found on the Microsoft website at HTTP://TECHNET.MICROSOFT.COM/EN-US/LIBRARY/CC794548.ASPX.

The first thing is that the only version supported on Hyper-V is Exchange Server 2007 SP1 in combination with Windows Server 2008 as the Child Operating System. This is mainly because Windows Server 2008 performs better than Windows Server 2003 using multiple virtual processors. The Exchange product team didn't want to spend any time on testing Exchange Server 2003 running on Hyper-V, so the official standpoint didn't change here. I'll refer to that later in this article.

Virtualizing Exchange Server is like designing a bare metal Exchange Server environment – it's all about performance. All design guides available for designing bare metal Exchange Server 2007 environments should be used for virtual Exchange Server 2007 environments as well. This goes for all Exchange 2007 roles except the Unified Messaging role. This role is not supported running under Hyper-V, due to the real-time speech recognition in the Unified Messaging role.

An Exchange Server 2007 running under Hyper-V can look something like this:

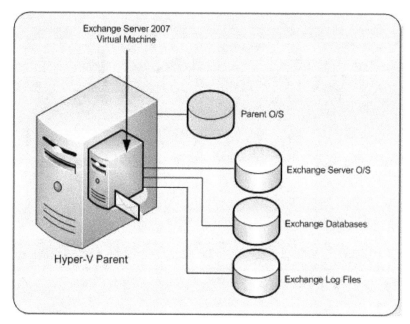

Figure 2:   Exchange Server 2007 SP1 runs on its own disks.

Before installing Windows Server 2008 as the child partition, a Virtual Hard Disk must be created. This can be a fixed size Virtual Hard Disk (.VHD file). Remember that dynamic .VHD files are not supported for Exchange Server 2007 SP1. A better solution is to use a dedicated or pass-through disk. This is a dedicated disk that can only be used by the Virtual Machine. Tests have shown that a dedicated disk under Hyper-V has a similar performance characteristic to a native disk in a non-virtualized Exchange Server.

Our server has two physical disks. The first disk is used for the Parent Partition which is, of course, running Windows Server 2008. The second disk will be dedicated to our Windows Server 2008 Child Partition where we install Exchange Server 2007 SP1.

First, bring the second physical disk offline; you can do this in the Disk Management option under Storage in Server Manager. By placing it offline, it is not available any more for other operating systems.

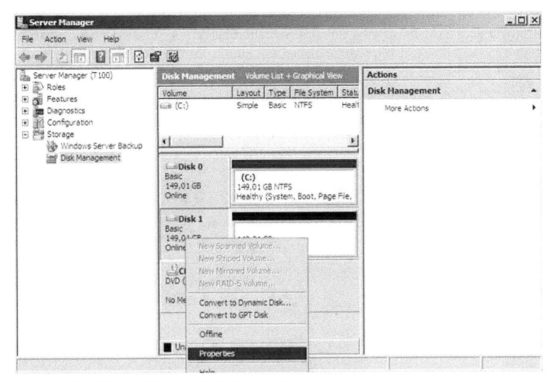

Figure 3:   Bring the disk in offline mode in Server Manager.

Now create a new Virtual Machine:

- Open the Hyper-V Manager in the Administrative Tools menu.

- In the **Tasks** pane click **New** and select **Virtual Machine**. The New Virtual Machine wizard starts and, after the welcome screen, you have to enter all kinds of information regarding the new Virtual Machine:

  - specify a name and location to store the Virtual Machine

  - assign it a certain amount of memory, for example, 4 GB

  - bind it to a publicly available network.

- At the **Connect Virtual Hard Disk** window select the **Attach a virtual hard disk later** option.

- Specify the ISO that will be used to install Windows Server 2008 x64.

- After reviewing the summary screen, click **Finish.**

Do not start the Virtual Machine at this point.

When finished, open the properties of the Virtual Machine, and go to the IDE Controller 0. This is the controller which the boot disk should be attached to. Check the **Physical Hard disk** option and select the physical disk we've put offline earlier. Click **OK** to save the configuration.

Unfortunately it is not possible to add a SCSI controller and the disk to this SCSI controller. The Hyper-V SCSI controller is part of the Integration Components, and thus runs against the VMBus structure. A very flexible solution, but only available when the Virtual Machine is up and running.

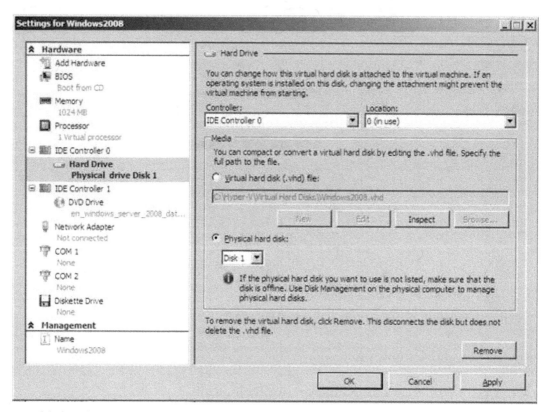

Figure 4:   Add the physical drive to the IDE Controller 0.

The new Virtual Machine is now ready to be installed; just power it on and install Windows Server 2008.

After installing and configuring the server, the server needs to be updated. The RTM version of Windows Server 2008 comes with a beta version of Hyper-V and this needs to be updated as soon as possible. When updating the Virtual Machine make sure that you install Microsoft Hotfix KB 950500. This hotfix brings the Virtual Machine to the RTM level of Hyper-V and thus includes the latest version of the Integration Components.

Installing the Integration Components in a new Virtual Machine can be challenging. Before the Integration Components are installed, there's no network available, and without a network it's impossible to copy drivers and updates to the Virtual Machine. It is a good idea to create an ISO image with the most important updates, including the Hyper-V RTM hotfix, and install this on the host server. This way you can always mount the ISO images and install the latest Integration Components.

After the Installation Components are installed and the server is brought up to date we have a fully functional Windows Server 2008 server. Assuming that you already have an Active Directory available on your network you can continue installing Exchange Server 2007 SP1.

Exchange database and log files

An Exchange server running on a server virtualization platform doesn't differ from a bare metal Exchange server and, as such, you need to place the Exchange database and the log files on separate spindles. This is both from a performance perspective as well as a disaster recovery perspective.

There are three ways to configure the database and the log files:

- **Use a fixed Virtual Hard Disk** – this is a preconfigured .VHD file with a fixed size placed on a separate disk.

- **Use a dedicated or pass-through disk** – this is identical to the disk we just installed Windows Server 2008 on. However, since we already have a running Windows Server 2008 Virtual Machine, we can add a SCSI controller to the Virtual Machine and attach the pass-through disk to the SCSI Controller. This is the preferred and recommended solution.

- **Use iSCSI LUNs** – using the Windows Server built-in iSCSI initiator, we can access LUNs on a storage device and place the database and log files on separate LUNs. Although using iSCSI within the Virtual Machine is a fully supported configuration, the performance is less than exposing an iSCSI LUN from the parent partition as a dedicated disk. This is due to the networking overhead within the child partition.

Again, there's no difference between designing a bare metal Exchange server and a virtual Exchange server. Always design your Exchange server with the best performance in mind!

It is not yet possible to use a fiber channel solution with Virtual Machines natively. The HBAs (Host Based Adapters) are not yet available for use with the VMBus structure. HBA vendors are working on this, however, but it is unknown yet (as of October 2008) when this will be available. It is possible, however, to use a fiber channel solution on the host system and expose LUNs on a SAN as disks that can be used using the pass-through mechanism.

Backup and restore

As explained in earlier articles on WWW.SIMPLE-TALK.COM, backup and restore is very important on Exchange servers. Running Exchange servers on Hyper-V make backups look very easy – just create a backup of your Virtual Hard Disk and that's it. Microsoft Server 2008 even supports VSS (Volume Shadow Copy Service) backups of the Virtual Hard Disk files.

Although this is true, you still have to be very careful with backing up your Exchange Server under Hyper-V. Not only do you have to back up your data, also the Exchange server's database needs to be checked for consistency, and the Exchange server's log files need to be purged.

The Hyper-V VSS writer that's part of Windows Server 2008 is communicating through the Integration Components with the Exchange writer in the Virtual Machine. Windows Server 2008 Backup (installed as a separate feature) can create VSS backups of the Virtual Machine running Exchange Server 2007 SP1. When checking the Exchange Server after a Hyper-V VSS backup is created, the Exchange database header show backup information, and also the log files are purged.

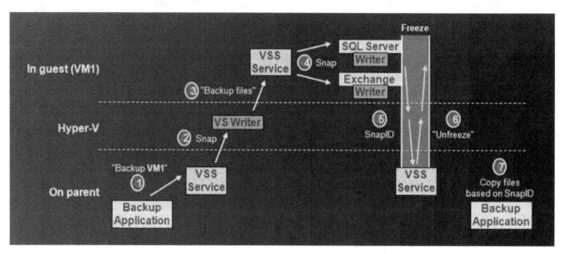

Figure 5:   Creating a Hyper-V VSS backup does interact with the Exchange server running in the Virtual Machine.

Although it is fully functional, it is not a very user-friendly solution. Microsoft is also offering a complete backup solution, Microsoft System Center Data Protection Manager (DPM) 2007. With the upcoming Service Pack 1 release of DPM, Microsoft is going to support VSS backups of Virtual Machines. The expected release of DPM 2007 Service Pack 1 is in the first quarter of 2009. Third-party vendors like Symantec offer VSS backups of both Hyper-V as well as VMware Virtual Machines in BackupExec 12.5 which was released early October 2008.

At this moment (November 2008) the recommended way to back up your virtualized Exchange Server 2007 environment is within the Virtual Machine itself. Install a DPM or other third-party backup agent in the Virtual Machine, and back it up from there.

Snapshots

A snapshot is a point-in-time copy of your system, in this case the Virtual Machine. After creating a snapshot of our Virtual Machine it is always possible to return to the state of this Virtual Machine at the moment of creation of the snapshot.

The following takes place during a snapshot:

• a copy of the configuration file is created

• the Virtual Machine's memory is flushed to disk

- a differencing disk is created and the original disk is set to read-only

- the Virtual Machine resumes operation.

While this is a great technology to return to a known state at a certain point in time, it is not supported for running Exchange Server 2007 SP1 in a production environment.

Exchange Server 2003

According to the earlier referenced Microsoft article, the only Exchange version officially supported under Hyper-V is Exchange Server 2007 SP1. If you want to virtualize Exchange Server 2003, the only official supported way to achieve this is to run it on Virtual Server 2005 R2 SP1.

Although not officially supported, Exchange Server 2003 runs great in a Virtual Machine under Hyper-V.

Conclusion

Microsoft now supports running Exchange Server 2007 in server virtualization environments. This is not only Hyper-V, but all vendors that have their solution validated in the Server Virtualization Validation Program (SVVP) are fully supported.

Important to remember, is that all design guidelines that are valid for a bare metal Exchange environment need to be used for a virtualized environment as well. Use disks that are capable of handling the expected I/O load; it is very likely that dynamic disks will not meet these requirements. Therefore, the use of dynamic disks is not officially supported by Microsoft when running Exchange Server 2007 SP1 under Hyper-V.

One should always take business requirements into account. Why do you want to virtualize, and what are the project goals, against which costs? I have seen customers returning from the virtualization twilight zone being very frustrated, and ending up in a bare metal environment. For larger environments I have seen a lot of large implementations where the Exchange Server 2007 Client Access Servers and Hub Transport Servers were running under VMware, but where the mailbox servers were running on bare metal. I have to admit, though, that these environments were larger than 4,000 mailboxes. For these environments, virtualizing the mailbox servers is questionable, but this might change in the future, and this is something that is hard to foresee.

Virtualizing Exchange: Points for Discussion

20 November 2008

by Nathan Winters

With the increasing acceptance of the use of Virtualization as a means of providing server infrastructure, this technology is being applied to production Exchange servers. This is a solution that is not just limited to the small shop, Nathan Winters discusses the pros, cons, and challenges that lie ahead in providing a flexible and highly available email system.

Introduction

The subject of virtualization has been a pretty hot topic for the last couple of years. It seems to offer a massive amount, for example, consolidating underused servers and therefore providing cost savings on hardware, rack space, electricity, and cooling. On top of that, virtualizing your server infrastructure brings other benefits such as the ability to easily move a Virtual Machine from one piece of physical hardware to another, and also to rapidly provision new servers where required.

Although this sounds great, there has been somewhat of a problem with virtualising Exchange 2007 because Microsoft has not, until very recently, supported Exchange 2007 on any virtualization platform. To be fair though, that has not stopped a lot of people from putting their Exchange servers on a virtual platform. In fact, it is something I have, myself, done for a handful of clients utilising the VMware ESX platform. However, as mentioned, the support situation has now changed, and these changes form the topic of the next section.

Is it supported?

In this rapidly changing marketplace, there is no straightforward answer to the question of support. Essentially, as far as Microsoft is concerned, this all boils down to what they have tested. Exchange 2003 has long been supported on the Microsoft Virtual Server platform, although only if you had a Microsoft Premier Support Contract. I have seen almost nobody using Virtual Server as anything other than a test platform, and other products like VMware Workstation were rather better for that. So why is Exchange 2007 different? It is because Exchange 2007 is the first Microsoft Server application which required a 64-bit (x64) operating system (OS). At the release of Exchange 2007, Microsoft still only had Virtual Server as their virtualization offering, which does not support the 64-bit OS required to run Exchange 2007. Therefore, Exchange 2007 was not supported in a virtual environment as Microsoft would have been reluctant to test on another company's virtualization platform!

331

Since July 2008, when Microsoft released Hyper-V, Microsoft's new hypervisor-based virtualization platform, it now has a virtualization platform capable of supporting 64-bit operating systems. It therefore came as no surprise that Microsoft issued a new support statement, *Microsoft Support Policies and Recommendations for Exchange Servers in Hardware Virtualization Environments*, in August 2008, which can be found at the link below:

HTTP://TECHNET.MICROSOFT.COM/EN-US/LIBRARY/CC794548%28EXCHG.80%29.ASPX.

Some of the key points are:

- The virtualization software must be one or other flavour of Hyper-V or, if third-party, must be listed on the Windows Server Virtualization Validation Program (SVVP).

- Exchange must be running on Windows Server 2008.

- The Unified Messaging role is not supported, although all others are.

- Virtual disks that dynamically expand are not supported by Exchange.

- Virtual disks that use differencing or delta mechanisms (such as Hyper-V's differencing VHDs or snapshots) are not supported.

- Snapshotting Exchange server Virtual Machines is not supported, as this is not an Exchange-aware backup mechanism.

- Both CCR and SCC are supported in hardware virtualization environments provided that the virtualization environment does not employ clustered virtualization servers.

The final issue listed here deserves some clarification as it has already caused some confusion. Essentially you can do one or the other of the following where the preference would be the second option: (1) cluster the hypervisor roots, or (2) cluster the guests (using multiple roots, for example, CCR where one node is a VM on one root and one node is a VM on another root). You cannot, however, combine the two, which suggests that using technology like VMware's VMotion and HA/DRS is not supported in conjunction with CCR or SCC. Perhaps this, again, will change when Microsoft release the Live Migration technology in R2 of Hyper-V. Having said that, Microsoft currently has Quick Migration, which also isn't supported when using Exchange clusters. We will simply have to wait and see.

Although the use of hypervisor high-availability techniques in conjunction with Exchange clusters is not actually supported, using VMware VMotion to move the active node in a CCR cluster does actually work (on a test system at least), and doesn't seem to cause a failover either! You do get a bunch of Event ID 1122 and 1123 messages telling you about the lost network connectivity, but things appear to keep working. Of course, this may well not be true for a heavily loaded system as, depending on the amount of time required to VMotion, a failover may be triggered. All in all, it isn't supported and, frankly, going to the trouble of setting up an high availability system, only to run it in an unsupported way, seems rather perverse to me!

Alongside the support announcement discussed above, Microsoft also changed some licensing conditions as the quote below from the Exchange team blog describes:

Microsoft is waiving its 90-day license reassignment policy to enable customers who virtualize Exchange to move their licenses between servers within a data farm as often as necessary.

So, all in all, this means that it is very much supported to run Exchange under the conditions stated on the Microsoft Hyper-V platform and to have flexibility to move Virtual Machines between physical hosts. What I guess a number of you are wondering is what this means for VMware support. Well, to answer that, we have to take a look at the Server Virtualization Validation Program or SVVP.

The website for SVVP is at: HTTP://WINDOWSSERVERCATALOG.COM/SVVP.ASPX?SVVPPAGE=SVVP.HTM.

Essentially, this is a way for Microsoft to certify whether third-party virtualization products can adequately serve Microsoft Windows and the Microsoft software which runs on Windows. VMware is on this list as supported. However, what is critical to note as regards Exchange is the supported processor architecture type. The link below lists the platforms which have met the requirements of the program for x64 processors:

HTTP://WINDOWSSERVERCATALOG.COM/RESULTS.ASPX?&BCATID=1521&CPID=0&AVC=0&AVA=23&AVQ=0&OR=1&PGS=25&READY=0.

Interestingly, this list changed during the writing of this article (Oct 2008). When I started the article, VMware was not on the list! However, during the first revision process, VMware became a supported x64 platform with the only caveat being that Virtual Machines can only have 16 GB of RAM allocated to them.

I hope that, having read the above, you have an understanding of the issues surrounding the support of Exchange on a virtualization platform. Before we move on, I would simply like to add that I and many other people have been running Exchange 2007 on various virtual platforms and it does generally work very well. The support issue is a risk, but often it is not a big enough risk to stop people making use of the benefits or virtualization technology. Having addressed the support issue, let's now move on to take a look at virtualizing Exchange in practice.

Virtualizing Exchange in practice

In this section, I will look at the pros and cons of virtualizing Exchange. I must make it clear at this point that I have not yet had the opportunity to deploy Exchange 2007 on Hyper-V, although I have deployed Exchange 2007 on VMware ESX. Therefore, my comments on Hyper-V are based on numerous discussions with trusted colleagues who are specialists in the virtualization field.

Benefits of Exchange virtualization

As you will know if you run an Exchange organization, Exchange is not a simple application. Exchange is a massive product, and getting familiar with it all is not easy. Therefore, the ability to have a replica of your production environment is extremely helpful when it comes to the testing and validation of upgrade and migration work. Virtualization makes this extremely simple, as copies of existing physical and Virtual Machines can be taken, and then run in isolation from the main network.

The introduction of multiple roles in Exchange 2007 has been very helpful in allowing Exchange to scale well, but it has also pushed up the server count dramatically. Virtualizing the Exchange environment allows these multiple roles to still run on separate Virtual Machines which can be tuned accordingly, whilst keeping down the number of physical machines required.

Following on from the flexibility of providing a test lab, it is common nowadays for this lab solution to be provided on equipment available for disaster recovery. The ability to move a Virtual Machine from one piece of hardware to another means that, in a disaster, getting the Exchange services up rapidly is much simpler than when relying on the correct physical hardware being available.

Interestingly, one area which I did not expect to put in the benefits section, is performance. It would appear that, when sized according to Microsoft Exchange sizing guidelines, a virtualized Exchange infrastructure can perform almost as well as a physical one. This was discussed at VMworld this year. In particular, it would seem that message throughput is actually slightly better on a virtual Hyper-V platform than on physical hardware.

Another area which could be considered both a benefit and a possible problem, is management. The reason I mention it as a possible problem is simply that it is another layer of management technology. However, once you accept the necessity, then management options are a definite benefit. It is one area in which Microsoft excel. Although VMware have their Virtual Center console, which is not a bad solution, the Microsoft solution, System Center Virtual Machine Manager (VMM), to give it its full name, gives you cradle-to-grave, hardware to application management. VMM 2008, like Virtual Center, has to be purchased.

What is brilliant, is the way it integrates with System Center Operations Manager 2007 using a connector/management pack. That gives you expertise on your infrastructure that's built into the network. Want to know which servers have spare resources to be potential hosts? Want to know which machines should be converted to VMs (and then P2V them). Want performance/health information in a single integrated management infrastructure (System Center)? This complete management solution is something the competition struggles to match.

Problems with Exchange virtualization

Of course there are some problems with virtualizing Exchange. It is important not to think that virtualization gives endless resources. It is absolutely critical to size the servers just like you would before. On top of this, running a virtual platform gives an added layer of complexity that must be understood and managed carefully, so as to provide a good platform for the Virtual Machines it supports.

Having mentioned performance in the benefits section, I think it is worth entering it here too. Why? Because I still feel that putting another layer underneath something that is already I/O- and memory-intensive isn't necessarily the greatest idea. After all, if you only run one VM on the box, why not just use physical hardware? I feel that this is particularly true when running the Exchange Mailbox server role on a virtualization platform.

Whilst it is true that when using pass-through disks performance is often within 1% of the physical hardware it is, however, still true that when load, in particular on the network cards, increases performance problems can occur. There will be improvements in this area soon, as new network cards increase throughput by implementing virtual switches in hardware. Whatever, it is not recommended to virtualize more than one Mailbox server on a single virtual host machine.

Still, there are benefits to virtualization so, at this point, it is perhaps a question of whether these outweigh the fact you may get fewer users on a VM than when using a physical machine. Looking at non-mailbox roles, Unified Messaging is simply not supported and really doesn't scale well, even if you try to put it in a virtual environment, as the audio playback can become rather choppy!

A possible barrier to virtualizing the Client Access and Hub Transport roles is the implementation of Windows Network Load Balancing (WNLB) on the virtualization platform. This is something that I have struggled with, however. It would seem that it is possible but that problems can occur unless things are configured correctly as described at the links below. To be fair, this is no different when in a physical environment.

Microsoft NLB not working properly in Unicast mode:
HTTP://KB.VMWARE.COM/SELFSERVICE/MICROSITES/SEARCH.DO?LANGUAGE=EN_US&CMD=DISPLAYKC&EXTERNALID=1556.

Exchange 2007 Unicast NLB issue on Hyper-V:
WWW.SHUDNOW.NET/2008/09/12/EXCHANGE-2007-UNICAST-NLB-ISSUE-ON-HYPER-V.

Although virtualization brings some benefits for disaster recovery, as mentioned above, you can't get away from the fact that by virtualizing you are putting a number of servers on a single physical piece of hardware. Obviously there is a need to mitigate this single point of failure, and one method is to use redundant hardware including PSUs and NICs. This is one area to be particularly careful of on the Hyper-V platform as physical NIC teaming is not currently supported under Hyper-V, so if you lose a NIC, everything on that machine loses connectivity!

Summary

Microsoft Hyper-V, VMware and other virtualization platforms provide a great platform for Exchange, especially as you now have the comfort of knowing that the solution is supported. Realistically, it is very likely that, as virtualization becomes more and more accepted as the normal way of providing server infrastructure, production Exchange servers will be virtualized.

In my opinion, there are clearly a few challenges to be faced when virtualizing Exchange but, so long as the challenges/limitations of the infrastructure are understood, the guidelines laid out by manufacturers are followed, and you thoroughly test the performance of the implementation before rolling it out in production, virtualizing Exchange can be very successful.

What is very clear is that virtualizing Exchange is no longer just an option for the small shop, but is now a solution for even the largest Exchange deployments looking to provide a flexible and highly available platform for their email systems.

Build Your Own Virtualized Test Lab

05 January 2009

by Desmond Lee

....

Desmond Lee explains the fundamentals of building a fully functional test lab for Windows Servers and enterprise applications (e.g. Exchange and Office Communications Server) from scratch with Hyper-V on a supported x64 machine. This will simulate a majority of test scenarios. He highlights the key points, and suggests tips and tricks to help to make the journey smoother.

....

If you are involved in supporting test, training or development servers, then you will find that server- or host-based virtualization will solve many of your problems. Instead of having to stock up several physical machines, each dedicated to certain roles and functionality, you will be able to consolidate them onto a number of powerful boxes with speedy multi-core processors, massive RAM memory, and fast disk drives with huge capacity. This will simplify administration, lessen the use of floor space, and reduce both costs and energy consumption.

In this article, I'll use Microsoft's host virtualization solution, Hyper-V, to build a representative test installation. Hyper-V is available as part of some editions of Windows Server 2008 or, more recently, as a free standalone product similar to VMware ESXi.

The big picture

Typically, a corporate infrastructure contains many servers providing core enterprise services such as network, directory, security, messaging, and file and print. Of late, the concept of Unified Communications (UC) has gathered a lot of attention within the industry. Unified Communications is a term for the technologies that aim to integrate and coordinate the systems that provide telephony, email, instant messaging, video, voicemail, and group chat, and ensure that the communications reach the recipients in the most effective and timely way.

One beauty of using Virtual Machines (VM) is the ease with which you can add, remove and edit virtualized hardware components such as network adapters, RAM memory, and hard drives at will. You can also roll back an installation should something go wrong, as long as you have taken point-in-time snapshots. The test lab is designed to run satisfactorily on up-to-date machines equipped with 2 GB or more RAM memory and plenty of disk storage on the host machine. You can then scale up the hardware to accommodate additional system demands and workload. Depending on the test scenarios being played out, the number of active running VMs can vary. Technically, there is no restriction imposed, but the licensing model may limit the number of VMs that can be deployed, depending on the Windows Server 2008 edition chosen. As a starting point, all VMs are created with the standard configuration of

337

default virtual devices, with the addition of the legacy network adapter set up to connect to one common internal, local-only (private) virtual network switch.

Although migrating Virtual Machine configuration (.vmc) and virtual hard disks (.vhd) created in Virtual PC or Virtual Server to Hyper-V is relatively painless, I shall instead cover the fundamentals of building the entire test lab from scratch with Hyper-V on a supported x64 machine. We'll have to assume that you know how to run setup, and accomplish basic tasks on your own without much hand-holding. I'll try to highlight key points, and suggest tips and tricks to help to make the journey a lot smoother.

All guest server VMs will be built using the SP1 version of Windows Server 2003, as it is so widely deployed. Hyper-V will support both x86 and x64 guest VMs (or child partitions) running side by side, but we'll choose the x86 edition, so as to keep the overall memory requirement to a manageable level with minimum overhead. All this is done without the risk of losing functionality in the sort of application that most organizations will be working with.

You can find a checklist summarizing the test lab machines in the following table.

Name	RAM (MB)	ip/24	Roles / services	Configuration
LABDC01	384	10.0.0.11	1. Windows Server 2003 SP1 x86 2. DC, DNS, GC 3. WWW only 4. Certificate Services CA and Certificate Services Web Enrollment Support	• FQDN = testlab.local • Raise domain functional level to "Windows Server 2003" • Enterprise root CA = TestLabRootCA • DNS SRV record = _sipinternaltls._tcp. domain.com:5061
LABEX01	768	10.0.0.12	1. Windows Server 2003 SP1 x86 2. WWW only 3. NET Framework v2.0 Redistributable Package x86 4. Windows PowerShell 1.0 RTW x86 5. KB926776. A hotfix rollup package for 913297, 913393, 918995, and 924895 6. December 2007 cumulative time zone update for Microsoft Windows operating systems (KB942763) 7. NET Framework 2.0 SP1 runtime x86 8. Windows Server 2003 SP2 x86 9. Exchange Server 2007 SP1 x86	• Exchange organization (native) = TestLabExchange • compatible with Outlook 2003 (public folder)

Name	RAM (MB)	ip/24	Roles / services	Configuration
LABOC01	512	10.0.0.13	1. Windows Server 2003 SP1 x86 2. WWW only 3. VC++ 2005 Redistributable 4. .NET Framework v2.0 Redistributable Package 5. Execute Step 1 to 8 in OCS setup. 6. Windows Server 2003 adminpak.msi	• testlab.local forest / Global Properties / Meetings tab / Default Policy / Edit / Check "Enable web conferencing" and "Enable program and desktop sharing"
LABXP01	384	10.0.0.51	1. Windows XP SP2 x86 2. Outlook 2003 3. Office Communicator 2007 client 4. Live Meeting 2007 client 5. Office Outlook Conferencing Add-in	
LABVT01	448	10.0.0.52	1. Windows Vista Ultimate SP1 x86 2. Outlook 2007 3. Office Communicator 2007 client 4. Live Meeting 2007 client 5. Office Outlook Conferencing Add-in	

The journey begins

Active Directory (AD) provides resource authentication and authorization for third-party solutions as well as all the Microsoft product family. You will need a solid Domain Naming Services network service to ensure problem-free operations across the entire AD forest. Therefore, the very first server (VM) should be set up as a Domain Controller (DC) and named as LABDC01 in our single forest, single domain infrastructure. For many good reasons, we must install the Microsoft DNS service and integrate it with Active Directory.

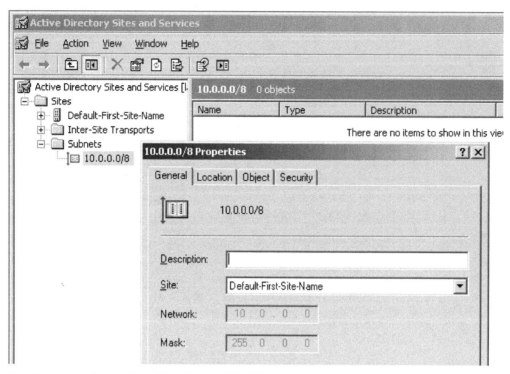

Figure 1:   Configure and associate IP subnet with AD site.

We use the fully qualified domain name (FQDN) of testlab.local to scope the authoritative DNS and AD name space to the private intranet. Being the first DC in the domain implies that the Global Catalog role will also be automatically enabled. As a best practice, create an IP subnet object (10.0.0.0/8) and associate it with the Default-First-Site-Name AD object from which all applications that use AD directory services will gain optimal traffic routing (see Figure 1).

The default AD domain and forest functional levels are set at those of **Windows 2000 mixed** and **Windows 2000** respectively. In order to introduce Exchange 2007 as the messaging service, the target domain that holds one or more Mailbox server role must be at the **Windows 2000 native** mode domain functional level or higher. Similarly, any AD domain with mailbox-enabled accounts (user, contact, etc.) – even with no Exchange 2007 Mailbox server role present – must be raised to this minimal domain functional level. To support Office Communications Server 2007, you will need to raise the domain functional level all the way to "Windows Server 2003."

Messaging service

The process of setting up Exchange Server 2007 with SP1 is a bit more tedious and time consuming. As a first step, you will need to install the WWW service from the Windows Server 2003 SP1 media. Unlike its predecessor, the SMTP service is not a requirement to set up Exchange 2007. You will save time and avoid frustration if you next download items 3 to 9 (listed in the bottom half of the table on page 338) from your administrative workstation.

When you are ready, install the files in the order listed onto the VM named LABEX01 that is joined to the domain. You will require SP2 for Windows Server 2003 in order to run Exchange Server 2007 SP1 on this version of Windows. Because the Microsoft Management Console 3.0 is shipped as an integral part of Windows Server 2003 SP1 and above, you won't need to install it separately. Likewise, all the prerequisites would have been met and you can straight away launch Step 4 (see Figure 5) as soon as you run the Exchange 2007 with integrated SP1 executable.

The typical Exchange Server installation option offers the minimal server roles that are compatible for setting up and running Exchange on the same machine, namely Client Access, Hub Transport, and Mailbox server roles. Throughout the installation process, accept all the proposed installation options except one, where you name the Exchange organization TestLabExchange.

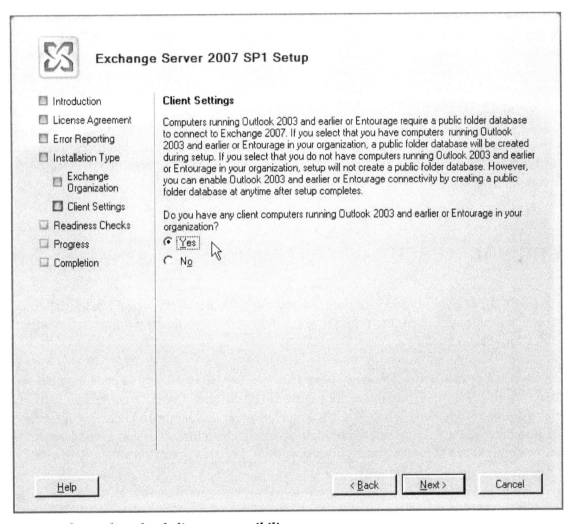

Figure 2: **Configure download client compatibility.**

To maintain compatibility with Outlook 2003 and earlier or Entourage clients, confirm that the **Yes** radio button is selected at the **Client Settings** page (see Figure 2); then you won't have to worry about any extra configuration steps later on. Updates to the Active Directory schema and configuration are part of the Exchange installation process so there is another one less thing to be concerned with.

When you've completed setup, and rebooted the machine as prompted, your messaging platform is almost ready for service. Start Exchange Management Console on LABEX01 and create two new mailbox-enabled user accounts, say, Alice and Bob. Next, we will mention the application clients.

The client side

To model real-world usage as far as possible, I suggest that you build two different client machines that run Windows XP SP2 and Vista SP1. Assign the names LABXP01 and LABVT01 and join them to the domain. On the respective systems, install the Outlook 2003 and 2007 clients. You may choose to set up other additional applications in the Office 2003/2007 suite. This will allow the Office 2007 applications to provide "click-to-dial" and to supply information about the users' presence to the Unified Communications system.

Next, log in to the XP desktop as Alice and Bob on Vista. Outlook 2007 on Bob's desktop will attempt to automatically locate, connect, and configure appropriate settings with the correct Exchange home server (LABEX01). In contrast, you will have to manually specify Alice's SAM account or display name, and the name of the home Exchange server, to achieve the same results. With this out of the way, you can then proceed to run functional tests for mail, calendaring, and scheduling. Then you can convince yourself that the core messaging services work as expected.

Extend your reach

Up to this point, the setup procedures for the basic test lab have been fairly straightforward. In order to provide Unified Communications functionality, you will have to face a lengthy setup process with Office Communications Server 2007.

Before we even begin, an internal Public Key Infrastructure (PKI) must already be present, unless you are going to use digital certificates from public root Certificate Authority (CA) such as Verisign and Thawte. This strict requirement guarantees that all OCS server-to-server and server-to-client communication channels are properly secured. You will usually save cost with this approach if you have a large number of servers or clients that will not be directly accessible by, or in communication with, the general public from the Internet.

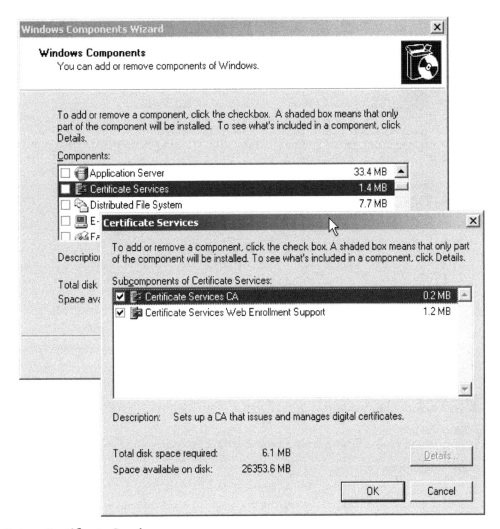

Figure 3: **Setup Certificate Services.**

For the test lab, it is sufficient to install the Certificate Services configured as an Enterprise root CA. Use the name TestLabRootCA with the default settings on the DC itself (see Figures 3 and 4). End-user or machine certificate application and enrollment can be greatly simplified through the use of the web front-end. For this reason, the WWW feature must be installed on the DC. In real practice, a separate member server will fulfill this special role.

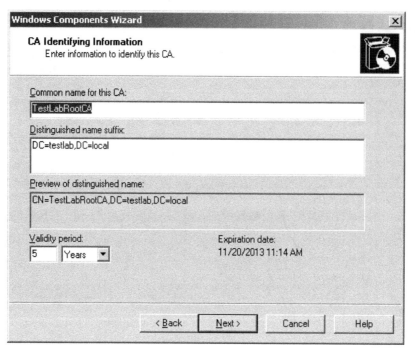

Figure 4: Configuring CA identifying information.

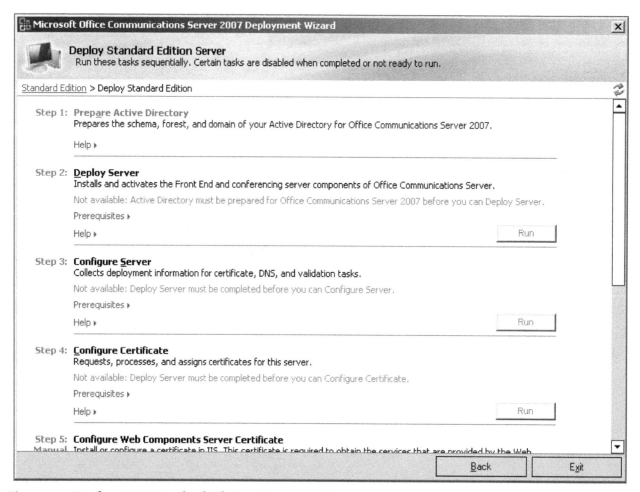

Figure 5: Deploy OCS Standard Edition (Steps 1 to 8).

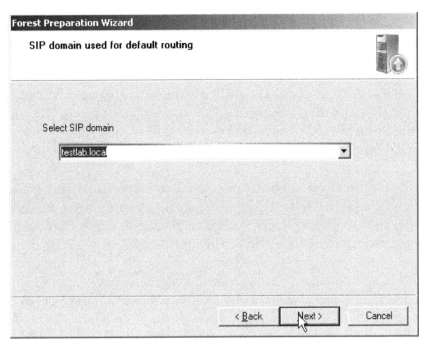

Figure 6: Configure SIP domain.

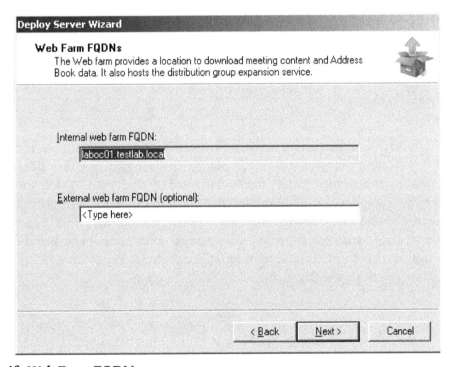

Figure 7: Specify Web Farm FQDN.

For a simple OCS standard edition deployment scenario for internal user access, the core set of features such as Instant Messaging, Audio/Video, and Web Conferencing all reside on the same machine. Again, the WWW service is featured prominently and must be installed ahead of time. Unlike Exchange Server 2007, OCS ships with all the prerequisite applications. Once you start setup, you will have the opportunity to install the Visual C++ 2005 Redistribution Kit, as well as the .NET Framework runtime. Similar to the other installations, you should login to LABOC01 with the built-in Administrator account in the domain. By default, this account has membership in the Domain Admins and Schema Admins groups. This permits you to execute Steps 1 through 8 in sequence without having to switch to and fro to the DC that holds the critical Schema Masters and other FSMO roles (LABDC01) (see Figure 5).

I recommend that you use testlab.local as the SIP domain and laboc01.testlab.local as the internal web farm FQDN to keep things simple (see Figures 6 and 7). Otherwise, it is enough to accept all the default settings during the OCS setup. Note that AD Domain and Forest preparation steps are an integral part of the OCS installation process.

At the termination of validation Step number 8, you can expect errors to surface because certain roles and features are not installed for a standard OCS setup. This can be safely ignored. Following that, pop in the Windows Server 2003 media and execute \i386\adminpak.msi. This is essential to enable user management and administration of OCS profile settings on LABOC01.

••

At the time of writing, Microsoft announced that OCS 2007 R2 will be released to manufacturing shortly. Like Exchange 2007, OCS R2 is supported only on the x64 platform in a production environment. What remains unclear is whether an x86 version will be made available for testing, evaluation and administration, as was the case with Exchange. Nevertheless, it should be easy to introduce OCS R2 into the OCS 2007 environment we are building here.

••

The final pieces

So that the Microsoft Office Communicator (MOC) client can automatically locate available OCS server pools without manual configuration, it is essential to set up the necessary SRV resource records in DNS. At a minimum, configure the **_sipinternaltls._tcp.testlab.local** to listen on TCP port 5061 on LABDC01 (see Figure 8). Once this is in place, go ahead and install items 3 to 5 in the table on both the LABXP01 and LABVT01 clients. The Live Meeting and Outlook Conferencing Add-in clients are extra components responsible for the web conferencing feature. In OCS R2, basic service or help desk in the form of a full remote desktop client control feature is built right into the updated MOC client. The standalone Live Meeting client is still required for the full, rich conferencing experience.

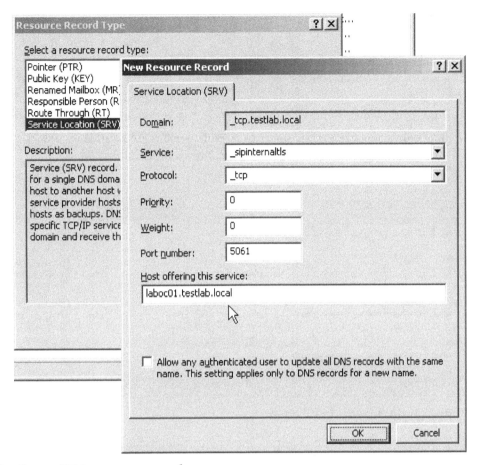

Figure 8: Configure SRV resource record.

You may want to restart the Windows client after installation completes. Although this is generally not required, you will then have the chance to identify any issues that typically surface only after a clean system shutdown and restart cycle is followed through. With a successful login to the domain, MOC queries DNS and your credentials will transparently be used to connect and sign in to OCS.

To conduct the functional tests, observe that rich presence information (Available, Busy, etc.) is shown in MOC, Outlook as well as locally installed Office applications (see Figures 9 and 10). You can start an Instant Messaging conversation between Alice and Bob, and escalate this to a collaborative web conferencing session. Using Outlook, it is possible to have appointments set up as ad hoc or scheduled web conferencing sessions. For this to work, you must make the configuration changes on LAB0C01 as described in the table.

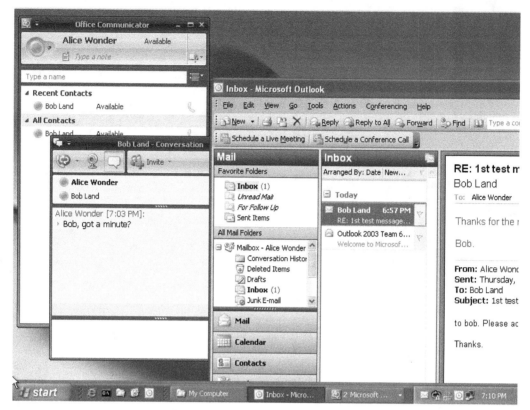

Figure 9: MOC and Outlook 2003 on XP client.

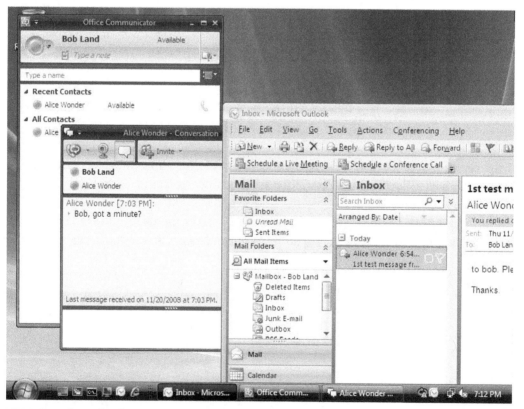

Figure 10: MOC and Outlook 2007 on Vista client.

Wrapping up

Generally, you should install the Hyper-V Integration Components into each guest VM. This is carried out to boost performance and enhance host-guest integration. Other than the machines with Vista SP1 and Windows Server 2003 SP2 in our test lab, all the other Windows operating systems do not fulfill the prerequisites to support the integration components. Therefore, the integration components are not installed in our test lab at the expense of VM performance improvements. This is a deliberate decision and does not affect the lab infrastructure.

Not surprisingly, there are already a number of patches and hotfixes since the official RTM of the various products. After you determine that functional tests of the enterprise services (directory, messaging, unified communications, etc.) perform as expected, consider applying the updates to bring the applications current. Before you do that, it is a good idea to save a working set of all the VMs by using Hyper-V's export feature. Subsequently, you can take a snapshot for each VM to enable quick rollback to a known state.

Using Hyper-V as the host virtualization solution is not without its shortcomings, though. Because there is no native support for built-in sound card and USB devices, you cannot extend the test lab to include scenarios that involve enterprise voice communications (VoIP), Exchange 2007 Unified Messaging, fax integration or any hardware dependent services. Moreover, Novell SUSE Linux Enterprise 10 is the only non-Windows operating system supported in Hyper-V. You will have to look elsewhere if you are considering building integration solutions based on other Linux distributions or operating systems. One good example is the recently released Cisco Unified Communications Server 7.0 family of products.

To overcome such constraints, you can set up another physical machine to run VMware Server 2.0 or VMware Workstation 6.5 hosted on Windows 2003/2008 x64 editions. Unfortunately, these products will not even install when Hyper-V is detected on the host machine, so this extra hardware investment is essential.

Parting words

By now, you should have a fully functional test lab to simulate a majority of real-world scenarios. All traffic is confined to the internal network (local only, private virtual network) and it does not take much to extend the test lab to cover external network segments. Subsequently, more VMs can be added to provide important services such as security, system configuration, monitoring and patch management. We'll look at these in a subsequent article.

A Beginner's Guide to Virtualizing Exchange Server: Part 1

05 May 2009

by Brien Posey

....

The advantage of virtualizing your servers is that it helps you make better use of your hardware resources, and reduces some of your licensing costs. However, there are disadvantages: With Exchange server, it isn't always obvious as to which server roles are suitable for virtualization, and it is rather hard to work out what system resources a virtual server is actually using. Brien Posey explains.

....

Virtualization is one of the hottest trends in IT today. Virtualization allows administrators to reduce costs by making better use of underused server hardware. Often times, virtualization has the added benefit of reducing server licensing costs as well. For all of its benefits, though, there are some downsides to virtualizing your servers. Capacity planning and scalability become much more important in virtualized environments, and yet measuring resource consumption becomes far more difficult. In this article series, I want to talk about server virtualization as it relates to Exchange Server.

Microsoft's support policy

Before I even get started, I want to address the issue of whether or not Microsoft supports virtualizing Exchange Server. There seems to be a lot of confusion around the issue, but the official word is that Microsoft does support Exchange Server virtualization, although with some heavy stipulations.

I don't want to get into all of the stipulations, but I will tell you that Exchange Server 2003 is only supported if you use Microsoft's Virtual Server as the virtualization platform. Microsoft does not support running Exchange Server 2003 in a Hyper-V environment.

I could never, with a clear conscience, tell you to deploy an unsupported configuration. I will admit, however, that I virtualized my production Exchange 2003 servers using Hyper-V before Microsoft announced that the configuration would not be supported. To this day, I am still using this configuration, and it has been performing flawlessly.

Exchange Server 2008 can be virtualized using any hypervisor-based virtualization platform that has been validated under Microsoft's Windows Server Virtualization Validation program (HTTP://GO.MICROSOFT. COM/FWLINK/?LINKID=125375) including Hyper-V and VMWare ESX.

There are a number of stipulations that you need to be aware of, though. These stipulations are all outlined in Microsoft's official support policy, which you can read at HTTP://TECHNET.MICROSOFT.COM/ EN-US/LIBRARY/CC794548.ASPX.

Server roles

One of the biggest considerations that you must take into account when you are planning to virtualize Exchange Server 2007 is which server roles you want to virtualize. Microsoft's official support policy states that they support the virtualization of all of Exchange Server's roles, except for the Unified Messaging role. As such, you would think that figuring out which roles are appropriate for virtualization would be relatively simple. Even so, this is a fiercely debated topic, and everyone seems to have their own opinion about the right way to do things.

Since I can't possibly tell you which roles you should virtualize without being ridiculed by the technical editors and receiving a flood of email from readers, I am simply going to explain the advantages and the disadvantages of virtualizing each role, and let you make up your own mind as to whether or not virtualizing the various roles is appropriate for your organization.

The Mailbox server role

The mailbox server role is probably the role that receives the most attention in the virtualization debate. Opponents of virtualizing mailbox servers argue that mailbox servers make poor virtualization candidates because they are CPU and I/O intensive, and because the virtualization infrastructure adds to the server's CPU overhead.

While it is true that mailbox servers are I/O intensive, that may not be a deal breaker when it comes to virtualization. Many larger organizations get around the I/O issue by storing the virtual hard drives used by the virtualized mailbox server on a SAN. Smaller organizations may be able to get around the I/O issue by using SCSI pass-through storage to host the mailbox database and the transaction logs.

I have seen several different benchmark tests that show that, while the abstraction layers used by the virtualization platform do place an increased load on the CPU, CPU utilization only goes up by about 5% (assuming that Hyper-V or VMWare ESX is being used).

The whole point of using virtualization is to make better use of underutilized hardware resources. Therefore, if your mailbox server is already running near capacity, then virtualizing it probably isn't such a good idea. Even in those types of situations, though, I have seen organizations implement CCR, and use a Virtual Machine to host the passive node, while the active node continues to run on a dedicated server.

The Hub Transport role

The Hub Transport server role is one of the most commonly virtualized Exchange 2007 roles. Even so, it is important to remember the critical nature of this server role. All messages pass through the Hub Transport server, and if the server crashes then mail flow stops.

When you are determining whether or not you want to virtualize a Hub Transport Server, it is important to make sure that you have some sort of fault tolerance in place. You should also use performance monitoring and capacity planning to ensure that the transport pipeline is not going to become a bottleneck once you virtualize the Hub Transport Server.

The Client Access server role

Whether or not the CAS server should be virtualized depends on a number of factors. For instance, many organizations choose to use CAS as an Exchange front end that allows users to access their mailboxes through OWA. If this is how you are using your CAS server, then you need to consider the number of requests that the CAS server is servicing. Some organizations receive so much OWA traffic that they need multiple front-end servers just to deal with it all. If your organization receives that much traffic, then you are probably better off not virtualizing your CAS servers.

On the other hand, if you only use CAS because it is a required role, or if your users don't generate an excessive number of OWA requests, then your CAS server might be an ideal candidate for virtualization. The only way to know for sure is to use the Performance Monitor to find out how many of your server's resources are being consumed. Performance monitoring is important because other functions such as legacy protocol proxying (Pop3/IMAP), Outlook Anywhere (RPC over HTTP), and mobile device support can also place a heavy workload on a CAS server.

The Edge Transport server role

The Edge Transport server is one of the more controversial roles when it comes to virtualization. Many administrators are reluctant to virtualize these servers because they fear an escape attack. An escape attack is an attack in which a hacker manages to somehow break out of the confines of a Virtual Machine and take control of the entire server. To the best of my knowledge, though, nobody has ever successfully performed an escape attack.

If you are concerned that someone might one day figure out how to perform an escape attack, but you want to virtualize your Edge Transport server, then my advice would be to carefully consider what other virtual servers you want to include on the server. The Edge Transport server is designed to sit in the DMZ, so if you are concerned about escape attacks, then why not reserve the physical server for only hosting Virtual Machines that are intended for use in the DMZ. That way, in the unlikely event that an escape attack ever does occur, you don't have to worry about the physical server containing any data.

The Unified Messaging server role

As I stated earlier, the Unified Messaging role is the only Exchange 2007 role that Microsoft does not support in a virtualized environment. Even so, I have known of a couple of very small organizations that have virtualized their Unified Messaging servers, and it seems to work for them. Personally, I have to side with Microsoft on this one, and say that just because you can virtualize a unified messaging server, doesn't mean that you should. Unified Messaging tends to be very CPU intensive, and I think that is probably the reason why Microsoft doesn't want you to virtualize it.

Resource consumption

Capacity planning is an important part of any Exchange Server deployment, but it becomes even more important when you bring virtualization into the picture. This is because virtualizing implies that your Exchange Server is only going to be able to use a fraction of the server's overall resources, and that the virtualized Exchange Server is going to have to compete with other Virtual Machines for a finite set of physical server resources. The problem with this is that it can be very tricky to figure out just how much of a server's resources your virtual Exchange Server is actually using.

To show you what I am talking about, I want to show you three screen captures. First, take a look at the screen capture that is shown in Figure A. This screen capture shows a lab machine that is running three virtual servers. One of these virtual servers is a domain controller, another is running OCS 2007, and the third is running an Exchange 2007 mailbox server (this is a sample configuration, not a recommendation).

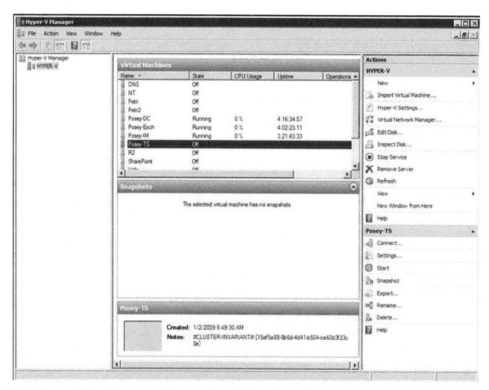

Figure A: This lab machine is currently running three virtual servers.

If you look at the figure, you will notice that all three machines are running, and have been running for a few days straight. You will also notice that the Hyper-V Manager reports each server as using 0% of the server's CPU resources. Granted, all three of these machines are basically idle, but there is no way that an Exchange 2007 mailbox server is not consuming at least some CPU resources.

The second screen capture that I want to show you is in Figure B. This screen capture was taken from the same server, but this time I put a load on my Exchange 2007 mailbox server. While doing so, I opened up two instances of the Performance Monitor. One instance is running within the host operating system, and the other is running within the virtual Exchange server. Even though these two screen captures were taken at exactly the same time, they paint a completely different picture of how the server's resources are being used. I will explain why this is the case later on, but you will notice that the host operating system reports much lower resource usage than the guest operating system does, even though there are a couple of other guest operating systems that are also running on the host.

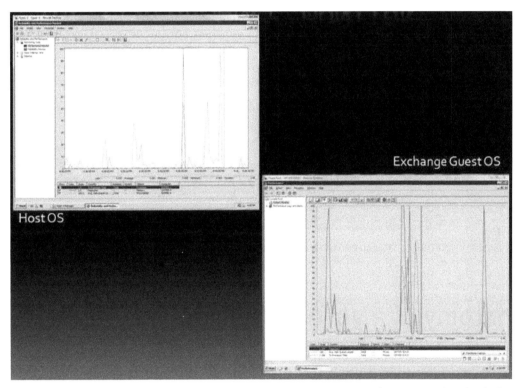

Figure B: The host operating system and the guest operating systems have completely different ideas about how resources are being used.

The last screen capture is shown in Figure C. What I wanted to show you in this screen capture is that even the Hyper-V Manager and the Windows Task Manager, which are both running within the host operating system can't agree on how hard the CPU is working. The Hyper-V Manager indicates that 5% of the CPU resources are being used, while the Windows Task Manager implies that 3% of the CPU resources are in use (97% of the CPU resources are free).

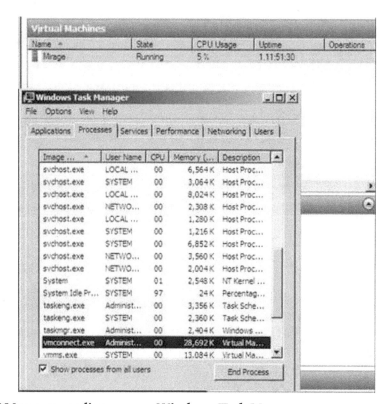

Figure C: Hyper-V Manager readings versus Windows Task Manager.

The anatomy of a Virtual Machine

So why do these discrepancies exist? In order to answer that question, you need to understand a little about the anatomy of a Virtual Machine. Before I get started, though, I need to point out that Virtual Machines are implemented differently, depending on which virtualization product is being used. For the sake of this discussion, I am going to be talking about Microsoft's Hyper-V.

As I'm sure you know, Hyper-V (like many other virtualization products) is classified as a hypervisor. Hyper-V is what is known as a type 2 hypervisor. A type 2 hypervisor sits on top of a host operating system, as opposed to a type 1 hypervisor, which sits beneath the server's operating system at the bare metal layer.

A type 2 hypervisor isn't to be confused with hosted solution-based virtualization products such as Microsoft's Virtual PC or Virtual Server. Such products typically pass all of their hardware requests through the host operating system, which sometimes results in poor overall performance.

In contrast, guest operating systems in a Hyper-V environment do reside on top of the host operating system, but Hyper-V is only minimally dependent on the host operating system (which must be a 64-bit version of Windows Server 2008). The host operating system connects to each Virtual Machine through a worker process. This process is used for keeping track of the Virtual Machine's heartbeat, taking snapshots of the Virtual Machine, emulating hardware, and similar tasks.

Now that I have explained some of the differences between a type 1 and a type 2 hypervisor, I want to talk about how the Virtual Machines function within Hyper-V. Hyper-V is designed to keep all the Virtual Machines isolated from each other. It accomplishes this isolation through the use of partitions. A partition is a logical unit of isolation that is supported by the hypervisor.

Hyper-V uses two different types of partitions. The parent partition (which is sometimes called the root partition) is the lower level of the hypervisor. The parent partition runs the virtualization stack, and it has direct access to the server's hardware.

The other type of partition that is used by Hyper-V is a child partition. Each of the guest operating systems resides in a dedicated child partition. Child partitions do not have direct hardware access, but there is always at least one virtual processor and a dedicated memory area that is set aside for each child partition.

Initially, Hyper-V treats each of the server's processor cores as a virtual processor. Therefore, a server with two quad core processors would have eight virtual processors. It is important to keep in mind, though, that Hyper-V does not force a one-to-one mapping of virtual processors to CPU cores. You can allocate more virtual processors than you have CPU cores, although Microsoft recommends that you do not exceed a two-to-one ratio.

Hyper-V manages memory differently from the way that it would be managed in a non-virtualized environment. Hyper-V uses an Input Output Memory Management Unit (IOMMU) as a mechanism for mapping and managing the memory addresses for each child partition. In a non-virtualized environment, low-level memory mapping is handled primarily at the hardware level (although the Windows operating system does perform some higher level memory mapping of its own).

Earlier, I mentioned that hypervisor-based virtualization products tend to be more efficient than hosted solution-based virtualization products, which pass all hardware calls through the host operating system. A big part of this efficiency is related to the root partition's ability to communicate directly with the server hardware. As you will recall, though, the guest operating systems reside in child partitions, which do not have the ability to talk directly to the server hardware. So what keeps the guest operating systems from suffering from poor performance?

There are several different mechanisms in place that help to improve the child partition's efficiency, but one of the primary things that helps with guest operating performance is something called "enlightenment." If you have ever installed a guest operating system in Hyper-V, then you know that one of the first things that you normally do after the operating system has been installed is to install the integration services. Technically, the integration services are not a requirement, and it's a good thing that they aren't. Many non-Windows operating systems, as well as most of the older versions of Windows don't support the integration services.

The first thing that most administrators notice after installing a guest operating system is that they can't access the network until the integration services have been installed. This is where enlightenment comes into play. After the integration services have been installed, the guest operating system is said to be "enlightened." What this really means is that the guest operating system becomes aware that it is running in a virtualized environment and, as such, is able to access something called the VM Bus. This makes it possible for the guest operating system to access hardware such as a network adapter or SCSI drives without having to fall back on an emulation layer. Incidentally, it is possible to access the network from a non-enlightened partition. You just have to use an emulated network adapter. In fact, I recently virtualized a server that was running Windows NT 4.0, and it is able to access the network by using the partition's emulation layer.

Let's get back to my original question. Why does the host operating system disagree with the guest operating systems about the amount of resources that are being used? The answer lies in the way that Hyper-V uses partitioning. Each partition is a completely isolated set of logical resources, and the host operating system lacks the ability to look inside individual partitions to see how resources are truly being consumed.

At first, this would seem to be irrelevant. After all, CPU usage is CPU usage, right? Remember, though, that child partitions use virtual processors instead of communicating directly with the physical processor. It is the hypervisor (not the host operating system) that is responsible for scheduling virtual processor threads on physical CPU cores.

Ever since the days of Windows NT, it has been possible to determine how much CPU time is being consumed by monitoring the **\Processor(*)\% Processor Time** counter in the Performance Monitor. When you bring Hyper-V into the equation, though, this counter becomes extremely unreliable from the standpoint of the system as a whole, as you have already seen.

If you monitor the **\% Processor Time** counter from within a guest operating system, you are seeing how hard the virtual processors are working, but in a view that is relative to that Virtual Machine, not the server as a whole. If you watch this counter on the host operating system, the Performance Monitor is not aware of CPU cycles related to the hypervisor.

As you will recall, the screen captures that I showed you earlier generally reflected extremely low CPU utilization for Virtual Machines. The fact that the host operating system isn't aware of CPU cycles related to hypervisor activity certainly accounts for at least some of that, but there are a number of other reasons why CPU utilization appears to be so low.

Hyper-V allows you to decide how many virtual processors you want to allocate to each virtual server. This can be a limiting factor in and of itself.

For instance, if a server has four CPU cores, and you only allocate one virtual processor to a child partition, then that partition can never consume more than 25% of the server's total CPU resources, regardless of how the partition's CPU usage is actually reported.

Things can get a little strange when you start trying to allocate more virtual processors than the number of physical CPU cores that the server has. For instance, suppose that you have a server with four CPU cores, and you allocate eight virtual processors. In this type of situation, the Virtual Machines will try to use double the amount of CPU time that is actually available. Since this is impossible, CPU time is allocated to each of the virtual processors in a round-robin fashion. When this occurs, CPU utilization is reported as being very low, because the workload is being spread across so many (virtual) processors.

In reality, the Virtual Machine's performance will be worse than it would have been had a fewer number of virtual processors been allocated. Allocating fewer virtual processors tends to cause CPU utilization to be reported as being higher than it would be, had more virtual processors been allocated, but performance ultimately improves because there is a significant amount of overhead involved in distributing the workload across, and then allocating CPU time to all those virtual processors.

Conclusion

As you can see, the values that are reported by the Performance Monitor and by other performance measuring mechanisms vary considerably, depending on where the measurement was taken. In Part 2, later in this book, I will show you why this is the case, and how you can more accurately figure out what system resources a virtual Exchange Server is actually consuming.

Windows Server Virtualisation: Introduction to Hyper-V

01 June 2009

by Jaap Wesselius

For SQL Server and Exchange Server, Windows Server Virtualization is going to be increasingly important as a way for the administrator to allocate hardware resources in the most efficient way, to offer more robust services, and for deploying services. Jaap Wesselius starts his new series on Hyper-V by explaining what Hyper-V is, how it relates to Windows Server 2008 and how it compares to ESX, Virtual Server, and Virtual PC.

Hyper-V introduction

Microsoft released Hyper-V, its hypervisor based virtualization product, in the summer of 2008; but what's the difference with Virtual Server? And why is Hyper-V a better product than Virtual Server? And what's the difference with VMware ESX for example? In a series of articles I'll try to explain what Hyper-V is, how it relates to other products, and I'll also try to give some best practices regarding the its use.

Windows architecture

Before we take a look at the Hyper-V architecture, we need to be clear about the architecture of Windows Server 2008 (and basically all Windows NT servers). When Windows Server 2008 is installed on appropriate hardware, two modes can be identified:

- **Kernel mode** – this is a protected space where the kernel, the "heart" of Windows Server 2008 is running, and where processes run that interact directly with the hardware, for example, the device drivers using buffers allocated in kernel mode. When such a process crashes, it is very likely that the server will crash as well, which will result in a blue screen of death.

- **User mode** – this is a more protected space where applications are running, for example, Microsoft Office, SQL Server, or Exchange Server. When an application in User Mode crashes, only the application stops and the server continues running.

361

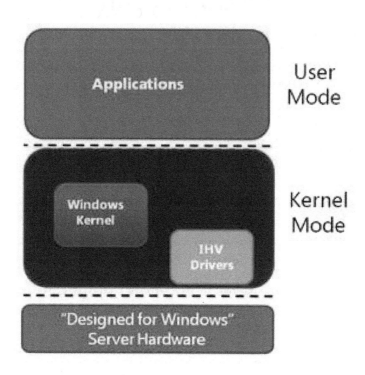

Figure 1: User and kernel modes running under Windows Server 2008.

When an application needs to access a piece of hardware, for example, the hard disk or the network interface, the application needs to communicate with the appropriate driver running in kernel mode. Switching from user mode to kernel mode is a costly process and consumes a considerable amount of processor cycles. This is known as "mode switching."

Virtual Server and Virtual PC are applications and, as such, are running in user mode, the complete environment where the Virtual Machine is emulated. After installing the Virtual Machine additions, or when using Hardware Assisted Virtualization, some kernel processes are handled directly by the processor. Every piece of hardware the Virtual Machine has to access has to go from user mode to kernel mode and vice versa. The overhead in this scenario is large and will have a large performance impact. The same is true for VMware Server and VMware workstation.

Hyper-V architecture

Hyper-V is a so-called hypervisor. The hypervisor is installed between the hardware and the operating system. Hyper-V is a role in Windows Server 2008 and can only be installed after Windows Server 2008 is installed. When installing the Hyper-V role, the hypervisor is "slid" between the hardware and the operating system. Besides the hypervisor, a little more is installed as well. The VMBus is installed which is running in kernel mode as well as a Virtual Storage Provider (VSP). Furthermore a WMI provider is installed which is running in user mode. A VMWorker process is spawned for every Virtual Machine that's started when Hyper-V is running.

Note

Hyper-V is only available on Windows Server 2008 X64 edition. Besides X64-capable hardware, the server should support hardware virtualization, and Data Execution Prevention (DEP) should be enabled on the server. The server's BIOS should support these settings as well.

After installing the Hyper-V role in Windows Server 2008, the server needs to be rebooted and is then operational. The original Windows Server 2008 that was installed is turned into a Virtual Machine as well, this one is called the "root" or the "parent partition." It is a very special Virtual Machine, since it controls the other Virtual Machines running on the server. I'll get back to this later in this article.

Virtual Machines and the parent partition on Hyper-V are running side by side as shown in Figure 2. Virtual Machines are called "child partitions." There are three types of Virtual Machines:

- Hypervisor aware Virtual Machines, like Windows Server 2003 and Windows Server 2008.

- Non-hypervisor aware Virtual Machines, like Windows Server 2000 and Windows NT4. These Virtual Machines run in an emulated environment.

- Xen-enabled Linux kernels (which also support the VMBus architecture). The only one that's available as a standard distribution at this point is SUSE Linux.

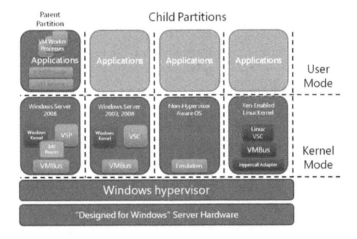

Figure 2:   The parent partitions and Virtual Machines in Hyper-V.

Now we're installing a Virtual Machine based on Windows Server 2008. This child partition is running on top of the hypervisor. When the Integration Components are installed, the new Virtual Machine can fully utilize the power of Hyper-V. The Integration Components are special Hyper-V drivers, the so-called synthetic drivers. Also, a Virtual Storage Client (VSC) is installed in the Virtual Machine. These drivers can use the VMBus structure. The VMBus is a point-to-point in-memory bus architecture, running fully in kernel mode. An application running in this Virtual Machine wants to access the network interface or a local disk on the parent partition and makes a request to do so. This request goes from user mode to kernel mode and is sent via the VSC over the VMBus to the VSP. From here, the request is sent to the appropriate device. No additional mode switching is needed, and this is truly a very fast solution.

363

A non hypervisor-aware Virtual Machine, for example a Windows NT4 server, does not have the Integration Components and a VSC. Everything is emulated, and it is emulated in the VMWorker processes. These processes are running in user mode on the parent partition.

When an application on this Virtual Machine makes a request to the local disk, the request is sent to the driver running in kernel mode in the Virtual Machine. This is intercepted and sent to the emulator on the parent partition which, in turn, sends it to the local disk. This means that three additional mode switches are needed. One in the Virtual Machine, from the Virtual Machine to the host partition, and on the actual host partition from user mode to kernel mode. This creates additional overhead which results in reduced performance for the emulated Virtual Machine. Virtual Server also makes use of a fully emulated environment and thus suffers from the same performance hit.

Virtual Machines running on SUSE Linux which have the Linux Integration Components installed can also fully utilize the new VMBus architecture and, thus, the server's resources. Other Linux clients use a fully emulated Virtual Machine, just like the NT4 example.

Micro-kernelized hypervisor

One difference between ESX and Hyper-V is the type of hypervisor. Microsoft uses a micro-kernelized hypervisor where VMware uses a monolithic hypervisor. So what are the differences between these two?

A micro-kernelized hypervisor is a very thin hypervisor (less then 800 Kb) with an absolute minimum of software in the hypervisor. Drivers, memory management, etc., needed for the Virtual Machines are installed in the parent partition. This means that Windows Server 2008 with the appropriate, certified hardware drivers can be used for a Hyper-V server.

A monolithic hypervisor is a hypervisor that contains more software and management interfaces. Network drivers and disk drivers, for example, are part of the hypervisor and not of the parent partition. This automatically means that only servers that are certified by VMware and have certified drivers can be used for an ESX Server.

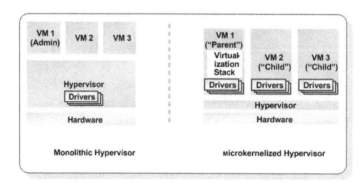

Figure 3: **Monolithic versus micro-kernelized hypervisor.**

Both solution have pros and cons, and time will tell which solution is the best one and offers the best performance and scalability.

Security

After the Hyper-V role is installed in Windows Server 2008, the original Windows installation automatically turns into a Virtual Machine, the so-called parent partition or root. After logging in to the parent partition this just looks like an ordinary Windows Server 2008. But it controls all other Virtual Machines running on the server, so special care needs to be taken.

When the parent partition is compromised with a virus or a Trojan horse, not only the parent partition is under somebody else's control, but potentially all Virtual Machines running on this server. The Hyper-V manager is available on this server, as well as all WMI interfaces that control the Virtual Machines running on this server. It is best practice to install no other software on the parent partition, and not to use it, for example, for browsing on the Internet. All applications and software should be installed on Virtual Machines and **not** on the parent partition.

A better solution is to use Windows Server 2008 Server Core. This is a very minimalist instance of Windows Server 2008, with few software or services installed. Also the Explorer is not present on the Server Core and, after logging in to this Server Core, only a Command Prompt is shown. Some small GUIs are available though, for example, the data-time applet to set the data and time on the server. Managing a Windows Server 2008 Server Core is definitely more difficult than managing a "normal" server with a Graphical User Interface (GUI) but, once you're used to it and can fully manage it, it is much safer due to the reduced attack surface.

Microsoft made a couple of design decisions with respect to security. Not using shared memory is one of these decisions. When using shared memory you can overcommit memory on your host server. Overcommitting is assigning more memory to Virtual Machines than there is available on the host server. By sharing memory pages between Virtual Machines it is possible to achieve this. Although this is definitely true, it was a security decision made by Microsoft to not use this feature.

Virtual Machines can be compromised as well, and this is also a situation you do not want to occur. But when a Virtual Machine is compromised it is not possible to access the hypervisor to take over the host server. It is also not possible to access other Virtual Machines.

This also means that when you have to copy data from one Virtual Machine to another, it's just like physical machines. You have to copy this data across the network using file shares. The only option that's possible is to copy plain text between your Parent Partition and a Virtual Machine using the **Copy Text** option in the Hyper-V Manager.

Integration components

When installing a Virtual Machine initially, this is running in an emulated environment. As explained earlier, this is not the most efficient way of running a Virtual Machine. After the initial installation, you have to install the Integration Components. Open the Hyper-V Manager, select the Virtual Machine, choose **Action** and select **Insert Integration Services Setup Disk**. This will install the Integration Components in your Virtual Machine. When finished, reboot the Virtual Machine and it's done.

When you install the Integration Components, the synthetic drivers are installed in the Virtual Machine, making it possible to have the Virtual Machine communicate via the VMBus architecture. This will speed up performance dramatically. You can see the Integration Components using the Virtual Machine's device manager in Figure 4.

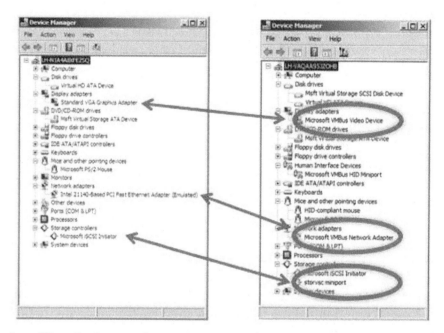

Figure 4: **After installing the Integration Components the emulated hardware is replaced by Hyper-V specific hardware.**

Besides the synthetic drivers the Integration Components offer more services to Virtual Machines, like time synchronization between the root partition and the Virtual Machine, backup options (volume snapshot) and operating system shutdown from the Hyper-V Manager.

Server Virtualization Validation Program

Microsoft has always been reluctant to support virtualized applications, especially in the timeframe before Hyper-V. In those days, Microsoft had only Virtual Server as virtualization software, while VMware was offering ESX Server.

When Hyper-V entered the virtualization market, Microsoft had not only to support their own software and applications running on Hyper-V, but also their applications running on other virtualization software, from other vendors. Microsoft has set up a program where other vendors can have their solutions validated. This program is known as the Server Virtualization Validation Program (SVVP). VMware's ESX Server, for example, is validated in this program, and all recommendations made for running Microsoft applications under Hyper-V also apply for running these applications under ESX Server. When issues are submitted by customers of Microsoft Product Support Services, Microsoft does not make a difference between ESX Server and Hyper-V when it comes to troubleshooting. You can find more information regarding the SVVP program on the Microsoft website at WWW.WINDOWSSERVERCATALOG.COM/SVVP.ASPX.

Conclusion

Microsoft Windows Server 2008 Hyper-V was released in the summer of 2008, and is Microsoft's first real hypervisor virtualization solution. It is not an emulated environment like Virtual Server or Virtual PC, but as a hypervisor solution it "sits" between the hardware and the operating system. With the Integration Components installed you can fully use the functionality offered by Hyper-V. You have to secure the Parent Partition as much as possible, to prevent compromising the complete system.

In further articles I will talk more about the Hyper-V best practices, deploying Virtual Machines, using the System Center Virtual Machine Manager (VMM) 2008 and the "high availability" options and why these aren't really high availability in the current release of Hyper-V.

Windows Server Virtualisation: Installing Hyper-V and Beyond

28 July 2009

by Jaap Wesselius

In his previous article, entitled Windows Server Virtualisation: Hyper-V, an Introduction, Jaap Wesselius explained about the Hypervisor, the parent partition, the child partition, and Integration Components. In this article, Jaap discusses installing Hyper-V, all kinds of Virtual Hard Disks, Virtual Networks, and some best practices.

Installing Hyper-V

Hyper-V is a Server Role within Windows Server 2008. This means that you have to install Windows Server 2008 before installing Hyper-V. The hardware requirements for installing Hyper-V are:

- the processor needs to support hardware virtualization (AMD-V or Intel VT)

- hardware enforced Data Execution Prevention (DEP); the Intel XD bit needs to be enabled or the AMD NX bit needs to be enabled

- the processor needs to be an X64 processor.

Furthermore you need plenty of physical memory in the server. For testing purposes, the absolute minimum is 4 GB of memory; the amount of memory needed in a production environment is dependent of the services you want to run.

Windows Server 2008 Hyper-V is a Server Role in the Standard Edition, Enterprise Edition and the Datacenter Edition. From a technical perspective there's no difference, it's a licensing issue.

- Install Standard Edition and you are allowed to run one Virtual Machine using the same license.

- Install Enterprise Edition and you are allowed to run four Virtual Machines using the same license.

- Install Datacenter Edition and you are allow to run as many Virtual Machines as the server can handle.

Note

There's also a Hyper-V Server available. This is a very small Operating System (command-line based) that's only capable of running the Hypervisor, nothing else. There are a few graphical UIs, like the date and time applet, but it's mainly command-line. Hyper-V Server is a free download, but when configuring Virtual Machines you need one license for each Virtual Machine!

Install Windows Server 2008 using your corporate standards, and bring it up to date with the latest hotfixes or service packs. Windows Server 2008 is now running on "bare metal" and there's no difference from any other Windows Server.

Log on to the server and open the Server Manager. In the left pane select **Roles** and in the right pane you'll see **Roles: 0 of 18 installed**. Click on **Add Roles** and select **Hyper-V** in the **Select Server Roles** Window.

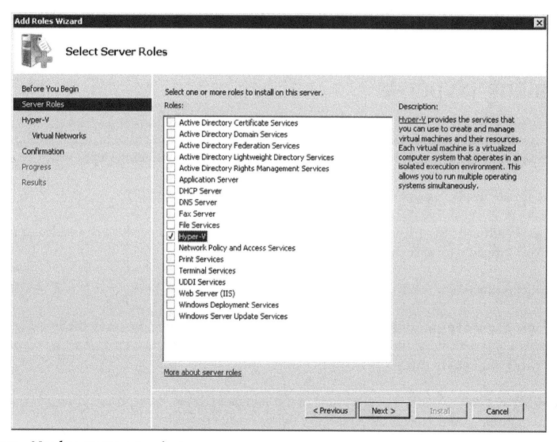

Figure 1: **Need to create a new image.**

Click **Next** to install the Hyper-V Server role. The wizard also includes the possibility to create Virtual Networks. We'll cover that later in this article so leave all options blank and click **Next** to continue.

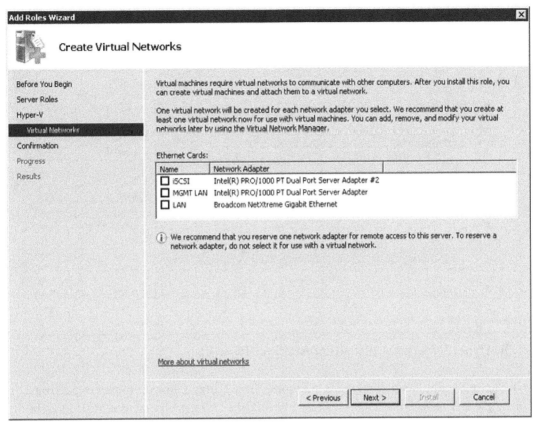

Figure 2: In the Add Roles wizard there's the possibility to create Virtual Networks. You can create these later, as well.

Right now, the actual Hypervisor "slides" under the Operating System, making the original Windows Server 2008 instance a Virtual Machine. Also the VM Worker processes (responsible for emulating devices), some WMI interfaces, the VM Bus, and the Virtual Storage Provider (VSP) are installed.

When finished the server needs to be rebooted. During the reboot process, the Hypervisor will be started initially which will hand over the boot process to Windows Server 2008, which is now the Parent Partition. The Parent Partition is also referred as the Root Partition.

When you log on after rebooting you'll see nothing special, it just looks like Windows Server 2008, and it is. The only new part is the Hyper-V Manager that can be found in the **Administrative Tools** menu.

The Hyper-V Manager is an MMC snap-in, with a server pane (left), a results pane (middle) and an actions pane (right). In the server pane you'll see only the server that you're logged on to, additional Hyper-V servers can be added later on.

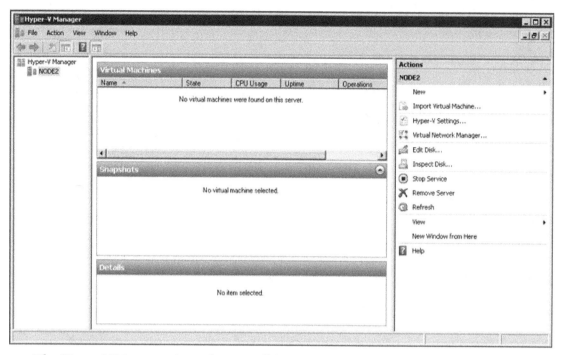

Figure 3: The Hyper-V Manager, just after installing Hyper-V.

One of the first things that has to be done is changing the settings. Click on **Hyper-V Settings...** in the actions pane and enter new paths for the Virtual Hard Disks and the Virtual Machine. By default, these will be placed on the C:\ drive, but from a performance perspective these should be configured on a separate drive. This can be a physical disk in the server, a storage cabinet attached to the server, or a SAN (iSCSI or Fiber).

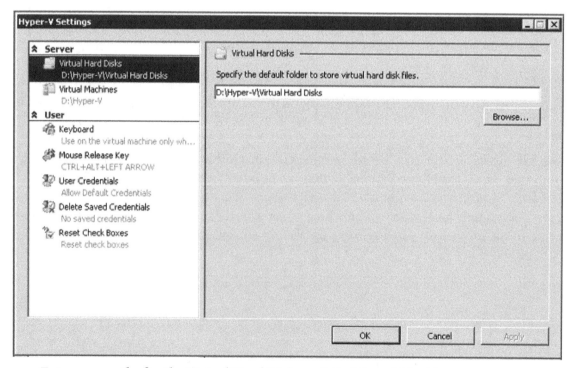

Figure 4: Enter new paths for the Virtual Hard Disks and the Virtual Machine.

The Virtual Machines are using the D:\Hyper-V directory in the example in Figure 4. This means that the configuration files will be placed in this directory. But snapshots will also be placed in this directory. Therefore, it is best practice not to place the Virtual Machines on the C:\ drive. When using snapshots extensively, this disk will fill up rapidly with snapshot information.

Virtual hard disks

Hyper-V uses Virtual Hard Disks for storing data. A Virtual Hard Disk is stored as a .VHD file on the disk of the Hyper-V server. There are three types of Virtual Hard Disks:

- **Dynamically Expanding Disks** – the dynamically expanding disk is a VHD file that's initially very small (2 MB) and that grows on demand. When more space is needed, Hyper-V will automatically assign more space to this VHD. A 50 GB disk will start as a 2 MB file, but the Virtual Machine will see it as a 50 GB disk. This is perfectly suited for test and development environments.

- **Fixed Size Disks** – the fixed size disk is a VHD file that has the complete size allocated before it can be used. A 50 GB disk also means a 50 GB VHD file. Pre-allocating 50 GB for a Virtual Disk can take a considerable amount of time. Microsoft recommends using fixed size disks for using Virtual Machine in a production environment, since it does not have the overhead of growing the VHD file.

- **Differencing Disks** – differencing disks consist of two virtual hard disks. One virtual hard disk is designated as a read-only disk, changes made by the Virtual Machine are written to the second disk. This will allow us to create a "master image" and use several Virtual Machines based on the master image. This is a perfect solution for creating a test environment within minutes.

There's also a fourth type of disk, the **pass-through** or **dedicated disk**. This is a dedicated disk on the Parent Partition that's connected to a disk controller of a Virtual Machine. The complete disk is used in this configuration without the VHD file. Therefore, it has no overhead. Besides the fixed-size disk, Microsoft also recommends using this kind of disk in a production environment. Check the Technet site for more information (HTTP://MSDN.MICROSOFT.COM/EN-US/LIBRARY/CC768529.ASPX).

The pass-through disk can be a physical hard disk in the Hyper-V host, but it can also be a LUN on an iSCSI or Fiber Channel SAN.

To create a new Virtual Hard Disk open the Hyper-V Manager, in the **Actions Pane** click **New** and select **Hard Disk...** . The New Virtual Hard Disk Wizard shows up with a welcome screen. Click **Next** to continue. In the **Choose Disk Type** window you can select what type of VHD needs to be created. Please be aware that creating a large fixed VHD file will take a considerable amount of time!

I will cover a dedicated or pass-through disk later in this article, after the creation of a Virtual Machine.

373

Virtual networks

By default, Virtual Machines are not connected to any network, so they are pretty useless actually. To connect Virtual Machine to each other, to the Parent Partition, or to the network outside the Hyper-V host, Virtual Networks need to be used.

Three types of Virtual Networks are available:

- **Private Virtual Network** – this is a virtual network that's only available for Virtual Machines running on the Hyper-V server. There's absolutely no possibility for the VMs to connect to the outside world, or to the Hyper-V server.

- **Internal Virtual Network** – this is a virtual network that's available for the Virtual Machines, but also for the Parent Partition. VMs can connect to the Parent Partition using the Internal Virtual Network. When Internet Connection Sharing (ICS) is enabled on the Parent Partition, the VMs can connect to the outside world using this connection.

- **External Virtual Network** – this is a virtual network that's connected to the network card on the Hyper-V server. Each Virtual Machine is capable using this network card to connect to the outside world. This also means that other computer on the network can "see" the Virtual Machines just as regular computers.

It is a Microsoft recommendation to use multiple network interfaces. One interface should be used for management purposes and be available only for the host. One network interface should be used for an External Virtual Network so that VMs can access the physical network as well. If you're using an iSCSI solution, an additional network interface for this should be used. For more information, check the Technet article, *7 Best Practices for Physical Servers Hosting Hyper-V Roles* (HTTP://TECHNET.MICROSOFT.COM/EN-US/MAGAZINE/DD744830.ASPX).

So, for having a Virtual Machine communicating with the outside world we have to create an External Virtual Network. Log on to the server and open the Hyper-V Manager. In the **Tasks** pane select the **Virtual Network Manager**.

Click **Add**, enter a name like *Public Virtual Network* and select the network interface that needs to be used by this Virtual Network. In this example this is the first Broadcom that's available.

When you click **OK**, the new Virtual Network will be created. A warning message will pop up indicating you may temporarily lose network connectivity with the Hyper-V host. If you're connected via a Remote Desktop session you may have to re-establish the connection.

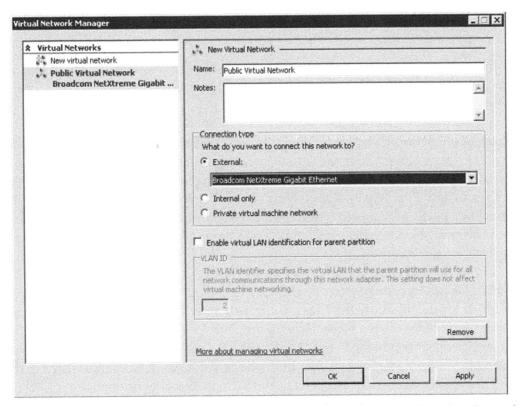

Figure 5: During the creation of an External Private Network you have to select the physical network interface.

When the new Virtual Network is created and you check the Network Connections, you'll notice a new entry; this is the new Virtual Network.

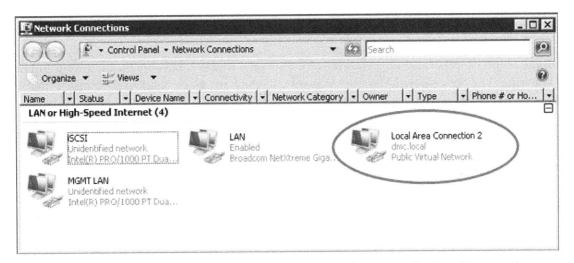

Figure 6: The new Network Connection after the creation of a External Virtual Network.

When you create a Virtual Machine and connect it to this new Virtual Network, the Virtual Machine will be able to access resources on the public network.

375

Virtual machines

On Hyper-V there are two types of Virtual machines, Supported and Unsupported Guest Operating Systems. This has nothing to do with the ability to run in a Hyper-V Virtual Machine, but whether it is directly supported by Microsoft:

- **Supported Guest Operating Systems** – these are Guest Operating Systems that are fully supported running on a Hyper-V server where the Guest Operating System can fully utilize the Hyper-V Infrastructure like the VMBus. Examples of these Operating Systems are: Windows Server 2008, Windows Server 2003 SP2, Windows 2000 Server with SP4, Windows Vista SP1, Windows XP Professional SP2 and SUSE Linux Enterprise Server 10 with Service Pack 2. For a complete list of all supported Operating Systems check the article, *Guest operating systems that are supported on a Hyper-V virtual machine* on the Microsoft site at HTTP://SUPPORT.MICROSOFT.COM/KB/954958.

- **Unsupported Guest Operating Systems** – these are Guest Operating Systems that can run on a Hyper-V server but do not utilize the Hyper-V infrastructure. These are running in an emulated environment and cannot use the native Hyper-V architecture. This is the VM Worker process. An emulated environment is running in User Mode in the Parent Partition. When a VM makes a call to, for example, a disk or a network, it goes through the VM, to the emulator and then to the actual hardware. This results in a serious I/O penalty, producing a slower performance.

Suse Linux Enterprise Server is a Supported Guest Operating System. This will run under Hyper-V, and if you encounter an issue you can call Microsoft Product Support. SCO Unix is an Unsupported Guest Operating System. This will run perfectly under Hyper-V but it is not supported by Microsoft, although it is fully supported by SCO. For more information check the SCO site.

Now we are going to create a Virtual Machine running Windows Server 2003 SP2. You can use the Windows installation CD or you can use an ISO image. The latter is usually faster.

Log on to the Hyper-V server and start the Hyper-V Manager. In the **Actions** pane click **New** and select **Virtual Machine**. The **New Virtual Machine Wizard** will show up. Click **Next** to continue. Enter a name for the new Virtual Machine, for example, *Windows Server 2003 X64*.

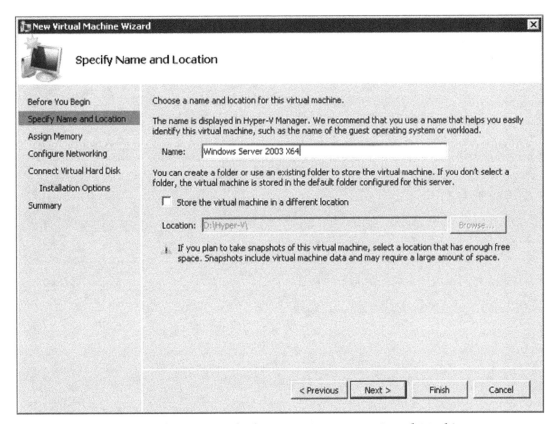

Figure 7: **The New Virtual Machine Wizard when creating a new Virtual Machine.**

The location will be same as we configured in the Hyper-V settings earlier in this article. You can check the **Store the virtual machine in a different location** check box if you want to have the new Virtual Machine on another location (i.e. another disk). Click **Next** to continue.

Enter the amount of memory that you want to assign to the VM. Please note that there's no real difference with a physical machine. If you fail to assign enough memory, the new Virtual Machine will be slow and sluggish. Another thing to remember is that, unlike VMWare, there's no way to overcommit memory. If you have 16 GB of RAM available, you can only assign 14 Virtual Machines 1 GB of RAM (assuming approximately 2 GB is used by the Parent Partition). The next stop is to connect the new Virtual Machine to a Virtual Network. Connect the Virtual Machine to the Public Virtual Network that we created earlier.

The new Virtual Machine needs a Virtual Hard Disk (VHD) to use. Since we did not create a VHD in advance use the default **Create a Virtual hard disk** setting.

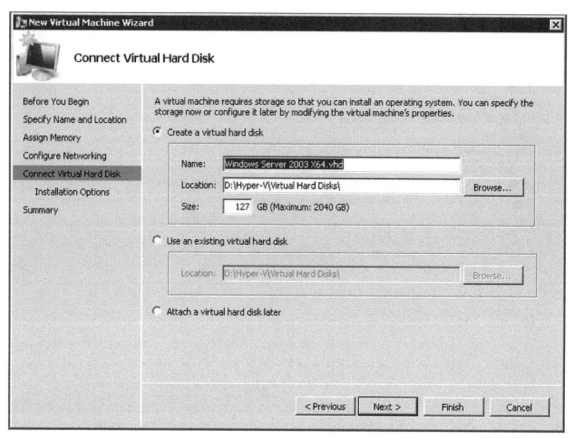

Figure 8:   A new Virtual Hard Disk will be created.

If you created a Virtual Hard Disk in advance, for example, a fixed size Virtual Hard Disk, you have to select Use an existing virtual hard disk and select the Virtual Hard Disk in the Location field. If you're using disk-intensive applications like SQL Server, MySQL or Exchange Server, fixed disks or pass-through disks should be used for best performance. Click **Next** to continue.

Since we will be installing a new Operating System we have to select the installation media. This can either be a CD/DVD or an ISO image, whichever you prefer.

Click **Finish** to end the New Virtual Machine Wizard. The new Virtual Machine is now ready to be booted, and we can continue to install the Operating System in the Virtual Machine.

Double-click on the new Virtual Machine in the Hyper-V Manager and press the **Virtual Power** button to boot the new Virtual Machine. Install Windows Server 2003 as usual.

***

Note

If you are accessing the Hyper-V server using Remote Desktop, it's not possible to use your mouse in the new Virtual Machine until you've installed the Integration Components. And Integration Components can only be installed after finalizing the setup of Windows, so the setup itself can be challenging. When you have access to the console itself then it's no problem, and the mouse works as expected.

***

Finishing the installation

When the setup of Windows Server 2003 in our example is finished, you have a new Virtual Machine that cannot do anything. When you check the Windows installation, for example, you'll notice that it doesn't have a network interface. The Virtual Machine is running in an "isolated box" and cannot do anything. The first thing you have to do is install the Integration Components. In Hyper-V, an introduction, (see the opening of this article) I covered the Virtual Storage Provider (VSP), the Virtual Storage Client (VSC) and the VM Bus. The Integration Components contain the software that's needed for working natively with Hyper-V. Open the Virtual Machine, select **Action** in the Virtual Machine menu and select **Insert Integration Services Setup Disk**. The Integration Components wizard will be started and the software will be installed. When finished, reboot the Virtual Machine and it will work just like a normal server!

Using a dedicated or pass-through disk

Creating a dedicated or pass-through disk requires a different approach. This is not really a Virtual Disk, but it is a physical disk connected to a virtual disk controller in a Virtual Machine. On the Hyper-V server, open the Server Manager and, under **Storage**, select **Disk Management**. Make sure that the disk you want to use as a dedicated disk is offline. This will ensure that the Parent Partition cannot access the disk. If it can access the disk, and write data on it, it will give unpredictable results in the Virtual Machine!

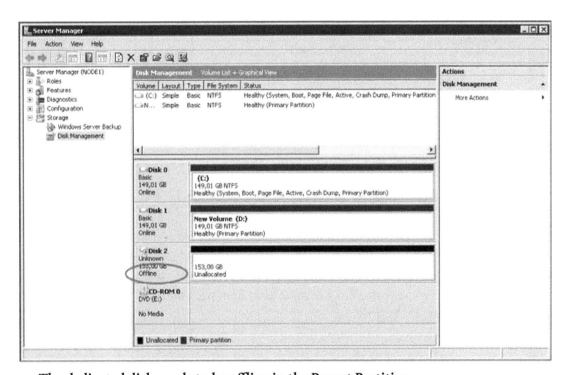

Figure 9: **The dedicated disk needs to be offline in the Parent Partition.**

In the Hyper-V Manager, right-click the Virtual Machine and select **Settings**. Select the **IDE Controller**, select Hard Drive and click Add. Under **Media** select **Physical Hard Disk** and select the disk you want to assign to this controller.

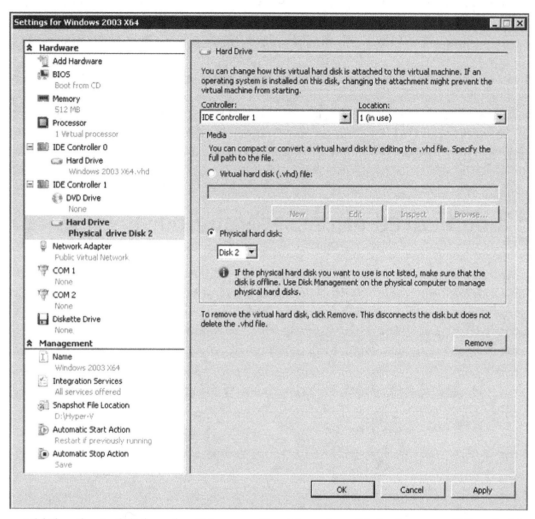

Figure 10: Add the physical disk to the disk controller. Note that this is the same disk as in Figure 8.

When you boot your Virtual Machine and open Disk Management the new disk will show up, ready to be partitioned and formatted.

Is it possible to boot from a pass-through disk? Yes, but only if assigned to the IDE controller. SCSI Controllers can be used for data disks. When creating a Virtual Machine that needs to boot from a pass-through disk you have to create the VM Configuration first, then add the pass-through disk to the IDE controller and then start up the VM.

Conclusion

In this article I have tried to give more information regarding the installation of Hyper-V, Hyper-V's Virtual Networks, Virtual Hard disks and Virtual Machines running under Hyper-V.

A Beginner's Guide to Virtualizing Exchange Server: Part 2

10 June 2009

by Brien Posey

It isn't easy to measure the consumption of physical resources by servers in Virtual Machines, since each partition has its own virtualised view of system resources. Not only that, but there is a subtle difference between virtual processors and physical processors. Brien Posey explains the special performance counters that can be used to get an accurate assessment, and goes on to describe how to test your physical servers to see if they are good candidates for virtualization.

If you read my first article in this series, you got something of a crash course in Hyper-V's architecture. Of everything that I covered in that article, though, there are two main points that you need to keep in mind:

- when it comes to virtualizing Exchange Server, it is critical that you monitor resource consumption so that you can ensure that there are sufficient hardware resources available to effectively service Exchange and any other Virtual Machines that may be running on the server

- each of the various resource monitoring mechanisms that I showed you tells a completely different story regarding how much of the server's physical resources are actually being consumed.

In other words, it is important to find out how much of the server's resources are being consumed, but you are not going to be able to do so in the usual way.

So why the discrepancy?

In my previous article, I showed you that when you monitor the amount of CPU time that the server is consuming, you will get different results, depending upon where the measurement was taken. I never really said why, though. The reason for this is that neither the root nor the child partitions control the APIC timer. In essence, this means that each partition has its own virtualized view of the system's available resources. It isn't that one set of performance counters is right and another set is wrong. All of the counters are correct from their own frame of reference. Remember that the goal of having multiple partitions is to isolate the Virtual Machines from one another. Therefore, no one single partition (including the root partition) has the full picture of how the system's resources are being used.

Monitoring CPU utilization

Traditionally, the **\Processor(*)\% Processor Time** performance monitor counter has been used to find out how much CPU time a server is consuming. As you have seen, though, this counter does not tell you the whole story when you use it in a Hyper-V environment.

There are ways of measuring CPU utilization in a Hyper-V environment but, before I show you how, it is important that you understand the difference between virtual processors and logical processors. Logical processors map directly to the number of CPU cores that are found in the system. For example, if you have a server that has two quad core CPUs installed, then the server has a total of eight CPU cores. Since logical processors correlate directly to the number of CPU cores, the server also has eight logical processors.

Hyper-V partitions do not directly use logical processors. Instead, they use virtual processors. As I explained in the first article, you can actually allocate more virtual processors to your partitions than the machine has logical processors. Therefore, if you want to know how much of the server's CPU resources are actually being consumed, you need to look specifically at the virtual processor utilization.

If you have ever used the Performance Monitor within the host operating system, you may have noticed that there are a number of Performance Monitor counters that are specifically related to Hyper-V. One of the most useful of these counters is the **\Hyper-V Hypervisor Logical Processor (_Total)\% Total Run Time** counter. This counter shows you the cumulative CPU consumption across all virtual processors. The output from this counter is presented as a percentage of the server's total CPU resources, just as the **\Processor(*)\% Processor Time** counter does on a non-virtualized system.

Microsoft even gives us some guidelines as to what is considered to be an acceptable level of utilization. According to Microsoft, if this counter is reflecting a value of 60% or less, then the server's CPU utilization is healthy. If the counter reflects a value of 60% to 89%, the server needs to be monitored, because it is in danger of exhausting available CPU resources. A value of 90% or above is considered to be a critical state in which the server's performance will suffer.

That is how you measure the server's CPU consumption as a whole. There are a couple of other Performance Monitor counters that you need to know about: the **\Hyper-V Hypervisor Logical Processor(_Total)\% Total Run Time** and **\Hyper-V Hypervisor Virtual Processor(_Total)\% Total Run Time** counters.

The **\Hyper-V Hypervisor Logical Processor(_Total)\% Total Run Time** counter shows you how hard the CPU is working from a logical processor standpoint, while the **\Hyper-V Hypervisor Virtual Processor (_Total)\% Total Run Time** counter looks at the workload from a virtual processor standpoint. Generally speaking, these two counters should be balanced so that they display roughly the same value.

If you find that logical CPU utilization is high, but that virtual CPU utilization is low, it is often a good indication that there are more virtual processors allocated to the server's partitions than the machine has logical processors. Although you can create more virtual CPUs than the number of logical CPUs that the server contains, you should try to use a one-to-one ratio when possible.

If you find that you have allocated an excessive number of virtual processors, Microsoft recommends using the **\Hyper-V Hypervisor Virtual Processor(*)\%Guest Run Time** counter to determine which virtual processors are consuming the most CPU resources. You can then begin removing lesser-used virtual processors from guest machines in an effort to try to reach a one-to-one virtual to logical processor ratio.

On the flip side, you may occasionally run into situations in which the logical processor utilization is low, but the virtual processor utilization is high. When this happens, you should consider allocating additional virtual processors to the partitions that need them most. Of course, you have to make sure that the operating system that is running within that partition will support the extra processors before you actually begin allocating any additional virtual processors. If you find that you have CPU resources to spare, but the guest operating systems do not support adding additional processors, then you might consider adding additional Virtual Machines to the physical server, to make better use of the server's resources.

Planning for Exchange

The techniques that I have shown you work well for figuring out how much of a server's resources are being consumed, but they may not do you a lot of good if you are trying to figure out whether or not a server has the resources to host a virtualized Exchange Server. Fortunately, there are a couple of tricks that you can use to gauge a server's capabilities before you try to virtualize your Exchange Server.

The first thing that you need to keep in mind is that, from a hardware requirement standpoint, Microsoft doesn't make any differentiation between a physical server and a virtual server. For instance, suppose that the Exchange Server role that you plan to deploy requires 2 GB of disk space. That 2 GB requirement remains the same whether you are going to be deploying Exchange on a physical server or on a virtual server.

Of course, adhering to the hardware requirements for Exchange Server will only get you so far. You have probably noticed that I have spent a whole lot of time in this series discussing how you can figure out how much of a server's CPU time is available. The reason for that is that Hyper-V makes it really easy to create a virtual server that adheres to specific hardware specifications. For instance, if you need a Virtual Machine with 2 GB of RAM, three hard drives that are 100 GB each, and two network adapters, then you can easily create such a machine by using the **Settings** option in the Hyper-V Manager.

CPU resources are a little bit more difficult to allocate, though. It's easy to tell Hyper-V how many virtual processors you want to assign to a Virtual Machine, and you even have the option of allocating CPU resources as a percentage of the server's total CPU resources. What you can't do, however, is tell Hyper-V to give your Virtual Machine the equivalent of a 2.8 GHz quad core processor. In other words, you can tell Hyper-V how many virtual processors to assign to a Virtual Machine, or you can tell it to use a percentage of the overall CPU resources, but there isn't a way of requesting a specific amount of processing power. That's why CPU monitoring and capacity planning is so important.

Of course this still leaves the question of how you can determine whether or not your host server is up to the job of running a virtualized instance of Exchange Server. If your Exchange Servers are currently running on physical hardware then the assessment process is easier than you might think.

The Microsoft Assessment and Planning Toolkit

Microsoft offers a free utility called the *Microsoft Assessment and Planning Toolkit* (HTTP://TECHNET. MICROSOFT.COM/EN-US/LIBRARY/CC936627.ASPX#_M). This utility can be used for a lot of different purposes, but one of the things that you can use it for is to test your physical servers to see if they are good candidates for virtualization.

Unfortunately, this utility isn't Exchange Server aware, so it isn't going to tell you that you can't virtualize one of your Exchange Servers because it isn't running a configuration that is supported in a virtual environment. What it will do, is collect performance data from your physical servers and then use that performance data to determine whether or not the server is a good candidate for virtualization based on its resource consumption, and on the resources that are provided by your host server.

I recommend running the Assessment and Planning Toolkit on a computer that's running Windows Vista, rather than running it directly on one of your servers. That way, you can minimize the utility's performance impact on the servers that you are going to be benchmarking. However, the machine that you run the utility on needs to have Microsoft Office installed. You won't even be able to install the utility unless you install Microsoft Office first.

Gathering performance data

The first step in analyzing your physical servers is to create a simple text file containing the NetBIOS names of the physical servers that you want to analyze. Just use Notepad to create the list, and put each server name on its own line.

Now that you have created a list of servers to analyze, open the Microsoft Assessment and Planning Solution Accelerator. When the console opens, click on the **Select a Database** link. You should now see a dialog box asking you if you would like to select an existing database, or if you would like to create a new database. Since this is the first time that we have used the Assessment and Planning Toolkit, choose the option to create a new database. Provide the database with a name, and click **OK**.

Next, select your newly created database from the console's **Assessment** pane, and then click the **Prepare Recommendations for Server Consolidation Using Windows Server 2008 Hyper-V or Virtual Server 2005 R2**. You will now see a message explaining that the wizard that you have chosen to use requires performance data. The message contains a link that you can use to capture performance data for your computers. Go ahead and click this link, and you will be prompted to supply the name and path of the text file that you created earlier.

After doing so, click **Next** and you will be prompted to provide a set of WMI credentials for the computers that you have specified. You can use the same credentials for each computer on the list, or you can specify separate credentials for each machine if necessary. When you are done, click **Next**.

You should now see a screen that asks you when the benchmark tests should complete. By default, the tests are set to run for an hour, but you can specify a different period of time if you wish. Keep in mind, though, that if you set the testing period to be too short, the wizard may not have enough data to make a good recommendation. Click **Next**, and you will see a summary of the settings that you have chosen. Take a moment to review these settings, and then click **Finish**. The performance monitoring process will now begin.

Analyzing the performance data

Now that we have completed the data collection process, it is time to analyze the results. To do so, click on the **Prepare Recommendations for Server Consolidation Using Windows Server 2008 Hyper-V or Virtual Server 2005 R2** link. When you do, Windows will launch the Server Virtualization and Consolidation Wizard.

The first thing that you will need to do when the wizard starts is to select the virtualization product that you plan on using. The wizard allows you to select either Hyper-V or Virtual Server 2005 R2.

Click **Next**, and you will be asked to provide some details regarding the host machine's CPUs. The wizard asks some fairly detailed questions regarding things like the sizes of the level 2 and level 3 caches, and the bus speed. Granted, answering these questions isn't rocket science, but it may require you to look up your server's specs. If you don't have a way of getting the specific details for your server's CPUs, then you can just select the make and model of the CPUs that the server is using, and the wizard will fill in the details for you. They might not be completely accurate in every situation, but they should at least be close enough to make the wizard's results reasonably accurate.

After you have filled in your CPU information, click **Next**, and you will be prompted to enter some details about your host server's disk configuration. This information is fairly easy to fill in. You just need to know the type and speed of the disks that will be used, and what type of array configuration (if any) will be used. When you are done, click **Next**.

The following screen prompts you to enter the number of network adapters that are installed in the host server, and the speed of those adapters. This screen is also the place where you tell the wizard how much memory is installed in your host server.

Click **Next**, and you will be asked if you would like to set a limit as to the number of Virtual Machines that the server can host. Personally, I recommend setting a limit, although the actual limit that you set is going to depend on what you feel comfortable with. I recommend setting a limit because the recommendations that the wizard is going to make are based on an hour's-worth of performance monitoring. Your peak usage may cause significantly higher resource consumption than what was recorded during the monitoring period. Besides that, though, it is smart to leave some room for future growth.

Click **Next**, and you will be asked to provide a text file containing a list of computer names. You should use the same text file that you used when you gathered performance data on your servers.

Click **Next** one more time, and you will see a screen that displays all of the settings that you have entered. Take a moment to verify that you have entered this information correctly, and then click **Finish**. The Microsoft Assessment and Planning Solution Accelerator will now create the requested reports.

Viewing the results

When the report generation process eventually completes, click **Close**, and you will be returned to the main console screen. You can access the reports by clicking the **View Saved Reports and Proposals** link. When you do, you will find that the wizard has created two documents. The first document is an Excel spreadsheet that contains the raw performance data from each of the servers that you are considering as virtualization candidates. The second document is a Microsoft Word document that contains detailed recommendations for virtualizing your proposed servers. These recommendations are based on the performance data that was collected and the information that you provided about your host server.

One thing that is important to understand is that the wizard does not perform any types of benchmarks on your host server. Therefore, the recommendations that the wizard makes are only as good as the information that you provide it with.

Conclusion

There are obviously many more virtual server resources that you can monitor, other than just the CPU. Keep in mind, though, that once you understand the basic concepts involved in monitoring CPU resources, many of those same concepts can be applied to monitoring other types of resources.

Increasing the Availability of Virtualized Applications and Services

22 October 2009

by Nirmal Sharma

By using a virtualized clustering computing environment with failover, you can improve server availability without using as many physical computers. A group of independent computers can work together to increase the availability of virtualised applications and services. If one of the cluster nodes fails, another node takes over to provide the service without disruption. Nirmal Sharma explains the failover process under Hyper-V, and how to improve the performance of a failover.

This article explains the internal process behind the Hyper-V Virtual Machine Resource DLL and the functions used to interact with cluster components to improve the failover process for Virtual Machines.

Most of the article talks about Hyper-V Resource DLL. It doesn't really show how to cluster Virtual Machines or how to configure Quick Migration in Hyper-V for Virtual Machines. Instead the article focuses more on the Hyper-V Resource DLL for Virtual Machines and the Failover Process for Virtual Machines running on Hyper-V Server.

Terms

Before we move ahead, let's define some important terms that we will be using.

Cluster Service
The Cluster Service is the main component of the Clustering Software which handles the communication between Resource Monitor and its managers. All the clustering managers run under the Cluster Service.

Resource Monitor
The Resource Monitor is part of the Clustering Software. This runs under the Cluster Service (Clussvc.exe) to handle the communications between the Resource DLL and the Clustering Software.

Resource DLL
The Resource DLL ships with cluster-aware applications. The functions executed by the Clustering Software are supported by the Resource DLL. The main function of the Resource DLL is to report the status of the application resources to the Clustering Software and execute the functions from its library as and when needed.

Cluster Configuration Database

The cluster configuration database is a registry hive that contains the state of the cluster. It is located at HKLM\Cluster at registry.

Resources

A resource is an entity that can provide a service to a client and can be taken offline and brought online by the Clustering Software. A resource must have its associated Resource DLL so that the Resource Monitor can communicate with the resources using this DLL. The Virtual Machines running on Hyper-V can be configured as a resource in the cluster. The Resource DLL for Virtual Machines is VMCLUSRES.DLL.

Windows clustering

Microsoft introduced its first version of clustering software in Windows NT 4.0 Enterprise Edition. Microsoft has significantly improved the clustering software in Windows 2000, Windows Server 2003, and Windows Server 2008. There are two types of clustering technologies: Server Cluster (formerly known as MSCS) and Network Load Balancing Cluster (NLB). MSCS or Server Cluster is basically used for High Availability. NLB is, of course, used to load balance the TCP/IP traffic. The MSCS or Server Cluster capability is also known as Failover Clustering. The support for Virtual Machines running on Hyper-V in a cluster is available only with Failover Clustering.

Virtual Machines and high availability

Support for clustering Virtual Machines was introduced in Windows Server 2008 running the Hyper-V role and has been continued in the versions that followed.

Windows Clustering includes many components such as Cluster Service, Resource Monitors, Node Manager, Membership Manager, Event Log Processor, Failover Manager, and Cluster Database Manager. The whole purpose of failover clustering is to provide high availability of application resources. Clustering doesn't get involved in deciding how much CPU and memory should be utilized by an application.

An application running in the clustering environment must be cluster-aware. A cluster-aware application supports the functions executed by the cluster service or its components as shown in Figure 1. There is no way for the Cluster Service to know about the availability of resources of an application in the cluster unless the application is cluster-aware. For example, if a node holding the application resources fails, the Cluster Service running on that node must be notified in order to start the failover process for the application's resources. The Cluster Service does this by receiving the responses from the Resource Monitor. The Resource Monitor tracks the Virtual Machines with the help of Resource DLLs provided by the Hyper-V role.

You cannot cluster Virtual Machines running on Virtual Server. The Virtual Machines running on Virtual Server do not provide any Resource DLL which can be used with the clustering software to make them highly available. On the other hand, the Virtual Machines running on Hyper-V are fully cluster-aware

Virtual Machines, supporting/responding to all functions executed by the cluster service. The Resource DLL of Hyper-V Virtual Machines, which supports all the functions, is **VMCLUSRES.DLL**. Hyper-V provides only one DLL for its Virtual Machines in the cluster. There are no other DLLs provided by the Hyper-V Role. We will discuss that DLL in detail in this article.

Tip

A Resource DLL is a separate application component that is specifically written to support cluster functions (for example, Open, Terminate, Online, Offline, Retry, and so on).

The Clustering Software Resource Monitor tracks the Hyper-V Virtual Machine's availability through VMCLUSRES.DLL by performing two checks: **IsAlive** and **LooksAlive**. Implementing these tests is application specific which is why cluster-aware applications are expected to provide their resource DLL. The Cluster Server doesn't need to know about application-specific functions. It just executes the functions provided by the Resource DLLs. Hyper-V implements many other functions in its Resource DLL. The functions are shown in Figure 1. These functions are Hyper-V Virtual Machine-specific and not related to clustering in any way.

Tip

*The two basic checks (**IsAlive** and **LooksAlive**) are supported by every Resource DLL or cluster-aware application.*

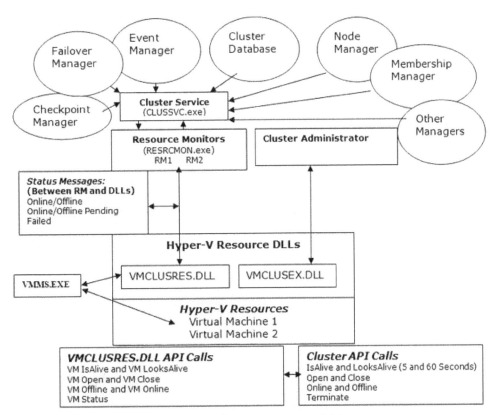

Figure 1:   Cluster components and Hyper-V Cluster Resource DLL.

In Figure 1 you can see the DLL VMCLUSRES.DLL is installed when the Hyper-V Role is enabled initially. Before you can cluster Virtual Machines running on Hyper-V, you need to install the Failover Clustering Software on Windows Server 2008 or 2008 R 64-bit edition. After installation is completed, you click on **Services and Applications** in Failover Cluster Management and then select the **Virtual Machines** as Cluster resource.

Tip

*If you don't see **Virtual Machines**, try running the commands below. This DLL must be registered before you can cluster Virtual Machines.*

Regsvr32.exe /u VMCLUSRES.DLL
Regsvr32.exe VMCLUSRES.DLL
The above command re-registers the VMCLUSRES.DLL with the Failover Clustering Software.

The next DLL is VMCLUSEX.DLL. This DLL works as a proxy between the Cluster Administrator and the Hyper-V Manager. The main function of this DLL is to provide interfaces to configure and control the Virtual Machines' configuration parameters and screens. If this DLL is missing or corrupted you can't access Virtual Machines. VMCLUSEX.DLL doesn't implement any cluster-specific control functions. As an example, when you right-click on a Virtual Machine resource using the Failover Cluster Manager, you will get the **Bring this Virtual Machine Online** option to start the Virtual Machine. The same will be reflected in Hyper-V Manager. You will see the Virtual Machine starting in the Hyper-V Manager also.

VMMS.EXE which is the main process of Hyper-V needs to know the status of Virtual Machines running on the Hyper-V Server. The Resource DLL is written to update the status of the Virtual Machines in a cluster to VMMS.EXE. VMMS.EXE, in turn, shows the status of each Virtual Machine in Hyper-V Manager.

VMCLUSRES.DLL which sits between Resource Monitor and Virtual Machines plays an important role in the failover process. Without this DLL Hyper-V cannot function as a cluster-aware application.

Tip

Malicious code running in your system may corrupt the DLL files.

- Re-run the Hyper-V Setup (disabling and enabling the role).

- Copy VMCLUSRES.DLL from a working computer.

Figure 1, above, also shows the functions defined in VMCLUSRES.DLL. The Hyper-V Virtual Machine-specific functions are mapped with the cluster-specific functions. For example, Cluster's **IsAlive** and **LooksAlive** functions are mapped with VM **IsAlive** and VM **LooksAlive** respectively. However, there are no static mappings defined within VMCLUSRES.DLL. VMCLUSRES.DLL knows which function to execute. In the same way, other Virtual Machines' functions are also mapped to related cluster functions as shown in Figure 1.

VM **IsAlive** and VM **LooksAlive** functions are executed by VMCLUSRES.DLL at a predefined interval. Most of the monitoring task is done by performing a VM **IsAlive** query. VM **IsAlive** is implemented in such a way that it performs all the checks for Hyper-V Virtual Machines. It checks to make sure all the Virtual Machines in cluster are online and configured with correct dependencies., and also that the registry entries for Virtual Machines' resources are configured correctly.

VM **LooksAlive** is used to perform a thorough check on the Virtual Machines in the cluster. This check might take some time, as it includes checking the configuration of Virtual Machine, Virtual Machine Configuration file location (XML), VHD location, etc. It might take some time for **LooksAlive** to perform these checks and report back the status to the Resource Monitor. To avoid the delays in reporting, the Resource Monitor cluster component depends on the results reported by **IsAlive**, which is configured to execute every 5 seconds by default. **IsAlive** only checks the status of Virtual Machine in the Cluster (e.g. Online or Failed). Based upon that, the action is taken by the Resource Monitor. Think of a situation where only **LooksAlive** is used to get the status of Virtual Machines in the Cluster. This may result in slightly more downtime of the Virtual Machines as **LooksAlive** calls are executed every 60 seconds! Now, you could ask, why not decrease the interval of **LooksAlive**? Well, if you do so, you will see a performance issue on the Cluster. Please note that the Resource Monitor component of Clustering Software executes **IsAlive** and **LooksAlive** queries against the whole Cluster Group. It is the responsibility of the Resource DLL (VMCLUSRES.DLL) to execute VM **IsAlive** and VM **LooksAlive** against its Virtual Machine resources. By default, the **IsAlive** check is performed every 5 seconds and **LooksAlive** check is performed every 60 seconds as shown in Figure 2, below.

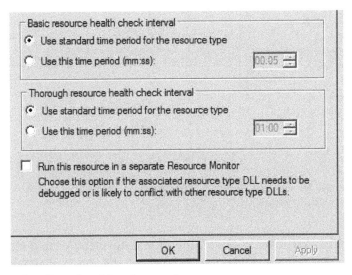

Figure 2: IsAlive and LooksAlive checking intervals.

The default interval can be changed per Virtual Machine to improve failover response time, as shown above in Figure 2.

In previous versions of Windows Clustering, it was not possible to define the **IsAlive** and **LooksAlive** interval per Resource. Now, starting with Windows Server 2008 cluster, it is possible to define the **IsAlive** and **LooksAlive** intervals per Resource.

When you set up a cluster for the first time, the Cluster Service running on the node takes a snapshot of the cluster configuration and saves it in HKLM\Cluster key. This key contains the cluster configuration such as the resource name, their GUID, node holding the resources, and status. This is generally called the cluster configuration database. As an example, for Virtual Machines it includes the following:

Resource Name	GUID		Node Name	Status	PersistentState
Virtual Machine 1	{GUID1}		Node1	Online	1
Virtual Machine 2	{GUID2}		Node1	Online	1
Virtual Machine 3	{GUID3}		Node1	Offline	0

The **PersistentState** keeps the status of the Resources or Virtual Machines in the Cluster. The above shown Status column is just for your reference. The **PersistentState** 1 means online and 0 means offline. The "Status" column is not stored as a registry entry.

This is also shown in the Cluster Registry hive:

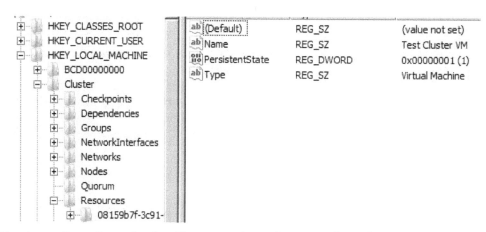

Figure 3: PersistentState Entry in the Cluster Registry for Virtual Machine.

As you can see in Figure 3, the **PersistentState** registry entry value of Virtual Machine "Test Cluster VM" is 1, which indicates that the Virtual Machine is online in the cluster.

Before the Resource Monitor executes any cluster function against the Virtual Machines or Cluster Groups, it looks at the cluster configuration database to check the status of all resources and their GUIDs. For example, let's say we have a cluster group named "HyperV VMs." All the Virtual Machines of Hyper-V reside in this group. When **IsAlive** interval expires (5 seconds by default), the Resource Monitor executes the **IsAlive** call against the "Hyper-V VMs" Cluster Group. It hands over the Resource GUID and Status to the Hyper-V Virtual Machines Resource DLL (VMCLUSRES.DLL). VMCLUSRES.DLL in turn executes the VM **IsAlive** call to check the Virtual Machines' availability. Please note that VMCLUSRES.DLL doesn't really know about the status of Virtual Machines. It is the Resource Monitor which supplies this information to VMCLUSRES.DLL.

Next, we look at VM Open, VM Close, VM Online and VM Offline. These functions are called whenever Virtual Machines are moved across Hyper-V Servers or taken offline/online, or when there is the need to call them. For example, you might want to take a Virtual Machine offline for maintenance purposes on a Hyper-V node. In that case, the Resource Monitor executes the Offline function and in turn VMCLUSRES.DLL executes the VM Offline function to take the Virtual Machine offline. The same will be updated to the VMMS.EXE process in background so that it is aware of the Virtual Machine status. We will discuss these functions later in this article. As a whole, these functions are executed by the Cluster Service and supported by the Hyper-V Resource DLL. That's why Hyper-V Virtualization is known as pure cluster-aware Virtualization Software!

The Resource Monitor determines the state of Virtual Machines by checking the **PersistentState** value at the registry. This value could be either 1 or 0. 1 is for online and 0 is for offline. For example, if you stop a Virtual Machine on a cluster node, the value 0 is set for that service or resource at the registry. If you stop the Virtual Machine using command line or Hyper-V Manager, the value is still updated in the cluster configuration database. It is because Resource DLL of Hyper-V and VMMS.EXE always talk to each other to get the status of Virtual Machines, and update accordingly in the cluster configuration database. When you stop a Virtual Machine using a command line or WMI Script, you are actually interacting with VMMS.EXE service which, in turn, executes the Stop command on your behalf. The status of Virtual Machine is updated in the cluster configuration database. This may not work for other applications in the cluster. As an example, Exchange Server Operations occurring out of the cluster for Exchange Server resources are not reflected at the cluster configuration database. In this case, the **IsAlive** query may not function correctly. The value supplied by the resource monitor will indicate that the resources are running. Thus, **IsAlive** will not take any action against the stopped Cluster Resources. The value is updated in the cluster configuration database only when the **LooksAlive** is executed, which performs a thorough check for the resources. The thorough check includes checking the Exchange Services.

How does Hyper-V Virtual Machine Resource DLL help in the failover process?

The status messages shown above Figure 1 are generated through **IsAlive** calls. When the **IsAlive** interval expires, the Resource Monitor executes the Cluster **IsAlive** calls. The Hyper-V Cluster Resource DLL in turn executes VM **IsAlive** against all Virtual Machine Resources. The messages returned by these calls include one of the following:

- online/offline

- online/offline pending

- failed.

The above status messages are passed back to the Resource Monitor. In turn, this reports the need to take any action to the Cluster Service.

As shown in Figure 1, the Resource Monitor sits between the Hyper-V Resource DLL and the Cluster Service. Any calls made to Hyper-V Virtual Machine Resources have to take place at VMCLUSRES.DLL first. For example, if the Cluster Service needs to check the availability of Hyper-V Virtual Machine

Resources, it will make a call to the Resource Monitor; this will ask VMCLUSRES.DLL to check the status of the Hyper-V Virtual Machine Resources and report back. If the Resource Monitor doesn't receive any response from VMCLUSRES.DLL or it cannot detect the Virtual Machine availability, it will pass the status back to Cluster Service. Cluster Service then passes this status message to related Managers as shown in Figure 4. Managers take the action as per the status passed by lower layer components. The status message could indicate a failure of Virtual Machine resources or could indicate a simple status message. These messages and cluster actions are discussed later in this article, with an example.

In addition, if functions executed by the Resource Monitor do not exist in the Resource DLL, the request is simply discarded and no operation is carried out.

Hyper-V Server doesn't really utilize its own mechanism to failover the Virtual Machines on the surviving node. Instead, Resource DLLs are written to "support" the failover process. Figure 4 shows a simple failover process.

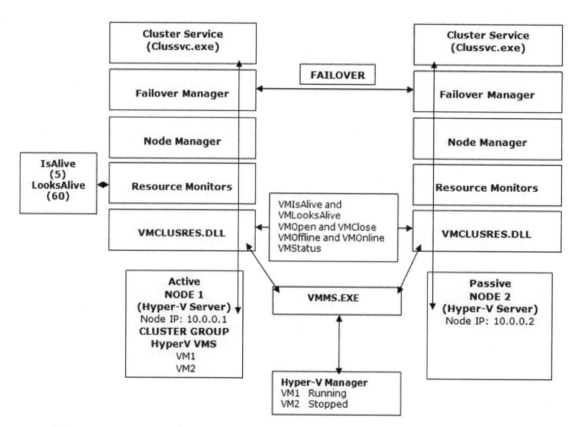

Figure 4: VMCLUSRES.DLL and status messages in Hyper-V Virtual Machines failover process.

- After **IsAlive** interval expires (by default every 5 seconds), Cluster Service asks the Resource Monitor to report the status of Virtual Machines.

- Resource Monitor checks the status of Virtual Machine Resources in cluster configuration database (HKLM\Cluster). It provides VMCLUSRES.DLL with the Virtual Machine Resources GUID and their current status (PersistenState).

- VMCLUSRES.DLL executes its own function (VM **IsAlive**) after it receives a signal from the Resource Monitor to perform a check on the Virtual Machines. It checks and reports back the status to Resource Monitor. VMCLUSRES.DLL will report the following status messages:

  - online/offline

  - online/offline pending

  - failed/stopped.

- After the Resource Monitor receives the status, it compares the status messages received from VMCLUSRES.DLL with the one stored in the Cluster configuration database. It then takes the action as per the status reported by the VMCLUSRES.DLL as listed below.

- If the comparison is successful, no action is taken. For example, the status message received in step 2 is **Online** and VM **IsAlive** query also reports the same status.

- If the comparison is unsuccessful, the following actions are taken:

  - If the status message received in step 2 is **Online** and VM **IsAlive** query reports **Offline**, the Resource Monitor executes an **Online** function. VMCLUSRES.DLL receives this message and executes VM Online function to bring the Virtual Machine online. This status message is also reported to the VMMS.EXE process.

....

Tip

*The Resource Monitor doesn't take any action for Online/Offline status messages because an Administrator might have stopped the resource for maintenance purposes, but the same should also be reflected in the cluster configuration database before **IsAlive** is called. The Resource Monitor only takes action when the comparison is not successful as stated above.*

*Furthermore, there shouldn't be any inconsistencies in the Cluster configuration database. If there were any, these wouldn't last longer than 5 seconds, since **IsAlive** calls always update the status at the Cluster configuration database.*
....

- The mechanism isn't really straightforward. There could be one more message returned by VMCLUSRES.DLL, that is, **Failed**. In this case, the Resource Monitor sends a message (**Restart**) back to VMCLUSRES.DLL to restart the Virtual Machine resource in the cluster. VMCLUSRES.DLL in turn executes the VM Online function to bring the failed Virtual Machines online.

....

Tip

VMCLUSRES.DLL doesn't actually implement a separate Restart function. Instead, it always uses its own implemented VM Online function. If a resource doesn't come online within the specified interval or after a few attempts, the resource is considered to be failed and then the failover process starts. The same is notified to the VMMS.EXE as it needs to keep the status of all the Virtual Machines running in the Cluster.
....

- After the Virtual Machine Resource has failed, the message is passed back to the Resource Monitor. The Cluster Service receives this message from the Resource Monitor and starts the failover process with the help of the Failover Manager. The Failover Manager on each node will communicate with the Failover Manager on another selected cluster node to improve the failover process. Before the Failover Manager on the node where the Virtual Machine resource has failed communicates with another Failover Manager, it needs to get the list of nodes available in the Cluster. This is where the Node Manager comes into the picture. It supplies the list of nodes available in the cluster, and the first available node at the top of the list will be selected for failover.

- Once the list of nodes has been obtained by the source Failover Manager, it will talk to the Failover Manager on the target node. The Failover Manager on the target node supplies the list of Virtual Machines Resources along with GUID and **PersistentState** to the Resource Monitor. Since this is a failover process, the Resource Monitor knows what to do next. It lists all the Virtual Machines with its flag (Online or Offline) and instructs the Resource DLL of Hyper-V to execute the VM Online function from its library.

- The Resource DLL, in turn, executes the VM Online function to bring the resources online on the target node. The same is updated to the VMMS.EXE process of Hyper-V.

- If the Virtual Machine is started successfully within a few attempts, the failover process doesn't occur.

Thus, if there is no Resource DLL for Hyper-V Virtual Machines, the failover process could take longer to move the resources from one node to another surviving node. Because Hyper-V Resource DLL is competent enough to handle the cluster functions executed by the Clustering Software, it doesn't need to wait to decide which action to take. As stated above, the cluster-aware functions are mapped with Hyper-V Resource DLL-specific functions, so it is easier for Hyper-V Resource DLL to execute these functions as soon as they are executed from the Resource Monitor.

In figure 4 you see VMMS.EXE and Hyper-V Manager. Every function executed by the VMCLUSRES.DLL is also notified to VMMS.EXE. VMMS.EXE, in turn, refreshes the status of its VMs on the Hyper-V Server. This is required in order to know the exact status of a VM running on the Hyper-V Server. As an example, an Administrator could open the Hyper-V Manager to get the status of all the Virtual Machines on the Hyper-V Server. If a Virtual Machine has failed and this is not communicated to VMMS.EXE, then there could be confusion, since the Failover Cluster Manager would report one status and the Hyper-V Manager would report a different status.

Tip

IsAlive is executed every 5 seconds for a Virtual Machine in the cluster. You could decrease this value to 1 or 2 to speed up the failover process.

Conclusion

To summarize, Virtual Machines running on Virtual Server are not cluster-aware because they do not provide any resource DLL. Virtual Machines running on Hyper-V are cluster-aware because they provide a resource DLL as they ship along with a cluster resource DLL.

We saw how the Cluster Service doesn't talk to VMCLUSRES.DLL directly. In fact, it uses its Resource Monitor. The status messages passed by the Hyper-V Resource DLL are received by the Resource Monitor to perform any appropriate action.

Finally, we also saw how the Hyper-V Resource DLL plays an important role for its Virtual Machines in the cluster. Resource DLLs allow Hyper-V Virtual Machines to be fully cluster-aware VMs. The functions executed by the Resource Monitor on behalf of the Cluster Service are supported by the Hyper-V Resource DLL. This makes the failover process faster.

Exchange and
SQL Server Tools
from Red Gate Software

Exchange Server Archiver

Email archiving software for Exchange

- ↗ Email archiving for Exchange Server

- ↗ Reduce size of information store – no more PSTs/mailbox quotas

- ↗ Archive only the mailboxes you want to

- ↗ Exchange, Outlook, and OWA 2003 and 2007 supported

- ↗ Transparent end-user experience – message preview, instant retrieval, and integrated search

> **"Exchange Server Archiver is almost 100% invisible to Outlook end-users. The tool is simple to install and manage. This combined with the ability to set up different rules depending on user mailbox, makes the system easy to configure for all types of situations. I'd recommend this product to anyone who needs to archive exchange email."**
>
> **Matthew Studer** Riverside Radiology Associates

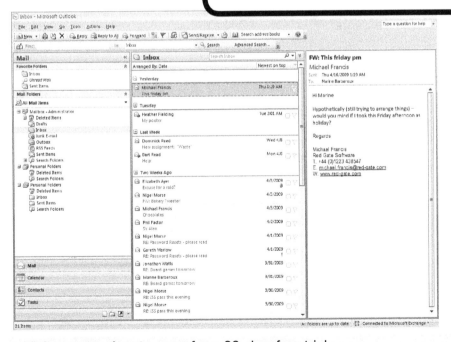

Visit **www.red-gate.com** for a 30-day, free trial

Exchange 2010 –
A Practical Approach
Jaap Wesselius

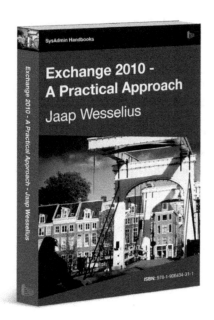

As a practical field-guide to Exchange Server 2010, this book will tell you exactly what you need to know to get started with upgrading, installing, configuring, and managing your new Exchange Server. If you need to get to grips with Exchange Server 2010 fast, or you want a short, to-the-point, practical guide to Microsoft's latest offering, then you should read this book.

ISBN: 978-1-906434-31-1
Published: December 2009

How to Become an
Exceptional DBA
Brad McGehee

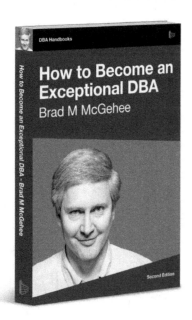

A career guide that will show you, step by step, exactly what you can do to differentiate yourself from the crowd so that you can be an Exceptional DBA. While Brad focuses on how to become an Exceptional SQL Server DBA, the advice in this book applies to any DBA, no matter what database software they use. If you are considering becoming a DBA, or you are a DBA and want to be more than an average DBA, this is the book to get you started.

ISBN: 978-1-906434-05-2
Published: July 2008

SQL Server Tacklebox
Rodney Landrum

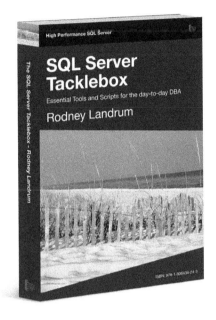

As a DBA, how well prepared are you to tackle "monsters" such as backup failure due to lack of disk space, or locking and blocking that is preventing critical business processes from running, or data corruption due to a power failure in the disk subsystem? If you have any hesitation in your answers to these questions, then Rodney Landrum's SQL Server Tacklebox is a must-read.

ISBN: 978-1-906434-25-0
Published: August 2009

Mastering SQL Server Profiler
Brad McGehee

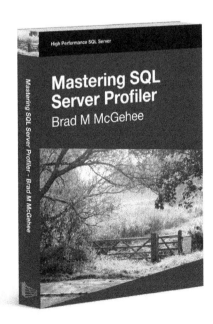

For such a potentially powerful tool, Profiler is surprisingly underused; unless you have a lot of experience as a DBA, it is often hard to analyze the data you capture. As such, many DBAs tend to ignore it and this is distressing, because Profiler has so much potential to make a DBA's life more productive. SQL Server Profiler records data about various SQL Server events, and this data can be used to troubleshoot a wide range of SQL Server issues, such as poorly-performing queries, locking and blocking, excessive table/index scanning, and a lot more.

ISBN: 978-1-906434-16-8
Published: January 2009